CompTIA Netwo W9-BRU-215

Student Manual

2009 Edition

CompTIA Network+, 2009 Edition

President & Chief Executive Officer:	Jon Winder
Vice President, Product Development:	Charles G. Blum
Vice President, Operations:	Josh Pincus
Director of Publishing Systems Development:	Dan Quackenbush
Developmental Editors:	Judi Kling and Andrew LaPage
Copyeditor:	Robert Tillett
Technical Editor:	Rozanne Murphy Whalen

Trademarks

ILT Series is a trademark of Axzo Press.

Some of the product names and company names used in this book have been used for identification purposes only and may be trademarks or registered trademarks of their respective manufacturers and sellers.

Disclaimer

We reserve the right to revise this publication and make changes from time to time in its content without notice.

ISBN 10: 1-4260-0608-X
ISBN 13: 978-1-4260-0608-1

Printed in the United States of America

4 5 6 7 8 9 10 GL 13 12 11

Contents

Introduction

After reading this introduction, you will know how to:

A Use ILT Series manuals in general.

B Use prerequisites, a target student description, course objectives, and a skills inventory to properly set your expectations for the course.

C Re-key this course after class.

Topic A: About the manual

ILT Series philosophy

Our manuals facilitate your learning by providing structured interaction with the software itself. While we provide text to explain difficult concepts, the hands-on activities are the focus of our courses. By paying close attention as your instructor leads you through these activities, you will learn the skills and concepts effectively.

We believe strongly in the instructor-led class. During class, focus on your instructor. Our manuals are designed and written to facilitate your interaction with your instructor, and not to call attention to manuals themselves.

We believe in the basic approach of setting expectations, delivering instruction, and providing summary and review afterwards. For this reason, lessons begin with objectives and end with summaries. We also provide overall course objectives and a course summary to provide both an introduction to and closure on the entire course.

Manual components

The manuals contain these major components:

- Table of contents
- Introduction
- Units
- Appendices
- Course summary
- Glossary
- Index

Each element is described below.

Table of contents

The table of contents acts as a learning roadmap.

Introduction

The introduction contains information about our training philosophy and our manual components, features, and conventions. It contains target student, prerequisite, objective, and setup information for the specific course.

Units

Units are the largest structural component of the course content. A unit begins with a title page that lists objectives for each major subdivision, or topic, within the unit. Within each topic, conceptual and explanatory information alternates with hands-on activities. Units conclude with a summary comprising one paragraph for each topic, and an independent practice activity that gives you an opportunity to practice the skills you've learned.

The conceptual information takes the form of text paragraphs, exhibits, lists, and tables. The activities are structured in two columns, one telling you what to do, the other providing explanations, descriptions, and graphics.

Appendices

An appendix is similar to a unit in that it contains objectives and conceptual explanations. However, an appendix does not include hands-on activities, a summary, or an independent practice activity.

Course summary

This section provides a text summary of the entire course. It is useful for providing closure at the end of the course. The course summary also indicates the next course in this series, if there is one, and lists additional resources you might find useful as you continue to learn about the software.

Glossary

The glossary provides definitions for all of the key terms used in this course.

Index

The index at the end of this manual makes it easy for you to find information about a particular software component, feature, or concept.

Manual conventions

We've tried to keep the number of elements and the types of formatting to a minimum in the manuals. This aids in clarity and makes the manuals more classically elegant looking. But there are some conventions and icons you should know about.

Item	Description
Italic text	In conceptual text, indicates a new term or feature.
Bold text	In unit summaries, indicates a key term or concept. In an independent practice activity, indicates an explicit item that you select, choose, or type.
`Code font`	Indicates code or syntax.
`Longer strings of ▶ code will look ▶ like this.`	In the hands-on activities, any code that's too long to fit on a single line is divided into segments by one or more continuation characters (▶). This code should be entered as a continuous string of text.
Select **bold item**	In the left column of hands-on activities, bold sans-serif text indicates an explicit item that you select, choose, or type.
Keycaps like (↵ ENTER)	Indicate a key on the keyboard you must press.

Hands-on activities

The hands-on activities are the most important parts of our manuals. They are divided into two primary columns. The "Here's how" column gives short instructions to you about what to do. The "Here's why" column provides explanations, graphics, and clarifications. Here's a sample:

Do it!

A-1: Creating a commission formula

Here's how	Here's why
1 Open Sales	This is an oversimplified sales compensation worksheet. It shows sales totals, commissions, and incentives for five sales reps.
2 Observe the contents of cell F4	F4 ▼ **=** =E4*C_Rate The commission rate formulas use the name "C_Rate" instead of a value for the commission rate.

For these activities, we have provided a collection of data files designed to help you learn each skill in a real-world business context. As you work through the activities, you will modify and update these files. Of course, you might make a mistake and therefore want to re-key the activity starting from scratch. To make it easy to start over, you will rename each data file at the end of the first activity in which the file is modified. Our convention for renaming files is to add the word "My" to the beginning of the file name. In the above activity, for example, a file called "Sales" is being used for the first time. At the end of this activity, you would save the file as "My sales," thus leaving the "Sales" file unchanged. If you make a mistake, you can start over using the original "Sales" file.

In some activities, however, it might not be practical to rename the data file. If you want to retry one of these activities, ask your instructor for a fresh copy of the original data file.

Topic B: Setting your expectations

Properly setting your expectations is essential to your success. This topic will help you do that by providing:

- Prerequisites for this course
- A description of the target student
- A list of the objectives for the course
- A skills assessment for the course

Course prerequisites

Before taking this course, you should have support-level experience with personal computers. It is helpful, but not required, that you've completed the following courses or have equivalent experience:

- *CompTIA A+ Certification: Essentials, 2nd Edition*
- *CompTIA A+ Certification: 220-602, 2nd Edition*

Target student

This course is designed to provide you with the foundation-level skills you need to install, operate, manage, maintain, and troubleshoot a corporate network. This course assists in preparing you for the *CompTIA Network+ (2009 Edition) Certification Examination*. It should be noted that a course alone cannot prepare you for any CompTIA exam. It's important that you have the recommended work experience in IT networking prior to taking the exam. For the *CompTIA Network+ (2009) Edition Certification*, CompTIA recommends you have 9 to 12 months of experience in the IT support industry.

CompTIA certification

This course will prepare students to pass the CompTIA Network+ (2009 Edition) certification exam. CompTIA is a non-profit information (IT) trade association. CompTIA's certifications are designed by subject matter experts from across the IT industry. Each CompTIA certification is vendor-neutral, covers multiple technologies, and requires demonstration of skills and knowledge widely sought after by the IT industry.

In order to become CompTIA certified, students must:

1 Select a certification exam provider. Form more information, students should visit: http://certification.comptia.org/resources/registration.aspx.
2 Register for and schedule a time to take the CompTIA certification exam(s) at a convenient location..
3 Read and sign the Candidate Agreement, which will be presented at the time of the exam. The complete text of the Candidate Agreement can be found at: http://certification.comptia.org/resources/canidate_agreement.aspx.
4 Take and pass the CompTIA certification exam(s).

For more information about CompTIA's certifications, such as its industry acceptance, benefits or program news, students should visit http://certification.comptia.org. To contact CompTIA with any questions or comments, please call 1-630-678-8300 or email questions@comptia.org.

Network+ 2009 Bridge Exam

The Network + Bridge Exam (BR0-002) is made available to those candidates already Network+ certified who are seeking to update their certification under the 2009 Network+ objectives. All objectives pertaining to the Bridge Exam (BR0-002) are denoted by the words "Bridge objective" next to the objectives at the beginning of each topic and in Appendix A.

Please note that this option is only for those individuals who are already Network+ certified. For more details please check the CompTIA certification website.

Course objectives

These overall course objectives will give you an idea about what to expect from the course. It is also possible that they will help you see that this course is not the right one for you. If you think you either lack the prerequisite knowledge or already know most of the subject matter to be covered, you should let your instructor know that you think you are misplaced in the class.

After completing this course, you will know how to:

- Describe the basic components and characteristics of a network.
- Identify wired network-to-network connections.
- Install LAN wiring components.
- Differentiate between wired internetworking devices.
- Configure the TCP/IP communication protocols for a wired connection.
- Install wireless networking components.
- Identify common security threats and mitigation techniques.
- Secure operating systems and network devices.
- Control access to the network.
- Monitor network resources.
- Troubleshoot the network.

Skills inventory

Use the following form to gauge your skill level entering the class. For each skill listed, rate your familiarity from 1 to 5, with five being the most familiar. *This is not a test.* Rather, it is intended to provide you with an idea of where you're starting from at the beginning of class. If you're wholly unfamiliar with all the skills, you might not be ready for the class. If you think you already understand all of the skills, you might need to move on to the next course in the series. In either case, you should let your instructor know as soon as possible.

Skill	1	2	3	4	5
Describing the basic components of a network		✓			
Identifying characteristics of various network technologies		✓			
Analyzing the OSI model	✓				
Identifying wired network cables and connectors			✓		
Installing and configuring network interface and modem PCI cards			✓		
Identifying network-to-network connection components	✓				
Installing LAN wiring	✓				
Identifying LAN wiring tests and equipment	✓				
Differentiating between basic internetworking devices		✓			
Identifying specialized internetworking devices	✓				
Describing the functions of the protocols in the TCP/IP protocol suite	✓				
Configuring TCP/IP	✓				
Installing and configuring DHCP and DHCPv6	✓				
Identifying the hardware components needed to create a wireless connection			✓		
Differentiating between the various communications standards used in wireless networks		✓			
Installing and configuring a wireless network connection	✓				
Identifying security threats	✓				
Identifying mitigation techniques	✓				
Updating and securing operating systems	✓				
Securing network devices	✓				

Skill	1	2	3	4	5
Identifying authentication techniques	✓				
Explaining PKI concepts	✓				
Explaining remote access security methods		✓			
Explaining wireless security methods		✓			
Monitoring network resources	✓				
Examining event logs		✓			
Describing a basic troubleshooting methodology	✓				
Troubleshooting the network	✓				
Applying troubleshooting techniques to a given scenario	✓				

Topic C: Re-keying the course

If you have the proper hardware and software, you can re-key this course after class. This section explains what you'll need in order to do so, and how to do it.

Hardware requirements

You'll need a computer to function as an Active Directory domain controller. This computer should have:

- A keyboard and a mouse
- At least 1 GHz 32-bit or 1.4 GHz 64-bit processor (2 GHz or faster recommended)
- At least 1 GB RAM (2 GB or greater recommended)
- At least 40 GB hard drive
- A DVD-ROM drive
- SVGA monitor at 1024×768

Your personal computer should have:

- A keyboard and a mouse
- At least 1 GHz 32-bit or 64-bit processor
- At least 1 GB RAM
- At least 50 GB hard drive with at least 15 GB of available space
- A DVD-ROM drive
- A graphics card that supports DirectX 9 graphics with:
  - WDDM driver
  - 128 MB of graphics memory (minimum)
  - Pixel Shader 2.0 in hardware
  - 32 bits-per-pixel
- SVGA monitor
- An available PCI slot

In addition to the above components, you will need the following hardware:

- Cable stripper, wire cutter, cable tester
- Network (protocol) analyzer (with load and throughput testing) and a Wi-Fi scanner. If you have only one, you can have students share
- BNC crimper, length of RG-58 coaxial cable—a foot or longer, and BNC connector
- RG-59 electronic component cable
- Twisted pair crimpers, length of twisted pair CAT 6 cable—a foot or longer, and RJ-45 modular plug
- Extra PCI NIC card compatible with Windows Vista
- PCI modem card compatible with Windows Vista
- CaT 5e/6 compatible punchdown block, length of twisted pair CAT 5e/6 cable—a foot or longer, and 788-impact tool

- Infrared, RF, and Bluetooth wireless devices and software
- Wireless client laptop
- Wireless access point and wireless PCI NIC card
- Any of the hardware tools listed in the CompTIA Network+ objectives and in the unit titled "Troubleshooting"

Software requirements

You will also need the following software:

- Windows Server 2008 Standard
- Windows Vista Ultimate
- Microsoft Virtual PC SP1
- Network Monitor 3.2
- Adobe Reader

Network requirements

The following network components and connectivity are also required for re-keying this course:

- Internet access, for the following purposes:
  - Downloading the latest critical updates and service packs from www.windowsupdate.com
  - Completing activities throughout the course
  - Downloading the Student Data files from www.axzopress.com (if necessary)
- Four sets of IPv4 addresses on the same subnet, for the following purposes:
  - To be handed out to your personal computer via the DHCP server. For example 192.168.157.001 to 192.168.157.050.
  - To be assigned to your Microsoft Vista host computer for a manual IPv4 address assignment activity. For example 192.168.157.051 to 192.168.157.099.
  - To be manually assigned to your Microsoft Windows Server 2008 virtual PC computer for a DHCP server installation activity. For example 192.168.157.100 to 192.168.157.150.
  - For the DHCP server scopes on your Microsoft Windows Server 2008 virtual PC computers. For example groups of ten addresses 192.168.157.151 to 192.168.157.254.

Setup instructions to re-key the course

Before you re-key the course, you will need to perform the following steps.

AD domain controller

You will need to perform the following steps to set up the AD domain controller.

1   Install Windows Server 2008 Standard using the following information.

    a   Don't go online to get the latest updates for installation.

    b   Select the appropriate language, time and currency format, and keyboard or input method.

    c   Select Windows Server 2008 Standard (Full Installation).

    d   Accept the license agreement.

    e   Choose a custom installation. Create at least a 25 GB partition and format it NTFS.

    f   When prompted, enter and confirm a password of !pass1234 for the Administrator account.

2   If necessary, change your display settings to 1024×768 or 1280×1024.

3   Configure the server using the Initial Configuration Tasks window.

    a   Set the correct time zone and time.

    b   Configure networking for the Local Area Connection:

- If necessary, install a driver for the network adapter.
- Specify the appropriate static IPv4 addressing parameters, including an IP address, subnet mask, and default gateway address.
- Use the server's IP address as its preferred DNS server address. Be sure to configure IP address settings that enable the server to connect to the Internet.
- Disable IPv6.

    c   Name the computer **netdc**. Restart when prompted.

    d   Don't configure automatic updating, and don't download or install updates. Note: This course was tested without any updates to the Windows Server 2008 Standard software. If you install updates, we can't guarantee the course will key as written.

    e   Install the DHCP server role.

- Under Customize This Server, click Add roles. Click Next.
- Select DHCP Server, and click Next twice.
- Verify the correct network connect is selected, and click Next.
- In the Parent Domain text box, type **networkplus.class**. In the Preferred DNS Server IPv4 Address text box, type the IP address of the server. Click Next twice.
- On the Add or Edit DHCP Scopes page, click Add. Create a name for the scope and configure it with enough IP addresses for all the students in class and the instructor. Enter the appropriate subnet mask and default gateway. From the Subnet Type list, select Wired. Click OK, and then click Next.
- Select "Disable DHCPv6 stateless mode for this server" and click Next.
- Click Install, and complete the installation.

    f   Install Active Directory Domain Services role.

- Under Customize This Server, click Add roles, and click Next.
- Select Active Directory Domain Services, and click Next twice. Click Install.
- Click Start, choose Run, and enter **dcpromo**. Click Next twice.
- Select "Create a new domain in a new forest" and click Next.
- In the FQDN text box, type **networkplus.class**, and click Next.
- In the Forest functional level list, select Windows Server 2008, and click Next.
- Verify that DNS server is selected, and click Next. Click Yes.
- Click Next to accept the default locations for the database folder, the log files folder, and the SYSVOL folder.
- Enter and confirm **!pass1234** as the restore mode administrator password. Click Next twice.
- Check "Reboot on completion."

4   Log back on as Administrator. In Initial Configuration Tasks, check "Do not show this window at logon," and click Close.

5   In Server Manager, expand Roles, DHCP Server, right-click the netdc.networkplus.class server and choose Authorize. Then expand IPv4. Right-click the scope and choose Refresh.

6   Create two user accounts in Active Directory for yourself.

    a   In Server Manager, expand Roles, Active Directory Domain Services, Active Directory Users and Computers, and the networkplus.class domain.

    b   In the Users folder, right-click a blank space and choose New, User.

    c   Enter a first name of **Net**, a last name of **Admin##**, where ## is the unique number assigned to the computer and student. Assign the instructor the Net Admin00 account.

    d   Enter a user logon name of **netadmin##**, where ## matches the unique number you assigned in the previous step. Click Next.

    e   Enter and confirm a password of **!pass1234**. Uncheck "User must change password at next logon." Check "User cannot change password" and "Password never expires." Click Next, and click Finish.

    f   Create another user account named **hostadmin##**, using the same procedure as above. You will use this to log on to their Windows Vista host computers.

    g   Add your Net Admin## and Host Admin## accounts to the Domain Admins group.

7   Close all open windows.

Your personal computer

You will need to perform the following steps to set up your personal computer.

1   Install Windows Vista Ultimate according to the software manufacturer's instructions on at least a 50 GB partition. This installation represents the "host" operating system on which you're going to install Microsoft Virtual PC 2007 SP1.

    a   When prompted, create a user named **Admin**. Create a password of **!pass1234**. This is a local administrative user.

    b   Name the computer **nethost##**, where ## is the unique number assigned to you. For example, nethost01, nethost02, and so on.

    c   When prompted to configure automatic updates, select "Ask me later."

    d   Set the appropriate date, time, and time zone.

    e   If prompted to choose a network location, select Work.

    f   Log in as Admin with a password of !pass1234.

    g   Verify that all devices are functional and install or update drivers as necessary.

    h   Use Display Settings in Control Panel to configure a screen resolution of 1024×768.

    i   In the Welcome Center, clear "Run at startup," and then close the window.

    j   Join the networkplus.class domain. Enter credentials for Administrator with a password of !pass1234.

2   Log on to the Windows Vista computer using the appropriate hostadmin## domain user account. (For example, on nethost01, you would log on as hostadmin01.) Install Microsoft Virtual PC 2007 SP1. Accept all installation defaults.

    a   Use the Network and Sharing Center to turn on both network discovery and file sharing.

3   Copy the Student Data files to the Windows Vista Host.

    If you don't have the data CD that came with this manual, download the Student Data files for the course. You can download the data directly to your personal computer, to a central location on your own network, or to a disk.

    a   Connect to www.axzopress.com.

    b   Under Downloads, click Instructor-Led Training.

    c   Browse the subject categories to locate your course. Then click the course title to display a list of available downloads. (You can also access these downloads through our Catalog listings.)

    d   Click the link(s) for downloading the Student Data files, and follow the instructions that appear on your screen.

4   Download and install Adobe Reader on the Windows Vista host. If you're using Internet Explorer, if prompted, in the Microsoft Phishing Filter dialog box, select "Turn on automatic Phishing Filter," and click OK. Do not install the Google toolbar from the Adobe web site.

5   Download and complete a typical install of Network Monitor 3.2 on the Vista Host. When prompted, don't use Microsoft Update.

6   Download and install Microsoft Virtual PC 2007 SP1. Accept all installation defaults.

7   Start Virtual PC and use the New Virtual Machine Wizard to create a new virtual machine.

    a   On the Virtual Machine Name and Location page, enter **Windows Server 2008** for the new virtual machine name.

    b   On the Operating System page, verify that Windows Server 2008 is selected in the Operating System drop-down list.

    c   On the Memory page, allocate at least 1 GB of RAM for the new virtual machine.

    d   On the Virtual Hard Disk Options page, select "A new virtual hard disk."

    e   On the Virtual Hard Disk Location page, in the Virtual hard disk size text box, type 25000 to allocate approximately 25 GB of disk space to this virtual machine.

8   Install Windows Server 2008 on the new virtual machine.

    a   Insert the Windows Server 2008 DVD. (On the Windows Vista host system, close the AutoPlay dialog box.)

    b   In the Virtual PC Console, verify that the Windows Server 2008 virtual machine is selected and then click Start. **Immediately press Delete to enter the BIOS Setup Utility.**

    c   Scroll to the right to select the Boot tab, and then press Enter to configure boot device priority.

    d   Scroll down to highlight CDROM and press + (plus sign) to move CDROM up to the top of the boot order. Press F10 to exit and save settings, and restart the virtual machine (press right Alt+Del).

    e   Choose CD, Use Physical Drive D, and restart the virtual machine (if necessary). The virtual machine should then boot to the Windows Server 2008 DVD.

    f   Install Windows Server 2008 into the new virtual machine using the information in the following table.

Installation Option	Configuration
Operating System	Windows Server 2008 Standard (Full Installation)
Installation Type	Custom
Partition	Install on a single partition and format it NTFS (the default).
Administrator Password	Change to **!pass1234**

g Use the Initial Configuration Tasks window to:
- Set the appropriate time zone.
- Verify that an IPv4 address has been assigned by DHCP.
- Name the computer **netsrv##**, where ## is the unique number assigned to the computer and student's user account. Add the Windows Server 2008 virtual machine to the networkplus.class domain. (You can use your netadmin## credentials.)
- Log back on to Windows Server 2008 in the Virtual PC as the domain user netadmin##.
- Verify that automatic updating is disabled and no updates have been downloaded.

h If prompted to fix display settings, click the button in the notification area to change the virtual machine window size to make it easier to work within the window.

i If necessary, activate your copy of Windows Server 2008.

9 Install the Virtual Machine Additions software by choosing Action, Install or Update Virtual Machine Additions. (Be sure you're logged on to the guest Windows Server 2008 operating system.) Accept all default settings for the installation. Restart when prompted. Log back on, and in the Initial Configuration Tasks window, check "Don't show this window at logon," and close the window. Leave Server Manager open.

10 Turn off Internet Explorer Enhanced Security Configuration.

a In Server Manager, select the Server Manager console root.

b Under Security Information, click "Configure IE ESC."

c Under Administrators, select Off. Under Users, select Off. Click OK.

d Leave Server Manager open.

11 Enable network sharing and discovery.

a Click Start, right-click Network, and choose Properties.

b Next to Network discovery, click Off. Select "Turn on network discovery," and click Apply. If prompted, click "No, make the network that I am connected to a private network."

c Next to File sharing, click Off. Select "Turn on file sharing," and click Apply.

d Click "No, make the network that I am connected to a private network."

e Close the Network and Sharing Center.

12 Add the Windows Server 2008 virtual machine to the networkplus.class domain. Log back on to Windows Server 2008 in the Virtual PC as the domain user netadmin##.

13 In Windows Server 2008- Microsoft Virtual PC 2007, choose Action, Close. Select "Save state" and click OK.

14 Close Virtual PC Console.

CertBlaster software

CertBlaster pre- and post-assessment software is available for this course. To download and install this free software, complete the following steps:

1   Go to www.axzopress.com.
2   Under Downloads, click CertBlaster.
3   Click the link for CompTIA Network+ 2009.
4   Save the .EXE file to a folder on your hard drive. (Note: If you skip this step, the CertBlaster software will not install correctly.)
5   Click Start and choose Run.
6   Click Browse and then navigate to the folder that contains the .EXE file.
7   Select the .EXE file and click Open.
8   Click OK and follow the on-screen instructions. When prompted for the password, enter **c_net+09**.

Unit 1

Network basics

Unit time: 150 minutes

Complete this unit, and you'll know how to:

A Describe the basic components of a network.

B Identify characteristics of network technologies.

C Analyze the OSI model.

Topic A: Network concepts

This topic covers the following CompTIA Network+ 2009 exam objectives.

#	Objective
Bridge objective → **1.1**	**Explain function of common networking protocols**
Bridge objective → **1.7**	**Compare the characteristics of wireless communication standards** • 802.11 a/b/g/n – Speeds
Bridge objective → **2.1**	**Categorize standard cable types and their properties** Type: • Serial • CAT3, CAT5, CAT5e, CAT6 • STP, UTP • Multimode fiber, single-mode fiber • Coaxial – RG-59 – RG-6 Properties: • Duplex • Noise immunity (security, EMI)
Bridge objective → **2.2**	**Identify common connector types** • RS-232
2.7	**Explain common logical network topologies and their characteristics** • Peer to peer • Client/Server
Bridge objective → **3.1**	**Install, configure and differentiate between common network devices** • Wireless access point

Networking models

Explanation

Nowadays, networks make the world go 'round. From the small home network to the larger networks at your doctor's office or your bank to the world-wide Internet, networks are involved in some way in almost all of the business activities and a good part of the leisure activities in the world today. A CompTIA Network+ technician must be able to support the interrelationships of all types and sizes of networks.

Local area network

A *local area network* (*LAN*) is a specifically designed configuration of computers and other devices located within a confined area, such as a home or office building, and connected by wires or radio waves that permit the devices to communicate with one another to share data and services. Computers and other devices connected on a LAN can send and receive information from one another without confusion. Each device with an address that can be accessed to send or receive information is a *node*. A *node* can be a computer, a router, a printer, a video camera, a controller, or any number of other electronic devices. A *host* is always a computer. The network directs the communication passing through it and acts as a sort of electronic traffic cop to prevent collisions or mixing of data.

A LAN can be connected to the Internet, either through a direct cable connection or by a telephone link through a modem, so that workstations on the LAN have access to all the networks and sites linked to the global Web. An example of the components on a LAN is shown in Exhibit 1-1. On the middle right is the server. The computers are workstations on the LAN and are connected with a media cable of some type. The second laptop is also a workstation on the LAN, but is connected through a wireless access point. The printer is a shared network printer available to clients on the LAN.

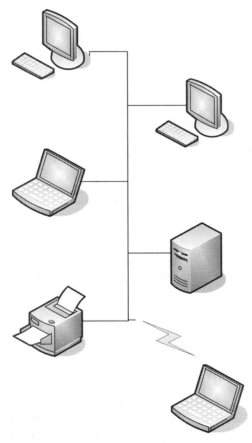

Exhibit 1-1: An example of a LAN

A host requires an operating system to manage its applications, hardware, and connection to the network. The operating system is also responsible for enabling the computers on the LAN to share their resources. The term *resource* refers to any files, databases, or printers installed on or attached to a host.

Basic network types

There are two basic types of networks that you'll encounter:

- **Peer-to-peer network**—Usually consists of several client computers that are connected to a network for simple file and printer sharing in a small office or home office. Each computer has a network card, which is connected to the network by a network cable or wireless network media. All the communication is between the client computers. There are often fewer than a dozen hosts on this type of network. You might also hear a peer-to-peer network described as decentralized networking model—you must administer each user and computer on the network individually.

- **Client/server network**—Computers called servers hold data and provide a wealth of services that users can share. Most of the communication on this type of network is between the client computers and the servers. Client/server networks scale much larger than peer-to-peer networks. You might also hear a client/server network described as a centralized networking model, because it enables you to administer computers and users as a group instead of individually.

Peer-to-peer model

In the *peer-to-peer networking model*, each host on the LAN has the same authority as other hosts. Each computer user is the administrator of his or her own computer and decides whether to share a resource on his or her computer (such as a file, database, or printer). The user is responsible for backing up data, installing software, sharing resources, enforcing security policies, and many other administrative tasks. All versions of Windows Vista, Windows XP, and Windows 2000 Professional are examples of client operating systems that support the peer-to-peer model.

In a peer-to-peer model, several hosts using different operating systems in a small business or home can be connected to form a small LAN, as shown in Exhibit 1-2. In this example, the hosts and other devices are physically connected using network cabling, but you can create a small LAN using wireless connections.

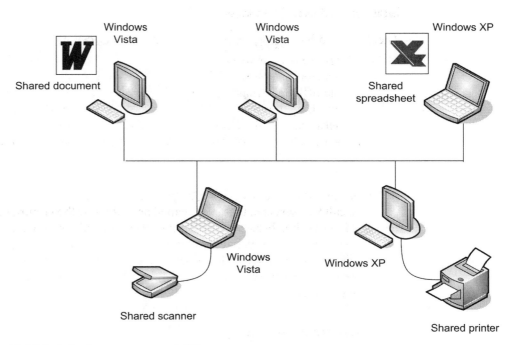

Exhibit 1-2: A peer-to-peer LAN

Peer-to-peer authentication

In a peer-to-peer LAN consisting of Windows 2000 Professional, Windows XP, and Windows Vista computers, each user has his or her own computer and must enter his or her valid user ID and password to use the computer. If the user doesn't enter a valid user ID and password, he or she can't use the computer. The process of entering a correct user ID and password and gaining access to a computer is called *authentication*, *validation*, or *logging on*. In the peer-to-peer model, a user ID and password is authenticated by the local client operating system.

All users have a user ID and password which allows them access only to their own computers. Using unique user IDs and passwords, they can't authenticate and gain access to someone else's computer. This is because their user accounts exist only on their own computers.

You can create additional local user accounts on a computer so that other users can access that computer's shared resources. A local user account is a collection of all the information that pertains to a user on a computer. This includes the user ID and password required for the user to authenticate and the permissions the user has for using and accessing resources on a computer.

Individual users in a peer-to-peer model can make resources on their computers available to other network users. Using Windows Vista, to use a shared resource:

1 Click Start and choose Network.

   All the Windows 2000 Professional, Windows XP, and Windows Vista computers on the LAN are displayed in the details pane.

2 Double-click the icon for the computer where the shared resource exists.

If the user of a computer hasn't shared any resources, when you double-click that computer icon, after a few moments you receive an error message stating that the computer isn't accessible and that you don't have permission to access this network resource.

Client/server model

A *network operating system* (*NOS*), such as Windows Server 2008 or 2003, Windows 2000 Server, UNIX, or Novell Open Enterprise Server or NetWare, can be installed on a server and used to manage network resources, including user accounts, printers, and file sharing across a LAN. User accounts are created on the NOS installed on a server. A trained system administrator is usually responsible for maintaining the server and NOS while managing resources to meet user needs. Users can authenticate and gain access to any host on the LAN by entering their single network user IDs and passwords. The user ID and password are authenticated against the NOS on the server instead of on each individual host.

In a client/server model, sometimes called a *domain model*, a server controls which resources on the LAN are shared and who can access these resources. In addition to creating user accounts in the NOS's directory, the system administrator assigns user permissions that control which resources users can access on the LAN. The server uses a database to store user account information, user permissions, security policies, printers, and other configuration settings. Software, files, printers, and other resources can be accessed by users on the LAN only when the system administrator has granted specific permission to a user account. An example of a client/server network is shown in Exhibit 1-3.

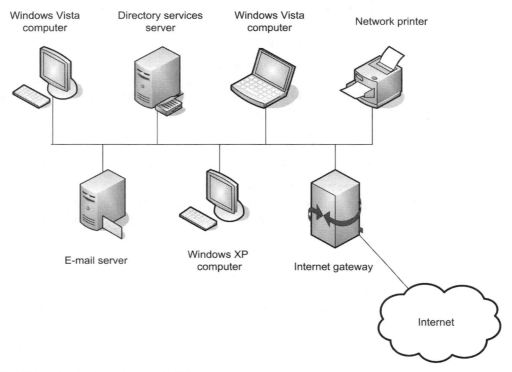

Exhibit 1-3: A client/server LAN

In the client/server model, the local client operating system isn't responsible for authenticating user IDs and passwords. Instead, the client OS sends this information to the NOS on the server, which verifies the information based upon the information stored in its database. It does this by using a *network client* that's installed on the client computer. The network client is responsible for communicating with the NOS on the server.

In the client/server model, an administrator assigns users their own user IDs and passwords. This process, in turn, allows them to authenticate against the NOS and log on to access network resources (also called logging on to the network). The logon process goes something like this:

1 The network client on the client computer displays a logon screen to the user.
2 The user enters his or her user ID and password at the logon screen and clicks OK.
3 The network client then sends this information to the NOS for authentication.
4 After the user ID and password have been authenticated, the user can gain access to the computer and to the network resources.

If Novell Open Enterprise Server or NetWare is the NOS on the server and Windows Vista, Windows 2000 Professional, or Windows XP is the client OS, the Novell Client for the client OS must be installed in order to serve as the network client. A server can be running Windows Server 2008 or 2003, or Windows 2000 Server as the NOS. In this case, the client OS (Windows Vista, Windows 2000 Professional, or Windows XP) is used as the network client.

Do it!

A-1:   Describing networking models and protocols

Questions and answers

1 How are client/server networks different from peer-to-peer networks?

2 Why would a company want to implement a client/server network?

3 What kind of company would implement a peer-to-peer network?

Do it!   **A-2: Identifying the basic components of a network**

Here's how	Here's why
1 Identify the server computer in your classroom	You'll identify components of your classroom network.
2 Identify the client workstations on your classroom network	
3 Identify nodes on your classroom network	
4 Determine whether you're using a physical or wireless communication channel in your classroom	

Segments and backbones

Explanation

Large networks are frequently broken down into manageable pieces called segments. A *segment* is the portion of the network on either side of two network transmission devices. Examples of network transmission devices include routers, bridges, repeaters, switches, and hubs. A network is segmented to extend allowable cable length, separate traffic to improve performance, and for security purposes.

Usually segments are connected directly to one another if they are in close proximity. In large buildings, or where the network spans more than one building, a backbone is constructed. The *backbone* is a high-speed network link connecting only segments (the nodes are connected to the segments).

With this design, only data destined for another segment travels across the backbone. Preventing a data packet from traveling over the entire network is a key element in a well-designed network. Directing data over the shortest possible route to the destination increases network availability on those segments it doesn't need to travel across. Exhibit 1-4 shows how segments are connected to a backbone.

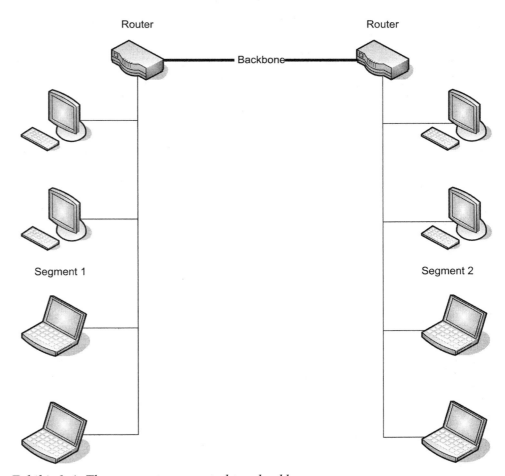

Exhibit 1-4: The segments connected to a backbone

Do it!

A-3: Identifying physical network segments

Here's how	Here's why
1 Identify the internetworking device connecting the network segment in your classroom to the organization's backbone	
2 Identify whether the classroom is set up as a single network segment or divided into multiple segments	

Network wiring

The computers in the network need a pathway to connect each other. This can be a physical connection of one type of wire or cabling or another. It can also be a connection through radio waves, infrared, or other wireless connection methods. Wiring is the heart of a network. It's also the part most vulnerable to performance problems caused by poor installation practices. Wiring in new construction is generally a straightforward process. Wiring in existing structures, whether done within the walls or on the surface, can be a frustrating experience. No network is better than the quality of the wiring on which it runs.

Fiber optic

Fiber optic cabling, which carries light-based data through strands of glass or plastic no thicker than a human hair, is currently the fastest and most expensive network transmission medium. Fiber optic cables are composed of a glass or a plastic strand through which light is transmitted. This core is clad in a glass tube designed to reflect the light back into the core, as the light bounces moving through the fiber core. An outer insulating, rubberized jacket covers the entire cable to protect it. An example of a single strand fiber optic cable is shown in Exhibit 1-5.

Exhibit 1-5: Example of a single strand fiber optic cable

There are two types of fiber optic cable: single-mode fiber (SMF) and multi-mode fiber (MMF). Optic fibers which support many transmission (propagation) paths are referred to as *multi-mode*. Optic fibers which support only a single transmission path are *single-mode*. Multimode optic fibers generally have a large-diameter core, and are used for short distances, typically less than 300 meters. You'll find single mode fibers used for most communication links longer than 300 meters.

Fiber optic cable is used by the telephone and cable companies to deliver information across long distances. Fiber optic cabling is also used as the *backbone* for networks. For an end-user to use fiber optics, they must purchase conversion equipment that changes electrical impulses into photons. At present, the price of these devices is costly, but is certain to decline as the technology matures. This makes their widespread use in the future more likely.

Twisted pair

Until recently, most networks have used *unshielded twisted pair* (*UTP*) or *shielded twisted pair* (*STP*) cabling to connect the nodes in the network. Both types of cable are composed of four pairs of wires. The wires in each pair are twisted around each other, and the pairs are twisted together and bundled within a covering, as shown in Exhibit 1-6. The two wires (two halves of a single circuit) are wound together in order to cancel out electromagnetic interference (EMI) from external sources.

Exhibit 1-6: UTP cable

UTP cable comes in categories. Each category has a specific use, number of twists per foot, and speed. The more twists, the less crosstalk and electrical magnetic interference (EMI) affects the data on the cable.

For networking, *Cat3* cable used to be acceptable. However, Cat3 operates at up to only 10 Mbps with about two or three twists per foot. Most networks now use at least *Cat5* cable, which operates at up to 100 Mbps, or *Cat5e*, which operates at up to 1 Gbps. Cat5 and Cat5e cables have 20 twists per foot. *Cat6* cables use higher quality materials and have the potential to operate at up to 2.5 Gbps. The number of twists in Cat6 cable can vary. All twisted pair cabling has a maximum run length of approximately 100 meters. There is also a *Cat6a* cable that provides performance of up to 10 Gbps. Cat7 is an emerging standard.

For the best wiring value and expansion capability, use *composite cable* (shown in Exhibit 1-7), which combines Cat5 or Cat6 and other transmission cables within a single PVC jacket. It makes multiple-wire installation easier and saves on the cost of future wiring. Some of these cables contain two Cat5 or Cat6 wires for the network and two shielded RG-6 coaxial cables for cable and satellite television. The top-of-the-line, "future-proof" version of this type of cable contains Cat5 or Cat6 and RG-6 wires, and a fiber optic line—the fastest available transmission medium.

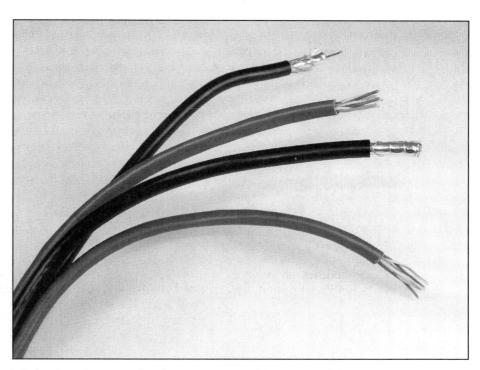

Exhibit 1-7: An example of a composite cable

Coaxial

Coax cables contain a layer of braided wire or foil between the core and the outside insulating layer. The shielding provided by this layer helps protect the data from EMI problems. Another layer of plastic or rubberized material separates the central core from the shielding layer since, if these two layers touch, the data signal is damaged or lost. The type used for Ethernet networking is marked *RG-58*, shown in Exhibit 1-8. It's important that you don't mistake RG-59 cable for RG-58.

RG-59 coaxial cable is used for low-power video and RF signal connections. You'll find it shipped with consumer electronic equipment, such as VCRs or digital cable and satellite receivers. In recent years, RG-6 type cables have become the standard for cable TV, replacing the smaller RG-59. RG-6 cables are most commonly used to deliver cable television signals to and within homes, and also aren't suitable for networking.

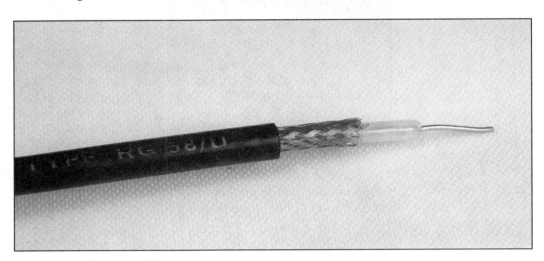

Exhibit 1-8: Thinnet cable

Thicknet cables are *RG-8* or *RG-11* cables. RG-8 cables, shown in Exhibit 1-9, are 50-ohm stranded core cables, and RG-11 are 75-ohm solid core cables with dual shielding (foil and braided wires). Neither RG-8 nor RG-11 bend easily, because both are 10 mm in diameter (four-tenths of an inch). These cables can carry signals up to about 500 meters, so they're typically used for Ethernet network backbones rather than for drops to network nodes.

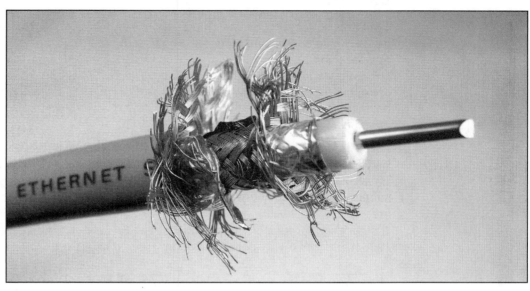

Exhibit 1-9: Thicknet cable

Thin Ethernet designs, wired with RG58/U coaxial cable, are limited by the attenuation (weakening due to distance traveled) of signals in the cable and can support network segments up to only 185 meters long. Thick Ethernet designs, wired with 50-ohm RG8/U coaxial, are more resistant to attenuation and can span up to 500 meters. Neither of these is being widely used now, because more advanced cable types can span distances up to 1,000 meters with less attenuation of network signals.

Serial

Using the serial ports on two computers, you can create a direct cable connection between two computers by using a single cable rather than a modem or other network interface device. In most cases, you make a direct cable connection with a null modem cable—a serial cable with RS-232 connectors on either end. Typical serial connectors are either 9-pin, shown in Exhibit 1-10, or 25-pin. A null modem cable differs from ordinary serial cables in that the transmit and receive lines on the ends are reversed to enable direct two-way communication.

Using the serial ports on two computers, you can create a direct cable connection between two computers by using a single cable rather than a modem or other network interface device. In most cases, you make a direct cable connection with a null modem cable—a serial cable with RS-232 connectors on either end. Typical serial connectors are either 9-pin, shown in Exhibit 1-10, or 25-pin. A null modem cable differs from ordinary serial cables in that the transmit and receive lines on the ends are reversed to enable direct two-way communication.

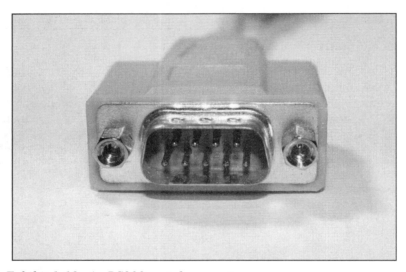

Exhibit 1-10: An RS232 serial connector

You can use this direct cable connection to transfer information between the computers to exchange files, access resources, and so on. The *Serial Direct Connection*, utilizing the COM ports of your computers, is a slow method of connecting computers. An RS-232 null modem cable transfers data at the rate of 115 Kbps. The fastest null modem cable, based on RS-422, supports up to 450 Kbps. That's pretty slow compared to a normal network connection.

Duplex

Data is transmitted as simplex, half-duplex, or full-duplex. In simplex, data is transmitted in a single direction. In half-duplex, data is transmitted across the medium in both directions, but only in one direction at a time. In full-duplex, data can be transmitted across the medium in both directions at the same time. Network transmissions can be either half-duplex or full-duplex, although the majority are half-duplex.

Data is transmitted as simplex, half-duplex, or full-duplex. In simplex, data is transmitted in a single direction. In half-duplex, data is transmitted across the medium in both directions, but only in one direction at a time. In full-duplex, data can be transmitted across the medium in both directions at the same time. Network transmissions can be either half-duplex or full-duplex, although the majority are half-duplex.

Do it!

A-4:   Identifying cable types

Here's how	Here's why
1 Examine the cable used to connect your computer to the network	
Identify its type	Cable type:
2 Record the backbone cabling used	Your instructor will describe the backbone cable used to connect network segments.

Wireless LAN

Wireless LAN (*WLAN*) technology uses radio waves or infrared light instead of cables to connect network nodes. Connections are made using a wireless NIC, which includes an antenna to send and receive signals. WLANs are popular in places where networking cables are difficult to install, such as outdoors or in a historic building with wiring restrictions, or where there are many mobile users, such as on a college campus. Wireless devices can communicate directly (for example, a handheld device communicating with a computer via an infrared connection), or they can connect to a LAN by way of a *wireless access point* (*WAP*). Access points are placed so that nodes can access at least one access point from anywhere in the covered area. When devices use an access point, they communicate through the access point instead of communicating directly. Exhibit 1-11 shows an example of a wired network with wireless segments.

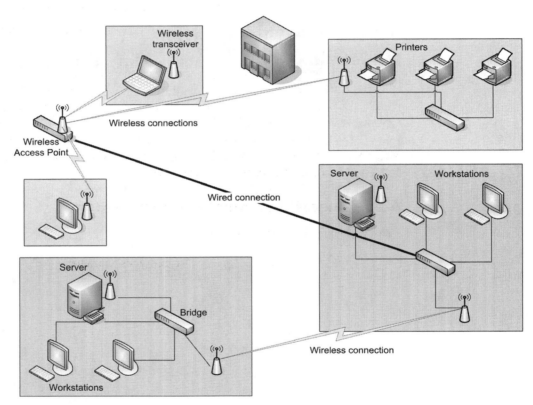

Exhibit 1-11: Wired network with wireless segments

Benefits/drawbacks of wireless networks

The benefits of WLAN technology are many. The most obvious benefit is the increased flexibility and mobility that's created when using WLANs. Employees can move freely around the organization without disconnection from the network. Examples of how wireless networking can benefit an organization include the following:

- Inventory is more convenient when employees can freely walk around the warehouse or organization.
- Portable devices such as personal digital assistants (PDAs) and Tablet PCs can be used in hospital wards to track patients and doctor visits.
- Mobile workers moving between offices and telecommuters coming into the office can easily connect to the LAN from almost anywhere.
- Online information is always available for research or information retrieval.
- Production on manufacturing shop floors can be readily evaluated.
- Wireless network infrastructure can be moved to a new building more easily.
- The cost of providing network access to buildings is substantially lowered.

Although WLANs have some obvious advantages in places where running cables would be difficult or expensive, WLANs tend to be slower than wired networks, especially when they're busy. Another problem with WLANs is security. Companies are reluctant to use them when it's possible for an unauthorized person with a receiving device to intercept wireless LAN transmissions. Security on a WLAN is accomplished by filtering the MAC addresses of wireless NICs that are allowed to use the access point and by encrypting data sent over the wireless LAN.

Do it!

A-5: Describing wireless networking

Questions and answers
1 In wireless communications, what replaces the wire?
2 What should you consider when determining which wireless technology to use?

Network protocols

Explanation

Network *protocols* are the languages that computers, servers, and network devices use to communicate with each other. Protocols send data across the network in units called *packets*. The following table lists some common network LAN protocols that you can use in Windows networks.

Protocol	Description
Transmission Control Protocol/Internet Protocol (TCP/IP)	A routable, non-proprietary protocol that's the predominant Windows network protocol. It's supported by all versions of Windows and most other non-Microsoft operating systems. TCP/IP is also the protocol of the Internet.
Internetwork Packet Exchange/Sequenced Packet Exchange (IPX/SPX)	A routable, proprietary protocol that was the native protocol in early versions of Novell NetWare. Later versions of NetWare supported TCP/IP as the native protocol. Windows computers can connect to IPX/SPX networks and NetWare servers by using Microsoft's version of IPX/SPX, called NWLink. To share files and printers on a NetWare server, you must install the Microsoft Client for NetWare.
AppleTalk	A routable network protocol supported by Apple Macintosh computers. Windows NT and Windows 2000 support AppleTalk. Mac OS X (10.2 and later) supports TCP/IP and can connect to Windows networks without requiring AppleTalk support.
	AppleTalk computers are called nodes and can be configured as part of zones for sharing resources. As with other networks, each node on an AppleTalk network must be configured with a unique network address.
NetBEUI	A non-routable, proprietary Microsoft protocol that's supported in Windows 9x/Me, Windows NT, and Windows 2000. NetBEUI uses Network Basic Input/Output System (NetBIOS) services to communicate with other computers on a network. (NetBIOS helps with computer names and some basic communication services.) Although it isn't technically supported in Windows XP, you can install NetBEUI by manually copying files from the installation CD-ROM.
	What's nice about NetBEUI is that it has no settings to configure. You install the protocol, connect the computer to the network, and it just works. The drawback is that it isn't routable, so it can't pass data from one network segment to another. This means that it can't be used for remote access or any communication outside a single segment.

Wireless network protocols

Wireless networks send and receive information using one of four major wireless protocols:

- *Wi-Fi* (*Wireless Fidelity*) is the most widely used wireless technology at present. Wi-Fi began as 802.11b IEEE standard, although most implementations have been upgraded to use the newer 802.11g IEEE standard. 802.11b and 802.11g have an indoor transmission range of up to 35 meters.

- *Bluetooth* is a short-range wireless technology limited to transmission distances of about 100 meters or less, which generally confines it to connecting nodes within a single room or adjacent rooms.

- *802.11a* is an improved version of the original Wi-Fi technology and is also based on the same IEEE 802 standard. 802.11a has an indoor transmission range of up to 35 meters. 802.11a isn't compatible with 802.11b.

- *WiMAX* (*IEEE 802.16 Air Interface Standard*) is a point-to-multipoint broadband wireless access standard. It's an emerging wireless connection standard for long distances.

Do it!

A-6: Comparing network protocols used on Windows clients

Questions and answers

1 Which protocol was used in early versions of Novell NetWare?

   A TCP/IP

   B NetBEUI

   C IPX/SPX

   D AppleTalk

2 What is the predominant protocol in Windows networks?

   A TCP/IP

   B NetBEUI

   C IPX/SPX

   D AppleTalk

3 Which protocol requires no configuration?

   A TCP/IP

   B NetBEUI

   C IPX/SPX

   D AppleTalk

4 List the major wireless protocols.

5 Are 802.11b products compatible with 802.11a products?

Topic B: Network architectures

This topic covers the following CompTIA Network+ 2009 exam objectives.

#	Objective
Bridge objective **1.7**	**Compare the characteristics of wireless communication standards** • 802.11 a/b/g/n – Speeds
Bridge objective **2.1**	**Categorize standard cable types and their properties** Type: • CAT3, CAT5, CAT5e, CAT6 • Multimode fiber, single-mode fiber Properties: • Transmission speeds • Distance • Duplex • Frequency
Bridge objective **2.3**	**Identify common physical network topologies** • Star • Bus • Ring • Point to point • Point to multipoint • Hybrid
Bridge objective **2.5**	**Categorize WAN technology types and properties** Type: • Frame relay • E1/T1 • E3/T3 • ATM Properties: • Packet switch • Speed • Transmission media • Distance

Bridge objective

#	Objective
2.5	**Categorize WAN technology types and properties**

Type:

- Frame relay
- E1/T1
- ADSL
- SDSL
- VDSL
- Cable modem
- Satellite
- E3/T3
- Wireless
- ATM
- IDSN BRI
- ISDN PRI
- POTS
- PSTN

Properties:

- Circuit switch
- Packet switch
- Speed
- Transmission media
- Distance

#	Objective
2.6	**Categorize LAN technology types and properties**

Bridge objective

Types:

- Ethernet
- 10BaseT
- 100BaseTX
- 100BaseFX
- 1000BaseT
- 1000BaseX
- 10GBaseSR
- 10GBaseLR
- 10GBaseER
- 10GBaseSW
- 10GBaseLW
- 10GBaseEW
- 10GBaseT

Properties:

- CSMA/CD
- Broadcast
- Collision
- Bonding
- Speed
- Distance

Bridge objective

#	Objective
2.7	**Explain common logical network topologies and their characteristics**

- VPN

#	Objective
3.1	**Install, configure and differentiate between common network devices**

- Wireless access point

Explanation

A network's architecture consists of:

- The design of its wiring or radio wave connections.
- The configuration of its other physical components.
- Its software (programming).
- The protocols by which it operates.

All of these parts must be tightly organized into a physical structure with consistent operating methodology to establish a communication system that works smoothly among all the devices connected to the network.

The most common types of network architecture used today are Ethernet, Token Ring, and wireless. Each has advantages and limitations. The bandwidth, that is, the amount of data (measured in megabits per second) that the network can handle at once, varies among these architectures.

Network designs

The design of a networks' wiring or radio wave connections is called its physical topology. It's helpful to think of a topology as a shape. Common network topologies include the star, bus, ring, and mesh.

The star

In a star topology, each node is connected to a central network transmission device such as a hub or a switch, which serves as a distribution device. The central network transmission device then passes the information packets it receives from any device to the other devices connected to it. In a star, each computer has its own wired or wireless connection to the hub, as shown in Exhibit 1-12. The benefit of the star design is that because each computer has its own connection to the central network transmission device, when a single connection fails, it doesn't affect the communication ability of other computers connected to the same network transmission device. However, if the central network transmission device fails, all of the computers connected to that device will no longer be able to communicate on the network. Currently the star design is the most popular LAN physical topology.

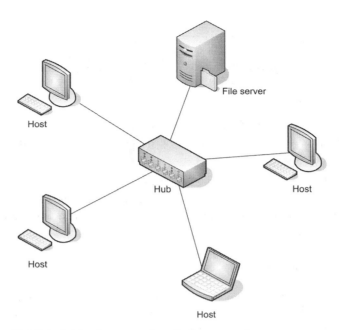

Exhibit 1-12: An example of a star topology

The bus

In a bus topology, each node is connected to the next by a direct line so that a continuous line is formed, as shown in Exhibit 1-13. There's no central point in this arrangement. Each node is simply connected to the next one on either side of it. The bus design incorporates coaxial cable and T connectors to connect the individual computers to the bus. When the end of the line is reached and there are no further nodes to be connected, the bus is closed off with a terminator device specific to the cabling used. In a bus Ethernet, data is sent on the network line in both directions from the source node. The data passes from one node to the next until it reaches the terminator at the end of the network. The terminator simply cancels the data signal, discarding the data so it can't echo back on the network line and head back to the node it just came from. All information on the network passes through each node but only once. There's no replication or broadcasting of data as in a star configuration. Each node determines if data it receives is addressed to it. If it is, the data is read and receipt is confirmed. If it isn't, the packet is passed on to the next node.

The benefit of a bus topology is that it's simple and inexpensive to set up. However, if there's a break in the line anywhere, all communication on that segment stops. The technology used is also not very scalable. Currently the bus design isn't used much in LAN physical topologies.

Exhibit 1-13: An example of a bus topology

The ring

In a ring topology, each node is connected to a central device by two wires, as shown in Exhibit 1-14. In Token Ring networks, this device is referred to as a multistation access unit (MSAU, although it is sometimes referred to as MAU). Communication is enabled by passing a token around the ring to each node—if a node has the token, it can transmit data. The token packet is always present somewhere on the network. It travels from the central device up one connecting wire to a node and back to the central device through the other wire, then up one wire to the next node and back through the other. It passes through the central device after each node and, after passing through all of them and returning to the central device, it travels back to its starting point at the other end of the central device through the main ring cable. The token travels in a circle or ring on the network in a single direction, even though the nodes are physically arranged as a star.

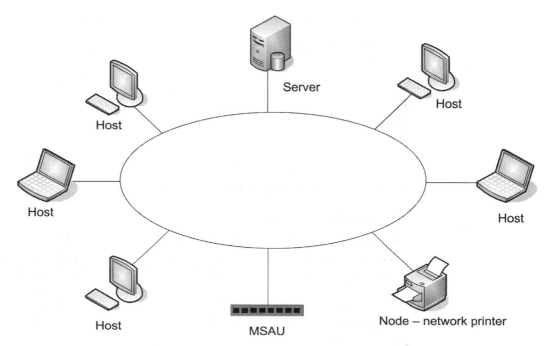

Exhibit 1-14: An example of a ring topology

The mesh

In a mesh topology, all nodes in the mesh have independent connections to all other nodes in the mesh, as shown in Exhibit 1-15. This configuration makes it very fault-tolerant and scalable. Mesh topologies require computers to have multiple network cards installed, and due to the complexity of wiring and support are rarely used for user computers.

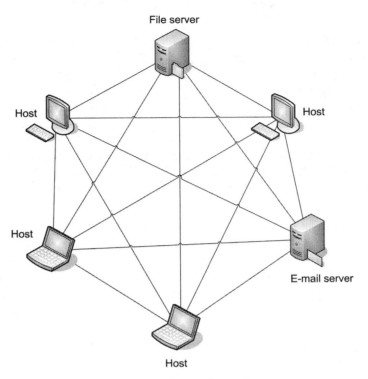

Exhibit 1-15: An example of a mesh topology

The hybrid

In a hybrid network topology two or more different types of network topologies are combined together into one network. For example, a large LAN might use a combination star and bus design with nodes connected to several hubs and the hubs connected in a bus configuration. This design is useful for constructing large networks with a minimum of wiring, but because all the hubs must still broadcast their data to the nodes, it tends to slow down as the amount of data flowing in it multiplies. Exhibit 1-16 shows a combined bus and star Ethernet design.

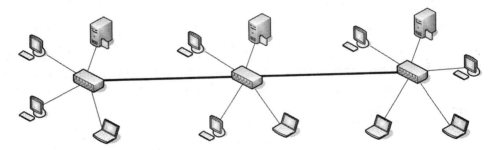

Exhibit 1-16: Combined bus and star Ethernet design

Notice the cable segments between hubs form the network backbone, which is the high-speed link between network segments.

Point-to-point versus point-to-multipoint

Each of the preceding network designs uses point-to-point or point-to-multipoint connections. In a point-to-point connection, there is a dedicated connection between two nodes—only those two nodes communicate over the connection. As shown in Exhibit 1-17, the connection between a wireless network and a LAN is typically a point-to-point connection—there's a dedicated communication line between the wireless access point and a LAN network transmission device. Another example of a point-to-point connection is the dial-up connection from a computer to an ISP.

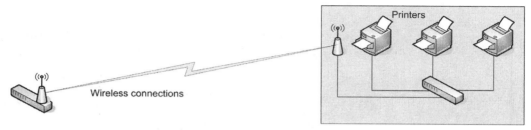

Exhibit 1-17: An example of a point-to-point connection

In a point-to-multipoint connection, there are multiple connections that connect a single node to multiple nodes. Network transmission devices, such as switches and hubs are point-to-multipoint devices.

Packet versus circuit switching networks

In a *packet switching network*, data is broken up into packets before it's sent over the network. Each packet is transmitted individually and is able to follow different routes to its destination. At the destination network node, the packets are queued as they arrive. Once all the packets forming the original data arrive at the destination, they're recompiled into the original form. In a *circuit switching network*, a dedicated line is allocated for the transmission of data between two network nodes.

Circuit-switching is the best choice when data needs to be transmitted quickly and must arrive in the same order in which it's sent, such as with most real-time data (live audio and video.) Packet switching is more efficient for data that can withstand delays in transmission, such as e-mail messages and Web pages.

Do it!

B-1: Describing physical network topologies

Questions and answers

1 Which physical network topologies make use of a central networking device?

2 Which physical network topology has the benefit that it's simple and inexpensive to set up?

3 In which physical network topology does all communication on that segment stop if there's a break in the line anywhere?

4 Which physical network topology is most fault-tolerant and scalable?

Mesh

5 What's the benefit of the hybrid network physical topology?

minimal wiring

6 How does a point-to-point connection differ from a point-to-multipoint connection?

Ethernet

Explanation

Ethernet is the most popular form of LAN in use today. It's popular because it strikes a good balance between ease of setup and use, speed, and cost. Four types of Ethernet architecture are available now. Each is distinguished primarily by the speed at which it operates.

- **10 Gigabit Ethernet** (also called *10GbE*) is the fastest of the Ethernet standards. With a data rate of 10 gigabits per second, it is ten times faster than Gigabit Ethernet.

- **1000-Mbps Ethernet** (also called *Gigabit Ethernet*) operates at a speed of 1000 Mbps (1 gigabit per second). It's used for large, high-speed LANs and heavy-traffic server connections. Few, if any, home networks require Gigabit Ethernet.

- **100-Mbps Ethernet** (also called *Fast Ethernet*) operates at a speed of 100 Mbps. It can also handle data at 10 Mbps, and this feature allows devices running at the slower speed to operate on the same network along with those operating at 100 Mbps.

- **10-Mbps Ethernet** (also called *Twisted Pair Ethernet*) operates at a speed of 10 megabits per second (Mbps) of data. The first Ethernet version was developed by the Xerox Corporation in the 1970s. It later became known as Ethernet IEEE 802.3.

Each Ethernet version can be set up using various types of wire or cable, but the different speeds of the versions and the conditions in which they operate usually dictate what type of connecting wires you need to use. Designations for the different Ethernet standards are based on the medium each standard uses:

- **BASE-X** and **BASE-R** standards—Run over fiber optic cable.

- **BASE-W** standards—Run over fiber optic cables; referred to as *Wide Area Network Physical Layer* (*WAN PHY*). Uses the same types of fiber and support the same distances as 10GBASE-R standards, however with these standards Ethernet frames are encapsulated in SONET frames.

- **BASE-T** standards—Run over twisted pair cable; shielded or unshielded.

- **BASE-CX** standards—Run over shielded copper twisted pair cable.

Most current Ethernet installations use shielded twisted-pair (STP) cable, unshielded twisted-pair (UTP) cable, or fiber optic cable. Older Ethernet installations used either 50-ohm RG58/U coaxial cable, also known as thin Ethernet and 10Base2, or 50-ohm RG8/U coaxial, known as thick Ethernet and 10Base5, but these are both obsolete now.

10 Gigabit Ethernet standards

The following table lists the 10 Gigabit Ethernet standards and their specifications.

Standard	Medium	Distance: up to	Notes
10GBASE-T	Copper twisted pair—shielded or unshielded	100 meters with CAT6a; up to 55 meters with CAT6	
10GBASE-SR 10GBASE-SW	Multi-mode fiber	26 meter or 82 meters depending on cable type 300 meters over 50 µm 2000 MHz·km OM3 multi-mode fiber	Preferred choice for optical cabling within buildings.
10GBASE-LR 10GBASE-LW	Single-mode fiber	10 kilometers	Used to connect transceivers.
10GBASE-ER 10GBASE-EW	Single-mode fiber	40 kilometers	
10GBASE-ZR 10GBASE-ZW	Single-mode fiber	80 km	Not specified in standards; built to Cisco optical specifications.

Gigabit Ethernet standards

The following table lists the gigabit Ethernet standards and their specifications.

Standard	Medium	Distance: up to	Notes
1000BASE-T	Unshielded twisted pair—CAT5, CAT5e, or CAT6	100 meters per network segment	Requires all four wire pairs.
1000BASE-CX	Balanced copper shielded twisted-pair	25 meters	An initial standard for gigabit Ethernet connections.
1000BASE-LX	Single-mode optic fiber	5 km *	(See paragraphs following table.)
1000BASE-LX10	Single-mode optic fiber	10 km	Wavelength of 1270 to 1355 nm.
1000BASE-BX10	Single-mode fiber, over single-strand fiber	10 km	Different wavelength going in each direction—1490 nm downstream, 1310 nm upstream.
1000BASE-LH	Single-mode optic fiber	10km	Wavelength of 1300 or 1310nm. Non-standard implementation. Very similar to 1000BASE-LX, but achieves longer distances due to higher quality optics. 1000BASE-LH is backwards compatible with 1000BASE-LX.
1000BASE-ZX	Single-mode optic fiber	70 km	1550 nm wavelength. Non-standard implementation.
1000BASE-SX	Multi-mode optic fiber	500 meters	

* The 1000BASE-LX standard specifies transmission over a single-mode optic fiber, at distances of up to 5 km over 9 µm (micron or micrometer). In practice, it often operates correctly over a much greater distance. Many manufacturers guarantee operation up to 10 to 20 km, provided that their equipment is used at both ends of the link.

1000BASE-LX can also run over multi-mode fiber with a maximum segment length of 550 m. Link distances greater than 300 m might require a special launch conditioning patch cord. The launch conditioning patch cord launches the laser at a precise offset from the center of the fiber. This causes the laser to spread across the diameter of the fiber core, reducing differential mode delay. Differential mode delay occurs when the laser couples onto a limited number of available modes in the multi-mode fiber.

Fast Ethernet standards

The following table lists the Fast Ethernet standards and their specifications.

Standard	Medium	Distance: up to	Notes
100BASE-TX	Twisted-pair copper—CAT5 or above	100 meters per network segment	Runs over two pairs—one pair of twisted wires in each direction. The most common Fast Ethernet.
100BASE-T4	Twisted-pair copper—CAT3		Requires four pairs—one pair for transmit, one for receiving, and remaining pairs switch direction as negotiated. An early implementation of Fast Ethernet.
100BASE-T2	Twisted-pair copper		Runs over two pairs.
100BASE-FX	Singe or multi-mode fiber	400 meters for half-duplex; 2 km for full-duplex over MMF	Uses two strands—one for receiving and one for transmitting. Not compatible with 10BASE-FL.
100BASE-SX	Multi-mode fiber	300 meters	Uses two strands of MMF—one for receiving and one for transmitting. Backwards-compatible with 10BASE-FL.
100BASE-BX	Single-mode fiber	20 km	Uses a single strand of SMF.

Ethernet bonding

Ethernet bonding combines the bandwidth of two network interface cards as a cost-effective way to increase bandwidth available for data transfers for critical servers, such as firewalls and production servers. Ethernet bonding can also provide fault tolerance, so that when one NIC fails, you can replace it without disabling client access to the server.

Do it!

B-2: Describing Ethernet standards

Questions and answers

1 Which is the fastest Ethernet standard?

10 GB

2 Which Ethernet standards run over fiber optic cables?

10 GB per sec

3 What type of cabling do most current Ethernet networks use?

100 unshielded twisted pair

4 Which 10 Gigabit Ethernet standard is capable of running the longest distance?

10 Base ER 2w

5 What type of cabling would you use for a 1000BASE-T Ethernet network?

Cut Fi 6 or cat Ft E

6 What difference in cabling use is there between 100BASE-TX and 1000BASE-T?

Ethernet networks

Explanation
Ethernet networks can be physically arranged in either of two configurations, which refer to how the nodes (devices) are connected to the Ethernet:

- Bus topology
- Star topology

A star Ethernet might be slower than a bus Ethernet, especially if there are many nodes on the network. This happens because the hub generates a lot of data traffic that isn't used. It replicates all the data it receives from any source and sends it to every node. The amount of data being sent increases for every node added to the network, even though most of the data sent to each node isn't intended for that node and is discarded on arrival.

A node on an Ethernet network waits to send information to the network until it determines that no other node is transmitting information, and then begins transmitting itself. During transmission, the system also listens in on the media. If it senses that another node is also transmitting, a collision event occurs, as shown in Exhibit 1-18. When this happens, the node quits transmitting for a random period of time and then checks the media again to see if it is okay to transmit. Any station might transmit when it senses that the carrier is free. If a collision is detected, each station will wait for a randomly determined interval before retransmitting.

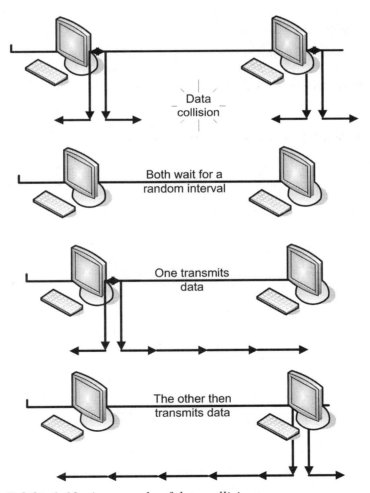

Exhibit 1-18: An example of data collision

As the amount of data sent increases, more and more data packets from different nodes competing for bandwidth on the LAN collide with one another. The network detects these collisions and resends the data packets involved, but the collisions and replication of data transmissions slow down the network. Most network operating systems track retransmissions, which are a good indication of the number of collisions occurring on the network.

Collisions slow cable throughput. At some point in its growth, an Ethernet network might encounter a reduction in performance. This depends on the amount of traffic generated by each workstation.

Channel access methods

The channel access method determines the physical methodology by which data is sent across the transmitting media. Today, there are various channel access methods through which conversation is made possible. These technologies are analogous to two of the ways that people communicate. For example, imagine that a specific problem and its possible resolutions are discussed in a meeting. This phase of the meeting is more of a free for all in which there might be moments where everyone talks and other times where most hold off speaking, yielding to only one speaker, after which everyone again attempts to communicate their thoughts. Now, consider yourself in a departmental staff meeting discussing project status. Each member of the team waits his turn to communicate the successes and failures for the week. After completing, the next person communicates his status. This process continues in an orderly fashion until all have had a chance to speak.

The example of several people talking at once is an example of a *Carrier Sense Multiple Access with Collision Detection (CSMA/CD) communications methodology*. CSMA/CD networks are more popularly known as Ethernet networks. CSMA/CD is the most common implementation of channel access.

- Carrier sensing—Listens for someone talking.
- Multiple access—All have concurrent access to the media.
- Collision detection—If two or more systems transmit at once, the system realizes the message did not get through and repeats the message.

Transmission failures can be caused by:

- Bad cabling
- Improper termination
- Collisions
- Improper cable length

The terms Ethernet and 802.3 are used interchangeably. There are some small differences, but both are CSMA/CD specifications. Ethernet was originally developed by Xerox, Intel, and DEC in the late 1970s, with specifications first released in 1980. The IEEE 802.3 specification differs from Ethernet primarily with respect to the frame format. Other differences involve pinouts and the Signal Quality Error (SQE) signal, also known as a heartbeat.

A variation on this theme is *Carrier Sense Multiple Access with Collision Avoidance (CSMA/CA)*. This methodology doesn't detect collisions as much as it attempts to avoid collisions. An alert message notifies nodes of an impending transmission. Any collisions that occur will be during this alert sequence rather than during actual data transmission. Because the alert sequence is shorter than an actual data transmission, the retransmit of lengthy data is avoided.

Token Ring networks

Token Ring LAN technology was developed by IBM Corporation. It operates at slower speeds than Ethernet, 4 Mbps or 16 Mbps depending on the Token Ring network, but it's physically arranged in a star topology, one of the designs also used by Ethernet. Token Ring LANs are so named because their protocol for data control uses a token, a small packet of data, to determine which node on the network can transmit data, and because all data actually travels in a circle or ring on the network.

In a Token Ring, each node is connected to a central device, referred to as a *Multistation Access Unit* (*MSAU*), by two wires. A token packet is always present somewhere on the network, traveling from the MSAU up one connecting wire to a node and back to the MSAU through the other wire, then up one wire to the next node and back through the other. It passes through the MSAU after each node and, after passing through all of them and returning to the MSAU, it travels back to its starting point at the other end of the MSAU through the Token Ring's main ring cable. While the Token Ring network physically appears to be a star, it's actually a ring. You can think of this design as a ring in a box. Exhibit 1-19 shows how a Token Ring network connects nodes through a MSAU. Token Ring networks are usually connected using shielded twisted pair cabling.

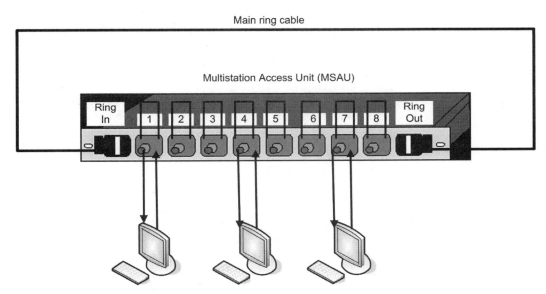

Exhibit 1-19: A Token Ring LAN

Wireless LANs

As their name suggests, wireless LANs don't use wires to connect the nodes of the network. The nodes aren't physically connected at all to one another or to a central device. They communicate with an access point or wireless hub using a wireless network interface card (NIC), which includes a transceiver and an antenna. The wireless NIC allows the node to communicate over relatively short distances using radio waves, which it sends to, and receives from, the nearest hub. Exhibit 1-20 shows how nodes on a wireless LAN connect by radio waves to access points or hubs that are wired to the network.

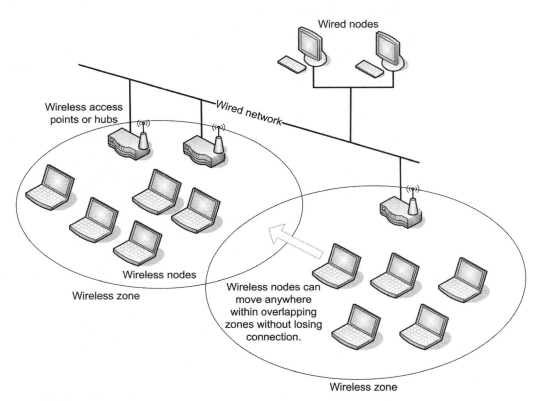

Exhibit 1-20: A wireless LAN design

Wireless connections can be made from a node to a hub through walls and other obstructions, because radio waves pass through solid obstructions fairly easily. This ability makes wireless LANs very useful and cost-effective in already finished buildings where retrofitting wiring is both difficult and expensive. It's also an advantage where hardwiring a network might be impossible, such as on the beach at a summer home, or to a boat tied up at a private dock. Wireless LANs are limited, however, both by the low transmitting power of their NICs and hubs and by the fact that dense metals, especially ferrous metals, as well as heavy layers of concrete, stone, brick, or dirt, absorb radio waves. These factors restrict the distance over which a wireless network can be extended and might require more hubs than anticipated to obtain full-area coverage.

Hubs or access points must be placed so that the wireless NICs of nodes can access at least one of them from any location within the LAN's defined area. Wireless networked nodes communicate with one another only through a hub, rather than directly node to node, as in a bus Ethernet. Hubs must be wired together or connected by wireless technology into a network that allows all hubs to communicate with one another and transmit the data they receive from their wireless nodes. A wireless LAN isn't entirely free of wired connections. It's usually connected to a cable network by its hubs, which constitute nodes on a wired LAN.

Do it!   **B-3:   Identifying the characteristics of the various physical architectures**

Here's how	Here's why
1 Examine the network in your classroom	You'll identify characteristics of physical architectures.
What's the physical architecture of the classroom network?	
2 If the architecture is Ethernet, which of the four types is being used?	
3 What's the medium used?	
4 What's the potential speed of the network?	
5 What's the physical topology of the classroom architecture?	
6 Could this network be a wireless network? Why or why not?	
7 What's the maximum network segment distance?	

WAN bandwidth technologies

Explanation

A wide area network (WAN) spans larger geographical distances and connects multiple LANs together using high-speed communication lines, as shown in Exhibit 1-21. Wide area networks expand the basic LAN model by linking LANs to communicate with one another. By traditional definition, a LAN becomes a WAN when you expand the network configuration beyond your own premises and many times lease data communication lines from a public carrier. WANs support data transmissions across public carriers by using facilities such as dial-up lines, dedicated lines, or packet switching.

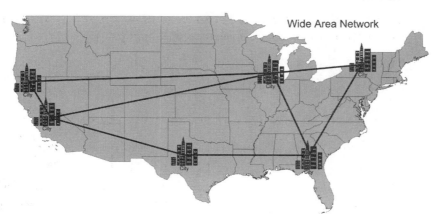

Exhibit 1-21: A wide area network (WAN)

There are several ways to create WAN connections, depending on location and available hardware:

- **Dial-up networking (DUN)**—Uses a modem to connect through regular, analog phone lines.
- **Virtual private network (VPN)**—A network connection that uses encryption and security protocols to create a private network over a public network.
- **Digital Subscriber Line (DSL)**—High-speed connections made over regular analog phone lines.
- **Cable**—Connections made over the same lines that carry cable television signals.
- **Satellite**—Connections made by sending and receiving signals from satellites in orbit around the earth.
- **Wireless**—Used to connect users in hotspots, where wireless Internet service is provided by an employer, business, or governmental unit, such as a city. Wireless connections can also be made over cellular telephone networks.
- **Cellular**—Connections made through a cell phone or laptop's cellular network PC card on a cellular phone network.

Faster WAN technologies are used to connect a small ISP or large business to a regional ISP, and a regional ISP to an Internet backbone. These technologies include the following:

- T lines and E lines
- X.25 and frame relay
- ATM

POTS/PSTN

The slowest but least expensive Internet connection to an ISP is affectionately known as *plain old telephone service* (*POTS*). Also referred to as the public switched telephone network (PSTN), it's the network of the world's public circuit-switched telephone networks. This is the most common method of home connection and uses a dialup system each time the connection to the ISP is made over the telephone line, as shown in Exhibit 1-22. The connection isn't continuous, and when the line isn't connected to an ISP, it can be used for regular telephone service or any other telecommunications function. Data speed on a regular telephone line is a maximum of 56 Kbps.

A technology called *modem bonding* allows multiple dial-up links over POTS to be combined for redundancy or increased throughput.

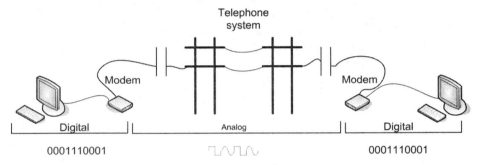

Exhibit 1-22: Communication via POTS/PSTN

ISDN

Integrated Services Digital Network (*ISDN*) technology also uses a telephone line to transmit data, but unlike POTS, the data isn't converted to analog form—the modem used must be a digital modem. An ISDN line is digital and consists of two phone circuits, both carried on one pair of wires along with a slower, third circuit used for control signals. Each data circuit can transmit data at up to 64 Kbps and the two circuits can be combined to move data at a speed of 128 Kbps. This configuration of an ISDN line is known as the *basic rate interface* (*BRI*) and is intended for home and small-business users. Another higher-cost ISDN level of service is called *primary service interface* (*PRI*) and is intended for larger users. It has 23 data channels and a control channel.

DSL

A *Digital Subscriber Line* (*DSL*) is a high-speed data and voice transmission line that still uses telephone wires for data transmission but carries the digital data at frequencies well above those used for voice transmission. This makes possible the transmission of voice and digital data on the same line at the same time. The regular voice telephone line must be dialed for each use, but the DSL part of the line is always connected to the computer. A DSL can transmit data at speeds up to 1.5 Mbps in both directions, or it can be set up as an asymmetric line (ADSL), which can transmit up to 640 Kbps upstream (to the ISP) and 7.1 Mbps downstream (from the ISP). Higher bandwidth can be achieved by bonding multiple DSL lines, similar to the modem bonding technology described for POTS.

Cable

A *cable modem* connects to the cable television line that's already installed or available in most homes. These devices are actually transceivers (transmitter/receivers), rather than modems, but are commonly known as cable modems. With a cable modem, digital data is converted to analog signals and placed on the cable at the same time as the incoming television signal. Incoming analog data signals are converted to digital for the computer by the modem. The data frequencies differ from the television signal frequencies, and the two signals don't interfere with one another on the cable. Depending on the individual configuration, a cable modem can transmit data at speeds from 500 Kbps up to 5 Mbps. Many cable companies now offer Voice over IP (VoIP) service, also known as digital phone service, to their users.

With VoIP, you can make telephone calls over a data network such as the Internet. VoIP converts the analog signals from digital back to voice at the other end so you can speak to anyone with a regular phone number.

An example of a cable connection is shown in Exhibit 1-23.

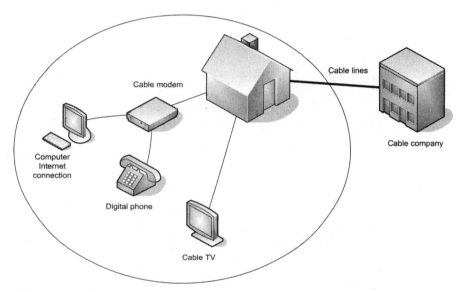

Exhibit 1-23: Cable connections

Satellite

A satellite link Internet connection to an ISP is now available nationwide. It's especially attractive in rural areas where telephone-based services may be limited, and cable sometimes isn't available. A satellite communication link uses a dish similar to a satellite television dish mounted on the building to communicate with a stationary satellite in orbit. The server is connected to the dish antenna. Incoming Internet data travels from the ISP to the satellite in orbit, then down to the dish and into the LAN server. The speed of the connection varies according to the ISP but can go up to 1.5 Mbps. The uplink connection from the LAN to the ISP is usually by a telephone line/modem connection and isn't as fast as the satellite downlink. A digital radio signal from the LAN up to the satellite, which in turn sends the signal to the ISP, is also available but at a much higher cost than the telephone connection, which is usually adequate for sent data. Exhibit 1-24 illustrates how a satellite ISP sends data at high speed to LANs via a stationary satellite and receives data from the LAN over a slower telephone/modem line.

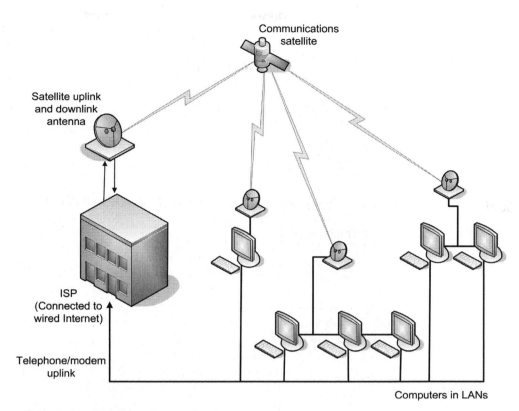

Exhibit 1-24: Satellite ISP configuration

Wireless

The term "wireless" refers to several technologies and systems that don't use cables for communication, including public radio, cellular telephones, one-way paging, satellite, infrared, and private, proprietary radio. With the expense and the concern that increasing the use of wireless might affect our health, airplane control systems, pacemakers, and other similar items, wireless isn't as popular as wired data transmission. Wireless is an important technology for mobile devices and for Internet access in remote locations where other methods aren't an option.

For Internet access, two popular applications of wireless are:

- Fixed-point wireless, sometimes called *Wireless Local Loop* (*WLL*)
- Mobile wireless

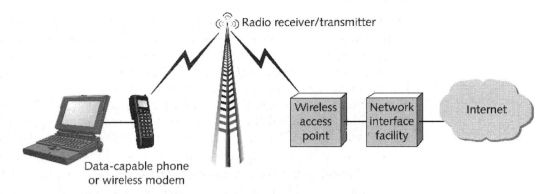

Exhibit 1-25: Wireless WAN

Cellular

All the major cellular phone companies now provide Internet connection service for their customers. Wherever you have cell phone service reception, you can connect to the Internet using your Internet capable phone or laptop using a cellular network PC card. Cell phone companies typically charge an additional monthly fee for this service. The connection speed for cellular Internet service is faster than dial-up, but is slower than DSL or cable. There are currently three connection technologies in use—*Enhanced Data rates for GSM Evolution* (*EDGE*), *Evolution-Data Optimized* (*EV-DO*), and *High-Speed Downlink Packet Access* (*HSDPA*).

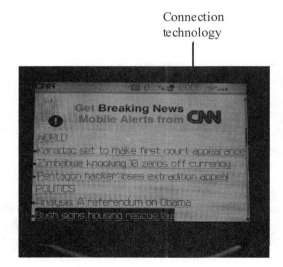

Exhibit 1-26: Cellular Internet access using EDGE

T lines and E lines

The first successful system that supported digitized voice transmission was introduced in the 1960s and was called a T-carrier. A T-carrier works with a leased digital communications line provided through a common carrier, such as BellSouth or AT&T. Although it was originally intended for voice, the line also works with data. The system has become a popular choice for Internet access for larger companies. The leased lines are permanent connections that use multiplexing, a process of dividing a single channel into multiple channels that can be used to carry voice, data, video, or other signals. Several variations of T-carrier lines are available; the most popular are T1 and T3 lines.

- For a T1 line, multiplexing allows the line to carry 24 channels, and each channel is capable of transmitting 64 Kbps. A 24-channel T1 line can transmit a total of 1.544 Mbps. If a T1 is used for voice only, it can support 24 separate telephone lines, one for each channel.
- A T3 line can carry 672 channels, giving it a throughput of 44.736 Mbps.

T1 and T3 lines can be used by a business to support both voice and data, with some channels allocated to each.

The E-carrier is the European equivalent of the American T-carrier. The E-carrier is a digital transmission format devised by ITU. The ITU Web site can be found at www.itu.int. An E1 line can transmit data at a rate of 2.048 Mbps, and an E3 line can work at speeds of 34.368 Mbps.

Both T-carriers and E-carriers use four wires, two for receiving and two for sending. Originally copper wires were used (telephone wiring), but digital signals require a clearer connection, so shielded twisted-pair wiring became the preferred wire. The carriers need repeaters that can regenerate the signal every 6,000 feet. Businesses with multiple T1 lines generally use coaxial, fiber optic, or microwave cabling, a high-end, high-performance cabling that can support microwave frequencies. With T3, microwave or fiber optic cabling is required.

A fractional T1 line is an option for organizations that don't need a full T1 line. The fractional T1 allows businesses to lease some of the channels of a T1 line rather than leasing all 24 channels. This arrangement is also good for businesses that expect to grow into a T1 line eventually. Each T1 channel has a throughput of 64 Kbps, so a fractional T1 can be leased in 64-Kbps increments.

X.25 and frame relay

Both X.25 and frame relay are packet-switching communication protocols designed for long-distance data transmission rather than the circuit-switching technology used by the telephone system. Packet-switching technology divides data into packets and sends each packet separately; it's the technology used by the Internet. Each packet might be sent on a different path. This technology works well, because it can use the bandwidth more efficiently.

Frame relay is based on X.25, but it's a digital version, whereas X.25 is an analog technology. Frame relay is digital, so it can support higher throughput of up to 1.544 Mbps, compared with X.25, which supports up to 56 Kbps. X.25 was popular for about 20 years and was the most common packet-switching technology used on WANs. Frame relay, which was standardized in 1984, has largely replaced X.25.

Both X.25 and frame relay use a *permanent virtual circuit* (*PVC*). PVC is a logical connection between two nodes. PVCs aren't dedicated lines, as the T-carriers are. Rather, when you lease a PVC, you specify the nodes (two endpoints) and the amount of bandwidth required, but the carrier reserves the right to send the data along any number of paths between the two stationary endpoints. You then share the bandwidth with other users who lease the X.25 or frame relay circuit.

The biggest advantage of X.25 and frame relay is that you have to pay for only the amount of bandwidth you require. Frame relay is less expensive than newer technologies, and it has worldwide standards already established. Both X.25 and frame relay use shared lines, so throughput decreases as traffic increases.

Circuits for X.25 aren't readily available in North America, but frame relay circuits can be found easily. International businesses that communicate overseas might use frame relay to connect offices.

ATM

Asynchronous Transfer Mode (*ATM*) is a very fast network technology that can be used with LANs as well as WANs. It uses fixed-length packets, called cells, to transmit data, voice, video, and frame relay traffic. Each cell is 53 bytes, 48 bytes of data plus a 5-byte header. The header contains the information necessary to route the packet. All the packets used by ATM are 53 bytes; it's easy to determine the number of packets and the traffic flow, which helps utilize bandwidth.

ATMs also use virtual circuits, meaning the two endpoints are stationary, but the paths between these two endpoints can change. They can use either PVCs or *switched virtual circuits* (*SVCs*). SVCs are logical, point-to-point connections that depend on the ATM to decide the best path along which to send the data. The routes are determined before the data is even sent. In contrast, an Ethernet network transmits the data before determining the route it takes; the routers and switches are responsible for deciding the paths.

ATMs achieve a throughput of 622 Mbps. This makes them popular for large LANs, because they're faster than Ethernet at 100 Mbps. An ATM network works best with fiber optic cable, so it can attain high throughput, however, it also works with coaxial or twisted-pair cable.

The following table compares a number of communication bandwidth technologies, their common uses, and their speeds.

Technology	Maximum throughput speed	Common uses and connection type
POTS	Up to 56 Kbps	Home and small business access to an ISP using a modem and a standard phone line.
ISDN	64 Kbps to 128 Kbps	Medium-level home and business access to an ISP using a Network Terminal Interface (NT1), terminal equipment (TE), and terminal adapter (TA).
Digital subscriber link (DSL)	Up to 1.5 Mbps	Home and business access to an ISP using a DSL transceiver and a standard phone line coming into the transceiver and either a USB or Ethernet RJ-45 connection to the computer.
DSL Lite or G.Lite	Up to 384 Kbps upstream; up to 6 Mbps downstream	Less expensive version of DSL for home and business using a DSL modem.

Technology	Maximum throughput speed	Common uses and connection type
Asymmetric digital subscriber line (ADSL)	640 Kbps upstream; up to 6.1 Mbps downstream	Home/business access with most bandwidth from ISP to user using an ADSL transceiver.
Symmetric digital subscriber line (SDSL)	1.544 Mbps	Home/business access; equal bandwidth in both directions using a single separate line from your standard phone line.
High-bit-rate DSL (HDSL)	1.5 Mbps	Home/business access using two separate lines from your standard phone line.
Very high-bit-rate DSL (VDSL)	Up to 52 Mbps downstream and 16 Mbps upstream	Home/business access using VDSL transceiver in your home and a VDSL gateway in the junction box.
Cable modem	512 Kbps to 5 Mbps	Home/business access to ISP using a cable modem and RG-59 cable going in and either Ethernet RJ-45, coax RG-58, or USB connection to the computer or a router.
802.11b wireless	5.5 Mbps or 11 Mbps	Home/business LANs using wireless router or wireless access point.
802.11g wireless	Up to 54 Mbps	Home/business access using wireless router or wireless access point.
802.11a wireless	Up to 54 Mbps	Home/business access using wireless router or wireless access point.
Enhanced Data rates for GSM Evolution (EDGE)	200 Kbps	Used by cellular phone companies that use Global System for Mobile Communications (GSM).
Evolution-Data Optimized (EV-DO)	300 to 400 Kbps upstream; 400 to 700 Kbps downstream	Used by cellular phone companies that use Code Division Multiple Access (CDMA).
High-Speed Downlink Packet Access (HSDPA)	384 Kbps upstream; 3.6 Mbps or higher downstream	Currently isn't in widespread use by cellular phone companies.
T1	1.544 Mbps	Shared leased line access for businesses supports both voice and data.
T3	44.736 Mbps	Shared leased line access for businesses supports both voice and data.
E1	2.048 Mbps	European equivalent of T1.
E3	34.368 Mbps	European equivalent of T3.
X.25	up to 56 Kbps	Packet-switching communication designed for long-distance data transmission.
Frame relay	up to 1.544 Mbps	Digital version of X.25.
ATM	622 Mbps	Popular for WANs and LANs. Works with fiber optic, twisted-pair, or coaxial cabling.

WAN mesh topology

Explanation   A mesh network topology is highly reliable and is used when the network reliability is critical and can justify the added expense. A mesh topology provides multiple point-to-point links between routers in a WAN, giving more than one choice on how data can travel from router to router. In a mesh topology, a router searches out multiple paths and determines the best one to take. Routers can make these decisions, based on how busy a network is, how many hops are between two remote networks, how much bandwidth is available, and the cost of using a network. A mesh topology offers added security, because routers can have their own dedicated line connections. A mesh topology also offers added reliability, because there's more than one option between routers.

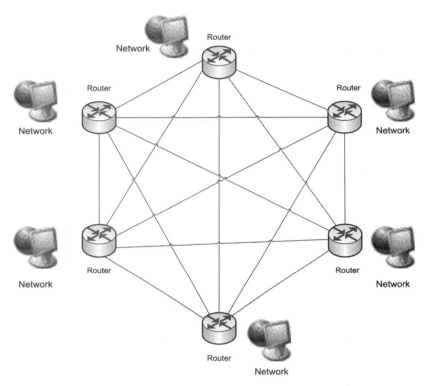

Exhibit 1-27: A mesh network

In addition, if one router fails, the WAN can still function. On the other hand, a mesh topology can be rather expensive, as added network cards and cabling are required. It's sometimes used on an ATM LAN or WAN.

Do it!   **B-4:   Discussing WAN bandwidth technologies**

Questions and answers

1 What's the difference between a T line and an E line?

US standard   European

2 How often is a repeater needed on a T line?

6000 ft

3 What's a fractional T1 line?

Less than 24 channel

4 What's packet-switching technology?

Cloud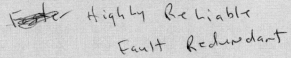

5 Name two packet-switching technologies.

X25   Relay Frame

6 What's ATM?

Fixed Length Packets

7 What's a benefit of ATM?

Voice + data

8 What are the benefits of mesh topology?

~~Faster~~ Highly Reliable
                 Fault Redundant

Topic C: The OSI model

This topic covers the following CompTIA Network+ 2009 exam objective.

#	Objective
4.1	**Explain the function of each layer of the OSI model**
	• Layer 1 – physical
	• Layer 2 – data link
	• Layer 3 – network
	• Layer 4 – transport
	• Layer 5 – session
	• Layer 6 – presentation
	• Layer 7 – application

Explanation

The *Open Systems Interconnection* (*OSI*) *model* is a standard means of describing a network operating system by defining it as a series of layers, each with specific input and output. It describes a theoretical model of what happens to information being sent from one computer to another on a network. The sending computer works from the Application layer down, and the receiving computer works on the transmitted data from the Physical layer up. The OSI model was developed by the International Standards Organization (ISO) and has seven layers that are numbered in order from the bottom (Layer 1) to the top (Layer 7).

The names of the various layers, starting from the top, are as follows:

- Layer 7—Application layer (top layer), the layer in which applications on a network node (computer) access network services, such as file transfers, electronic mail, and database access.

- Layer 6—Presentation layer, the layer that translates application layer data to an intermediate form that provides security, encryption, and compression for the data.

- Layer 5—Session layer, the layer that establishes and controls data communication between applications operating on two different computers, regulating when each can send data and how much.

- Layer 4—Transport layer, the layer that divides long communications into smaller data packages, handles error recognition and correction, and acknowledges the correct receipt of data.

- Layer 3—Network layer, the layer that addresses data messages, translates logical addresses into actual physical addresses, and routes data to addresses on the network.

- Layer 2—Data Link layer, the layer that packages bits of data from the physical layer into frames (logical, structured data packets), transfers them from one computer to another, and receives acknowledgement from the addressed computer.

- Layer 1—Physical layer (bottom layer), the layer that transmits bits (binary digits) from one computer to another and regulates the transmission stream over a medium (wire, fiber optics, or radio waves).

All parts of network operating systems function in one of these seven layers. If you can visualize the layer in which an operating system functions, you have a clearer understanding of how it relates to the rest of the network operating system.

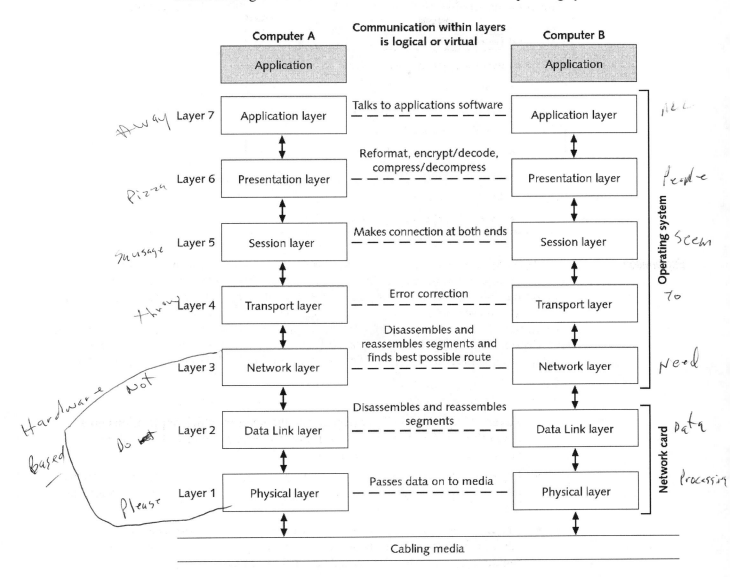

Exhibit 1-28: The OSI model

The OSI model applied to local area networking

The applications, operating systems, and network technology you choose determine how the OSI model is applied to your network.

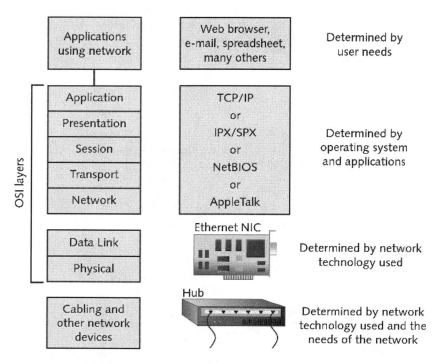

Exhibit 1-29: A LAN compared with the OSI model

Do it!

C-1:   **Analyzing the OSI model**

1 Use the following clues to complete the crossword.

ACROSS:

    2. Layer that transmits bits from one computer to another and regulates the transmission stream over a medium.

    3. Layer in which programs on a network node access network services.

    6. Layer that divides long communications into smaller data packages, handles error recognition and correction, and acknowledges the correct receipt of data.

DOWN:

    1. Layer that packages bits of data from the physical layer into frames, transfers them from one computer to another, and receives acknowledgement from the addressed computer.

    2. Layer that translates application layer data to an intermediate form that provides security, encryption, and compression for the data.

    4. Layer that establishes and controls data communication between applications operating on two different computers, regulating when each can send data and how much.

    5. Layer that addresses data messages, translates logical addresses into actual physical addresses, and routes data to addresses on the network.

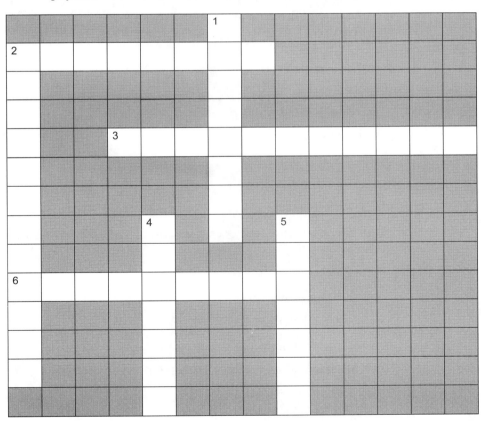

Unit summary: Network basics

Topic A   In this topic, you learned the basic components of a network. You learned the differences between a **LAN** and a **WAN**. You learned about the differences between the two basic types of networks—**peer-to-peer** and **client/server**, including the differences in authentication. You saw how larger networks are broken up into smaller pieces called **segments** and then connected together by a **backbone**. You examine three different types of network wiring—**fiber optic**, **twisted pair** (both shielded and unshielded), and **coaxial cables**. You also learned how wireless LANs create connections without physical wires. Finally, you learned about some common communication protocols used on wired and wireless networks.

Topic B   In this topic, you learned a network's architecture consists of the design of its wiring or radio wave connections, the configuration of its other physical components, its software, and the protocols by which it operates. You examined the **physical topologies** that you can configure your network in—**star**, **bus**, **ring**, **mesh**, or **hybrid**. You also learned how packet- and circuit-switching networks use different methods for data transmission. You learned the differences between the **10GbE**, **Gigabyte Ethernet**, **Fast Ethernet**, and **10-Mbps Ethernet** standards. You examined how Ethernet and Token Ring networks communicate based on their architecture. Finally, you looked at WAN bandwidth technologies—**POTS/PSTN**, **ISDN**, **DSL**, **cable**, **satellite**, **wireless**, **cellular**, **T and E lines**, **X.25**, **frame relay**, and **ATM**.

Topic C   In this topic, you examined the seven layers of the **Open Systems Interconnection (OSI) model**. You learned that this model is used to describe a theoretical representation of what happens to information being sent from one computer to another on a network.

Review questions

1 Which network type is a specifically designed configuration of computers and other devices located within a confined area?

   A Peer-to-peer network

   B Local area network

   C Client/server network

   D Wide area network

2 In which network type does each host on the LAN has the same authority as other hosts?

   A Peer-to-peer network

   B Local area network

   C Client/server network

   D Wide area network

3 Which network type requires a network operating system (NOS)?

   A Peer-to-peer network

   B Local area network

   C Client/server network

   D Wide area network

4 Large networks are frequently broken down into manageable pieces called
segments .

5 Which network component is most vulnerable to performance problems caused by poor installation practices?

A Clients

B Servers

C Wiring

D Network transmission devices

6 Which network medium carries light-based data through strands of glass or plastic no thicker than a human hair?

A Coaxial

B Twisted pair

C Fiber optic

D Wireless

7 Which network medium is composed of four pairs of wires, where the pairs are twisted together and bundled within a covering?

A Coaxial

B Twisted pair

C Fiber optic

D Wireless

8 Which network medium contains a layer of braided wire or foil between the core and the outside insulating layer, plus another layer of plastic or rubberized material that separates the central core from the shielding layer?

A Coaxial

B Twisted pair

C Fiber optic

D Wireless

9 Which network medium is a popular choice for outdoors or in an historic building?

A Coaxial

B Twisted pair

C Fiber optic

D Wireless

10 Fiber optic cabling is often used as the _Backbone_ for networks.

11 _Composite_ cable has the best wiring value and expansion capability.

12 Which type of coaxial cable is used for low-power video and RF signal connections?

 A RG-6

 B RG-8

 C RG-11

 D RG-58

 E RG-59

13 Thicknet cables are which type? (Choose all that apply.)

 A RG-6

 B RG-8

 C RG-11

 D RG-58

 E RG-59

14 Security on a WLAN is accomplished by ___Filtering___ the MAC addresses of wireless NICs that are allowed to use the access point and by encrypting data sent over the wireless LAN.

15 Which wireless protocol is a short-range wireless technology limited to transmission distances of about 100 meters or less?

 A 802.11a

 B Bluetooth

 C Wi-Fi

 D WiMAX

16 In which network topology is each node connected to a central network transmission device such as a hub or a switch?

 A Bus

 B Mesh

 C Ring

 D Star

17 In which network topology is each node connected to the next by a direct line so that a continuous line is formed?

 A Bus

 B Mesh

 C Ring

 D Star

18 In which network topology is each node connected to a central device by two wires?

    A Bus

    B Mesh

    C Ring

    D Star

19 In which network topology do all nodes have independent connections to all other nodes?

    A Bus

    B Mesh

    C Ring

    D Star

20 True or false? The network topology shown in the graphic is an example of the mesh topology.

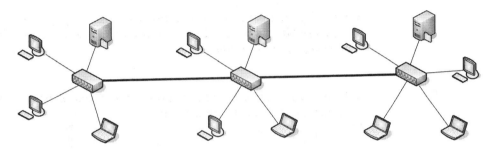

21 True or false? In a star topology, when a single connection fails, it doesn't affect the communication ability of other computers.

22 The benefit of a ___bus___ topology is that it's simple and inexpensive to set up.

23 True or false? The star topology uses a central networking device called a multistation access unit (MSAU).

24 The ___mesh___ topology is extremely fault tolerant, but expensive to implement.

25 An example of a ___point-to-point___ connection is the dial-up connection from a computer to an ISP.

26 In which type of network is data is broken up into packets before it's sent over the network?

   A Point-to-point

   B Point-to-multipoint

   C Packet-switching

   D Circuit-switching

27 Which Ethernet standard is the fastest?

   A Twisted Pair Ethernet

   B Fast Ethernet

   C Gigabyte Ethernet

   D 10GbE

28 Which Ethernet standard designates fiber optic cabling as its required medium? (Choose all that apply.)

   A BASE-CX

   B BASE-R

   C BASE-T

   D BASE-W

   E BASE-X

29 Ethernet _____ *Bonding* combines the bandwidth of two network interface cards as a cost-effective way to increase bandwidth available for data transfers for critical servers, such as firewalls and production servers.

30 True or false? A star Ethernet might be faster than a bus Ethernet, especially if there are many nodes on the network.

31 Which network topologies can you use with Ethernet networks? (Choose all that apply.)

   A Bus

   B Mesh

   C Ring

   D Star

32 ____ *CSMA/* *collision avoidance* is an acronym for the channel access method that avoids collisions rather than detecting them.

33 In order to transmit data on a Token Ring network, a node must have possession of the ___ *token*.

34 In a WLAN, the wireless NIC allows nodes to communicate over _short_ distances using radio waves, which it sends to, and receives, from the hub.

35 (True)or false? A LAN becomes a WAN when you expand the network configuration beyond your own premises and must lease data communication lines from a public carrier.

36 Which is WAN connection technology that uses encryption and security protocols to create a private network over a public network?

    A Cable

    B Cellular

    C DSL

    D DUN

    E Satellite

    F VPN

    G Wireless

37 Which is WAN connection technology that uses high-speed connections made over regular analog phone lines?

    A Cable

    B Cellular

    C DSL

    D DUN

    E Satellite

    F VPN

    G Wireless

38 Which WAN connection technology is shown in the following graphic?

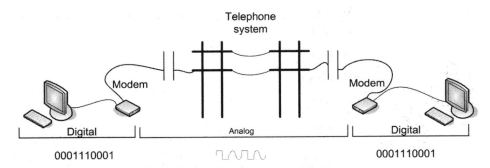

    A Cellular

    B DSL

    C ISDN

    D POTS/PSTN

39 Which WAN connection technology currently uses Enhanced Data rates for GSM Evolution (EDGE), Evolution-Data Optimized (EV-DO), or High-Speed Downlink Packet Access (HSDPA)?

    A Cable

    B Cellular

    C DSL

    D DUN

    E Satellite

    F VPN

    G Wireless

40 Which WAN technology that's used to connect a small ISP or large business to a regional ISP, and a regional ISP to an Internet backbone, uses fixed-length packets, called cells, to transmit data, voice, video, and frame relay traffic?

    A ATM

    B E1/E3

    C Frame relay

    D T1/T3

    E X.25

41 Which OSI layer provides security, encryption, and compression for the data?

    A Layer 1—Physical

    B Layer 2—Data Link

    C Layer 3—Network

    D Layer 4—Transport

    E Layer 5—Session

    F Layer 6—Presentation

    G Layer 7—Application

42 Which OSI layer divides long communications into smaller data packages, handles error recognition and correction, and acknowledges the correct receipt of data?

    A Layer 1—Physical

    B Layer 2—Data Link

    C Layer 3—Network

    D Layer 4—Transport

    E Layer 5—Session

    F Layer 6—Presentation

    G Layer 7—Application

43 Which OSI layer addresses data messages, translates logical addresses into actual physical addresses, and routes data to addresses on the network?

   A Layer 1—Physical

   B Layer 2—Data Link

   C Layer 3—Network

   D Layer 4—Transport

   E Layer 5—Session

   F Layer 6—Presentation

   G Layer 7—Application

44 Which OSI layer transmits bits from one computer to another and regulates the transmission stream over a medium?

   A Layer 1—Physical

   B Layer 2—Data Link

   C Layer 3—Network

   D Layer 4—Transport

   E Layer 5—Session

   F Layer 6—Presentation

   G Layer 7—Application

Independent practice activity

There is no independent practice activity for this unit.

Unit 2

Wired computer-to-computer connections

Unit time: 135 minutes

Complete this unit, and you'll know how to:

A Identify wired network cables and connectors.

B Install and configure network interface and modem PCI cards.

Topic A: Wired network connections

This topic covers the following CompTIA Network+ 2009 exam objectives.

#	Objective
Bridge objective **2.1**	**Categorize standard cable types and their properties**
	Type:
	• CAT3, CAT5, CAT5e, CAT6
	• Multi-mode fiber, single-mode fiber
	• Coaxial
	– RG-59
	– RG-6
	• Plenum vs. Non-plenum
	Properties:
	• Transmission speeds
	• Distance
	• Noise immunity (security, EMI)
	• Frequency
Bridge objective **2.2**	**Identify common connector types**
	• RJ-11
	• RJ-45
	• BNC
	• SC
	• ST
	• LC
	• RJ-59
	• RJ-6
Bridge objective **2.4**	**Given a scenario, differentiate and implement appropriate wiring standards**
	• 568A
	• 568B
	• Straight vs. cross-over
	• Rollover
	• Loopback
Bridge objective **2.5**	**Categorize WAN technology types and properties**
	• OC-x
	• SONET

#	Objective
Bridge objective	**4.7** **Given a scenario, troubleshoot common connectivity issues and select an appropriate solution** Physical issues: • Crosstalk • Attenuation
Bridge objective	**5.3** **Given a scenario, utilize the appropriate hardware tools** • Cable testers • Cable stripper

Explanation

As computer networks have evolved over the last two decades, the need to connect machines miles apart has become just as important as connecting a machine to the printer down the hall. To accomplish these tasks, the computer industry has developed a wide array of cables, connectors, and media access protocols suited for either long distance or short run communications. You'll find network cabling generally grouped as fiber optic and copper, with copper divided into two subgroups—twisted pair and coaxial.

Fiber optic wired connections

Fiber optic cable is wide-spread in the telecommunications industry. It carries digital signals in the form of pulses of light. It has many benefits over metal-based wiring such as coaxial or twisted-pair, which transmits data using electrical impulses:

- Thinner and lighter weight—It's possible to manufacture optical fibers which have smaller diameters and weigh less than the comparable copper wire cable. Fiber optic cables are classified based on the diameter of their core:
  - Single-mode fiber optic cable has a diameter of 8.3 to 10 microns, and light travels down the cable in a single ray.
  - Multi-mode fiber optic cables are common in diameters of 50-to-100 microns. In U.S. LAN network applications, the most common size is 62.5 microns. The outside diameter of the cable is also expressed in microns, such as 125 microns. You'll see fiber optic cable with a light fiber diameter of 62.5 and an outside diameter of 125, expressed as 62.5/125 fiber. Multi-mode fiber works with LED light sources of different wave lengths depending on the speed required.
- Higher carrying capacity—Optical fibers are thinner than copper wires, so more fibers can be bundled together into a cable jacket than copper wires. Fiber optic cable supports data rates up to 10 Gbps over distances ranging from 2 meters to 40 kilometers, depending on the media type used (10GBase-SR/SW, 10GBase-LR/LW, 10GBase-ER/EW). Some manufacturers have shown 40 Gbps speeds possible, and are working on 1 terabit per second (Tbps) speeds.
- Use of digital signals—Optical fibers are ideal for carrying digital information, which makes them useful in computer networks. Both multi-mode and single-mode fibers are used in communications.

- Less signal degradation—The loss of signal in optical fiber is less than in copper wire. Because signals in optical fibers degrade less, you can use lower-power transmitters instead of the high-voltage electrical transmitters you need for copper wires. The fibers used in long-distance communications are always glass because it has lower optical attenuation.
  - Multi-mode fiber is used mostly for short distances (up to 500 m), and single-mode fiber is used for longer distance links.
  - Single-mode fiber has a higher transmission rate and up to 50 times more potential distance than multi-mode, but it costs more. Because of the tighter tolerances required to couple light in single-mode fibers, single-mode transmitters, receivers, amplifiers and other components are typically more expensive than multi-mode components.

- Less interference—Fiber is resistant to electrical interference, which prevents cross-talk between signals in different cables and pickup of environmental noise. Unlike electrical signals in copper wires, light signals from one fiber don't interfere with those of other fibers in the same cable.

- Non-flammable—You can run fiber optic cabling in hazardous, high-voltage environments because it doesn't carry electricity. You can also use fiber cables where explosive fumes are present, without danger of ignition because no electricity passes through optical fibers.

- More secure—Wiretapping fiber optic cabling is more difficult compared to cables which use electrical connections. There are concentric dual core fibers that are advertised as tap-proof.

The bulk of the expense that characterizes fiber optic cabling systems can be attributed to the interface devices that convert computer signals to and from light pulses.

SONET

Synchronous Optical NETwork (*SONET*) is an ANSI standard protocol for signal transmission on optical networks. The standard is divided into categories based on a base signal (Synchronous Transport Signal or STS) and an optical carrier (OC) level. The following table lists the various categories of SONET.

Signal	Rate
STS-1, OC-1	51.8 Mbps
STS-3, OC-3	155.5 Mbps
STS-12, OC-12	622.0 Mbps
STS-48, OC-48	2.48 Gbps
STS-192, OC-192	9.95 Gbps
STS-768, OC-768	39.81 Gbps

Fiber optic connectors

Joining lengths of optical fiber is more complex than joining electrical wire or cable. The ends of the fibers must be carefully cleaved, and then spliced together either mechanically or by fusing them together with an electric arc. A *ferrule* is a cap placed over the end of an object to prevent splitting. The purpose of a cable connector (ferrule) is to terminate the end of the cable and allow for ease in connecting and disconnecting the cable from network devices to avoid splicing. Fiber optic connectors must be designed to connect and align the fibers' cores so that light can pass through correctly. Some of the more common fiber optic connectors include:

- *ST* (*straight tip*) *connectors* are the most popular connection type for fiber optic cables. These come in a few varieties. One is a slotted bayonet with a 2.5 mm cylindrical ferule that screws on to the cable. The drawback of this is that it can cause scratches on the fiber. Another ST type is a feed-through mechanism in which the cable passes through the connector.
- *SC* (*standard connector*) *connectors* use a 2.5 mm ferrule that snaps into a network device with a simple push/pull motion. It's standardized in TIA-568-A.
- *LC* (*local connector*) *connectors* are half the size of SC connectors with a 1.25 mm snap-in type ferrule.
- *FC connectors* have been mostly replaced with SC and LC connectors. The FC connector uses a 2.5 mm ferrule that is keyed to align in the connection slot and then screw tightened.
- *MT-RJ* (*mechanical transfer registered jack*) *connectors* are duplex connectors with both fibers in a single ferrule. It has male and female (plug and jack) connections, snaps in to connect, and uses pins for alignment. You may hear these connectors incorrectly referred to as RJ-45.
- *FDDI connectors* have two 2.5 mm ferrules with a fixed shroud covering the ferrules. FDDI connectors snap-in and are generally used to connect network to a wall connection.
- *Opti-jack connectors* have two ST-type ferrules in a fixed shroud the size of a twisted-pair RJ-45 connector. Like the MT-RJ connector, the Opti-jack connector snaps-in and has both male and female connections.
- *MU connectors* are snap-in connectors similar to SC connectors but with a 1.25 mm ferrule.
- *Volition connectors* are made by 3M. They don't use a ferrule. Instead you align fibers in a V-grove like a splice. It connects using a snap-in and comes in both male and female connections.
- *LX-5 connectors* use the same ferrule as the LC connector, but it includes a shutter over the end of the fiber. It also connects using a snap-in.

Examples of the common fiber optic connectors are shown in Exhibit 2-1.

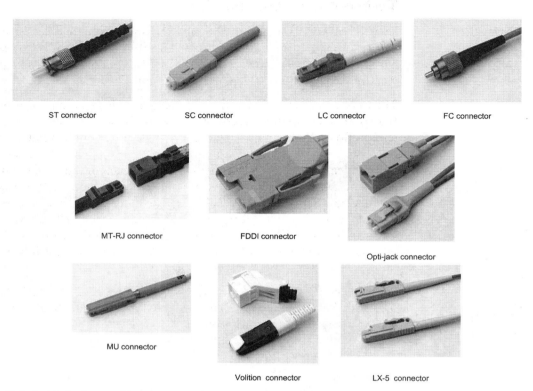

ST connector   SC connector   LC connector   FC connector

MT-RJ connector   FDDI connector

Opti-jack connector

MU connector

Volition connector   LX-5 connector

Exhibit 2-1: Examples of some common fiber optic connectors

Fiber optic connectors that are now obsolete include: Biconic, Deutsch 1000, NEC D4, Optimate, and SMA.

Do it!

A-1: Discussing fiber optic cables and connectors

Questions and answers

1 What speeds do fiber optic cable support? 39.8` GBps

2 How long can fiber optic cables be?

3 List some of the fiber optic connectors you might encounter.

Twisted pair connections

Explanation

Twisted pair cable is common in many business applications to deliver both voice and data information from one location to another. Selection of the proper cable type is based on the cable's electrical characteristics, conductor size, and ability to resist electromagnetic interference (called crosstalk or noise).

The twisted pair cable used for networking has three to four pairs of wires. The pairs are twisted together to prevent crosstalk. *Crosstalk* occurs because alternating electrical current flowing through a wire creates an electromagnetic field around the wire. This field then affects the current flow in any adjacent cables. When you place two wires in an electrical circuit close together, as done in each of the twisted wire pairs, their electromagnetic fields are the exact opposite of each other. The magnetic field in one wire cancels the other wire's field out. The more twists you have in a cable, the better it is at reducing crosstalk. However, there is a drawback. When you increase the twists, you also increase the distance signals must travel down the cable, thus increasing attenuation. *Attenuation* is a decrease in strength of the electrical signal as it travels farther down the cable.

As you learned in a previous unit, there are two types of twisted pair cabling—unshielded twisted pair (UTP) and shielded twisted pair (STP). The shielding for STP can be either foil or braided wire.

The following table lists the UTP categories of twisted-pair cabling.

Category	Speed and Frequency	Typical use
CAT 1	Up to 1 Mbps	Analog telephone networks. Not suitable for data networks.
CAT 2	4 Mbps	Voice and low-speed data transmission. Mainly found in IBM Token Ring networks.
CAT 3	16 Mbps; 10 MHz	Voice in newer telephone systems. The minimum category you can use for data networks. Most often found in 10BASE-T networks. Ethernet, Fast Ethernet, and Token Ring all support CAT3.
CAT 4	20 Mbps; 20 MHz	Data and voice in Token Ring networks. Ethernet, Fast Ethernet, and Token Ring all support CAT4. CAT4 is a standard which wasn't widely implemented.
CAT 5	100 Mbps; 100 MHz 155 Mbps ATM	Used for data and voice in Ethernet networks running at running at 10 or 100 Mbps. Ethernet, Fast Ethernet, Gigabit Ethernet, Token Ring, and ATM all support CAT5.
CAT 5e	1000 Mbps; 200 MHz 155 Mbps ATM	Used for data and voice in Fast Ethernet and Gigabit Ethernet networks. Ethernet, Fast Ethernet, Gigabit Ethernet, Token Ring and ATM all support CAT5e.
CAT 6	1000 Mbps; 250 MHz 155 Mbps ATM	Used for data in Fast Ethernet and Gigabit Ethernet networks. Currently the fastest UTP standard. Ethernet, Fast Ethernet, Gigabit Ethernet, Token Ring and ATM all support CAT6.
CAT 6e	10 Gbps; 550 MHz	Used in Gigabit Ethernet networks. This standard was published in Feb. 2008. Cabling can be shielded (STP, ScTP, S/FTP) or unshielded (UTP).
CAT 7	10 Gbps; 600 MHz	Used for full-motion video, teleradiology, and government and manufacturing environments. You'll also hear this category referred to as ISO Class F.

Currently, when you go to purchase CAT twisted pair cabling, you'll find two categories—solid and stranded. Solid cabling has a thicker, more protective covering making it less flexible. It's best for longer network runs and for fixed wiring applications. Stranded cabling has a thinner protective covering, making it more pliable and useful for shorter-distances and movable wiring applications such patch cables.

Twisted pair connectors

There are four types of connectors used on unshielded twisted pair cabling—RJ-11, RJ-14, RJ-25, and RJ-45. The "RJ" in the jack's designation simply means "Registered Jack," and the number refers to the specific wiring pattern used for jacks and connectors. You'll find RJ-11, RJ-14, and RJ-25 connectors used for telephone and dial-up modem connections. Twisted pair network cables use RJ-45 connectors, which look a lot like the other RJ snap-in connectors except they're larger. Examples of RJ-45 and RJ-11 cables are shown in Exhibit 2-2.

Exhibit 2-2: RJ-45 connector at left and RJ-11 at right

The RJ-11 connector has a total of 6 connector pins. However, in an RJ-11 connector, also referred to as a *6P2C connector*, only 2 of the wires in the twisted pair cable are actually used. They are connected to pins 3 and 4. The oldest style of residential twisted pair wiring consisted of just two wires, typically wrapped in brown insulation. Later, two-pair wires wrapped in colored plastic insulation was used. In this configuration of wires, green-red and black-yellow pairs provide the option for two lines or one line plus intercom or buzzer service and use an RJ-14 connector, also referred to as *6P4C connector*.

Modern residential wiring is accomplished with four-pair (or larger) cable using modern, fire-resistant "plenum" insulation wrapped tightly around the conductors to eliminate the flow of fire within the cable. Current telephone wire typically contains two pairs of wires—pair 1 is blue and blue/white, pair 2 is orange and orange/white. If a third pair of wires is included, it is green and green/white, and attaches to an RJ-25 connector, also known as a *6P6C connector*. The pairs connect to the RJ-25 connector as shown in Exhibit 2-3. Pins 3 and 4 are used for line 1, pins 2 and 5 are used for line 2, and pins 1 and 6 are used for line 3.

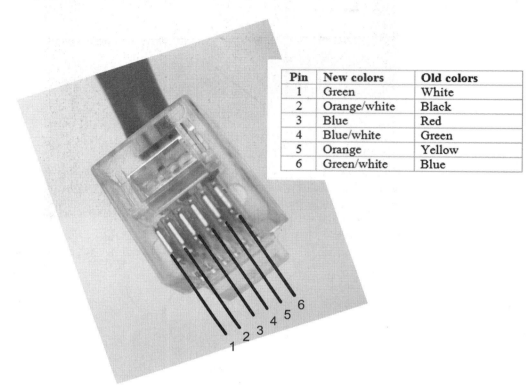

Pin	New colors	Old colors
1	Green	White
2	Orange/white	Black
3	Blue	Red
4	Blue/white	Green
5	Orange	Yellow
6	Green/white	Blue

Exhibit 2-3: RJ-25 pinout

The RJ-45 connector attaches to eight wires, as opposed to the four or six in the RJ-11. The jacks, with which the two types of connectors mate, have corresponding conductor counts and are also different sizes. An RJ-45 connector won't fit into an RJ-11 jack. The EIA/TIA-568-A standard defines two wiring patterns for Ethernet CAT cabling: T568A and T568B. These standards specify the pattern in which the color-coded wires in a twisted pair cable are connected to the pins of the RJ-45 connector or the jack. The T568A standard is preferred for residential application and T568B for commercial applications. Both, however, are electrically identical, as long as you use the same color pattern to connect both ends of a given cable. If you're consistent in this, pin 1 at one end of the cable is always connected to pin 1 at the other end, and pin 2 on one end is connected to pin 2 on the other end, and so on, regardless of which of the two color patterns you use.

If you hold an RJ-45 connector in your hand with the tab side down and the cable opening towards you, the pins are numbered, from left to right, 1 through 8, as shown in Exhibit 2-4. The pin numbers connect to the following colored wires in the cable for T568A or T568B.

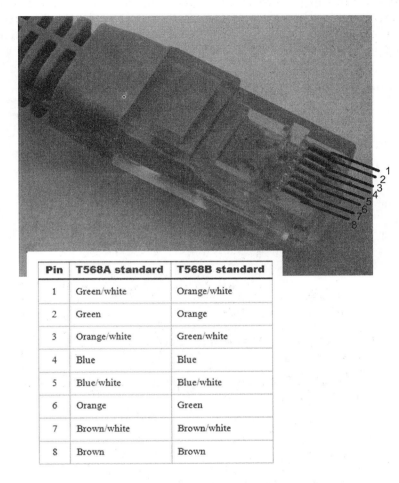

Pin	T568A standard	T568B standard
1	Green/white	Orange/white
2	Green	Orange
3	Orange/white	Green/white
4	Blue	Blue
5	Blue/white	Blue/white
6	Orange	Green
7	Brown/white	Brown/white
8	Brown	Brown

Exhibit 2-4: The pin numbering of an RJ-45 connector

For the network you're working on, pick one standard and use it for all the wiring. It doesn't matter which you choose. If you were to buy a pre-made CAT6 patch cable that has been made to the other standard, it still works on the network because both ends of the cable are wired to the same standard.

The RJ-48 connector is used to provide the connection for shielded twisted pair cabling. RJ-48 is an 8P8C connector. You'll find it providing connections for T1 and ISDN services.

Straight-through, cross-over, and rollover cables

A *straight-through cable* is a TP cable where both ends follow either 568A or 568B wiring standard. You use straight-through cables to connect computers to a hub or a switch. This is in contrast to a *cross-over TP cable* where one end is wired using 568A and the other using 568B. A cross-over cable lets you directly connect two computers together. A *rollover TP cable* is used to connect a computer's serial port to the console port of a router or managed switch. Rollover cables are wired with the ends the reverse of one another other:

End 1	End 2
Pin 1	Pin 8
Pin 2	Pin 7
Pin 3	Pin 6
Pin 4	Pin 5
Pin 5	Pin 4
Pin 6	Pin 3
Pin 7	Pin 2
Pin 8	Pin 1

Do it!

A-2: Examining twisted pair cables and connectors

Here's how	Here's why
1 Locate a segment of twisted pair cabling	
2 Verify that it has an RJ-45 connector	RJ-45 has 8 wires, whereas RJ-11 has only 6.
3 If the connector is clear, examine the color of each wire to the pins	
What T568 standard is being used?	

Terminating CatX to RJ-45 connectors

Explanation   To terminate CAT6 or similar cable to an RJ-45 connector, you must use an RJ-45 stripper/crimping tool, which can be purchased in a wide range of qualities and prices from $10 to $90.

To terminate a CAT6 or similar cable:

1 Remove about 1-1/2 inches of jacket from the cable.
2 Untwist the full length of the exposed wire pairs.
3 Place the cable end on to the connector and arrange the wires into the slots on the connector using the color code for T568A or T568B.

    The jacketed portion of the cable must go all the way up into the connector. Don't leave any of the twisted wires in the cable exposed without a jacket covering them.
4 Using the stripper/crimper tool, press the tool's bit down on to the terminal with the side of the bit that cuts the wire pointed to the outside of the connector.
5 Press down on the tool to compress the spring until the tool hammers down the wire into the terminals slot. At the same time, the hammer action drives down the cutting edge of the bit to terminate and cut the wires.

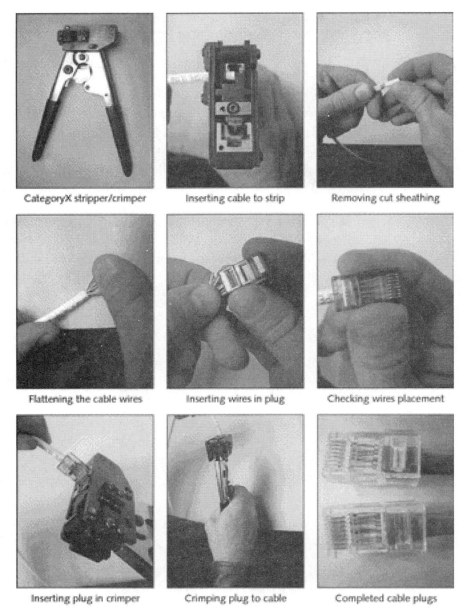

Exhibit 2-5: Terminating cable to an RJ-45 plug

Do it!

A-3: Terminating with an RJ-45 connector (optional)

Here's how	Here's why
1 Review the cable specifications	There are several different grades of cable. The markings on the outer PVC covering inform you of the exact cable grade. LAN cables that are used to connect workstations and hubs to wall jacks usually use the CM communications-grade UTP, which is found in most office buildings.
2 Using the crimper or wire cutters, carefully slice open the PVC sheath	Use Exhibit 2-5 as a guide through these steps. The slit should be approximately 1.5 cm from the tip of the cable.
3 Spread the wires apart so that you can see the color assignments	This cable is engineered with the same color scheme for all eight wires: green, white/green, orange, white/orange, blue, white/blue, brown, white/brown.
4 Arrange the wires in the order shown in the table	

Pair	Color
1	Blue
2	Orange
3	Green
4	Brown

The solid color is placed before the matching striped wire.

Here's how	Here's why
5 Choose one of the cabling schemes	There are several commonly used configuration schemes; however, it is essential that the scheme chosen be consistent throughout the entire implementation. Otherwise, you could run the risk of your data highway traffic lane abruptly terminating. The two most popular pin-out configurations are T568A and T568B (as shown in Exhibit 2-4).
6 Make sure that the edges of the cable are smooth, not frayed	
Strip/unsheathe the plastic casing without cutting internal wiring (1.2 cm-1.5 cm)	
Spread the cables	Pulling gently out of sheath. Then straighten the wires.
7 Organize the colors according to chosen standard scheme	Pull the wires out to verify color.
8 Position the wires as closely as possible and parallel	Clip to even out the wires.

9	Slide the wires into the module plug	Clip them on the bottom, wires 1-8, left to right.
	Verify that the copper wires are fully inserted into plug, their ends covering the metallic teeth, and their casing firmly under the crimp wedge	
10	Insert the modular plug into the crimp tool while maintaining pressure on the cable	
11	Press hard and remove the modular plug	
	Verify that the casing is firmly bit and against the wall of the chamber	All teeth should be chomped into the cable.
12	Gently tug on the cable to verify the crimp	
13	When you're finished, your instructor will use a cable tester to check the continuity of your connection	

Coaxial connections

Explanation

Twisted pair and fiber optic cabling is used most often in today's networks, but if you're supporting older networks, you might run into some coaxial cable. Coaxial cable ("coax" for short) comes in many variations. As you learned in a previous unit, the type used for Ethernet networking is marked RG-8, RG-11, or RG-58. The RG in the designation stands for "Radio Guide," which was originally based on now-obsolete military specifications. RG cable might also have letters after the number that help you identify whether the inner conductor is solid or stranded, and its impedance (specified in ohms). Just like twisted pair cable, stranded coax is more flexible. The design of coax cable restricts the electromagnetic wave used to transmit data to the area between the center conductor and the shield, thus allowing the cable to bend and be attached to conduit supports without affecting the signal.

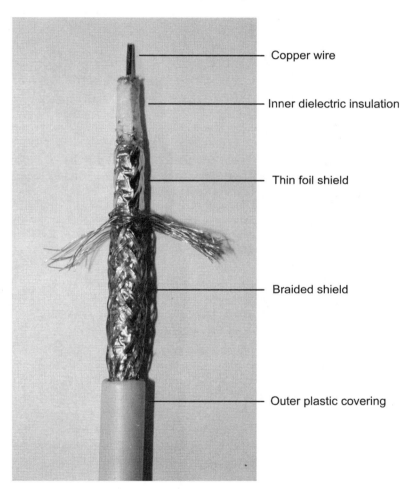

Copper wire

Inner dielectric insulation

Thin foil shield

Braided shield

Outer plastic covering

Exhibit 2-6: Common components of a coaxial cable

The different RG standards are described in the following table.

Standard	Impedance	Core size	Uses
RG-6/U	75 Ω	1.0 mm	Cable and satellite television; cable modems.
RG-6/UQ	75 Ω	1.0 mm	Q stands for quad – four layers of shielding, compared to RG-6/U, which has two.
RG-8/U	50 Ω	2.17 mm	Thicknet network backbones; amateur radio.
RG-9/U	51 Ω	2.17 mm	Thicknet network backbones.
RG-11/U	75 Ω	1.63 mm	Long drops and underground.
RG-58/U	50 Ω	0.9 mm	Thin Ethernet; radio; amateur radio.
RG-59/U	75 Ω	0.81 mm	Baseband video in closed-circuit television; cable television.

Another coax cable you might encounter is marked RG-62/U. This is used for the older network technology ARCnet. This cable has 93 Ω impedance, and uses AWG 22 gauge wire with a .64 mm core.

Coax connectors

Thinnet cables connect to the computer with a BNC barrel connector. The standard BNC is considered a 2-pin connector—pin 1 is the center conductor which carries the data signal, and pin 2 is the tinned copper braid which provides the ground. Segments of coax cable for networks are connected with T-connectors. The end of the line ends in a terminator, which is needed to keep the signal from reflecting back down the cable and corrupting data. Examples of these connectors are shown in Exhibit 2-7.

Exhibit 2-7: Coax cable connectors

Thicknet cables connect to computers using a *vampire tap*. The name comes from the fact that the tap contains metal spikes, which penetrate the cable to make the connection to the cable within the layers. A transceiver device is then connected to the cable and to the computer or other network device via an *Attachment Unit Interface* (*AUI*) port or *DIX* connector. An example of a thicknet vampire tap connector is shown in Exhibit 2-8. AUI is a 15-pin connector.

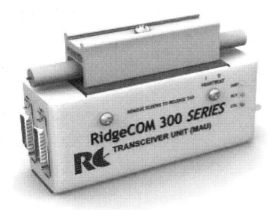

Exhibit 2-8: Thicknet vampire tap

Do it!

A-4:   Examining coaxial cables and connectors

Here's how	Here's why
1 Locate a network coaxial cable	
Locate a cable television coaxial cable	
What's the difference between the two cables?	
2 What type of connector is attached to the cable?	
3 What are some other coax cable types that won't work for Ethernet networking?	
4 Where's thicknet coax cable typically used?	

Terminating coax to BNC connectors

Explanation

To terminate coaxial thinnet cable to a BNC connector, you should have a cable stripper and a BNC crimper. You'll use the BNC crimper twice in the connection process. The first time is to crimp the BNC pin to the main conductor. The second time is to crimp the collar over the outer insulation. Some people try to make the crimp using a pair of pliers, but it works best if you use an actual crimping tool. Getting a good quality crimp can be the difference between a connector that works and one that doesn't.

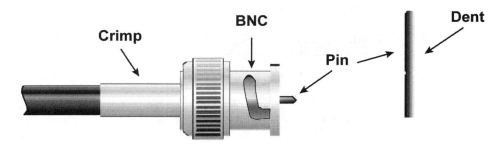

Exhibit 2-9: A BNC cable connector

Do it!   **A-5:   Terminating with a BNC connector (optional)**

Here's how	Here's why
1 Slide the crimp onto the coaxial cable	Refer to Exhibit 2-9.
2 Use the cable stripper to strip off a section of the outer sheath ¾ the length of the crimp	
3 Pull the braided outer conductor back over the stripped cable to expose the insulator surrounding the center conductor	Be careful not to cut off the braid.
4 Observe the dent in the pin Remove a piece of insulator that is as long as the length of the pin from its bottom to the bottom of the dent	
5 Insert the center conductor fully into the pin	Make sure that the pin is held tight.
6 Use the BNC crimper to crimp the pin to the center conductor	
7 Slide the crimp up over the braid and over the base of the BNC so that the braid is between the crimp and the BNC base	Make sure that none of the braid is protruding from the top or bottom of the crimp. If even a single thread of the braid or filament of foil touches the center conductor, the signal shorts, causing significant or total signal loss. This problem is most often caused by improperly installed connectors and splices.
8 Use the BNC crimper to secure the crimp to the cable	
9 When you're finished, your instructor will use a cable tester to check the continuity of your connection	

Plenum wiring

A *plenum* is an enclosure in a building that's used to move air for heating, cooling, or humidity control. It might be created by a false ceiling, a false floor, metal duct work, or a variety of other construction methods, but its main purpose is to move air that's environmentally controlled in some manner. A secondary purpose of a plenum might be to contain high- or low-voltage wiring. Because plenums often connect rooms in a building, they provide convenient paths through which to run wiring.

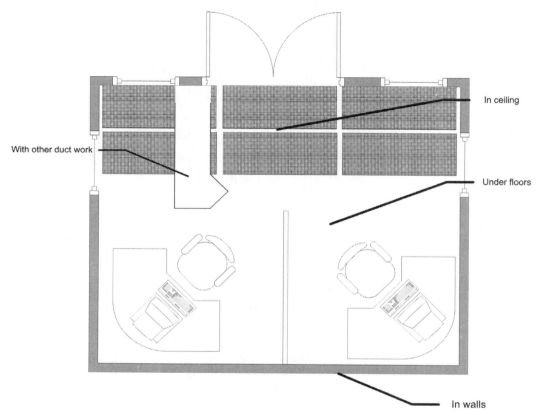

Exhibit 2-10: Examples of plenum spaces in an office

Cables that run in plenums must meet applicable fire protection and environmental requirements. These are important because the plenum-run cables might be subjected to temperature and humidity extremes not encountered in normal wiring paths. *Plenum wiring* also poses a greater hazard than wiring run inside walls because, if a fire occurs in the plenum-run wiring, smoke and heat is carried by the moving air in the plenum to other parts of the building, thus spreading the fire faster than it would otherwise move.

Protection for plenum-run cables might mean enclosing them in conduit (inside the plenum) or using cables having jackets and other components made of materials that are resistant to open flame and are nontoxic at high temperatures. Plenum cabling is often covered with Teflon and is more expensive than ordinary cabling. In the event of fire, its outer material is more resistant to flames and, when burning, produces less smoke and fewer noxious fumes than ordinary cabling. Twisted pair and coaxial cable are both made in plenum cable versions.

Do it!

A-6: Researching plenum wiring

Here's how	Here's why
1 If necessary, boot your computer and log in using the following domain user credentials: User name: **hostadmin##** Password: **!pass1234**	Where ## is your assigned student number.
2 Open Internet Explorer	
3 Use your preferred search engine to determine which categories of network cable are available in plenum grade	
4 What is the price difference between plenum-grade cabling and the general purpose cabling?	
5 What is typical temperature rating for plenum grade CAT cable?	
6 Close Internet Explorer	

Topic B: Network interface cards and modems

This topic covers the following CompTIA Network+ 2009 exam objectives.

#	Objective
1.1	**Explain the function of common networking protocols** • DNS
1.3	**Identify the following address formats** • IPv6 • IPv4 • MAC addressing
3.1	**Install, configure and differentiate between common network devices** • Modem • NIC
4.7	**Given a scenario, troubleshoot common connectivity issues and select an appropriate solution** Physical issues: • Interference

Bridge objective (1.1)

Bridge objective (3.1)

Bridge objective (4.7)

Explanation

A network adapter, also referred to as a network board or Network Interface Card (NIC), provides a communication channel between your computer's motherboard and the network. The function of a NIC is to send and receive information from the system bus in parallel and to send and receive information from the network in series. The NIC also converts the data that it receives from the system into a signal that's appropriate to the network. For an Ethernet card, this means converting the data from the 5-volt signal used on the computer's motherboard into the voltage used by UTP cables. The component on the NIC that makes this conversion is a transceiver.

Computer network connection

In most cases, the NIC is an adapter card that plugs into one of the expansion slots that all PCs have on their motherboards or attaches to the computer through an external port, such as a USB 2.0 or IEEE 1394 (sometimes referred to as FireWire) port. The NIC will have one or more ports built into it that are used to connect the NIC and its computer to a network using a cable that plugs into the port or wireless radio waves. The type of connector on the card varies with the type of network medium being used, as shown in Exhibit 2-11.

a. FDDI

b. Token Ring

c. Ethernet

d. Wireless

Exhibit 2-11: Examples of NICs for different network media

Most new network adapter cards you'll install will be PCI Ethernet cards with an RJ-45 port to connect to unshielded twisted pair (UTP) cabling. A NIC might have ports that can accept more than one type of cable connection. For example, on the ISA (Industry Standard Architecture) Ethernet card pictured in Exhibit 2-12, it has two transceivers—one to convert data into the appropriate voltage for UTP and a second to convert data for thinnet coaxial cable.

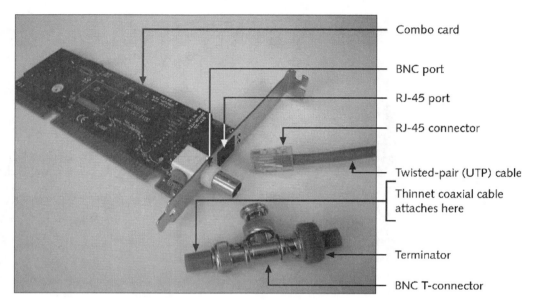

Exhibit 2-12: An Ethernet combo NIC

Notebook computers

Network adapters are standard equipment on notebook computers now. They used to be PC Cards that you added to a computer. Now they're typically built into the notebook computer. Ethernet 10/100 cards are the network adapters found in most cases. For notebooks without a built-in network adapter, PCMCIA adapters, also called PC card adapters, are most common. These cards are relatively simple to install. Usually when a PC card NIC is inserted in the slot, the system recognizes it and loads the appropriate drivers, or the OS prompts you for the driver location. Most PC cards are hot swappable—meaning you don't need to power down the computer to insert or remove them. On Windows computers, prior to removing a PC Card, you should stop its services by using the "Safely Remove Hardware" icon in the System tray. Then you press the eject button on the case to pop the card out of the slot.

NIC selection

When selecting a NIC, it's critical to match it with the following:

- The network architecture to which it connects
- The specific type of cable connection it uses
- The type of slot in the computer (PCI or ISA) in which it's installed

All internal cards for desktop systems are PCI cards at this point. If you're supporting older equipment, you might encounter some ISA or EISA cards in which you need to configure the IRQ, DMA, and I/O addresses. A utility from the manufacturer is used to configure the settings on those cards.

Do it!   **B-1:   Installing a NIC**

Here's how	Here's why
1 On your Windows Vista computer, click **Start** and choose **Control Panel**	You'll disable the existing NIC and then install a second NIC in your computer.
Click **Network and Internet**	
Click **Network and Sharing Center**	
Under Tasks, click **Manage network connections**	
2 Right-click **Local Area Connection** and choose **Disable**	You're going to disable the working NIC so that you can easily view the results of installing the second NIC card.
Click **Continue**	To allow Windows to complete the task.
Close all open windows	
3 Shut down the computer	
Unplug the computer from its power source	Many components, including network cards, continue to receive power even if the computer isn't turned on, so it's best practice to unplug the computer in addition to turning it off.
Unplug any peripherals from the computer	Remember to remove the cable from the network card.
4 Remove the case to access the slots on the motherboard	
Remove the slot cover from an empty PCI slot	
5 Install the new NIC into the slot	Be sure it's fully seated into the slot.
Attach the NIC to the case	If there's no screw, just be sure that the card is fully seated in the slot.
6 Replace the case	
7 Reattach any peripherals to the computer	
8 Plug the computer into the power source	

9   Connect the network cable to the
    network card

10 Turn on the computer

    Log on using the following   Where ## is your assigned student number.
    domain credentials:
    User name: **hostadmin##**
    Password: **!pass1234**

11 If prompted to install drivers,
    follow the prompts to do so

Addressing

Explanation

Every device on a network has a unique address. On a network, different methods are used to identify devices and programs, as shown in Exhibit 2-13:

- **Media Access Control (MAC) address**—A unique address permanently embedded in a NIC by the manufacturer. It identifies devices on a LAN. A MAC address is a unique value expressed as six pairs of hexadecimal numbers, often separated by hyphens or colons. (In a hexadecimal number, a base of 16 rather than 10 is used to represent numbers. Hexadecimal numbers consist of a combination of numerals and letters.) Part of the address contains the manufacturer identifier, and the rest is a unique number. No two NICs have the same identifying code. The MAC address is used only by devices inside the LAN and isn't used outside the LAN. Also referred to as physical or adapter addresses, or Ethernet addresses.

- **IPv4 address**—A 32-bit address consisting of a series of four 8-bit numbers separated by periods. An IP address identifies a computer, printer, or other device on a TCP/IP network, such as the Internet or an intranet. The largest possible 8-bit number is 255, so each of the four numbers can be no larger than 255. An example of an IP address is 109.168.0.104. Consider a MAC address a local address and an IP address a long-distance address.

- **IPv6 address**—A 128-bit address, which enables it to support a much greater pool of available addresses than IPv4. IPv6 addresses are written in the hexadecimal equivalent values for each of its 16 bytes.

- **Character-based names**—Include domain names, host names, and NetBIOS names used to identify a computer on a network with easy-to-remember letters rather than numbers.

- **Port address**—A number between 0 and 65,535 that identifies a program running on a computer.

OSI model	Protocols	Identifying address
Application Presentation Session	HTTP, SMTP, POP, IRC, FTP	Port address and IP address (or domain name)
Transport	TCP or UDP	IP address (or domain name)
Network (or Internet)	IP	
Data Link Physical	Ethernet	MAC address

Exhibit 2-13: Identifying addresses

MAC addresses

MAC addresses function at the lowest (Data Link) networking level. If a host doesn't know the MAC address of another host on a local area network, it uses the operating system to discover the MAC address. Computers on different networks, however, can't use their MAC addresses to enable communication because the hardware protocol (for example, Ethernet) controls traffic only on its own network. For the host to communicate with a host on another LAN across the corporate intranet or Internet, it must know the IP address of the host. Three important things to remember about MAC addresses:

- Unlike other addresses, MAC addresses are absolute—a MAC address on a host normally doesn't change as long as the NIC doesn't change.
- All hosts on a local area network must communicate by their MAC addresses, which are managed by the Data Link layer protocol that controls the network.
- MAC addresses alone can't be used to communicate between two computers on different LANs.

IP addresses

All the protocols of the TCP/IP suite identify a device on the Internet or an intranet by its IP address.

IPv4

An *IPv4 address* is 32 bits long, made up of 4 bytes separated by periods. For example, a decimal version of an IP address might be 190.180.40.120. The largest possible 8-bit number is, in binary form, 11111111, which is equal to 255 in decimal. Then the largest possible decimal IP address is 255.255.255.255. In binary, it's 11111111.11111111.11111111.11111111.

Within an IPv4 address, each of the four numbers separated by periods is called an octet (for 8 bits), and, in decimal form, can be any number from 0 to 255, making for a total of 4.3 billion potential IP addresses ($256 \times 256 \times 256 \times 256$). With the allocation scheme used to assign these addresses, not all IP addresses are available for use.

The first part of an IP address identifies the network, and the last part identifies the host. When data is routed over interconnected networks, the network portion of the IP address is used to locate the right network. After the data arrives at the LAN, the host portion of the IP address identifies the one computer on the network that's to receive the data. Finally, the IP address of the host must be used to identify its MAC address so the data can travel on the host's LAN to that host.

IPv6

IP version 6 is a 128-bit address. These 16 byte addresses are displayed in hexadecimal rather than decimal. In hexadecimal, you represent the first four bits in a byte (which means there are 16 possible values for those four bits) using the numbers 0 to 9 and the letters A through F. You then represent the remaining four bits in a byte with their hexadecimal equivalent value. Thus, for each byte, you see two numbers, with the first number identifying the first four bits and the second number identifying the remaining four bits.

You write an IPv6 IP address by grouping the address in hexadecimal, two bytes at a time, and separating these groups by colons (:). For example, you might see an IPv6 address of 3FFE:FFFF:0000:2F3B:02AA:00FF:FE28:9C5A. You can remove any leading zeroes in an IPv6 address. If a two byte block of an IPv6 address consists of all zeroes, you can "compress" the address by using double colons (::) to indicate those bytes. This means that with the address in our previous example, we could rewrite it using the format 3FFE:FFFF::2F3B:02AA:00FF:FE28:9C5A.

Character-based names

Computers use numeric network addresses to communicate with each other. People prefer to use names, such as host or NetBIOS names, to describe the computers on the network. Most likely, when you direct your computer to connect to a remote computer, you provide a name for that remote computer. Your computer must resolve, or determine, the name of the target computer.

- TCP/IP supports a naming service called the *Domain Name System* (*DNS*). DNS servers resolve host names to IP addresses.
- Windows computers support *NetBIOS* names—A 16-character name with the first 15 characters available for the name and the 16th character reserved to describe a particular service or functionality.

Domain Name System

DNS servers match host names to IP addresses. These specialized servers maintain databases of IP addresses and their corresponding domain names. For example, you could use DNS to determine that the name www.microsoft.com corresponds to the IP address 207.46.19.60.

DNS naming hierarchy

DNS names are typically composed of three parts: a computer name, a domain name, and a top-level domain name. For example, in the name www.microsoft.com, "www" is the computer's name (or at least an alias name for the actual name), "microsoft" is the domain, and "com" is the top-level domain.

With this scheme, many computers can be called "www" without causing naming conflicts. Additionally, there can be many computers within the microsoft domain, each with a different name. There might also be more than one microsoft domain, as long as each is contained in a different top-level domain.

It's also possible to use subdomains. For example, in www.corporate.microsoft.com, "corporate" is a domain within the microsoft domain. Four-part names such as this aren't rare, but you probably won't see further divisions beyond that.

Top-level domains

Top-level domains (*TLDs*) constitute the suffix at the end of a DNS name. The original specifications called for the following TLDs, each meant to contain domains with the following purpose:

- .com for general business
- .org for nonprofit organizations
- .edu for educational organizations
- .gov for government organizations
- .mil for military organizations
- .net for Internet organizations (hosting companies and ISPs)
- .int for international

As more countries joined the Internet, new TLDs were added for each country. A few examples of these two letter (digraph) TLDs are in the following list, and a complete list can be found at www.iana.org/cctld/cctld-whois.htm:

- .ar for Argentina
- .be for Belgium
- .ca for Canada
- .de for Germany
- .cn for China
- .ve for Venezuela

The Internet Corporation for Assigned Names and Numbers (ICANN) regulates TLDs. It has recently created several new TLDs to keep pace with the demands of the growing Internet. These include:

- .biz for businesses
- .name for individuals
- .museum for museums
- .pro for professionals
- .aero for aviation
- .coop for cooperatives
- .info for general information

NetBIOS

A *NetBIOS* name is a 16-character name, with the first 15 characters available for the name and the 16th character reserved to describe a particular service or functionality. A NetBIOS name can consist of letters, numbers, and the following special characters:

> ! @ # $ % ^ & ( ) - _ ` { } . ~

NetBIOS names, however, must be unique and can't contain spaces or any of the following special characters:

> \ * + = | : ; " ? < > ,

NetBIOS names aren't case-sensitive, which means "A" is equivalent to "a." Some examples of valid NetBIOS names are SUPERCORP, SERVER01, and INSTRUCTOR.

In a NetBIOS name, the reserved 16th character is typically expressed as a hexadecimal number surrounded by angle brackets at the end of the name. For example, the NetBIOS name SUPERCORP<1C> would represent a request for the SUPERCORP domain controllers. When you try to access a given service, you don't have to append a NetBIOS suffix manually; Windows does this automatically. When setting the NetBIOS name on a domain or computer, it's entered without the 16th character because a single NetBIOS name can be used to represent many different services on the same system.

NetBIOS names exist at the same level—a concept referred to as a flat namespace— even if the computers to which they're assigned are arranged in a network hierarchy. All NetBIOS names are in one big pool, so without any identification as to what part of the network the name belongs to. For example, SERVER01 and SERVER02 are both valid NetBIOS names. By looking at the names, however, it's impossible to tell that SERVER01 is a member of the domain CHILD01 and SERVER02 is a member of CHILD02. With the flat name structure, it becomes much more difficult to manage a large network environment.

Resolving NetBIOS names

The simplest way for a computer to resolve a NetBIOS name to a numeric address is to send a network broadcast, as shown in Exhibit 2-14. A *broadcast* is a message destined for all computers on a given network. The name request broadcast message includes the NetBIOS name the computer is looking for, the type of service, represented by the 16th character, and the address of the computer sending the broadcast. In this way, the computer with the requested NetBIOS name can respond to the request. If a computer with a matching NetBIOS name and service type receives the broadcast message, it responds directly to the computer that sent the broadcast message.

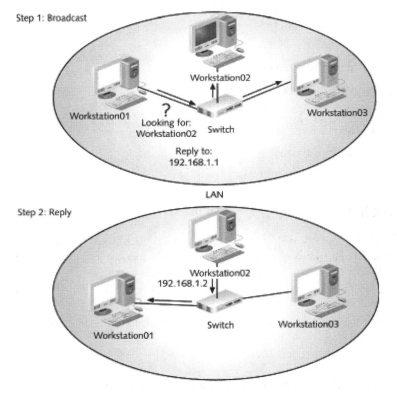

Exhibit 2-14: NetBIOS name resolution, using broadcast

Once the two computers know each other's IP addresses, they can communicate directly with one another. In order to improve performance and reduce network traffic, IP addresses associated with resolved NetBIOS names are cached for 10 minutes.

Although using broadcasts to resolve NetBIOS names is simple, it isn't efficient. Network devices, such as routers, which are used to control traffic among various parts of a network, usually don't forward broadcasts. Two computers on different physical networks separated by a router can't resolve each other's NetBIOS names. To overcome some of these problems, Microsoft introduced the *Windows Internet Name Service* (*WINS*).

WINS is a database that all the computers on a network register their NetBIOS names with. In order for computers to register with WINS, they must be configured with the IP address of one or more WINS servers on the network. When a computer needs to resolve a NetBIOS name to an IP address, it sends a request directly to a WINS server instead of sending a broadcast to the entire network. If the WINS server finds a matching name in its database, it responds with the IP address of the computer being sought.

Due to issues, such as excessive broadcasts and the inability of broadcasts to cross routers, and in acknowledgement of the dominant role the Internet plays in today's networks, Microsoft switched to DNS (Domain Name System) as the primary name resolution system on Windows networks, starting with Windows 2000.

Port addresses

One of the defining characteristics of Transport layer protocols is the use of port numbers. Each service running on a server listens at a port number. Port numbers 0 to 1024 are reserved for privileged services (well-known ports). Each Transport layer protocol knows which service to deliver the packet. The combination of an IP address and a port number is referred to as a *socket*.

Do it!

B-2: Examining addresses

Here's how	Here's why
1 On your Windows Vista computer, click **Start** and right-click **Computer**	
Choose **Properties**	
2 Examine the "Computer name" and "Full computer name" lines	This information relates to the character-based name your computer is using.
3 Close the System window	
4 Click **Start** and choose **Control Panel**	
5 Click **Network and Internet** and **Network and Sharing Center**	

6	Examine the networkplus.class (Domain network) section	It shows you have Local and Internet Access and one network connection currently enabled.
		The graphic at the top of the box visually shows you have a connection to both the internal network and the Internet.
7	Next to Connection, click **View status**	
	Click **Details**	
8	Examine the Physical Address line	This is your network card's MAC address.
9	Examine the DHCP Enabled line	This value is Yes, so your computer gets assigned its IP address from a central server. If this value was No, a computer administrator would manually assign your computer an IP address.
10	Examine the IPv4 Address line	This is the IP address your computer is using.
11	Examine the IPv4 Subnet Mask line	This number works with the IP address to separate the network portion of the address from the host portion.
12	Examine the IPv4 DNS Server line	This is the IP address of the server your computer is using to resolve DNS character-based names to IP addresses.
13	Examine the IPv4 WINS Server line	In the classroom, your computer is using broadcasts on the local subnet to resolve NetBIOS names. Your computer isn't configured to use a WINS server.
14	Examine the "NetBIOS over Tcpip Enabled" line	It is set to Yes. NetBIOS is an older application programming interface. Examples of Windows applications and services that use NetBIOS are file and printer sharing and the Computer Browser service.
15	Click **Close** twice	
	Close the Network and Sharing Center window	
16	Click **Start**	
	In the Start Search box, type **cmd**	
	Press (↵ ENTER)	To open a command prompt window.

17 At the command prompt, type **netstat –an |find /i "listening"**

Press (↵ ENTER)   The first column shows the service, and the second column shows the port the service is listening on.

```
C:\Users\VistaHost>netstat -an |find /i "listening"
  TCP    0.0.0.0:135            0.0.0.0:0              LISTENING
  TCP    0.0.0.0:445            0.0.0.0:0              LISTENING
  TCP    0.0.0.0:5357           0.0.0.0:0              LISTENING
  TCP    0.0.0.0:49152          0.0.0.0:0              LISTENING
  TCP    0.0.0.0:49153          0.0.0.0:0              LISTENING
  TCP    0.0.0.0:49154          0.0.0.0:0              LISTENING
  TCP    0.0.0.0:49155          0.0.0.0:0              LISTENING
  TCP    0.0.0.0:49156          0.0.0.0:0              LISTENING
  TCP    127.0.0.1:12025        0.0.0.0:0              LISTENING
  TCP    127.0.0.1:12080        0.0.0.0:0              LISTENING
  TCP    127.0.0.1:12110        0.0.0.0:0              LISTENING
  TCP    127.0.0.1:12119        0.0.0.0:0              LISTENING
  TCP    127.0.0.1:12143        0.0.0.0:0              LISTENING
  TCP    192.168.157.4:139      0.0.0.0:0              LISTENING
  TCP    [::]:135               [::]:0                 LISTENING
  TCP    [::]:445               [::]:0                 LISTENING
  TCP    [::]:5357              [::]:0                 LISTENING
  TCP    [::]:49152             [::]:0                 LISTENING
  TCP    [::]:49153             [::]:0                 LISTENING
  TCP    [::]:49154             [::]:0                 LISTENING
  TCP    [::]:49155             [::]:0                 LISTENING
  TCP    [::]:49156             [::]:0                 LISTENING
```

18 At the command prompt, type **exit**

Press (↵ ENTER)   To close the Command Prompt window.

19 Open Internet Explorer and verify you have Internet connectivity

20 Close Internet Explorer

Do it!

B-3: Removing a NIC

Here's how	Here's why
1 Click **Start** and choose **Control Panel**	You'll disable and remove the second NIC in your computer.
Click **Network and Internet**	
Click **Network and Sharing Center**	
Under Tasks, click **Manage network connections**	
2 Right-click **Local Area Connection** and choose **Enable**	To enable your original NIC.
Click **Continue**	To allow Windows to complete the task.

3 Right-click **Local Area Connection 2** and choose **Disable**

To disable the second NIC you just installed.

Click **Continue**

To allow Windows to complete the task.

Close all open windows

4 Shut down the computer

Unplug the computer from its power source

Unplug any peripherals from the computer

Remember to remove the cables from the network cards.

5 Remove the case to access the slots on the motherboard

6 Remove the new NIC from its slot

7 Replace the case

8 Reattach any peripherals to the computer

9 Plug the computer into the power source

10 Connect the network cable to the original network card

11 Turn on the computer

Log on using the following domain credentials:
User name: **hostadmin##**
Password: **!pass1234**

Where ## is your assigned student number.

Modems

Modems are devices that enable you to connect your computer to another computer through a phone line. A modem can be an external device (Exhibit 2-15) connected to a USB or serial port. It can also be a modem card (Exhibit 2-16) using PCI slot, or in older computers, an ISA slot. The modem in the sending computer must convert the digital signals within the computer to analog signals that are compatible with the phone system. The receiving modem must convert analog signals to digital signals.

Exhibit 2-15: SupraSonic external modem

Flash ROM microchip

Exhibit 2-16: 3Com U.S. Robotics 56K Win modem card

Modulation and demodulation

Computers are digital, and regular phone lines are analog. Data stored inside a PC is communicated to a modem as binary, or digital, data (0s and 1s). A modem converts this data into an analog signal, in a process called *modulation*, which can travel over a phone line. The modem at the receiving end converts the signal back to digital data, in a process called *demodulation*, before passing it on to the receiving PC. The two processes of MOdulation/DEModulation lead to the name of the device: modem.

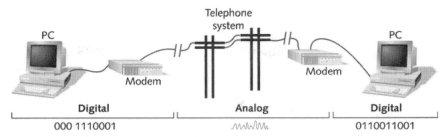

Exhibit 2-17: Modems convert digital signals to analog and then back to digital

Sound traveling over regular phone lines is transmitted as analog signals. PC data must be converted from two simple states or measurements, 0 and 1, or off and on, to waves, like sound waves, that have a potentially infinite number of states or measurements. Modems use different characteristics of waves to correspond to the zeros and ones of digital communication.

On a PC, the modem provides a connection for a regular phone line—an RJ-11 connection—which is the same type of connection that you see for a regular phone wall outlet (Exhibit 2-18). In addition to a line-in connection from the wall outlet, a modem usually has an RJ-11 connection for a telephone.

Exhibit 2-18: RJ-11 connection on a modem

A modem must be able to both receive and transmit data. Communication in which transmission can occur in only one direction at a time is called *half-duplex*; an example of this type of communication is a CB radio. A modem that can communicate in only one direction at a time is called a *half-duplex modem*. Communication that allows transmission in both directions at the same time is called *full-duplex*, a regular voice phone conversation is an example of full-duplex communication. If a modem can communicate in both directions at the same time, it is a full-duplex modem. Most modems today are full-duplex.

Forms

A modem can be an external component that you connect to your PC through a serial port. (In fact, that was the original purpose of serial ports on PCs.) Internal modems are also common. These modems can be built into the motherboard, implemented on an adapter card that you insert into your PC's expansion bus, or implemented on a card that you insert into a riser slot.

Riser cards

The early internal modems were implemented as adapter cards that plugged into a PC/XT or ISA slot. While PCI-based internal modems are still sold, many modern computers use special expansion buses designed specifically for internal modems. The most popular are:

- The Audio Modem Riser (AMR) slot
- The Communications and Networking Riser (CNR) slot
- The Advanced Communications Riser (ACR) slot

AMR

Intel developed this riser slot standard to support modems and audio cards. This slot moved analog input/output functions off of the motherboard and onto an external card.

An AMR-compatible motherboard includes no other analog I/O functions. Such motherboards don't have to be subjected to time-consuming Federal Communications Commission (FCC) certification tests. Thus, AMR-compatible motherboards are faster and cheaper to produce. An example of an audio/modem riser slot is shown in Exhibit 2-19.

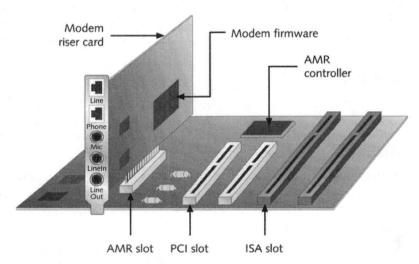

Exhibit 2-19: An audio/modem riser slot

CNR

Intel developed the CNR riser slot standard as an expansion of the AMR slot idea. This expansion slot supports specialized modems, audio cards, and network cards. CNR also provides for extensions that would enable manufacturers to create CNR-based cards that support new technologies, such as cable modems or DSL modems.

ACR

Motherboards from ASUSTeK Computer Inc. (ASUS), sometimes come with a proprietary riser slot called the Advanced Communications Riser slot. This expansion slot supports specialized modems, audio cards, and network cards. This slot type is not nearly as popular as the other, standardized, riser types.

Physical comparisons

Holding an AMR card vertically while looking at the faceplate (slot) cover, you'll see that its components are located on the right side of the circuit board. CNR cards have their components on the left when held the same way.

AMR slots are typically located in the middle of the motherboard. CNR slots are normally near the edge of the motherboard. A motherboard will have either an AMR or CNR slot, not both.

CNR and AMR slots are normally brown. ACR slots are normally white like the PCI slots they mimic.

Benefits of riser cards

Any of these riser slots are designed with the goal of simplifying the expansion card, thus lowering its price. The tradeoff is that the CPU must perform many of the functions that a dedicated controller chip would handle on a "normal" expansion card.

The CPU must handle all the processing for an AMR, CNR, or ACR modem, sound card, or network card. The result is that modems for these slots cost a few dollars while PCI or ISA-based modems typically cost tens of dollars.

Most times, a computer's manufacturer will populate a riser slot with a modem or other add-on card. Riser slot-based aftermarket add-ons are less popular. Unless one fails, you might never need to install a riser slot-based modem or expansion device.

Softmodems

Whether they are implemented with a riser slot or PCI slot, modems must perform some basic core functions. These include modulating and demodulating the signal, as well as interfacing with the operating system. This latter function includes things like error correction, compression, command set interpretation, and so forth.

A modem could implement all those functions with hardware, and many do. Another approach is to implement those functions in software. The most popular software-based modem, or softmodem, is the WinModem.

A *WinModem* is Windows-based combination of simple hardware (basically, just physical components to interface with the motherboard and phone lines) and modem function emulation software. The term linmodem (all lowercase) is sometimes used to describe a Linux-based softmodem.

Benefits

Softmodems are inexpensive because less hardware is required. Additionally, you can easily upgrade softmodems by installing new software.

Detractions

Softmodems are tied to their operating systems. You might be able to run a Windows XP-based WinModem under Windows Vista, or you might not. Only with extreme efforts can you run a WinModem under Linux or another non-Windows operating system.

Additionally, software is slower than hardware. Softmodems are slower as a result. To make matters worse, softmodems use CPU power that could be dedicated to other applications running on your computer.

When a modem isn't a modem

The term modem is sometimes used in inappropriate ways. The term is an abbreviation of modulate/demodulate, which is a digital-to-analog (or vice-versa) conversion process. Modems for use over telephone lines do just that. However, the term is sometimes applied to cable and DSL (digital subscriber line) Internet connectivity devices.

Cable and DSL are digital media. There is no need to modulate and demodulate signals sent over those lines. Thus, the connectivity devices you use with those media should not be called modems. Technically, such devices are transceivers. However, most people still call them modems, as in cable modem or DSL modem.

Modem installation

As with any add-on hardware, internal modems require device drivers. Softmodems require their software to be installed, for without it, the hardware components are worthless. And in most cases, you can't use the functions of a modem without communications software to provide the dialing and connection management functions you need to actually connect to a remote computer.

Typically, you install the drivers to your system before installing the hardware. This puts the driver files where Windows, specifically Plug and Play, can find them after you install the card.

Do it!

B-4:   Installing a PCI internal modem

Here's how	Here's why
1 If specified by the adapter's manufacturer, run the adapter's setup utility	To copy the driver installation files to your hard disk where Windows can locate them.
2 Shut down the computer	
Unplug the computer from its power source	
Unplug any peripherals from the computer	Remember to remove the cables from the network cards.
3 Remove the case to access the slots on the motherboard	
4 Install the modem card	
5 Replace the case	
6 Reattach any peripherals to the computer	
7 Plug the computer into the power source	
8 Connect the network cable to the network card	
9 Turn on the computer	
Log on using the following domain credentials: User name: **hostadmin##** Password: **!pass1234**	Where ## is your assigned student number.
10 If prompted to locate and install drivers, follow the prompts to do so	

Dial-up connection creation

Explanation

Many home users use a dial-up connection to connect to their Internet Service Provider (ISP). Once you've installed a modem on your computer, you can establish a connection to an ISP's dial-up server by using the "Set up a connection or network" wizard. In Windows Vista, to create a dial-up connection:

1 Open the Network and Sharing Center.

2 In the Tasks list in the left pane of the Network and Sharing Center, click the "Set up a connection or network" link to start the "Set up a connection or network" wizard.

3 On the "Choose a connection option" page, select "Set up a dial-up connection" and then click Next.

4 On the "Type the information from your Internet service provider (ISP)" page, enter the telephone number, your user name and password, and a name for the dial-up connection so that you can easily identify it in the Network Connections window.

5 You can use the Show characters checkbox, shown in Exhibit 2-20, to show the characters of your password as you enter it.

6 You can use the Remember this password checkbox, to have the connection remember your password so you don't have to enter it each time you connect.

7 If you want to make this connection object available to all users of the computer, select the "Allow other people to use this connection" checkbox. Then click Continue.

8 Click Connect.

9 If you don't want to immediately connect to the remote access server after you define this connection, click Skip.

10 Click Create to create the dial-up connection object, and then click Close.

Exhibit 2-20: Creating a dial-up connection

After you create a dial-up connection object, you can establish a connection with the dial-up server by double-clicking on the object in the Network Connections window.

Connecting to a remote access server

Some organizations require users to connect to remote access servers via dial-up connections in order to increase the security of their communications. You can establish a connection to a company's remote access server by using the "Set up a connection or network" wizard. To use the wizard to connect to a remote access server via a dial-up connection, use the following steps:

1   Open the Network and Sharing Center.

2   In the Tasks list in the left pane of the Network and Sharing Center, click the "Set up a connection or network" link to start the "Set up a connection or network" wizard.

3   On the "Choose a connection option" page, select "Connect to a workplace" and then click Next.

4   On the "Do you want to use a connection that you already have?" page, verify that "No, create a new connection" is selected and click Next.

5   On the "How do you want to connect?" page, click Dial directly.

6   On the "Type the telephone number to connect to" page, type the telephone number and a name for the dial-up connection so that you can easily identify it in the Network Connections window.

7 If you want to make this connection object available to all users of the computer, select the "Allow other people to use this connection" check box, as shown in Exhibit 2-21. You can optionally select the "Use a smart card" check box if the remote access server requires a smart card for authentication purposes.

8 If you don't want to immediately connect to the remote access server after you define this connection, select the "Don't connect now; just set it up so I can connect later" check box. Click Next.

9 On the "Type your user name and password" page, type your user name, password, and the name of the domain in which the remote access server resides (if necessary).

10 Click Create to create the dial-up connection object, and then click Close.

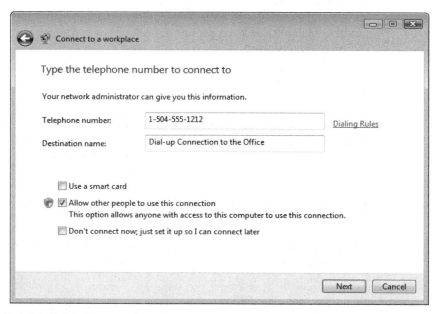

Exhibit 2-21: Connecting to a remote server

Do it!

B-5: Creating a dial-up connection

Here's how	Here's why
1 Open the Network and Sharing Center	
2 Under Tasks, click **Set up a connection or network**	
3 Select **Set up a dial-up connection** Click **Next**	
4 On the "Type the information from your Internet service provider (ISP)" page, in the "Dial-up phone number" box, type **555-555-5555**	The classroom doesn't actually have a dial-up server configured to accept connections from the students' modems. You'll create the connection, but won't actually connect.

5 Click **Dialing Rules**

This is where you set the Location Information for all modem connections.

6 Enter your area code

What area code (or city code) are you in now?

585

7 Observe the other settings

You can change our country/region, specify a carrier code, and specify a number to dial to get an outside line (such as 9). You can switch between tone and pulse dialing.

Click **OK** twice

8 In the User name box, type **MyIspUserName**

9 In the Password box, type **MyPassword**

10 Check **Show characters** and **Remember this password**

Show characters allows you to verify you entered your password correctly. Remember this password is handy for users, but isn't especially secure.

11 In the Connection name box, type **ISP Connection**

12 Check **Allow other people to use this connection**

Anyone who can log on to this computer, can connect to the dial-up server using this connection.

Click **Continue**

Your screen looks like Exhibit 2-20.

13 Click **Connect**

Windows uses your modem to dial the phone number you entered. Because the modem isn't plugged into a phone line and the phone number you entered isn't for a real dial-up server, the connection fails.

14 Click **Set up the connection anyway**

Click **Close**

15 In Network and Sharing Center, under Tasks, click **Manage network connections**

Dial-up (1)
ISP Connection
Disconnected
Standard 9600 bps Modem

The dial-up connection you just created is listed above your LAN connection.

Dial-up connection object management

Explanation

After you define a dial-up connection, you can use the connection's Properties dialog box to modify its properties. You do so by right-clicking on the dial-up connection within the Network Connections window and choosing Properties. The following table describes the key properties you might configure for a dial-up connection along with the tab on which these properties are located.

Tab	Property	Use to
General	Phone number	Specify the phone number of the remote access server.
	Dialing rules	Set and enable dialing rules for the connection.
Options	Dialing options	Specify prompts and display items for the connection.
	Redial attempts	Configure the dial-up connection to retry connecting to the dial-up server in the event the first connection attempt fails.
Security	Advanced (custom settings)	Define the security protocols necessary for connecting to the remote access server. By default, Windows Vista configures the dial-up connection to use encryption only if the remote access server requires it and to support three different authentication protocols. The only scenario in which you will need to modify the authentication protocol is if the remote access server requires the use of the Extensible Authentication Protocol (EAP).
Networking	Protocols and services	Specify and configure the protocols and services the connection uses.
Sharing	Internet connection sharing	Allow other network users to connect to the Internet through this computer's dial-up connection.

Do it!

B-6: Examining a dial-up connection object's properties

Here's how	Here's why
1 Right-click **ISP Connection** and choose **Properties**	
Click **Continue**	
2 On the General tab, observe the Phone number text box	If the phone number for the remote access server changes, you can use the Phone number text box to change the phone number stored in the dial-up connection object.
3 Check **Use dialing rules**	The options for editing the dialing rules become available.
4 Activate the **Options** tab	
5 Observe the Dialing options that are checked by default	Windows will display its progress while making the connection. Before making the connection, it will display the connection dialog box where you can enter user credentials and a different phone number if you'd like.
6 Observe the Redial attempts text box	By default, Windows Vista configures the dial-up connection to redial three times.
7 Activate the **Security** tab	
8 In the "Verify my identity as follows" drop-down list, observe the default selected option	By default, Windows Vista configures a dial-up connection to send the user's password in plain text (unencrypted). This is because it's much more difficult for a hacker to eavesdrop on a telephone connection than it is on a VPN connection over the Internet.
9 Activate the **Networking** tab	This connection is set up to use the IPv4 and IPv6 protocols, the QoS Packet Scheduler, and Virtual Machine Services.
10 Active the **Sharing** tab	Currently this computer is not sharing its dial-up connection with other network computers.
11 Click **Cancel**	To close the Headquarters Dial-up Connection Properties dialog box.

12 Double-click **ISP Connection**	
	These are the prompts that were checked on the Options tab of the connection's Properties sheet. You can access the Properties sheet by clicking Properties.
13 Click **Cancel**	To close the dialog box.
14 Right-click **ISP Connection** and choose **Delete**	
Click **Yes**	
Click **Continue**	
15 Close Network Connections and Network and Sharing Center	
16 Shut down your computer	
17 Remove the modem card	
18 Turn on the computer	
Log on using the following domain credentials: User name: **hostadmin##** Password: **!pass1234**	Where ## is your assigned student number.

Unit summary: Wired computer-to-computer connections

Topic A   In this topic, you learned how to categorize the standard cable types of **fiber optic**, **twisted pair**, and **coaxial**, and identify their associated properties. You examined the common **connector types** for each of these three cable types. You identified the different **wiring standards** for the cables and connectors.

Topic B   In this topic, you learned how to install a **network interface card** in a PC. You looked at the different **addressing standards** for NICs—**MAC address, IPv4, IPv6, NetBIOS, DNS**, and port. You also learned how to install **modem PCI cards** and create a **dial-up connection** to a remote server.

Review questions

1 Which type of network cable transmits digital signals in the form of pulses of light?

   A Coaxial

   B Unshielded Twisted Pair (UTP)

   C Shield Twisted Pair (STP)

   D Fiber Optic

2 Which occurs because alternating electrical current flowing through a wire creates an electromagnetic field around the wire?

   A Attenuation

   B Crosstalk

   C Interference

   D Shorts

3 Which categories of UTP cabling can be used in Gigabit Ethernet networks? (Select all that apply.)

   A CAT 1

   B CAT 2

   C CAT 3

   D CAT 4

   E CAT 5

   F CAT 5e

   G CAT 6

   H CAT 6e

   I   CAT 7

4 The diameter of fiber optic cable is expressed in which measurement?

A Centimeters

B Microns

C Millimeters

D Ohms

5 _____multi mode_____ fiber optic cable is used mostly for short distances (up to 500 m).

6 Which of the following Radio Guide cable categories is used for Ethernet networking? (Select all that apply.)

A RG-6

B RG-8

C RG-9

D RG-11

E RG-58

F RG-59

7 Which of the following fiber optic cable connectors is an example of a ST (straight tip) connector?

A

B

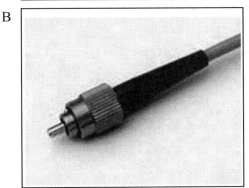

C

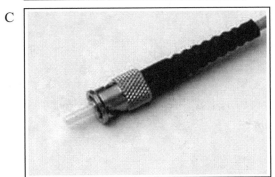

D

8 Twisted pair network cable uses which RJ connector?

   A RJ-11

   B RJ-14

   C RJ-25

   D RJ-45

9 An RJ-11 connector is which type?

A 6P2C

B 6P4C

C 6P6C

D 8P8C

10 What is the pinout difference between the T568A and T568B standards? (Select all that apply.)

A The wire color attached to pin 1

B The wire color attached to pin 2

C The wire color attached to pin 3

D The wire color attached to pin 4

E The wire color attached to pin 5

F The wire color attached to pin 6

G The wire color attached to pin 7

H The wire color attached to pin 8

11 The standard BNC barrel connector is considered a how-many-pin connector?

A 1

B 2

C 3

D 4

12 Impedance is measured in which of the following?

A Nanoseconds

B Ohms

C Millimeters

D Volts

13 Cables that run in _____ must meet applicable fire protection and environmental requirements.

14 The device on a NIC card that converts the data that it receives from the system into a signal that's appropriate to the network is called a _____.

A Port

B PROM chip

C Receiver

D Transceiver

15 True or false? On the majority of today's laptop computers, the network adapters are PC Cards.

16 The built-in identifying address coded into the NIC by the manufacturers is called which of the following?

   A IPv4 address

   B IPv6 address

   C MAC address

   D Port address

17 A 16-byte address displayed in hexadecimal is called which of the following?

   A IPv4 address

   B IPv6 address

   C MAC address

   D Port address

18 ___D＋S___ servers match host names to IP addresses.

19 A ___Net Bios___ name is a 16-character name, with the first 15 characters available for the name and the 16th character reserved to describe a particular service or functionality.

20 True or false? The purpose of a modem is to convert digital data signals from the computer into analog signals for transmission over the phone line.

21 Modems use which RJ connector?

   A RJ-11

   B RJ-14

   C RJ-25

   D RJ-45

22 True or false? PCI-based modems are less expensive to purchase because the CPU must handle all the processing, making them cheaper to produce.

23 True or false? In Windows Vista, you use the software that comes with your modem to create dial-up connections to remote servers.

Independent practice activity

In this activity, you'll practice creating a working network connection.

1 Disable your current network card.

2 Install a second PCI NIC.

3 Identify the addresses assigned to this NIC and network connection.

MAC address:

IP version:

IP address:

Character-based names (type and name):

4 Verify you have Internet connectivity.

5 Rename your new LAN connection **LAN 2 – PCI Card**.

6 Disable LAN 2 – PCI Card and enable Local Area Connection.

7 Verify you have Internet connectivity.

Unit 3

Network-to-network connections

Unit time: 135 minutes

Complete this unit, and you'll know how to:

A Identify network-to-network connection components.

B Install LAN wiring.

C Identify LAN wiring tests and equipment.

Topic A: Network-to-network connection components

This topic covers the following CompTIA Network+ 2009 exam objectives.

#	Objective
2.8	**Install components of wiring distribution**
	• Vertical and horizontal cross connects
	• Patch panels
	• 66 block
	• MDFs
	• IDFs
	• 25 pair
	• 100 pair
	• 110 block
	• Demarc
	• Demarc extension
	• Smart jack
3.1	**Install, configure and differentiate between common network devices**
	• Basic router
3.2	**Identify the functions of specialized network devices**
	• CSU/DSU

Bridge objective (2.8)

Bridge objective (3.1)

Bridge objective (3.2)

Connection responsibility

Explanation

Some of the network connections required to connect your computers with other computers are your responsibility; other connections you lease. In this topic, you'll examine the connections from major Internet connection points, all the way down to an individual computer.

Network Access Points (NAPs)

A *Network Access Point* (*NAP*) is a major Internet connection point that's used to connect and route traffic between smaller commercial backbones. Exhibit 3-1 shows the location of the four original NAPs. The NAPs in San José, CA, and Washington, DC, are called MAE West and MAE East, respectively. An *MAE* (*Metropolitan Area Exchange*) is an interconnection point within a metropolitan area. The other two NAPs are in Chicago, IL, and New Jersey, although the New Jersey NAP most often is called the New York NAP. These four NAPs originally were managed by Metropolitan Fiber Systems (MFS), American Advanced Data Systems (AADS), Sprint, and Pacific Bell.

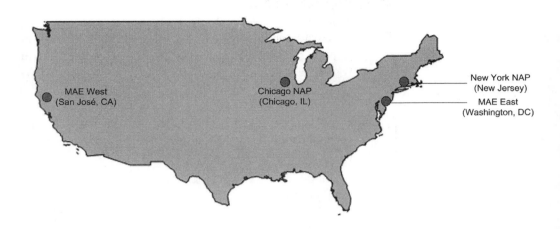

Exhibit 3-1: The original four major NAPs

Although the four original NAPs continue to be major Internet connection points or *Internet exchange points*, more than these four exist today. The original four are called *public Internet exchange points*, and others, built by privately owned companies, are called *private Internet exchange points*. Some of the private Internet exchange points are owned by *Commercial Internet Exchange* (*CIX*), an organization established in 1991 by several commercial enterprises to provide exchange points for commercial traffic. Another organization, the *Federal Internet Exchange* (*FIX*), is responsible for connection points for the network of federal agencies. In some cases, less significant exchange points are used to connect two backbones; such exchange points only exist to move traffic from one backbone to the other backbone. Today, many backbones are owned and managed by a variety of companies.

Internet service providers (ISPs)

Large companies that have access to high-speed equipment can connect directly to one of these commercial backbones, but smaller companies and individuals use a provider company to make the connection to a commercial backbone.

An Internet service provider (ISP) is a business that provides connectivity to the Internet. ISPs can be a small business that provides connectivity in only one city, or a large company with access points in many cities and countries.

ISP services

The primary service an ISP provides is access to the Internet. To connect to the Internet, a computer needs:

- A physical connection to the ISP—To connect to an ISP, a computer must be using an operating system that supports the TCP/IP communication protocol. Windows Vista, Windows Server 2008, Windows Server 2003, Windows XP, Windows 2000 Server and Professional, Windows 98, Windows 95, Windows Me, Windows NT Server and Workstation, Linux, and the Macintosh operating systems support TCP/IP.

- Software to communicate over the Internet—Application software such as Internet Explorer, which accesses the World Wide Web, is already part today's Windows operating systems.

- A unique IP address so others on the Internet can identify the computer. In many small companies, these addresses are assigned to gateways that other company computers use to access the Internet.

An ISP can supply all three of these components.

How an ISP works

You connect to an ISP, then the ISP connects you to the Internet. The ISP's equipment can be simple or complex, depending on the ISP's size.

A small ISP

Exhibit 3-2 shows an example of how a small ISP might connect to the Internet. Because a small ISP is not likely to have the high-speed equipment necessary to connect directly to a commercial backbone, it most likely subscribes to a regional ISP who makes the commercial backbone connection.

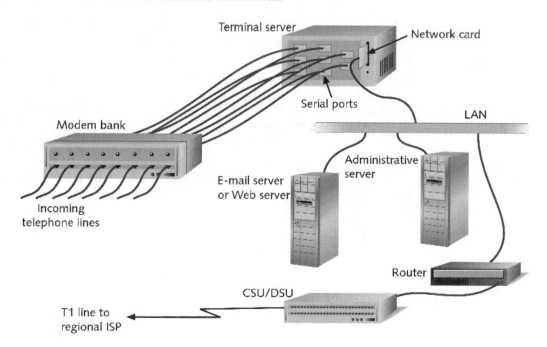

Exhibit 3-2: A small ISP

The small ISP uses a T1 line to connect to the regional ISP. A *T1 line* is a digital, dedicated circuit leased from the telephone company that carries the equivalent of 24 telephone circuits and can transmit data at 1.5 million bps. Prices for T1 lines vary and are around $550 per month.

The individual telephone lines coming in from customers connect to a modem bank. A *modem bank* is a box that contains several modem cards similar to a modem card that is installed in a regular computer. It takes one modem card to manage one telephone line. The modem converts the analog signal from the telephone line to digital before it moves the signal on to the terminal server. For each modem card in the modem bank, there is one serial cable connecting the modem bank to the terminal server.

Each of these serial cables then connects to a separate serial port on the terminal server. A single network card in the terminal server consolidates all these lines into a single line, which then connects the terminal server to the local network. The network cable leaving the terminal server connects to the ISP's local area network. A local area network (LAN) is a group of computers and other devices networked together that are confined to a small area, such as one building.

The LAN can have one or more servers connected to it. For example, if the ISP provides e-mail and Web site services to its customers, the LAN might include a server that manages both these services. Depending on the size of the ISP, these services might exist on a single server, or each service might have its own dedicated server. In addition, there most likely will be another server, called the *administrative server*, that manages customer accounts, including managing the process when the customer logs on to the ISP.

The router in Exhibit 3-2 is responsible for connecting the LAN at the ISP to the network of the regional ISP. A *router* is a device that connects two or more networks and can intelligently make decisions about the best way to send data over these networks. The two networks shown in Exhibit 3-2 are the ISP's LAN and the regional ISP's network. This regional network is an example of a *wide area network* (*WAN*), a network that covers a large geographical area and might use a number of communications technologies.

Before data gets onto a T1 line, it must be cleaned and formatted by a device called a *CSU/DSU*, which is really two devices in one. The *Channel Service Unit* (*CSU*) acts as a safe electrical buffer between the LAN and a public network accessed by the T1 line. A *Digital Service Unit or Data Service Unit* (*DSU*) ensures that the data is formatted correctly before it's allowed on the T1 line.

A regional ISP

The ISP illustrated in Exhibit 3-3 supports several small ISPs and medium-sized companies that all connect to it using T1 lines or DSL lines. At the same time, the regional ISP also has its own group of individual customers that connect using regular dial-up lines or DSL lines. The regional ISP connects to a backbone using a T3 line. A T3 line transmits digital data at 44.7 Mbps and is fast enough to connect to a backbone. The T3 line enters a data communications center and connects to a backbone by way of a router that belongs to the commercial backbone operator (for example, AT&T or UUNET).

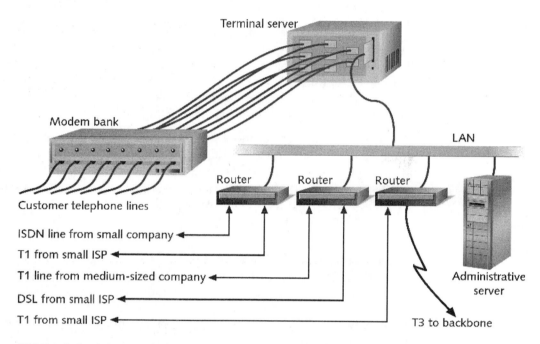

Exhibit 3-3: A regional ISP

Do it!

A-1: Identifying the connection components of an ISP

Questions and answers

1 What are the three components a client needs to connect to the Internet?

computer

software

I/p address

2 Which device is responsible for determining the best path for data to pass between networks?

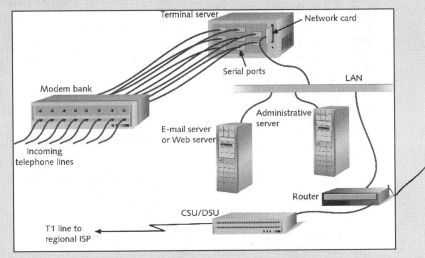

Which device acts as a safe electrical buffer between the LAN and the public network?

Which device is responsible for verifying that data is formatted correctly before it is sent onto the T1 line? *psu*

3 Identify the customers that might be coming into the routers at a regional ISP.

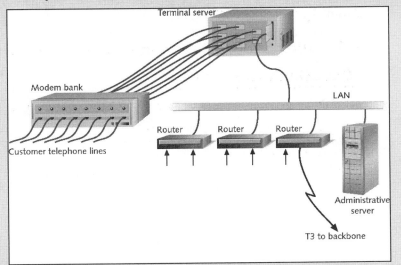

LAN installation components

Officially, the definition of a *demarcation point* (*demarc*) is the point at which the communications network owned by one company connects to the communications network owned by another company. In terms of your company's data network, the demarc is the point at which your organization's network connects to your ISP. A *demarc terminating device* is responsible for the code and protocol conversions, as well as the buffering required for communications to and from an ISP and your internal network. You might hear the demarc device referred to as the *network terminating interface* (*NTI*), *network terminating unit* (*NTU*), *network terminating device* (*NTD*), *smart jack*, or an *MPOE* (*minimum point of entry*). The demarc terminating device is the starting point for your network wiring installation. The actual demarc terminating device depends on the type of WAN connection used. For example with a T1 connection, the device is a CSU/DSU connected to a terminating router. It's from this point inward that you are responsible for the installation and maintenance of the network.

As shown in Exhibit 3-4, the demarc is connected to your network's *main cross-connect*. In general terms, a *cross-connect* is defined as the location where signals are distributed to various destinations. If for some reason, the demarc isn't in the same location as the main cross-connect, you need to request a *demarc extension*. This is typically done by the ISP and may involve an additional charge. At the main cross-connect, is a *main distribution frame* (*MDF*). The MDF is a network rack that contains the devices used to manage the connections between external communication cables and the cables of your internal network.

In a multi-story building, network backbone cabling is run from floor to floor connecting the main cross-connect to *intermediate cross-connects* on each floor. You might hear these runs referred to as *vertical cabling* due to direction in which they're run to connect floors. In a secure environment, this wiring is housed in locked rooms with limited access. For this course, we'll use the term "telecommunications room" to refer to these rooms. In each floor's telecommunications room are *intermediate distribution frames* (*IDFs*), which are network racks containing the devices connecting each floor's internal wiring to the MDF. As shown in Exhibit 3-5, you can create these hub-to-hub connections in a daisy-chain or a star configuration.

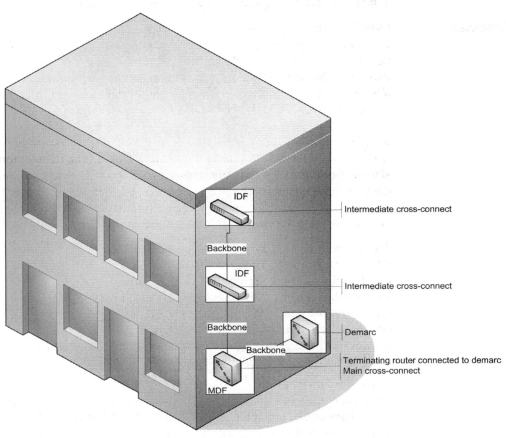

Exhibit 3-4: Main and intermediate cross-connects

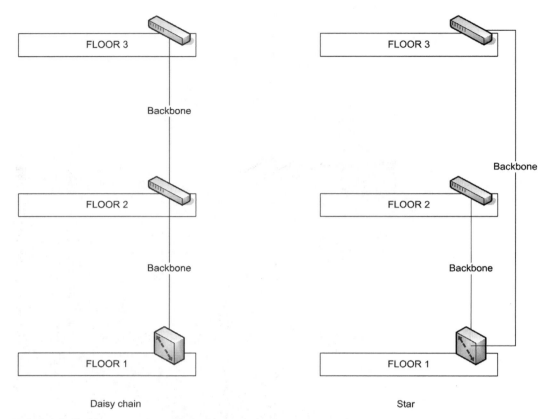

Exhibit 3-5: Connecting intermediate cross-connects to the main cross-connect

TIA/EIA-569-A sets standards for the entrance facility, equipment room, backbone pathways, telecommunications room, and horizontal pathways. It also discusses recommended space requirements for the designated rooms.

From the telecommunications rooms on each floor, horizontal cables are run without splice points, cable junctures, or taps to each individual workstation. Exhibit 3-6 shows these runs, also referred to as *workstation* or *station drops*. The junction point for the workstation cables is called a *horizontal cross-connect*. TIA/EIA-568-C specifies UTP standards for workstation runs. The cables for the workstation runs come into the telecommunications room and are organized onto a wiring board (typically a 4' x 8' color-coded plywood board attached to the wall) or routed into cable trays in racks.

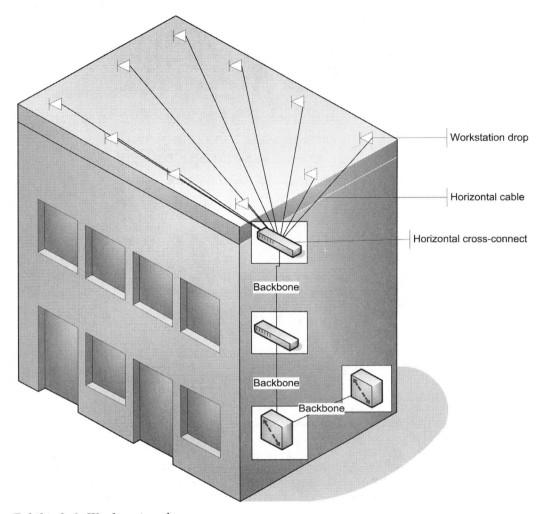

Exhibit 3-6: Workstation drops

From the horizontal cross-connect comes the wiring for that particular floor's network wiring. A typical UTP installation might include:

- A multiport hub
- Patch cables
- A terminating block/patch panel
- Drop cables
- Wall jacks

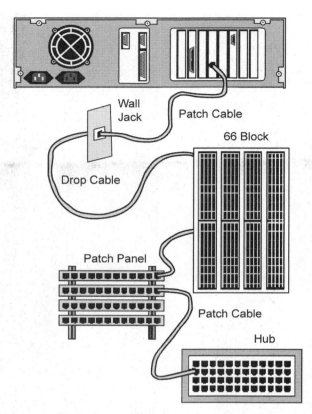

Exhibit 3-7: A sample UTP installation

In Exhibit 3-7, which shows a sample UTP installation, a *patch cable* runs from the node's network card to the RJ-45 wall jack. You'll also hear this cable referred to as a user cable, because it runs from the wall jack to the equipment in the user's workstation. *Drop cables* from the RJ-45 wall jacks run to a *termination block* found in your telecommunications room. The total length of the drop, including patch and equipment cables, can't exceed the total maximum cable length for the chosen media. For example, as you learned in a previous unit, all twisted pair cabling has a maximum run length of approximately 100 meters.

Telecommunications room

The telecommunications room is where network wiring is terminated. You have two choices as your method of termination—punchdown termination with cross-connect wiring, as shown in Exhibit 3-8, or termination directly into a patch panel, shown in Exhibit 3-9. The *punchdown terminal* or *patch panel* can be mounted directly to the wall or set in a rack or cabinet. You use the same patch panel or punchdown to terminate both workstation drops and backbone wiring. Direct patch panel terminations are most often found in Cat 5e or Cat 6 installations.

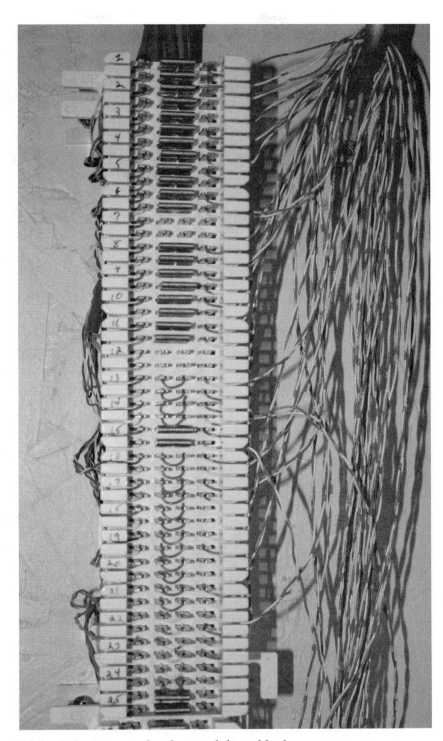

Exhibit 3-8: An example of a punchdown block

Exhibit 3-9: An example of a patch panel with connectors instead of individual wire termination

Punchdown block

The main component in the telecommunications room is the *punchdown block*, which is used to terminate station cables and cross-connect to other punchdown locations. There are two types—the *110 block* and the older *66M block*. There are two components to the 110 block—the 110 wiring block and the 110C connecting block, shown in Exhibit 3-10. The purpose of the *110 wiring block* is to hold wires in place. It's a molded plastic mounting block with horizontal index strips. The space between the horizontal strips is used to organize and secure incoming cables. The 25-pair block secures 25 cable pairs or 50 wires; the 100-pair block has 4 horizontal index strips to organize 100 cable pairs or 200 wires; the 300-pair block has 12 horizontal strips to organize 300 cable pairs or 600 wires. The purpose of the *100C connecting block* is to electronically terminate cables. It consists of a small plastic housing with metal contact strips, color-coded to assist you with correct wire placement. Each 110C connecting block can terminate 3 to 5 pairs of AWG 22 to 26 gauge solid cable.

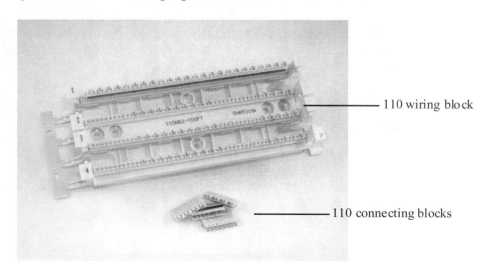

110 wiring block

110 connecting blocks

Exhibit 3-10: An example of the components of the 110 block

As shown in Exhibit 3-11, you terminate the workstation run cables at the rear of the 110 block. Cross-connects are made at the front.

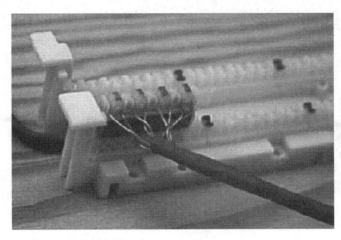

Exhibit 3-11: 110 block termination

The 66 block originated with telephone cabling. Its purpose was to terminate a 25-pair phone trunk cable in a wiring closet; then individual 4-pair wires would go from there to the user's desk. The 66 and 110 termination blocks are used in data networking but not as often as networking specific versions because each punched down connection at the termination block adds potential for noise and effectively increases the length of the network cable. Many times, workstation drops simply go to the patch panel.

Exhibit 3-7 shows a separate *patch panel*. In reality today, the termination block and patch panel are one unit. The patch panel houses the cable connections. It's from here that a network technician can quickly change the path of select connections. The patch panel can be manufactured to connect individual wires similar to a terminating block, or it can have female connectors that are identical to the ones at the workstation outlet jacks.

The patch panel is then connected to the multiport hub by *patch cables*—one for each network drop—thus connecting the nodes on one section of the network with other sections of the network. This allows a network engineer to easily move a user's network drop between hubs or ports without requiring any rewiring. Just unplug a patch cable and plug it in someplace else.

Do it!

A-2: Examining telecommunication room connection components (optional)

Here's how
1 If the security policy of the training center allows it, you'll view the following network components and answer questions about them:
Demarc
Main cross-connect
If used, intermediate cross-connect
Identify the wiring board
Does the training center use a punchdown block or a patch panel for termination?
2 Is the demarc in the same location as the main cross-connect?
3 Does the training center have intermediate cross-connects? If so, how many?
4 If multiple intermediate cross-connects are used, how are they connected?
5 What color is the wiring board?
6 What type of termination does the training center use?
7 If they use a punchdown block, what type is it?
8 If there's a punchdown block, what type of cabling is it used for?
9 If they use a patch panel, what type of media is used?

Topic B: LAN wiring

This topic covers the following CompTIA Network+ 2009 exam objectives.

#	Objective
Bridge objective **2.6**	**Categorize LAN technology types and properties** Properties: • Distance
Bridge objective **2.8**	**Install components of wiring distribution** • Vertical and horizontal cross connects • Patch panels • 66 block • 25 pair • 100 pair • 110 block
Bridge objective **3.2**	**Identify the functions of specialized network devices** • CSU/DSU
Bridge objective **4.7**	**Given a scenario, troubleshoot common connectivity issues and select an appropriate solution** Physical issues: • Near End crosstalk • Shorts
Bridge objective **5.3**	**Given a scenario, utilize the appropriate hardware tools** • Punch down tool • Cable stripper

Network cable installation

Explanation
In your LAN, there are two different types of wiring needs—permanent wiring, which includes backbones, workstation runs, and cross connects, and movable wiring, which includes user and patch cords terminated with an RJ-45 connector. If you're using copper cable, use solid cable for permanent wiring and stranded cable for user and patch cords. Solid wire wraps and bends easier than stranded cable without kinking, binding, or creating sharp bends. Stranded cable is more flexible, so you have less control over how it lies. No matter which media type you're using, you should follow these general guidelines to properly route cables:

- Avoid proximity to electromagnetic fields, by running cables away from:
  — Motors
  — Pipes
  — Structural steel
  — Power lines
- Minimize sharp bends in the cable, which can distort the electrical characteristics of the cable.
- Don't run spans of unsupported cables.
- When bundling cables with tie wraps, avoid over-tightening, which can also distort the electrical characteristics of the cable; use hook and loop (Velcro) tie wraps instead of common nylon ones.

You can use cable trays and hangers to prevent unsupported spans of cables, sharp bends, kinks, binds, nicks, and the need for tie wraps. It's much easier to properly wire a building under construction, than to retrofit an existing building.

Backbone installation

When choosing a location for telecommunications rooms on multiple floors, the best choice is to locate them one above the other with a utility shaft between them. You can run the network backbone cabling through the utility shaft and into each telecommunications room.

Many companies run fiber optic cabling as their backbone media. It has a much longer maximum allowable distance from the main cross-connect to the first intermediate cross-connect. You can run fiber 2000 meters compared to 800 meters for twisted pair. This distance does decrease for linking intermediate cross-connects. Fiber backbone requires a special two fiber connection in the telecommunications room, where twisted pair can be terminated in the same block as your workstation drops. With the fiber connector, one connection sends and the other receives. This is referred to as *polarity*. 568SC and FDDI standards govern dual-fiber connectors to maintain polarity.

Workstation runs

You can route your workstation runs through metal floor or ceiling supports. You can use hangers, clips, or trays to support the cables. Trays are very popular as they prevent kinks and sharp bends in your cables. Hangers and clips are best for straight runs from the telecommunications room to each workstation. Remember your workstation runs must not exceed the maximum length of your chosen media. In a UTP installation, you don't want to exceed a 100 meter distance from the user's equipment to the final termination point in the telecommunications room. A standard UTP installation will have no more than 90 meters for the horizontal run with 10 meters reserved to split between the telecommunications room drop and the workstation drop. Remember that this is only a guideline, as some office configurations need as much as 8 meters at the user end. To calculate the length of each workstation run:

1 Determine the length of the ceiling or floor (horizontal) run, as shown in Exhibit 3-12.

2 For straight runs, add 2-5% to the measurement to accommodate running cable around obstacles.

3 Determine the length of the vertical drop in the telecommunications room to the *final* termination point—remember to include in your measurement routing cables through equipment and rack channels.

4 Determine the length of the vertical drop to the workstation outlet.

5 Add 18" extra to the workstation outlet vertical drop.

If a workstation run will exceed the maximum distance for the media, you need to add an additional telecommunications room on the floor, or, if possible, relocate the telecommunications room to a more central location. Again, this is easier during the construction stage of a building, rather than attempting it as a retrofit.

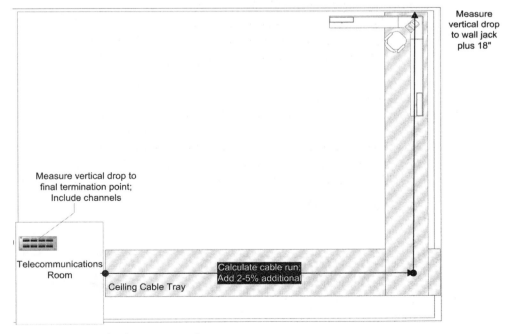

Exhibit 3-12: Calculating a workstation run

When retrofitting an existing building with workstation runs, sometimes you need to run cables along baseboards and around doorways. This method of running cables generally increases the length of the run. You should always cover this cable with metal channel guides to protect the cable itself from damage and users from tripping hazards.

Another item to consider when determining the configuration of your workstation runs is expansion and growth. Two drops per workstation is standard—this gives each user phone and network service—but as equipment needs increase, you will find this configuration doesn't allow for increased network demands. It's recommended that you overwire each workstation drop with at least one additional network cable anticipating future needs.

Modular office systems

Many modern offices are configured using modular office systems, consisting of movable partitions and furniture. Although these systems provide flexibility in arranging and rearranging office spaces based on changing needs, they can be a nightmare for the LAN wiring professional. As shown in Exhibit 3-13, the arrangement of cubicles is not always against a wall where outlets are typically permanently mounted. With modular office systems, the outlets are manufactured into the panels. You run your cables in narrow channels within the panels and connect them to the panel's outlets.

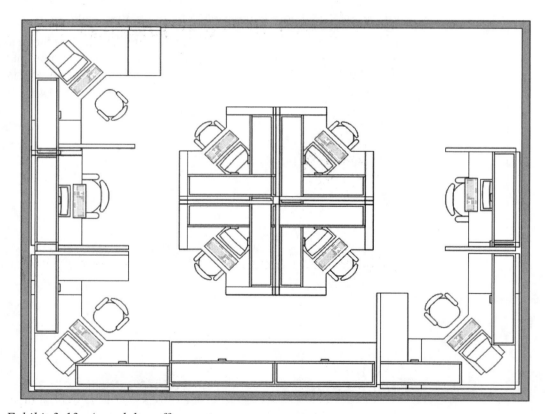

Exhibit 3-13: A modular office system

A disadvantage of the modular office system is that you must install your workstation runs after the furniture is installed, instead of during construction. To compensate, if you have a blue print/plan of the modular system layout, you can run your workstation cables prior to assembling the modular systems, leaving enough wire coiled at the end of the ceiling or floor run to stretch to the modular units. Another issue for networking is that if the modular office systems are rearranged, the existing workstation runs might not connect to the new locations.

TIA-568 Telecommunications Service Bulletin (TSB)-75 establishes guidelines for horizontal cabling in open offices (offices with modular office systems). There are two popular options for horizontal runs to modular office systems: the consolidation point and the multiuser outlet.

- *Consolidation point*—The point in a horizontal run where two cables are interconnected using a reusable connector such as a punch-down block. This isn't considered a "splice." The consolidation point must be at least 15 meters from the telecommunications room. You are allowed to coil extra cable to meet the 15 meter distance. All other cable distance maximums remain the same. From the consolidation point, workstation runs can be punched down and run to the outlet.

- *Multiuser telecommunications outlet assembly* (*MUTOA*)—This method creates centrally mounted workstation outlets (in a wall, not the ceiling), then employs longer user cables to reach from each workstation's equipment to the MUTOA. There is a 20 meter maximum for the user cables, and the extra length of the user cables reduces the maximum distance you have available for the horizontal cable. The TSB provides a formula that calculates the available horizontal run distance slightly less than simple subtraction to compensate for the decreased transmission rate in the longer stranded user cable.

Telecommunications room

It's important to keep cables in your telecommunications room orderly. You should clearly identify every cable, termination fixture, patch panel, and cross-connect following TIA/EIA-606 guidelines. Use the color coding specifications in TIA/EIA-569-A to designate wire termination areas.

You can use standoffs and distribution rings to route cables to their appropriate location. When available, run cables along rack and equipment wiring channels to keep them out of the way. It's also a good idea to secure them in place where possible to prevent someone accidently snagging them. Some wire management panels have covers that keep wires out of sight.

When calculating cable distances, remember to allow for 2 to 3½ meters for the vertical drop from the ceiling to your wall mount patch panel. Add extra for routing cables if you're using a rack mount.

Do it!

B-1: Running network cabling

Here's how	Here's why
1 If necessary, log on using the following domain credentials: User name: **hostadmin##** Password: **!pass1234**	Where ## is your assigned student number.
2 From the Student Data folder for this unit, open **FloorPlan.pdf**	(If necessary, accept the license agreement.)
3 Zoom the view so you can read the callouts	
4 Answer the following questions based on the floor plan What special considerations do you need to make for this particular office style? Other than straight runs to each workstation, what other options do you have? Where can you find out more information regarding these options?	
5 If you have a printer available, print FloorPlan.pdf Draw on the floor plan where you might place cable trays, consolidation points, or multiuser outlets	
6 Close FloorPlan.pdf	

7 From the Student Data folder for
   this unit, open **CableTrays.pdf**

   If you were to run cable trays to
   hold your UTP cabling from the
   telecommunications room along
   the outside walls, how would you
   calculate an estimate for
   maximum size of the main room?

   What change could you make if
   running UTP from the
   telecommunications room along
   the outside walls to any of the
   workstations along the back wall
   would exceed 90 meters?

8 Close CableTrays.pdf

Telecommunications room equipment

Explanation

The best configuration in your telecommunication room is one where your LAN hubs and punchdown block/patch panel wiring are close together. This can be tricky as LAN hubs and other equipment need power and ventilation, as well as connectivity. As shown in Exhibit 3-14, when you terminate workstation cables on a punchdown block, you must connect each cable to its final destination (the LAN hub or switch) using a cross-connect jumper. A cross-connect jumper is unjacketed solid twisted pair wires loosely spiraled around each other. It's available in 1, 2, 3, and 4-pair 22, 24, or 26 AWG, with 24 being the most common. For LAN cross-connects, you'll use the 4-pair cable. If you have separate racks for these items, you'll need to run longer patch cables between the two, which isn't ideal.

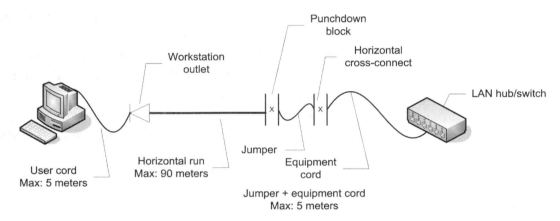

Exhibit 3-14: Punchdown block requires a cross-connect

Another guideline to follow in your telecommunications room is to color code the cross-connects. TIA/EIA-569 recommends using different cable sheath colors to accomplish this; however, the standard doesn't differentiate between telephone and LAN wires, or take into account that plenum-rated cabling comes standard in gray.

Each workstation cable is connected to an internetworking device such as a hub or concentrator. This device electrically terminates the cable.

Patch panel versus connecting blocks

As described earlier, you can choose to use a patch panel or a connecting block to terminate your workstation runs. Let's look at the advantages and disadvantages of each.

With a patch panel, each jack on the patch panel corresponds with a single workstation outlet. 18 and 24 jack patch panels are common. Most patch panels are designed to be mounted in 19" racks in your telecommunications room. They can be wired for either the T568-A or T568-B standard, so make sure you've chosen the correct one. Some patch panels come with jacks instead of punchdowns for individual cable wires.

The advantages of using a patch panel include:

- It's a permanent link.
- Channel testing is easier.
- It's a solid connection.
- Moves easily.

Disadvantages of using a patch panel include:
- The panel itself is an added equipment expense.
- It adds more wires to your telecommunications room.
- The modular connections create crosstalk.

When using a connecting block, the station cables are cross-connected to a mass termination connector for the LAN hub/switch. Connecting blocks have the following advantages over patch panels:
- Long-term corrosion is rare.
- Signal deterioration doesn't occur.

However, connecting blocks do have their disadvantages:
- Troubleshooting is more difficult because you can't just "unplug" the modular connector from the patch panel.
- It's more difficult to locate individual workstation cables.
- There's an increased potential for installation mistakes because of:
  — The incoming connection at the connection block.
  — Two connections for the cross-connect jumper.
  — The multi-circuit termination leading to the LAN hub/switch.

Using a punchdown tool

When wiring a punchdown block, remove the cable jacket only to the length needed to terminate the pairs, about 25mm. Make sure that you preserve the wire twists. In Cat 5e/6 cable, you can untwist the cables a maximum of 13mm according to TIA/EIA-568-C.

You trim and insert incoming workstation cables into a 66 or 110 block using a punchdown tool. There are two common types: the 788-type impact tool, shown in Exhibit 3-15, which you can use to connect up to 5 pairs of wires at a time; and the single pair version shown in Exhibit 3-16. When using a punchdown tool, make sure to use the correct blade (66 and 110 blocks require different blades) and that the side labeled "CUT" is down.

Exhibit 3-15: 5-pair 788 punchdown tool

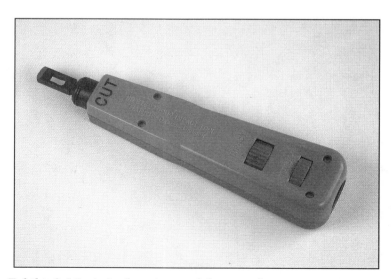

Exhibit 3-16: A single pair punchdown tool

To use the tool:

1 Insert the wire between the two metal blades on the punchdown block. There is one wire per contact in the punchdown block.

2 Place the punchdown tool on top of the wire. (Remember to have the correct side of the tool facing up.)

3 Apply pressure to the wire until you hear an audible snap. This snap is from the spring mechanism inside the tool.

The tool strips the wire and creates the contacts in the block. The color coding for a 66 or 110 block is shown in the following table.

Contact row	Contact pair	4-pair colors	3-pair colors	2-pair colors
1	1	White/Blue	White/Blue	White/Blue
2		Blue	Blue	Blue
3	2	White/Orange	White/Orange	White/Orange
4		Orange	Orange	Orange
5	3	White/Green	White/Green	White/Blue
6		Green	Green	Blue
7	4	White/Brown	White/Blue	White/Orange
8		Brown	Blue	Orange
9	5	White/Blue	White/Orange	White/Blue
10		Blue	Orange	Blue
11	6	White/Orange	White/Green	White/Orange
12		Orange	Green	Orange
13	7	White/Green	White/Blue	White/Blue
14		Green	Blue	Blue
15	8	White/Brown	White/Orange	White/Orange
16		Brown	Orange	Orange
17	9	White/Blue	White/Green	White/Blue
18		Blue	Green	Blue
19	10	White/Orange	White/Blue	White/Orange
20		Orange	Blue	Orange
21	11	White/Green	White/Orange	White/Blue
22		Green	Orange	Blue
23	12	White/Brown	White/Green	White/Orange

Contact row	Contact pair	4-pair colors	3-pair colors	2-pair colors
24		Brown	Green	Orange
25	13	White/Blue	White/Blue	White/Blue
26		Blue	Blue	Blue
27	14	White/Orange	White/Orange	White/Orange
28		Orange	Orange	Orange
29	15	White/Green	White/Green	White/Blue
30		Green	Green	Blue
31	16	White/Brown	White/Blue	White/Orange
32		Brown	Blue	Orange
33	17	White/Blue	White/Orange	White/Blue
34		Blue	Orange	Blue
35	18	White/Orange	White/Green	White/Orange
36		Orange	Green	Orange
37	19	White/Green	White/Blue	White/Blue
38		Green	Blue	Blue
39	20	White/Brown	White/Orange	White/Orange
40		Brown	Orange	Orange
41	21	White/Blue	White/Green	White/Blue
42		Blue	Green	Blue
43	22	White/Orange	White/Blue	White/Orange
44		Orange	Blue	Orange
45	23	White/Green	White/Orange	White/Blue
46		Green	Orange	Blue
47	24	White/Brown	White/Green	White/Orange
48		Brown	Green	Orange
49*	25			
50*				

* The 49th and 50th contact rows are used with a 25-pair wire.

Do it!   **B-2:** **Terminating a Cat 5e or Cat 6 cable in a punchdown block**

Here's how	Here's why
1 When terminating a Cat5e or Cat6 cable, how far should you remove the cable jacket?	
2 Remove the shielding (cable jacket) from your cable	
3 When terminating Cat 5e or Cat 6 cable, how far are you allowed to untwist the pairs?	
4 Untwist the cable pairs	
5 Determine the wire color for contact row 1 and contact row 2	
6 Place the appropriate wire over contact row 1 on the punchdown block	
Place the appropriate wire over contact row 2 on the punchdown block	
7 Use your punchdown tool to trim and insert the wires in contact rows 1 and 2	
8 Repeat for the remaining 3 wire pairs	

Topic C: LAN wiring tests

This topic covers the following CompTIA Network+ 2009 exam objectives.

#	Objective
Bridge objective — 2.4	**Given a scenario, differentiate and implement appropriate wiring standards** • Loopback
Bridge objective — 2.8	**Install components of wiring distribution** • Verify wiring installation • Verify wiring termination
Bridge objective — 4.7	**Given a scenario, troubleshoot connectivity issues and select an appropriate solution** Physical issues: • Near End crosstalk • Shorts
Bridge objective — 5.3	**Given a scenario, utilize the appropriate hardware tools** • TDR • OTDR

LAN tests

Explanation Full LAN wiring installation testing is best done by a certified company. Testing to TIA-568-B and C standards includes:

- Each individual cable link.
- Permanent link from the workstation outlet to the cross-connect block or patch panel.
- Channel testing of user and patch cords and cross-connect wires.

A wire map is also completed, which checks for wiring errors and cable faults such as:

- Continuity issues
- Shorts
- Crossed pairs
- Reverse pairs
- Split pairs

All wiring is measured electronically to verify maximum lengths aren't exceeded. Attenuation on all permanent and channel links is also tested using the formulas provided in TSB-67.

Near end crosstalk (*NEXT*) occurs when the signal from one pair of wires interferes with the signal on another pair of wires. This makes it difficult for a device to distinguish far-end signals from its own transmission. LAN wiring installation testing will measure NEXT loss in both directions on the cable link.

Testing equipment

For smaller-scope tests, you can purchase some simple testing equipment. Testing equipment ranges from basic wiring verification tools to the more expensive electrical-powered field testers, which automate testing and store their results. Both are used to pinpoint problem locations in your LAN wiring. Descriptions of some of the common testing equipment used for LAN wiring installations are provided in the following table.

Equipment	Description
Continuity tester	Verifies an electrical connection between two points.
Cable wire map tester	Verifies each TP wire is connected to the correct pin.
Cable tracer	Detects cables hidden behind walls or underground.
Cable scanner	Used to find cable faults. Comes in analog and digital versions.
Loopback connector	Checks cables for broken or shorted wires, and wall jack to network switch connections. Used when you need a network card to operate as though it has a live network connection, without it actually being connected to a network.
Time domain reflector (TDR)	Verifies impedance and termination in a cable.
Fiber optic tester	Optical time-domain reflectometer (OTDR) – version of TDR for optical cable.

Do it!

C-1: Researching LAN wiring test equipment

Here's how	Here's why
1 Open Internet Explorer	
2 Use any comparison shopping site to determine a cost estimate for the following LAN wiring test equipment:	www.google.com/products; shopping.msn.com, www.bizrate.com
Continuity tester	
Cable wire map tester	
Cable tracer	
Cable scanner	
Loopback adapter	
TDR	
OTDR	
3 Close Internet Explorer	

Unit summary: Network-to-network connections

Topic A   In this topic, you identified **network-to-network connection components** from an Internet backbone through to your own company's workstations. You saw how these components are connected together, and learned which connections are your responsibility and which you lease.

Topic B   In this topic, you learned how to install the **LAN wiring connections** that are your responsibility in the network-to-network connection scheme. You learned the standards that govern **LAN installations** and how they are applied in your network.

Topic C   In this topic, you learned the tests that are performed to verify a **LAN wiring installation**. You examined the various equipment used for the tests, as well as what type of test each device performs.

Review questions

1 Which of the following cities hosts one of the four original NAPs? (Choose all that apply.)

   A San Francisco, CA

   B Washington, DC

   C New York, NY

   D Seattle, WA

   E Chicago, IL

2 The original four NAPs are called what?

   A Public Internet exchange points

   B Private Internet exchange points

   C Commercial Internet Exchange (CIX) points

   D Federal Internet Exchange (FIX) points

3 Smaller companies and individuals use a(n) _____ to make the connection to a commercial backbone.

4 Before data gets onto a T1 line, it must be cleaned and formatted by a device called what?

   A CSU/DSU

   B Router

   C Hub

   D Demarc device

5 The point at which the communications network owned by one company connects to the communications network owned by another company is called what?

A Cross-connect

B Demarc

C Entrance facility

D Main distribution frame

6 Network backbone cabling run from floor to floor connecting the main cross-connect to intermediate cross-connects on each floor is referred to as _vertical_ cabling. *(cable)*

7 Which standard addresses the entrance facility, equipment room, backbone pathways, telecommunications room, and horizontal pathways?

A TIA/EIA-568-C

B TIA/EIA-569-A

C TIA/EIA-606

D There is no standard for these components.

8 Which standard specifies UTP standards for workstation runs?

A TIA/EIA-568-C

B TIA/EIA-569-A

C TIA/EIA-606

D There is no standard for these components.

9 What are the two choices you have for terminating network wiring in the telecommunications room? (Choose two.)

A Cross-connect

B LAN router

C Patch panel

D Punchdown terminal

10 True or false? You terminate both workstation drops and backbone wiring using the same device. *True*

11 The patch panel is then connected to the multiport hub by _Patch_ cables.

12 Backbones, workstation runs, and cross connects are part of what type of wiring?

A Horizontal runs

B Movable wiring

C Permanent wiring

D Vertical cabling

13 If you're using copper cable, what type of cable do you use for user and patch cords?

    A Solid

    B Stranded

14 Many companies run what type of cabling as their backbone media?

    A Fiber optic

    B Solid twisted pair

    C Stranded twisted pair

    D Coaxial

15 Minimize sharp bends in the cable, which can distort the __electrical__ characteristics of the cable.

16 In a UTP installation, you don't want to exceed what distance from the user's equipment to the final termination point in the telecommunications room?

    A 10 meters

    B 90 meters

    C 100 meters

    D 1000 meters

17 What are two popular options for horizontal runs to modular office systems? (Select two.)

    A Cable trays

    B Consolidation points

    C Multiuser outlets

    D Straight runs

    E Splices

18 What AWG gauge is most common for cross-connect jumpers?

    A 20

    B 22

    C 24

    D 26

19 For LAN cross-connects, how many pairs of wires are in the cable?

    A One

    B Two

    C Three

    D Four

20 Which terminating device has the following advantages?

- It's a permanent link.
- Channel testing is easier.
- It's a solid connection.
- Moves easily.

A Connecting block

B Patch panel

21 A wire map test checks for wiring errors and _Cable_ faults.

22 When the signal from one pair of wires interferes with the signal on another pair of wires, it's called what?

A Attenuation

B Impedance

C Near End Crosstalk

D Signal degradation

Independent practice activity

There is no independent practice activity for this unit.

Unit 4

Wired internetworking devices

Unit time: 180 minutes

Complete this unit, and you'll know how to:

A Differentiate between basic internetworking devices.

B Identify specialized internetworking devices.

Topic A: Basic internetworking devices

This topic covers the following CompTIA Network+ 2009 exam objectives.

#	Objective
Bridge objective	**1.1** **Explain the function of common networking protocols** • SNMP2/3
Bridge objective	**1.4** **Given a scenario, evaluate the proper use of the following addressing technologies and addressing schemes** Addressing schemes • Broadcast
Bridge objective	**1.5** **Identify common IPv4 and IPv6 routing protocols** Link state: • OSPF Distance vector: • RIP • RIPv2
Bridge objective	**1.6** **Explain the purpose of routing** • Static vs. dynamic
Bridge objective	**3.1** **Install, configure and differentiate between common network devices** • Hub • Repeater • Media converters • Basic switch • Bridge • Basic router • Basic firewall • Proxy server
Bridge objective	**3.3** **Explain the features of a switch** • PoE • Spanning tree • VLAN • Trunking
Bridge objective	**6.1** **Explain the function of hardware and software security devices** • Network based firewall • Host based firewall

Internetworking devices

Explanation

Internetworking can be defined as the technology and devices by which computers can communicate across differing types of networks. For example, let's say you have a computer on a Token Ring network in Washington that needs to access data on a file server resident in San Diego that participates on an Ethernet network. The two networks are tied together by WAN links maintained by a telecommunications provider. To achieve your goal, you must have a good understanding of how to internetwork the Token Ring LAN, the WAN links, and the Ethernet LAN.

Four common types of devices used to form an internetwork are:

- Repeaters ✓
- Bridges ✓
- Routers ✓
- Gateways ✓

Repeaters, bridges, routers, and brouters, which combine the characteristics of bridges and routers, play an important role in network management. On a technical level, these devices are distinguished by the OSI level at which they function (see Exhibit 4-1).

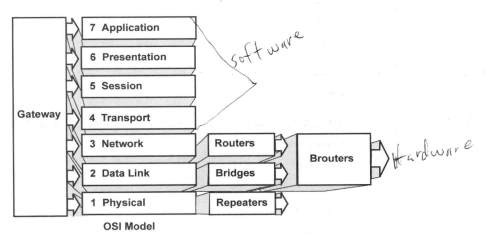

Exhibit 4-1: Internetworking devices

Device	Level	Layer
Repeater	1	Physical
Bridge	2	Data link
Router	3	Network
Brouter	2 & 3	Data link & Network

It's important that you understand the role of each internetworking device to be able to select the correct device to meet network requirements. Network performance is directly related to the number of computers on a cable segment and to the route data has to take to get to its destination. Careful planning and proper implementation of internetworking devices can help you build an efficient communications environment.

✓Repeaters

A *repeater* is one of the most basic internetworking devices. It boosts the electronic signal from one network cable segment or wireless LAN and passes it to another, helping you to physically extend network segments or wireless coverage. There are two kinds of repeaters:

- An *amplifier repeater* simply amplifies all incoming signals.
- A *signal-regenerating repeater* (also called an *intelligent repeater*) reads the signal and then creates an exact duplicate of the original signal before sending it on, as shown in Exhibit 4-2.

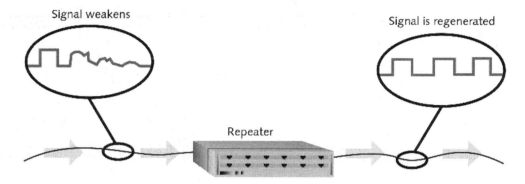

Exhibit 4-2: Data traffic through a repeater

A repeater connects network segments of similar media, as shown in Exhibit 4-3, or extends the reach of a wireless LAN, as shown in Exhibit 4-4. Historically, repeaters have been used on bus networks. To get the best signal quality, you should place the repeater so that the two network segments connected are approximately the same length.

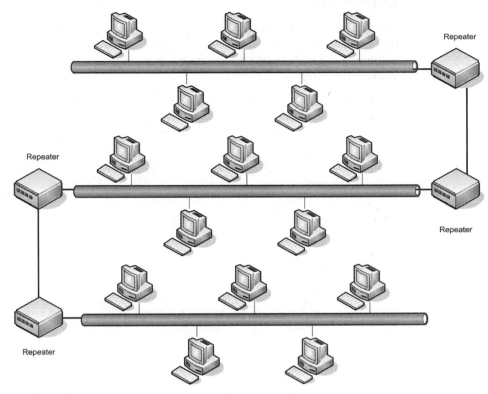

Exhibit 4-3: A repeater connects similar network segments

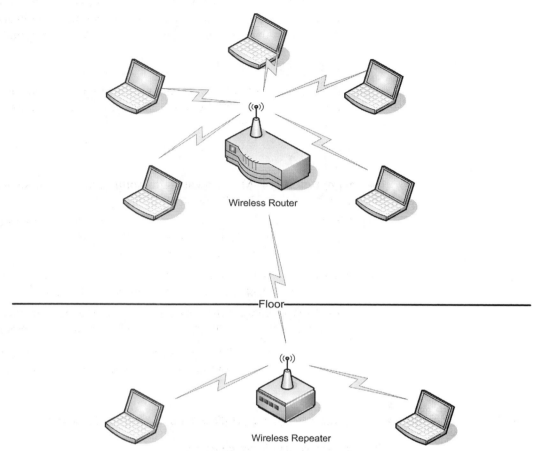

Exhibit 4-4: A wireless repeater extends wireless coverage

Repeaters operate at the Physical layer of the OSI Model, as shown in Exhibit 4-5. Repeaters aren't sensitive to higher-layer protocol attributes because they take a signal from one side and amplify it on the other side. In addition to amplifying the signal, a repeater also amplifies noise. As a result, there will be a limit to the number of repeaters that might be used in a given network segment. Intelligent repeaters regenerate the digital signal and are immune to the limitations of increasing attenuation over distance.

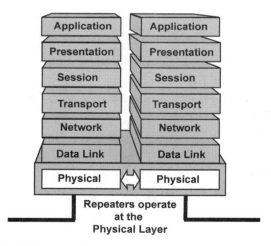

Exhibit 4-5: A repeater connecting network segments

Repeaters extend baseband networks that use one signal. Broadband networks support multiple signal transmissions simultaneously. An example of a broadband network is cable TV. Broadband networks use *amplifiers* to extend their signal transmissions.

Repeaters and their roles

All network media has a maximum transmission length. The earliest functional role of repeaters was to simply extend the physical length of a LAN. This is still one of the primary benefits of a repeater.

There are, however, several potential problem areas that aren't addressed by repeaters. These include:

- **Signal quality**—Most repeaters do nothing to filter noise out of the line, so noise is amplified and sent on with the signal.
- **Time delays**—Time delays can occur as signals are generated over greater distances. These delays might eventually generate time-out errors, keeping repeaters from being used for remote links.
- **Network traffic**—Because they don't have the capacity to filter traffic, repeaters do nothing to reduce the network traffic load.
- **Node limitations**—Repeaters are invisible to access protocols. All nodes added through a repeater count toward the total that can be supported in a subnet.

In today's networks, a repeater as a single network device is rarely used. The functions of a repeater have been incorporated into other devices, such as active and switching hubs.

Do it!

A-1: Discussing internetworking basics

Questions and answers

1 Define "internetworking."

2 Name the devices used to form an internetwork.

Router
Bridges
Repeater

(Switches multiport)

gateway (open gate) out of yard

3 A repeater boosts the electronic signal from one network cable segment and passes it to another.

4 What is the primary benefit of a repeater?

Extend range or clear signal

Bridges

Explanation   A *bridge* is an internetworking device that connects two different LANs and makes them appear to be one, or segments a larger LAN into two smaller pieces. Bridges, as shown in Exhibit 4-6, are more intelligent than repeaters. Bridges can read the specific physical address of devices on one network and filter information before passing it on to another network segment. This keeps local traffic from one segment from going beyond the segment, as well as prevents traffic addressed to one network segment from being sent out to all segments. Like intelligent repeaters, they go beyond amplifying the signal and are able to regenerate it. Rather than passing on line noise, a clean signal is sent out.

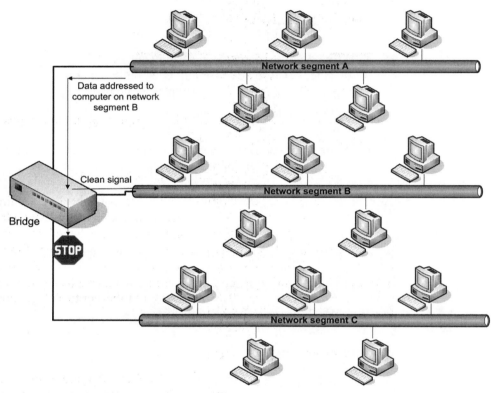

Exhibit 4-6: A bridge can filter traffic

As shown in Exhibit 4-7, bridges operate at the data link layer, or more precisely, at the Media Access Control (MAC) sub layer. In general, bridges:

- Are transparent to higher-level protocols. Segments connected through a bridge remain part of the same logical network.
- Can filter traffic based on addresses. Thus, a bridge can reduce traffic between segments. This feature can also be used to improve security by selecting the packets that can be passed.

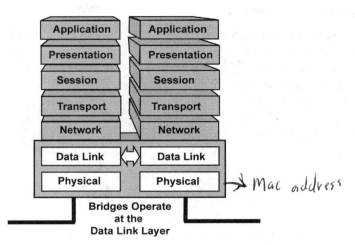

Exhibit 4-7: A bridge operating at the data link layer

There are a number of other terms and concepts relating to bridges and how they operate that follow.

Translating Heterogeneous (translating) bridges

A bridge reads a MAC layer frame. Therefore, some bridges are limited to linking similar MAC layer protocols. In special cases, where physical addressing is similar and the logical link services are identical, hybrid bridges have been developed to link between dissimilar MAC layer protocols. Because a number of the 802 series of protocols share the common 802.2 Logical Link Control (LLC) layer, it's possible for bridges to interconnect different types of networks such as Ethernet and Token Ring. One example of this is the IBM model 8209 Ethernet to Token Ring Bridge. Bridges of this type are also called *translating bridges*.

Encapsulating bridges

In *encapsulating* mode, a bridge packages frames of one format into the format of another. For example, Token Ring frames might be encapsulated in Ethernet frames and passed out onto the Ethernet network.

Presumably, there is another Ethernet-Token Ring bridge that de-encapsulates the packets and puts them on a second Token Ring network where they are read by a destination station. To stations on the intermediate Ethernet, these encapsulated frames are unrecognizable because there's no lower-level address translation being performed by the bridge.

In the example shown in Exhibit 4-8, packets from LAN A can be read by nodes on LAN C because they share a common addressing scheme. Nodes on LAN B can't read the packets.

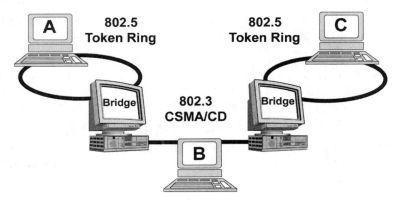

Exhibit 4-8: An example of encapsulation

Encapsulation is faster than translation. It helps the LAN to pass data quickly when the packets have to pass through multiple LANs.

A learning (transparent) bridge

Modern bridges are usually known as learning bridges because they are capable of automatically identifying devices on the segments they connect. A *learning bridge* listens to each of the attached cable segments and creates a table of addresses originating on each segment. It does this by listening to the replies. Until it knows where a destination station is, it forwards all of the packets for that station.

In the example shown in Exhibit 4-9, A's initial message to B might go out on the backbone, but B's reply teaches the bridge not to forward packets which are sent from A to B, or B to A. In the same manner, a reply from C teaches the bridge C's location.

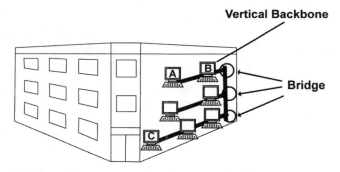

Exhibit 4-9: An example of learning bridge

When a learning bridge receives a frame from Station A, it records A's source address as a node on LAN 1. The bridge does this for all frames coming from LAN 1. For any frame that comes from LAN 1, if the destination address is one of the addresses recorded on LAN 1, the frame is simply discarded instead of broadcast on the backbone. Only unrecognized frames from LAN 1 are forwarded to the backbone.

This filtering process means that all local traffic from LAN 1 remains on LAN 1 and doesn't hit the backbone. A learning bridge's filtering effect on local traffic can be significant.

Bridge routing management

In complex internetworks, any LAN segment might have multiple paths to reach a given destination. When such choices arise, two critical issues are confronted:

- First, flow control information is necessary to know the relative capacities of each of the various bridge segments.

- Second, some form of routing control is necessary to make sure that segments with multiple links don't reproduce and distribute the same information. In this case, it's possible that two bridged segments will transmit the same frame, leading to a redundant message arriving at the destination node. This can cause serious operational confusion in any network system.

Flow control is especially important on large, active networks. Many studies suggest that 80% or more of the total traffic in a bridged network is local traffic. Less than 20% of the total traffic needs to be broadcast on the backbone.

No aspect of bridging is more confusing than routing protocols that relate to bridges and not routers. The purpose of these routing protocols is to eliminate the possibility of duplicate frames that might be generated by having segments with multiple links that form loops in a bridged network. Packets can circulate within a segment of the network and ultimately clog the network by using these loops.

Spanning tree routing algorithm

Bridges that support the spanning tree algorithm are able to communicate with each other and negotiate which bridge(s) will remain in a blocking mode (not forward packets) to prevent the formation of loops in the network. The bridges in the blocking mode continue to monitor the network. When they notice that another bridge has failed, they come back online and maintain the network connections.

Source routing algorithm   *Read all*

Source routing is found in IBM's Token Ring networks. In this environment, a workstation determines the routes to other workstations with which it wants to communicate by transmitting an all-routes broadcast frame, which propagates throughout the network. The second station's reply to the broadcast includes the route that the original frame took, and from that point on, that route is specified by the initial station (the source) for the duration of communications between the stations.

As a result, bridges in a Token Ring environment rely on the source to supply the routing information to be able to forward frames to other networks.

Source routing transparent bridges have been proposed by IBM, which will forward other types of frames, as well as those with source routing information.

Additional filtering and intelligence

Many vendors realized that the processor resources necessary to read frame addresses can be put to extended use and thus have created bridge filtering. Bridge filtering consists of looking for other patterns within the frame to selectively control the frames, which are forwarded.

This additional capability in a bridge has raised confusion over the technical definition of a bridge. The standards-oriented technicians are inclined to say that looking at information within the frame envelope for such patterns is a higher-level service, which, indeed, it is. However, these services can be layered effectively in bridge devices.

Note: Given the ability to identify patterns within the frames, bridge filtering might be deployed to selectively bridge only certain protocols.

Local and remote bridges

In addition to filtering and learning capabilities, bridges are also categorized based on the linkage between the two network segments.

When a bridge has a LAN link directly attached on each side, it's known as a *local bridge*. Local bridges are characterized by comparable input and output channel capacities.

When a bridge must link a local network across a wide area segment, it's known as a *remote bridge*. The output channel from the remote bridge is usually of dramatically lower bandwidth capacity.

This difference in relative bandwidth capacity on the input and output channels makes remote bridges significantly more complex to design and manage. They must be able to buffer inbound traffic and manage time-out errors. It's also necessary to design your network to keep traffic requirements over the remote link to a minimum.

Layer 2 switches

The term *Layer 2 switch* (also known as a *data switch* or simply *switch*) is generally a more modern term for multiport bridge. Like bridges, switches operate at the data link layer of the OSI model. However, although their basic functionality is the same, switches implement additional advanced filtering techniques to optimize performance. These filtering techniques are called *Virtual LAN* (*VLAN*) features and enable the implementation of a VLAN. In a VLAN, computers that are connected to separate segments appear and behave as if they're on the same segment. Although most VLAN filtering techniques have no universally accepted standard, they tend to fall into a few categories:

- Port-based grouping—Certain ports can be assigned to a specific VLAN. Packets will be kept local to the VLAN.

- Address-based grouping—Certain addresses can also be assigned to a specific VLAN. Packets will be forwarded only to the appropriate VLAN.

- Protocol-based grouping—The switch can examine the access protocol and forward the packet accordingly. This is Level 3 switching.

- Subnet-based grouping—If you are using TCP/IP, some switches might be able to identify the appropriate subnet and forward the packet accordingly. This is Level 3 switching.

Power over Ethernet

Power over Ethernet (PoE) technology is a method for transferring both electrical power and data to remote devices over twisted-pair cable in an Ethernet network. This technology allows you to place network switches in locations where it would inconvenient or impossible to run electrical power for the device. Cat 5e and Cat 6 cable both use 24 AWG conductors, which can safely carry power to remote network switches.

Bridges versus switches

Similar to repeaters, bridges aren't used very often in modern networks. Their features have been incorporated into switches. One of the benefits of a switch over a bridge is that bridges have fewer ports to connect network segments.

Modern switches also have the capability for *VLAN trunking*. When you connect multiple network segments together, it requires an internetworking device with multiple network interfaces—one for each network segment. With VLAN trunking, a single network adapter can virtualize "n" number of network adapters. "n" has a theoretical limit of 4096, but is typically limited to 1000 different VLAN network segments. Switches then use the *VLAN trunking protocol* (*VTP*) to communicate with each other about VLAN configuration.

Let's take a look at an example of VLAN trunking. In Exhibit 4-10, each switch is connected to two network segments, labeled "VLAN #" in the exhibit. On switch #2, VLAN #3 and VLAN #4 are sent through a single port (trunked) to the router and through another port to switch #1. VLAN #1 and VLAN #2 are trunked from the switch #2 to switch #1, and through switch #2 to the router. This trunk is able to transmit traffic from all four VLANs. The trunk link from switch #2 to the router can also carry all four VLANs. This single connection to the router allows the router to appear as if it was physically connected to all four network segments, just like it had four different physical ports connected to each switch.

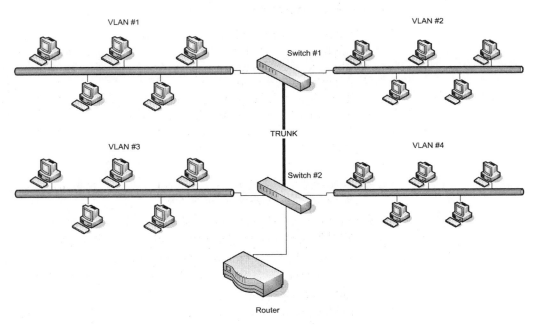

Exhibit 4-10: VLAN trunking

The VLANs communicate with each other via the trunking connection between the two switches using the router. For example, data from a computer on VLAN #3 that needs to communicate with a computer on any of the other VLANs must travel from the switch to the router and back again to the switch. Because of the transparent bridging algorithm and trunking, both computers and the router operate as if they are on the same physical network segment.

Other internetworking devices that are also now able to utilize VLAN trunking include:

- Routers
- Firewalls (software or hardware)
- Proxy servers
- VMWare hosts
- Wireless Access Points

Do it!

A-2: Identifying types of bridges and switches

Questions and answers

1 A bridge operates at which layer of the OSI model? *Layer 2*

2 What's a defining characteristic of a heterogeneous bridge? *Mac address*

3 You have two Ethernet networks connected by an intermediate Token Ring segment. The computers on the Ethernet segment need to communicate with each other. However, they don't need to communicate with computers on the Token Ring network. Which device is the best choice for connecting the three segments?

A   Router

B   Translating bridge

C   Transparent bridge

D   Encapsulating bridge

4 What's a translating bridge?

5 What's a learning bridge? *No vertual same as switch - multiple ports*

6 What's a switch? *multiple Bridge*

7 What's one of the differences between a bridge and a switch?

Routers   — Hop devices   I.P. address used
                                                    By

Explanation

As networks become more complex, simple bridging doesn't provide enough control of the flow of traffic. For example, broadcasts in a bridged network might propagate unnecessarily throughout the network. As shown in Exhibit 4-11, you can segment an extended internetwork into manageable, logical subnets by using routers.

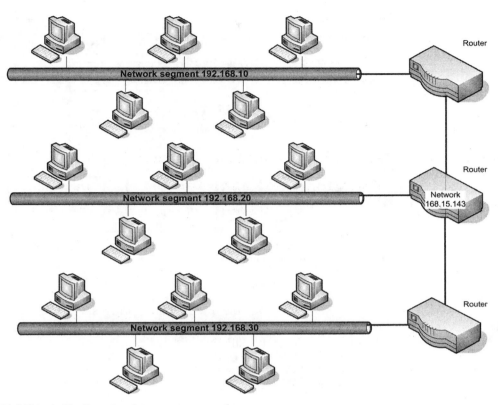

Exhibit 4-11: Routing between network segments

Routers are fundamentally different from bridges because they operate at the network layer, as shown in Exhibit 4-12. This means that a router opens the MAC (Media Access Control) layer envelope and looks at the contents of the packet delivered at the MAC layer. The contents of the MAC layer envelope are used to make routing decisions. This also means that protocols must have network layer addressing to be routable.

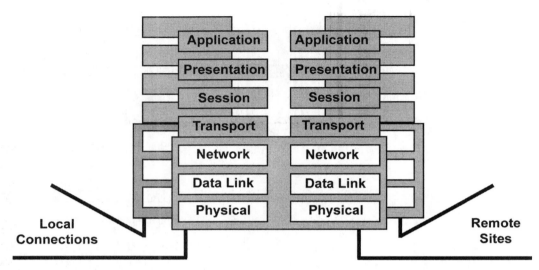

Exhibit 4-12: A router operating at the network layer

Routers might not match the throughput of bridges. A router activity needs more processor time, more memory, and multiple network connections. Current routers have enough speed to handle Ethernet and Token Ring traffic without dropping packets.

About routers

Early routers supported a single protocol, such as TCP/IP or XNS. Today, multiple-protocol routers might support 15 to 20 protocols simultaneously. The rise of networks running multiple protocols on the same wire is leading to the increased use of third-party multiple-protocol routers.

When a router receives a packet, it will generally forward it to the appropriate network based on a table maintained in the router. There are two types of tables:

- A *static table* is maintained by a system manager and is updated manually as the network is modified.
- A *dynamic table* is updated automatically as routers converse among themselves, by using a common routing protocol.

Bandwidth is cheaper on the LAN. Modern backbone networks are now migrating to 100-megabit speeds and above. The need for flow control, multiple-path management, and routing decision rules arises primarily in wide area links.

A wide area connection generally needs a routable protocol, such as TCP/IP or IPX. That is, the protocol must add information to the packet that differentiates between a destination on the local network and one on a different network. Microsoft's NetBEUI protocol is an example of a non-routable protocol. Each network segment is a separate logical network and might be administered independently. This also provides easier fault isolation.

The additional intelligence of routers provides for multiple (redundant) paths between locations, which provide both backup and the ability to do load balancing, and makes full use of available bandwidth. With bridges, multiple paths have to be avoided. Spanning tree, for example, shuts down redundant links until they are needed.

Offsetting the higher cost of managing and coordinating these more complex connections is the increased functionality that includes the ability to isolate individual workgroup networks as unique subnets. The router provides a port of entry that can control entrance and exit of traffic to and from the subnet. This segmentation is vital in organizations that rely on department-level network management. It also improves security and reduces congestion across the internetwork.

The programmable features of routers provide for effective management of remote links. Because these wide area connections are the most expensive components of the network, proper management and prioritization of traffic on these links is a vital concern for multi-site organizations.

Router features

The features of a router are:

- Inclusion of processor/memory/storage
- Multiple physical interfaces (ports) support
- Multiple protocol support
- Configuration/management (open/proprietary) interface

Processor/memory/storage

Routers are actually specialized microcomputers with highly tailored I/O capabilities. Memory is especially important because it is used to buffer packets in times of congestion.

Routers are contained in a box about the size of a PC. In some cases they might be an actual PC, such as a Novell Open Enterprise Server or Windows Server product configured as a router. There is also a trend toward router cards used in hubs or wiring concentrators.

Physical interfaces (ports)

These might vary considerably from vendor to vendor. In some cases, the router might be a simple box with multiple ports from which two or three specific ports might be selected. Other boxes might be expanded through the addition of cards supporting specific interfaces.

On the LAN side, there might be the common Ethernet, Token Ring, or ARCnet interfaces. Connections to the wide area (telecommunications) network might include RS-232, V.35, and RS-442 interfaces. Other possible interfaces include FDDI and broadband.

Because hardware is similar for bridges, routers, and brouters, upgrades might need new software.

Protocols

Multiprotocol routers support most of the common network protocols including, but not limited to, TCP/IP, Xerox XNS, and other XNS-based protocols such as Ungermann-Bass, Banyan VINES, Novell's IPX, the ISO CLNS, DECnet, HP Advancenet, SDLC, and AppleTalk.

In the wide area, protocols to consider include X.25, Frame Relay, and Switched Multimegabit Data Services (SMDS), in addition to dedicated lines ranging up to 56 Kb or T3 speeds.

Protocols used between routers to communicate routing table information include Routing Information Protocol (RIP), Open Shortest Path First (OSPF), the End System-Intermediate System protocol (OSI ES-IS), and the Intermediate System-Intermediate System protocol (OSI IS-IS), as well as proprietary vendor protocols.

LAN protocols	Router protocols	WAN protocols
TCP/IP	RIP	ATM
XNS	OSPF	X-25
IPX	OSI-ES-IS	Frame relay
Apple Talk	OSI-IS-IS	SMDS

Configuration/management (open/proprietary)

Most routers have a simple (RS-232) serial port to provide terminal access to the router, either directly or by modem. This provides a simple, generally character-oriented interface for configuring and managing the router. There might also be the possibility of connecting across the network to manage the router remotely.

Security with respect to managing the router might consist of simple password protection, but it might be possible to restrict access to specific network addresses or only the serial port. Many routers help in the use of filters or access lists to limit access to or from a specific router. This feature makes it possible to isolate specific subnets or to restrict access to the wider network to specific users or stations.

Simple Network Management Protocol (*SNMP*) is a TCP/IP-based management protocol that might be implemented on routers. With SNMP, it might be possible to show or set various characteristics of a router to an SNMP-based management station. The difficulty with SNMP is that it does not provide for security, so the ability to set the parameters of routers by using SNMP is avoided. SNMP has evolved through three different versions—v1, v2, and the current version as of 2004, v3.

OSI standards for network management are expected to provide more in the way of security. *Common Management Information Protocol* (*CMIP*) is the OSI-based protocol expected to provide standard management of network devices in general. CMOT (CMIP over TCP/IP) is an implementation of CMIP by using TCP/IP as a transport for use in managing TCP/IP networks specifically. Until CMIP is widely available, proprietary offerings might be the best alternatives where security is an issue.

Some key points to remember about routers include:

- A router connects two or more subnetworks.
- A router might be configured to support a single protocol or multiple protocols.
- A router will only process packets specifically addressing it as a destination.
- Packets destined for a locally connected subnetwork are passed to that network.
- Packets destined for a remote subnetwork are passed to the next router in the path.
- A router that exists in the same subnet as a host can be configured as a default gateway.

Note: The term "gateway" is also used to refer to a network device used to connect dissimilar systems or protocols.

Routers are intelligent devices. Many can dynamically determine the best route to a destination subnetwork. They can also inform the originating host if any problems occur during transmission.

Types of routers

Static routers

While still used in some situations, most static routers have been replaced by dynamic routers. Static routers are more difficult to manage and less efficient than their dynamic counterparts, for several reasons:

- Manual configuration—Each entry in the routing table must be made manually. In a large network, this can be a time-consuming process.
- Manual updates—If there are changes to the network, such as subnets added or removed or other router configurations changed, these must be entered into the routing table manually. The more dynamic the network, the more time that must be spent configuring routers.
- Changing environments—A static router cannot compensate for a failed route or high levels of traffic on a primary route. This means that data might be lost, or might be delayed over an inefficient route.

Static routers might provide an inexpensive solution on small networks, but it can become difficult to manage them efficiently on a larger network. Use of default routers is also critical to avoid losing packets whose destination has not been configured on the router.

Dynamic routers

Dynamic routers use an Interior Gateway Protocol (IGP) to communicate with each other. Some common Interior Gateway protocols are described in the following table.

IGP	Description
Routing Information Protocol (RIP)	Routers use RIP to keep each other informed about routing destinations. It is based on a Distance Vector algorithm that normally uses the fewest hops (router transversals) to determine the best path. RIP is a classful protocol, which means it doesn't support subnet masks, so all addresses within the same address class are considered to have the same subnet mask. RIPv2 improves on the RIP standard, including providing support for classless routing and increased maximum hop count. The version of RIP adapted for IPv6 is known as RIPng.
Open Shortest Path First (OSPF)	OSPF uses a Link State algorithm that provides for configuration of hierarchical topologies and helps quick response to changing network conditions. It is considered a more advanced routing technique than RIP. The current version is OSPFv2, with OSPFv3 adapted for use with IPv6. OSPF is the most widely used IGP.
Interior Gateway Routing Protocol (IGRP)	A proprietary Cisco protocol, it was created to overcome some of RIP's shortcomings, including its limited maximum number of hops. IGRP is another classful protocol and is considered by some to be an obsolete protocol.
Enhanced Interior Gateway Routing Protocol (EIGRP)	Another Cisco proprietary protocol, EIGRP was created to address some of the limitations of IGRP and include support for variable length subnet masks (VLSMs).

In a network connected to the Internet, it would clearly be impossible for any routing table to contain a list of all the available networks. Only information about networks on the network's own side of the Internet gateway is exchanged by using the IGP. When all routers in a network have received and processed all updates, the network is said to be *converged*, or in a steady state.

Path vector protocols

Path vector protocols are designed to interconnect autonomous domains (networks). In general, they operate like distance vector algorithms. A single "speaker node" in each domain shares its routing data with a speaker node in other domains.

The information shared is different. Instead of sharing node-level connectivity information, speaker nodes share large-scale path information. Such information is sufficient to get a packet from domain to domain, after which the intra-domain routing protocol (a distance vector or link-state algorithm) is used to route the packet to its ultimate destination.

Path vector protocols scale to the largest networks. The *Border Gateway Protocol* (*BGP*) is an implementation of a path vector algorithm.

Default gateway

Gateway-to-Gateway Protocol is used to update the massive routing tables maintained on routers within the Internet. To access the Internet, routers are configured with a default gateway (or smart gateway). Any requests for networks to which a route is not known are forwarded to the default gateway.

Routing tables

Both static and dynamic routers use routing tables to pass packets on to remote subnetworks. The only difference is whether the table is created manually or automatically. In either case, the routing table will contain the same information such as:

- The destination network IP address
- The destination network subnet mask
- The router interface used to get to the network
- The IP address of the next router in the path to the destination
- The number of hops to the destination

The number of hops refers to the number of intermediate networks (other routers) that must be crossed to reach the destination. Each packet will have a Time to Live (TTL) value that is decremented with each hop. When TTL reaches zero, the packet is dropped.

An IPv4 address of 0.0.0.0 refers to a default router. A default router intercepts all packets destined for networks not specifically designated in the routing table

Routing examples

Some specific situations are handled as follows:

- Local destination—The packet will be addressed for the destination host. Any other systems, including routers, will ignore the packet.
- Remote destination, next hop known—The source host will place the IP address for the next router as the immediate destination. That router will then pass the packet on to the following hop, if known. If not known, the router will pass the packet to its default gateway.
- Remote destination, next hop unknown—The source host will place the IP address for the default gateway as the immediate destination. That router will then pass the packet on to the following hop, if known. If not known, the router will pass the packet to its default gateway.

If a packet reaches a point where no routing is available to the next hop, the packet is destroyed and an ICMP message returned. ICMP (Internet Control Message Protocol) provides error reporting during datagram processing. This is a means by which dynamic routers can update their routing tables. If the TTL value reaches zero, indicating that the packet is likely lost and being bounced between default gateways, the packet is destroyed and an ICMP message generated.

Brouters

Brouters operate at both the network layer for routable protocols and at the data link layer for non-routable protocols.

As networks continue to become more complex, a mix of routable and non-routable protocols has led to the need for the combined features of bridges and routers. Brouters handle both routable and non-routable features by acting as routers for routable protocols and bridges for non-routable protocols. Bridged protocols might propagate throughout the network, but techniques such as filtering and learning might be used to reduce potential congestion.

Bridges vs. routers

Routers should be given preference over bridges when designing and configuring WANs. Bridges, by design, can escalate a transient reliability problem into a serious network failure.

Frequently, a host will use broadcast transmissions if there is an unexplained loss of contact with another host. Routers do not propagate these broadcasts.

Remote bridges, on the other hand, pass on all broadcasts. Every host receiving the broadcast must process it, if only to reject it. As broadcasts go above a certain level, the performance loss due to broadcast can lead to further broadcasts. This can lead to a broadcast storm, which can result in a complete breakdown of network communications.

Do it!

A-3: Discussing routers and brouters

Questions and answers
1 True or false? Static routers are more efficient than their dynamic counterparts.
2 What is the basic difference between static and dynamic routers?
3 Name a non-routable protocol.
4 List three features of routers.
5 Define the purpose of a router. *Data Flow   Prop Broadcast Traffic*

Wired internetworking devices

6 Name the protocol used to update the massive routing tables maintained on routers within the Internet. *Gateway to Gateway*

7 True or false? Only dynamic routers use routing tables to pass packets on to remote subnetworks.

8 A device that can handle both routable and non-routable protocols is called a *Brouter* .

   A Bridge

   B Repeater

   C Brouter

   D Router

9 A router operates at which layer of the OSI Model?

   A LLC

   B Data link

   C Network

   D Physical

   E B, C, and D

10 What is Common Management Information Protocol (CMIP)? *OSI protocol*

11 A node has ten packets worth of data to send to a remote host. There are multiple potential routes between the nodes. Will all of those packets take the same route across the network? *No - probably*

Ethernet hubs

Explanation To connect computers together in a network, in addition to cabling, connection devices are also necessary. These vary depending on the transport protocol used.

When wiring Ethernet in a star topology, it is necessary to use a device that will take the signal transmitted from one computer and propagate it to all the other computers on the network. This device is called an *Ethernet hub*. Hubs operate at the Physical layer of the OSI model.

A *hub* is a network device that can be used to connect devices that use a BNC or RJ-45 connector. A hub is generally inexpensive and is best suited for a small, simple network. These devices can include computers, servers, or printers.

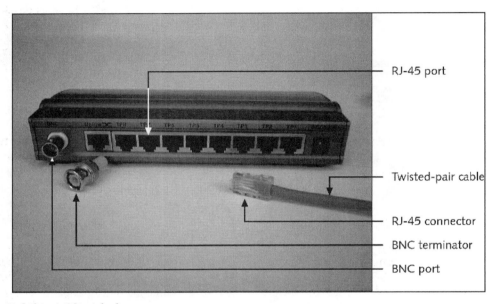

Exhibit 4-13: A hub

Hubs are easy to configure because they broadcast data packets to every device at once. Think of a hub as just a pass-through and distribution point for every device connected to it. The hub does not pay attention to the kind of data passing through it, nor to where the data might be going. When Computer A sends data to the hub, the hub replicates the data and sends it on every device connected to it. Computers B, C, and D all get a copy of the data. It's up to these computers to decide if the data is intended for them. For this reason, a hub can generate a lot of unnecessary traffic on a LAN, which can result in slow performance when a lot of nodes are connected to a hub.

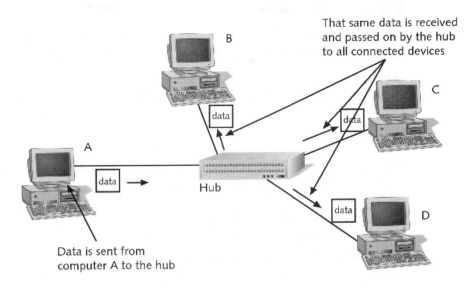

Exhibit 4-14: Data traffic through a hub

There are several types of hubs on the market, of which the important ones are of four types. Each has features of its own, but just about any combination of these feature sets can be found in a single hybrid device. When purchasing a hub, make sure to perform sufficient research to get a combination of necessary features.

Passive hubs

This is the most basic distribution device. Sometimes referred to as a concentrator, it might not even have a power source, although most do. A *passive hub* takes incoming electrical signals on one port and passes them down the cable on its other ports. In this way, all nodes see the signal just as if they were all connected on a physical bus topology.

Many passive hubs have indicator lights for power, network traffic, link state per port, and collision. Some also provide a BNC connector so that the hub can be connected to a 10Base2 backbone or an AUI port so that you can connect a transceiver of your choice.

Active hubs

Active hubs do more than simply rebroadcast incoming traffic. These hubs repair weak signals by actually retransmitting the data with proper transmission voltage and current. This essentially resets the cable length limitations for each port on the hub. For example, in a 10BaseT network the maximum transmission length is 100 m. Because the data is actually retransmitted on each port, a 100-m cable run can be attached to each port.

Other active hubs have the ability to resynchronize data that has been received from a NIC whose transmissions are not within standard timing specifications. This can help prevent data loss due to lost packets and improve the end-to-end reliability of network transmissions. Some active hubs will even alert you to this condition in a NIC so that the hardware can be replaced.

Switching hubs

A *switching hub* builds on the features of an active hub. Each port on a switching hub is isolated from the other ports. When a switching hub is first powered on, it listens to each port and makes a record of the NIC hardware address attached. A switching hub takes an incoming packet of data and actually looks inside at the destination hardware address. Then instead of rebroadcasting this packet on all the ports, the hub sends the packet out to only the port connected to the destination machine.

This is an effective method of avoiding collisions on the network. Each computer is free to transmit whenever it needs to. The switching hub will buffer the packets when more than one computer transmits simultaneously. It then propagates them as needed, giving each machine the impression that it is the only transmitter on the network.

Switching hubs can also make changes in transmission speeds. It is possible to connect both 10-Mbps and 100-Mbps NICs to the same hub. This auto-sense capability gives you flexibility to install faster 100-Mbps NICs in machines that need them and less expensive 10-Mbps NICs in those that do not. The switching hub uses its memory buffer space to hold incoming packets and then retransmits them at a slower or faster rate as needed.

Intelligent hubs

The term intelligent hub is more nebulous than the terms discussed up to this point. An intelligent hub might have management features that help it to report on traffic statistics, retransmission errors, or port connects/disconnects. It might support the TCP/IP Simple Network Management Protocol (SNMP).

You might be able to log into the hub itself and perform tasks, such as disabling/enabling ports, resetting ports, or monitoring traffic on an individual port in real-time. These hubs might have advanced features, such as built-in routing or bridging functions.

Because there is no standard definition, make sure you understand the features of a hub when it is termed intelligent.

Do it!   **A-4: Discussing Ethernet devices**

Questions and answers

1 Which of the following is a defining characteristic of an active hub?

   A   Retransmits lost packets

   B   Resets transmission to correct voltage and current

   C   Provides bridging functions

   D   Does not have a power source

2 You are installing a hub at a small remote office. There is no IT staff at this location. Which hub feature would you consider for this application?

   Intelligence

3 You have a 10BaseT network node connected 97 m from a passive hub, which drops its network connection regularly. What might you do to improve performance? *Active hub + repeater*

4 You have a 10BaseT network node connected 90 m from the central patch panel. A patch cable of 15 m runs from the patch panel to a switching hub. The network node has frequent problems accessing the network. What is a possible cause of this problem?

Token Ring Multi-station Access Unit

Explanation

Token Ring networks have some specific devices that are analogous to Ethernet hubs—MSAUs.

Token Ring media

Token Ring can be installed by using:

- Unshielded twisted pair in star or modified star configuration at 4 Mbps
- Shielded twisted pair in star or modified star configuration at 4 or 16 Mbps

Some facts to remember about Token Ring installations include:

- Multistation Access Unit (MSAU) supports up to 8 nodes.
- Maximum 12 MSAUs per ring.
- Local Ring Hub permits four node connections on one MSAU port cable.
- 64 - 72 (max.) nodes recommended per ring for optimal performance.

Maximum distances on a Token Ring network are illustrated in the following table.

Item	Distance
Station to MSAU	45 m
MSAU to MSAU	120 m
MSAU to repeater	600 m
Maximum Network Length	750 m (Type 1 cabling)
MSAU to Fiber Optic Repeater	1.5 km (max. net. 4,000 m)

MSAUs

Even though most Token Ring networks look like a star, they work as a ring. The Multistation Access Unit (MSAU) makes this possible.

Note: Originally, a multistation access unit was abbreviated as MAU. But this became confusing as a media access unit (transceiver) was also called a MAU. It is generally accepted that a multistation access unit is now abbreviated MSAU to avoid this confusion. Be alert that you might find MAU still in use, and you'll have to make a determination of its meaning from the context of use.

When a device connects to a MSAU, a cable with two twisted pairs is used. One pair transmits from the device to the MSAU, the other from the MSAU to the device. As each device is connected and initialized, you can hear the click as the MSAU makes a physical relay connection.

In Exhibit 4-15, the MSAU is wired to provide a local loop through an internal backup path. When multiple MSAUs are used, the Ring Out of each is plugged into the Ring In of the next until the ring is completed.

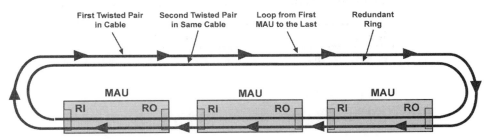

Exhibit 4-15: MSAU providing a local loop through an internal backup path

Two rings are actually completed. One is used for token passing between the devices. The second is a loop of all of the MSAU backup paths. This is known as a *redundant ring*.

The redundant ring is used when there is a break in the cable. The MSAUs on either side of the break will recognize it and set up a ring wrap connection. When the token gets to the last station in the ring, it is routed to the first station by way of the MSAU's backup path.

Media converters

Media converters provide a connection between one network media type and another without changing the channel access method. Physically, a media converter is usually a small box approximately $3 \times 2 \times 0.5$ in. It has an AUI port on one side and any one of a number of connectors on the other side.

A media converter might be used to connect a fiber optic backbone to a twisted pair hub. This is a change in media (fiber optic to twisted pair) but not a change in access method (both are Ethernet). Media converters are available with 10Base2, 10Base5, RJ-45, and fiber optic connections. When used in Token Ring applications, media converters are commonly referred to as media filters.

Do it! **A-5: Discussing Token Ring and other devices**

Questions and answers

1 A transceiver is used to

   A Connect segments with different network addresses.

   B Receive and transmit data on a patch panel.

   C Convert between different media types by using the same channel access method.

   D Connect a NIC to a managed hub.

2 What is the maximum number of MSAUs on a single Token Ring?

3 What is a redundant ring?

Firewalls   *Stateful   Inspection*

Explanation   A *firewall* is software or hardware used to control information that's sent and received from outside the network. The firewall resides on the network's gateway, which is the connection point between the internal network and outside communication. The firewall ensures that all communication is received from outside users and computers that are legitimate. A firewall can be installed on several different types of gateways, including a router, server, or computer. An example of a hardware firewall is shown in Exhibit 4-16. Firewalls can be used to help prevent Denial of Service (DoS) attacks and infections from a viruses, worms, or Trojan horses.

Exhibit 4-16: Hardware firewall

Various types of firewalls can function in several ways:

- Firewalls can filter data packets, examining the destination IP address or source IP address or the type of protocol used by the packet, for example, TCP or UDP.
- Firewalls can filter ports so outside clients can't communicate with inside services listening at these ports.
- Firewalls can filter applications, such as FTP, so that users inside the firewall can't use this service over the Internet.
- Some firewalls can filter information such as inappropriate Web content for children or employees.

In addition, some firewalls can set off alarms when suspicious activities happen and track this activity in log files. Several variations of firewalls are available, from personal firewalls to protect a single computer up to expensive firewall solutions for large corporations. When selecting a firewall, know what's being filtered, how it's filtered, and what options the firewall offers.

Hardware firewall

A good firewall solution is a hardware firewall that stands between a LAN and the Internet, as shown in Exhibit 4-17. A hardware firewall is ideal for a home network consisting of two or more computers, because it protects the entire network. For most home and small-office LANs that connect to the Internet through a single cable modem or DSL converter, a broadband router is used as a hardware firewall. You can buy a broadband router with enough ports to connect several computers and perhaps a network printer to it. Some broadband routers also serve double duty as a wireless access point to the network, DHCP server, and proxy server. The broadband router connects directly to the cable modem or DSL converter. Note that some DSL devices are also broadband routers and include embedded firewall firmware.

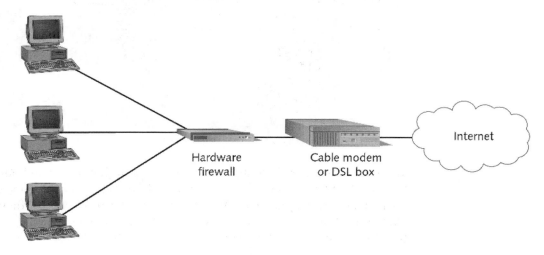

Exhibit 4-17: A hardware firewall

Software firewall

When a home or business computer has an "always on" connection to the Internet, such as a cable modem or DSL, it's a good idea to install a software firewall in addition to a hardware firewall. Firewall software can be installed on a computer connected directly to the Internet. For a LAN, you can install firewall software on each computer on the LAN. The firewall also requests permission from the user prior to allowing any programs access to the Internet. All open ports are blocked, as are any probes from Web sites.

Beginning with Service Pack 2 for Windows XP, Microsoft included the security enhancement Windows Firewall. Unlike most firewalls, Windows Firewall can be configured to block only incoming network traffic on your computer. All outgoing network traffic is allowed to travel, unrestricted, from your computer to its destination. Windows Firewall offers many new features, such as allowing incoming network connections based upon software or services running on a user's computer and the ability to block network connections based upon its source—the Internet, your local area network, or a specific range of IP addresses. By default, Windows Firewall turns on when Windows XP Service Pack 2 or a later version of Windows is installed.

Proxy server

A *proxy server* is a server that acts as an intermediary between computers on a network and the Internet. In the corporate environment, the main purpose of a proxy server is to provide Web access for computers that are located behind a corporate firewall, as shown in Exhibit 4-18.

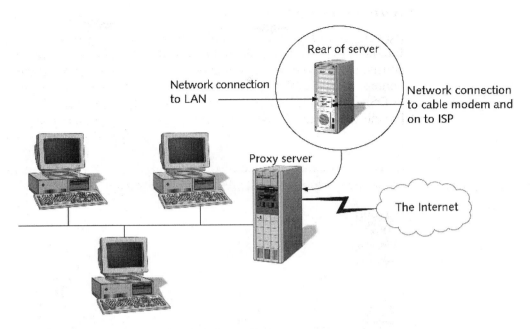

Exhibit 4-18: A proxy server as a firewall

When a proxy server is acting as a firewall, it can filter traffic in both directions. It can filter traffic that's coming into the network from outside computers, and it can filter traffic that's leaving the network. One way to filter incoming traffic is to limit communication from the outside to specific ports on the inside of the private network. Some firewalls maintain a list of ports to which they prevent access.

Firewalls filter outgoing traffic through a variety of methods. One method is to examine the IP address of the destination Web site against a list of either allowed addresses or forbidden addresses.

Port and packet filters

When a firewall filters ports, it prevents software on the outside from using certain ports on the network, even though those ports have services listening to them. For example, if you have an intranet Web site that's to be used only by your employees inside the network, you can set your firewall to filter port 80. Those on the intranet can access your Web server using port 80 as normal, but those outside can't reach your Web server.

When a router also acts as a firewall, it's called a *screening router*. Sometimes, screening routers can use a technique called stateful inspection. The router keeps track of all TCP sessions currently made and allows only those packets to pass that have been requested inside the network for these open sessions.

Sometimes, a problem arises when you want to allow certain ports to be accessed but others to be filtered or to allow packets that aren't a part of a current TCP session, such as when there's a videoconference. Employees on the inside of your firewall need to participate in a videoconference on the Internet, but when you tell your firewall software to allow these ports needed for the conference to be exposed to the Internet or to allow certain type of packets but not others, sometimes the firewall software doesn't respond properly. In this case, some system administrators temporarily "drop their shields" and remove port and packet filtering altogether, so the conference can take place. During these times, the network is vulnerable to an attack.

Do it!

A-6: Examining Firewall products

Here's how	Here's why
1 If necessary, log on using the following domain credentials: User name: **hostadmin##** Password: **!pass1234**	Where ## is your assigned student number.
2 Open Internet Explorer	
3 Go to **www.google.com** Click **Shopping**	
4 In the Google search box, type **hardware firewall**	
5 How reasonably priced is a hardware firewall for home use?	
6 What's the cost of a hardware firewall for enterprise use?	
7 Search for the cost of software firewall products	Popular companies include Symantec, CA, and Norton.
8 What's different about software firewall products compared to hardware firewall products?	
9 Access the Cisco Web site at **www.cisco.com** Under Products & Services, select **Security** Under Firewalls, click **View Products** Use the links to examine the features and functions provided by a Cisco hardware firewall	
10 Close Internet Explorer	

Topic B: Specialized internetworking devices

This topic covers the following CompTIA Network+ 2009 exam objectives.

#	Objective
2.5	**Categorize WAN technology types and properties**
	• MPLS
3.2	**Identify the functions of specialized network devices**
	• Multilayer switch
	• Content switch
	• IDS/IPS
	• Load balancer
	• Multifunction network devices
	• Bandwidth shaper
3.3	**Explain the features of a switch**
	• Port mirroring
4.5	**Explain different methods and rationales for network performance optimization**
	Methods:
	• Traffic shaping
	• Load balancing
5.2	**Explain the purpose of network scanners**
	• Intrusion detection software
	• Intrusion prevention software
6.1	**Explain the function of hardware and software security devices**
	• IDS
	• IPS

Bridge objective — 2.5
Bridge objective — 3.2
Bridge objective — 3.3
Bridge objective — 4.5
Bridge objective — 5.2
Bridge objective — 6.1

Higher-level switches

Explanation

A *multilayer switch* (*MLS*) is an internetworking device that operates at OSI Layer 2 like a basic switch, but provides additional functions at higher OSI layers. Multilayer switches combine Layer 2 data switching with Layer 3 routing using an application-specific integrated circuit (ASIC). (An *application-specific integrated circuit* is one that has been customized for a specific purpose.) This allows data packets to be directed to their destinations at a higher speed (referred to as *wirespeed*) than with normal routing. An example of a Layer 3 switch is shown in Exhibit 4-19.

Exhibit 4-19: A NetGear FSM7352S managed Layer 3 switch

Some switches can implement data packet switching based on information up to OSI layer 7. You'll hear these switches referred to as *Layer 4-7 switches*, *content switches*, *content services switches*, *web switches* or *application switches*. We'll use the term content switch in this material. Layer 4 switches use packet information identifying the application it belongs to. It uses this information to prioritize packets for routing. Layer 5 switches use information from the Session layer to route packets using URLs.

You use content switches for HTTP, HTTPS, VPN, and TCP/IP traffic *load balancing* among your servers and avoid a single point of failure. Load balancing utilizes network address translation so that clients aren't aware of which server is handling its requests. They simply send a request using a *virtual IP address* (*VIP*) assigned to the content switch, and it distributes the requests among your servers based on one of three methods:

- Least connections—The content switch sends the request to the server with least number of current open sessions. This method indirectly accounts for differences in server processor speeds. Because more powerful servers tend to close sessions quicker than less powerful ones, the content switch ends up sending more new sessions to the faster servers .

- Round Robin—The content switch sends new sessions to each server in turn. This method doesn't account for server processor speed differences. The content switch sends the same number of new sessions to each of your servers regardless of their capabilities.

- Weighting—With most content switches, you can configure a weighting factor to least connections or round robin to control the allocation of resources better. For example, your content switch might still use the round robin process, but you can specify that it direct twice as many new sessions to a high-end server compared to a slower, older server.

One of the benefits of a content switch is that many times it can perform network address translation at wirespeed. You can also use content switches to provide other higher-level services, such as SSL encryption/decryption and the centralized management of digital certificates. By having the content switch perform these functions, you can reduce the load on the servers receiving the data requests.

Do it!

B-1: Researching multilayer switches

Here's how	Here's why
1 Open Internet Explorer	
2 Access **www.cisco.com**	
In the Search box, type **multilayer switch** and click **Go**	
If prompted, respond to the Information Bar message	
3 Click the link for one of the returned search items	
4 Use the links on the page to identify answers to the following questions:	
What multilayer switch did you select?	
How many ports are available on the multilayer switch?	
How do you configure the multilayer switch you selected?	
What additional features are included with the switch?	
	Keep Internet Explorer open on the Cisco site for the next activity.

IDS and IPS

Explanation

Like a basic firewall, intrusion detection systems (IDS) and intrusion prevention systems (IPS) are hardware devices used to protect your network from unauthorized external access. You install an IDS device inside your network to monitor both internal traffic and traffic that has passed through your firewall. You install an IPS device on the perimeter of your network to monitor for and stop threats before they are passed on your network. Both are recommended to protect your LAN.

IDS

An IDS device uses a monitoring port to look at data packets sent on the network. A network switch sends a copy of all network packets it receives on a particular port or from a particular VLAN to the network monitoring connection on an IDS device—this is called port mirroring. The IDS device compares the traffic it receives from the switch to configurable rules, and if it detects suspicious traffic it logs the activity and triggers an alarm to let a network administrator know of suspicious activity. Most IDS devices use signature-based and anomaly-based detection methods, as well as stateful protocol analysis to identify threats. With stateful protocol analysis, the IDS device knows how TCP and UDP traffic—including DNS, FTP, HTTP and SMTP protocols—work. It examines data traffic to look for any values that don't meet the standard. Malicious traffic that would normally slip through your firewall detected by an IDS includes:

- Network attacks against services
- Data-driven attacks on applications
- Host-based attacks such as unauthorized logins
- Malware such as viruses, Trojan horses, and worms

One drawback of IDS devices is that they can erroneously trigger alarms for legitimate traffic.

IPS

An IPS device takes the IDS functions one step further. It can actually shut down suspicious traffic on the wire by:

- Terminating the network connection or user session.
- Blocking access to the targeted host, service, or application from a specific user account, IP address, or other attribute.
- Blocking all access to the targeted host, service, or application.
- Reconfiguring other devices, such as a firewall or router, to block an attack.

Some higher-end IPS devices can:

- Apply security patches for a known vulnerability to network hosts.
- Remove the malicious content of an attack, for example deleting an infected attachment prior to delivering an e-mail to a user.

Do it!

B-2:   Examining IDS and IPS products

Here's how	Here's why
1 Go to **www.cisco.com**	
2 Select **Product & Services**, **Security**	This page contains information on Cisco's Security Products.
3 Use the links to determine what types of IPS products Cisco offers	
	Keep Internet Explorer open on the Cisco site for the next activity.

Traffic shaper

Explanation

A *traffic shaper*, also called a *bandwidth shaper*; is software that controls network traffic in order to optimize performance or increase usable bandwidth. A traffic shaper controls the traffic by delaying packets that meet criteria that you set. You classify traffic according to categories such as port number or protocol. You then set rules for how each particular traffic class should be treated.

MPLS

Multiprotocol Label Switching (MPLS) is a protocol that operates between the definitions of OSI Model Layer 2 and Layer 3. You might hear it referred to as a *Layer 2.5 protocol*. It can transport data for both circuit and packet-switching clients in an IPv4 or IPv6 network. MPLS works in conjunction with the IP protocol and IGP routing protocols, providing networks with a more efficient way to manage applications and move information between locations. Its features include simple traffic shaping and the ability to create Layer 3 (IP) Virtual Private Networks.

Do it!

B-3: Comparing traffic shaper configuration

Here's how	Here's why
1 Go to **http://www.cisco.com/univercd/cc/td/doc/product/atm/►8110/8110/8110trfc.pdf**	
	This page describes how to configure traffic shaping on Cisco's 8110 Broadband Network Termination Unit.
2 Skim the material to get a general idea of how to accomplish traffic shaping on this particular device	
3 Go to **http://www.softperfect.com/products/bandwidth/**	
	This page describes a software product for Windows computers that you can use to limit bandwidth and manage traffic.
4 Skim the material to get a general idea of how to accomplish traffic shaping with this software	
5 Close Internet Explorer	

Multifunction network devices

Explanation

In order to save space in telecommunications room, many vendors have combined the functionality of multiple internetworking devices into one compact unit. These devices, known as *multifunction network devices*, are useful in tight spaces. However, as you add functionality to a single device, its management becomes more complicated and if the device fails, multiple functions on your network go down instead of just one.

Unit summary: Wired internetworking devices

Topic A   In this topic, you learned how to differentiate between basic internetworking devices, such as a **repeater**, **bridge**, **router**, **switch**, **firewall**, **proxy server**, and **media converters**. You learned the function each type of device provides to create an interconnected network of computers. You also identified where each type of device is installed on your network.

Topic B   In this topic, you identified specialized internetworking devices, such as a **multilayer** or **content switch**, **Intrusion Detection System** and **Intrusion Prevention System**, **load balancer**, **bandwidth shaper**, and multifunction network devices. You learned how each is installed and configured on your network to provide services to optimize your network traffic.

Review questions

1 *Reentove* _____ combine the characteristics of bridges and routers. *4-3*
   Brouter

2 Repeaters operate at which OSI layer?

   A Layer 1 – Physical

   B Layer 2 – Data link.

   C Layer 3 – Network

   D Layer 4 – Transport

3 Repeaters are typically used on what type of network?

   A Bus

   B Star

   C Ring

   D Hybrid

4 What type of repeater is shown in the following graphic?

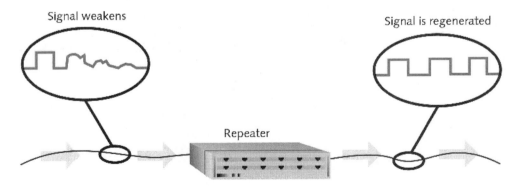

   A Amplifying

   B Basic

   C Intelligent

   D Multifunction

5 Bridges operate at which OSI layer?

   A Layer 1 – Physical

   B Layer 2 – Data link.

   C Layer 3 – Network

   D Layer 4 – Transport

6 Bridges filter based on which of the following?

   A Host name

   B Domain

   C Physical address

   D Signal quality

7 What type of bridge can package frames of one format into the format of another?

   A Encapsulating

   B Heterogeneous

   C Translating

   D Transparent

8 When a bridge has a LAN link directly attached on each side, it's known as a
   _____ bridge.

9 Routers operate at which OSI layer?

   A Layer 1 – Physical

   B Layer 2 – Data link.

   C Layer 3 – Network

   D Layer 4 – Transport

10 Which internetworking device makes computers that are connected to separate
    segments appear and behave as if they're on the same segment?

    A Bridge

    B Hub

    C Router

    D Switch

11 With VLAN trunking, a single network adapter can virtualize "n" number of
    network adapters. "n" has a theoretical limit of what?

    A 90

    B 1000

    C 4096

    D 5012

12 True or false? Routers were designed to prevent unnecessary broadcasts in bridged
    networks

13 True or false? Routers have a lower throughput than bridges.

14 Which of the following are router protocols? (Choose all that apply.)

A ATM

B Frame relay

C IPX

D RIP

E OSPF

F TCP/IP

G X-25

15 Which TCP/IP-based management protocol implemented on routers provides for security?

A CMIP over TCP/IP (CMOT)

B Common Management Information Protocol (CMIP)

C Simple Network Management Protocol (SNMP)

D SNMPv3

16 The two most common Interior Gateway protocols are:

A NAT

B OSPF

C RIP

D SNMP

17 When wiring Ethernet in a star topology, the internetworking device you use to take the signal transmitted from one computer and propagate it to all the other computers on the network is which of the following?

A Bridge

B Hub

C Repeater

D Switch

18 True or false? Brouters operate at both the network layer for routable protocols and at the data link layer for non-routable protocols.

19 Which type of hubs repairs weak signals by actually retransmitting the data with proper transmission voltage and current?

A Active

B Intelligent

C Passive

D Switching

20 Which type of hub is yet to be defined, but might include management features and support the TCP/IP Simple Network Management Protocol (SNMP)?

   A Active

   B Intelligent

   C Passive

   D Switching

21 True or false? The internetworking device used to connect computers on a Token Ring network is called a Token Ring hub.

22 Physically, Token Ring networks look like a star, but they operate like which topology?

   A Bus

   B Hybrid

   C Ring

23 True or false? Firewalls are hardware devices.

24 When a router also acts as a firewall, it's called a ___Screening___ router.

25 Multilayer switches combine Layer 2 data switching with Layer 3 routing using which of the following?

   A Application-specific integrated circuit (ASIC)

   B MPLS

   C Round robin

   D Specialized software

26 Which content switch load balancing method indirectly accounts for differences in server processor speeds?

   A Least connections

   B Round robin

   C Weighting

27 You install a(n) ___IPS___ device on the perimeter of your network to monitor for and stop threats before they are passed on your network.

28 A(n) ___IPS___ device can terminate a network connection or user session.

29 True or false? A traffic shaper can limit the amount of bandwidth a certain type of traffic is allowed to use.

Independent practice activity

In this activity, you'll research different types of internetworking devices.

1   Use Internet Explorer and a search engine to determine three different manufacturers of internetworking devices.

2   Pick one of the companies and examine their product line. What types of internetworking devices do they offer that you learned about in this unit?

3   Examine the technical documentation and support provided by the company. What types of things do they offer?

4   Search any of the manufacturers' Web sites for a case study document pertaining to the implementation of an internetworking device discussed in this unit. Read the document.

5   Close Internet Explorer.

Unit 5

Wired communication standards

Unit time: 195 minutes

Complete this unit, and you'll know how to:

A Describe the functions of the protocols in the TCP/IP protocol suite.

B Configure TCP/IP.

C Install and configure DHCP and DHCPv6.

Topic A: The TCP/IP protocol suite

This topic covers the following CompTIA Network+ 2009 exam objectives.

#	Objective
Bridge objective — 1.1	**Explain function of common networking protocols**
	• TCP
	• FTP
	• UDP
	• TCP/IP suite
	• TFTP
	• HTTP (S)
	• ARP
	• SIP (VoIP)
	• RTP (VoIP)
	• SSH
	• POP3
	• NTP
	• IMAP4
	• Telnet
	• SMTP
	• ICMP
	• IGMP
Bridge objective — 1.2	**Identify commonly used TCP and UDP default ports**
	TCP ports:
	• FTP – 20, 21
	• SSH – 22
	• TELNET – 23
	• SMTP – 25
	• DNS – 53
	• HTTP – 80
	• POP3 – 110
	• NTP – 123
	• IMAP4 – 143
	• HTTPS – 443
	UDP ports:
	• TFTP – 69
	• DNS – 53
	• BOOTPS/DHCP – 67
	• SNMP – 161

#	Objective
1.3	**Identify the following address formats**
	• MAC addressing
1.5	**Identify common IPv4 and IPv6 routing protocols**
	Link state:
	• OSPF
	Distance vector:
	• RIP
	• RIPv2
5.1	**Given a scenario, select the appropriate command line interface tool and interpret the output to verify functionality**
	• Ipconfig
	• Ifconfig
	• Ping
	• Arp
5.3	**Given a scenario, utilize the appropriate hardware tools**
	• Protocol analyzer

Bridge objective (1.5)

Bridge objective (5.1)

Bridge objective (5.3)

Explanation

Computers and devices that are connected via network media require a method for communicating with other computers and devices on the network. In order for communication to occur, there must be a set of rules or protocols. *Network communication protocols* establish the rules and formats that must be followed for effective communication between networks, as well as from one network node to another. A network communication protocol formats information into packages of information called *packets*. The media access method, for example Ethernet or Token Ring, is then used to send these packets onto the media itself.

The TCP/IP suite

The most common LAN protocol used today is actually a suite of protocols called TCP/IP, which stands for two of the primary protocols it uses: Transmission Control Protocol and Internet Protocol.

TCP/IP architecture

A four-layer reference model is used to describe the TCP/IP protocol architecture. This model can be compared to the OSI model. The four architectural layers in the TCP/IP model are:

- Application
- Transport
- Internet
- Network Interface

The Application, Transport, and Internet architectural layers contain the TCP/IP protocols that make up the TCP/IP protocol suite. The TCP/IP model is also referred to as the *TCP/IP stack*.

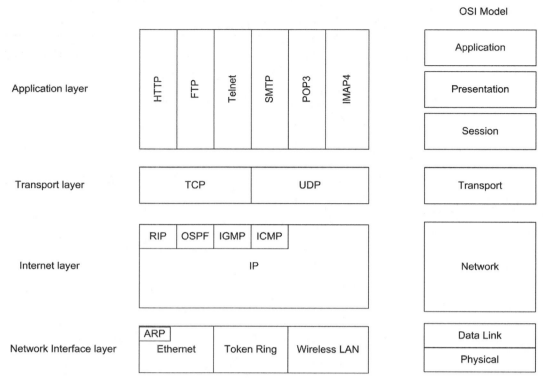

Exhibit 5-1: TCP/IP architecture

The TCP/IP architecture *Application layer* provides access to network resources. It defines the rules, commands, and procedures that client software uses to talk to a service running on a server. It also contains a series of protocols that are useful on TCP/IP networks such as the Internet. As an example, the HTTP protocol is an application layer protocol that defines how Web browsers and Web servers communicate.

The TCP/IP architecture *Transport layer* is responsible for preparing data to be transported across the network. This layer breaks large messages into smaller packets of information and tracks whether they arrived at their final destination.

The TCP/IP architecture *Internet layer* is responsible for logical addressing and routing. IP addresses are logical addresses.

The TCP/IP architecture *Network Interface layer* consists of the network card driver and the circuitry on the network card itself.

Do it!   **A-1:   Discussing the TCP/IP architecture**

Questions and answers

1 At which layer of the TCP/IP model does the network card operate?

   A   Application

   B   Transport

   C   Internet

   D   Network interface

2 To which layer in the OSI model does the TCP/IP Internet layer correspond?

   A   Application

   B   Transport

   C   Network

   D   Physical

IEEE Network Interface layer protocols

Explanation

The Institute of Electrical and Electronics Engineers (IEEE) defines most of the common TCP/IP architecture Network Interface layer protocols. The IEEE has a system of numbered committees; each defines a different Network Interface layer protocol.

The following table lists some of the IEEE Network Interface layer protocols.

Protocol	Description
802.3	Ethernet
802.5	Token Ring
802.11	Wireless LAN
802.15	Wireless personal area network

ARP

Address Resolution Protocol (*ARP*) is used to convert logical IP addresses to physical MAC addresses. This is an essential part of the packet delivery process. *Reverse Address Resolution Protocol* (*RARP*) does the opposite—converting physical MAC addresses to logical IP addresses. ARP and RARP operate at the OSI Data Link layer and are implemented by the network protocol driver.

Network cards use a MAC address to filter irrelevant packets. When a packet is received, the network card verifies that the destination MAC address matches the MAC address of the network card or is a broadcast MAC address. For example, if the receiving computer has a MAC address of A1:B2:C3:D4:E5:F6, then the network card of the receiving computer passes the packet up to IP if the destination MAC address of the packet is A1:B2:C3:D4:E5:F6 or FF:FF:FF:FF:FF:FF (broadcast MAC address). This process offloads the responsibility for analyzing all the network packets from IP to the network card. This reduces CPU utilization on the computer.

Data packets have four addresses: source IP address, destination IP address, source MAC address, and destination MAC address. When a packet is created, the source computer must find the MAC address of the destination computer based on the destination IP address.

ARP uses a two-packet process to find the MAC address of the destination computer. The first packet is an ARP Request that is broadcast to all computers on the local network asking for the MAC address of the computer with the destination IP address. The destination computer sees this packet and sends an ARP Reply containing its MAC address. The sending computer can then create data packets using the destination MAC address. Exhibit 5-2 shows an example of a small computer network. Computer A needs to find the MAC address of Computer B before data packets can be delivered.

IP Address: 192.30.0.24   IP Address: 172.30.0.25
MAC: 00:10:5A:5D:BA:62   MAC: 00:50:DA:23:15:2D

Exhibit 5-2: Computer A communicates with Computer B

Exhibit 5-3 shows the structure of an ARP Request packet sent as the first step of the resolution process. The ETHERNET section of the packet contains the MAC address information used by network cards when analyzing whether the packet should be passed up to IP. In this packet, the source MAC address is the MAC address of computer A, and the destination MAC address is the broadcast MAC address of FF:FF:FF:FF:FF:FF. All computers on the local segment process this packet and pass it up to ARP because the broadcast MAC address is the destination MAC address.

```
⊞ FRAME: Base frame properties
⊟ ETHERNET:   EType = ARP
   ⊞ ETHERNET: Destination address = FFFFFFFFFFFF
   ⊞ ETHERNET: Source address = 0000F81F35A6
   ⌐ ETHERNET: Ethernet Type : 0x0806 (ARP)
⊟ ARP_RARP: ARP: Request, Target IP: 192.168.1.66
   ⌐ ARP_RARP: Hardware Type = Ethernet (10Mb)
   ⌐ ARP_RARP: Protocol Type = 2048 (0x800)
   ⌐ ARP_RARP: Hardware Address Length = 6 (0x6)
   ⌐ ARP_RARP: Protocol Address Length = 4 (0x4)
   ⌐ ARP_RARP: Opcode = Request
   ⌐ ARP_RARP: Sender's Hardware Address = 0000F81F35A6
   ⌐ ARP_RARP: Sender's Protocol Address = 192.168.1.33
   ⌐ ARP_RARP: Target's Hardware Address = 000000000000
   ⌐ ARP_RARP: Target's Protocol Address = 192.168.1.66
```

Exhibit 5-3: ARP Request packet

The ARP_RARP section of the packet as shown in Exhibit 5-3 is the ARP information that is processed by ARP on the receiving computer. The most important information in this part of the packet is the Target's Protocol Address. This is the IP address of the destination computer. If the Target's Protocol Address matches the IP address of Computer B, then an ARP Reply packet is created. If the Target's Protocol Address does not match the IP address of Computer B, then the packet is discarded.

Exhibit 5-4 shows the structure of an ARP Reply packet sent as the second step of the resolution process. The ETHERNET section of the packet contains the MAC address information used by network cards when analyzing whether the packet should be passed up to IP. In this packet, the source MAC address is the MAC address of computer B, and the destination MAC address is the MAC address of computer A. The ARP_RARP section of the packet has the ARP information required by Computer A to create proper data packets. The Sender's Hardware Address is the MAC address that is required by Computer A.

```
⊞ FRAME: Base frame properties
⊟ ETHERNET:  EType = ARP
   ⊞ ETHERNET: Destination address = 0000F81F35A6
   ⊞ ETHERNET: Source address = 0080C876AA8A
   └ ETHERNET: Ethernet Type : 0x0806 (ARP)
⊟ ARP_RARP: ARP: Reply, Target IP: 192.168.1.33 Target Hdwr Addr: 0000F81F35A6
   ┈ ARP_RARP: Hardware Type = Ethernet (10Mb)
   ┈ ARP_RARP: Protocol Type = 2048 (0x800)
   ┈ ARP_RARP: Hardware Address Length = 6 (0x6)
   ┈ ARP_RARP: Protocol Address Length = 4 (0x4)
   ┈ ARP_RARP: Opcode = Reply
   ┈ ARP_RARP: Sender's Hardware Address = 0080C876AA8A
   ┈ ARP_RARP: Sender's Protocol Address = 192.168.1.66
   ┈ ARP_RARP: Target's Hardware Address = 0000F81F35A6
   ┈ ARP_RARP: Target's Protocol Address = 192.168.1.33
   └ ARP_RARP: Frame Padding
```

Exhibit 5-4: ARP Reply packet

If the sender determines that a packet's destination IP address is on a remote network, then the ARP process is modified. The first ARP Request is for the default gateway, then the ARP Response includes the MAC address of the router. The data packet is then built and sent to the router. The router removes and then replaces the source MAC address with its own and uses ARP to find the MAC address of the next router, if required, or the final destination host.

In Exhibit 5-5, Computer A is sending a data packet to Computer B. The data packet is addressed to Computer B at the IP layer, but must be given to the router for delivery. The MAC address is used to deliver the packet to the router.

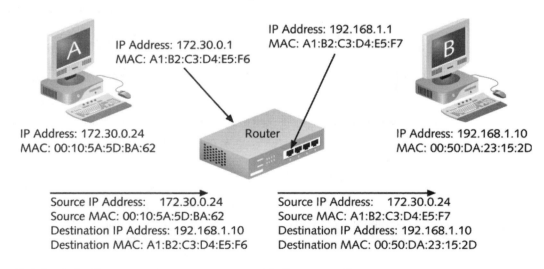

Exhibit 5-5: Computer A communicates with Computer B across a router

The router removes the MAC address information from the data packet and replaces it with the MAC addresses required to deliver it to Computer B. The source and destination IP addresses of the packet do not change.

ARP/RARP can be used in any type of broadcast network. The fields in the ARP packet specify the type of MAC address and protocol address. ARP is most often used in IEEE 802.x LAN media networks. It can also be used with FDDI, Token Ring, and Fast Ethernet.

IPCONFIG

You can use the command-line utility IPCONFIG to retrieve a computer's IP configuration. The IPCONFIG utility can display and modify the current TCP/IP stack. There are several switches you can add to the ipconfig command. `ipconfig /all` displays the current IP configuration information. For information on additional switches, enter `ipconfig /?` at the command prompt.

IFCONFIG

The ifconfig command provides a similar functionality to ipconfig, but for UNIX-based hosts. It can disable and enable network cards and release and renew the IP addresses assigned to those cards.

Do it!

A-2: Using IPCONFIG to view IP configuration

Here's how	Here's why
1 If necessary, log on using the following domain credentials: User name: **hostadmin##** Password: **!pass1234**	Where ## is your assigned student number.
2 Click **Start** and in the Start Search box, type **cmd**	
Press (↵ ENTER)	
3 Type **ipconfig /all**	To view your IP configuration settings.
Press (↵ ENTER)	
Record your IP address	IP address: _____
Share your address with your partner	My partner's IP address: _____
4 Close the command prompt window	

Do it!

A-3: Viewing the ARP cache

Here's how	Here's why
1 Click **Start** and right-click **Command Prompt**, choose **Run as administrator**	(If the Command Prompt doesn't appear on the Start menu, you'll find it under All Programs, Accessories.)
Click **Continue**	You'll view the contents of the ARP cache and clear the cache to force the rebuilding of the cache information. Clearing the ARP cache requires elevated permissions.
2 Enter **arp –a**	To view the contents of the ARP cache.
3 Enter **netsh interface ip delete arpcache**	
	To clear the contents of the ARP cache.
4 Enter **arp –a**	To view the contents of the ARP cache. It's now empty.
5 Enter **ping [partner's_IPaddress]**	
6 Enter **arp –g**	(To view the contents of the ARP cache.) Right now it shows the IP address and MAC address of your partner's computer.
7 Enter **ping www.yahoo.com**	
8 Enter **arp –g**	Notice that the cache does not have an entry for www.yahoo.com. Because www.yahoo.com is on a remote network, the cache has a new entry for your default gateway and the DNS server used to resolve the name.
9 Close the command prompt window	

Internet layer protocols

Explanation

Internet layer protocols in the TCP/IP architecture are responsible for all tasks related to logical addressing. An IP address is a logical address. Any protocol that is aware of other networks, as in how to find them and how to reach them, exists at this layer. Each Internet layer protocol is very specialized. They include: IP, RIP, OSPF, ICMP, IGMP, and SSH.

IP

The *Internet Protocol* (*IP*) is an unreliable connectionless protocol, functioning at the Network layer of the OSI model. IP doesn't verify that a specific packet of data has reached its destination. The sole function of the IP protocol is to transmit TCP, UDP, and other higher-level protocol packets, making the protocol routable.

Internet Protocol (IP) is responsible for the logical addressing of each packet created by the Transport layer. As each packet is built, IP adds the source and destination IP addresses to the packet.

When a packet is received from the network, IP verifies that it is addressed to this computer. IP looks at the destination IP address of the packet to verify that it is the same as the IP address of the receiving computer, or a broadcast address of which this computer is a part of the broadcast domain. For example, if a computer has an IP address of 192.168.1.50/24, then IP would accept packets addressed to 192.168.1.50, 192.168.1.255, and 255.255.255.255.

It's important to note that IP must have a Transport layer service to either guarantee the data delivery or not guarantee delivery.

RIP/RIPv2 and OSPF

Routing Information Protocol (*RIP*), its newer version *RIPv2*, and *Open Shortest Path First* (*OSPF*) are routing protocols. They are responsible for defining how paths are chosen through the internetworking of one computer subnet to another. They also define how routers can share information about the networks of which they are aware. These protocols operate at the Network layer of the OSI model.

ICMP/ICMPv6

Internet Control Messaging Protocol (*ICMP*) and the newer version *ICMPv6* are used to send IP error and control messages between routers and hosts. ICMP is an OSI Network layer protocol. The most common use of ICMP is the ping utility.

The ping utility uses ICMP packets to test connectivity between hosts. When you use ping to communicate with a host, your computer sends an ICMP Echo Request packet. The host that you are pinging sends an ICMP Echo Response packet back. If there is a response, you can be sure that the host you have pinged is up and functional. However, if a host does not respond, that does not guarantee it is nonfunctional. Many firewalls are configured to block ICMP packets.

IGMP

Internet Group Management Protocol (*IGMP*) is used for the management of multicast groups. Hosts use IGMP to inform routers of their membership in multicast groups. Routers use IGMP to announce that their networks have members in particular multicast groups. The use of IGMP allows multicast packets to be distributed only to routers that have interested hosts connected. ICMP operates at the OSI Network layer.

SSH

Secure Shell (*SSH*) exchanges data between two network nodes over a secure channel. It operates at the OSI Network layer. SSH was designed as a replacement for Telnet and other insecure remote shells, which sent data (including passwords) in plaintext. This left the data open for interception. SSH encryption provides data confidentiality and integrity over an insecure network, such as the Internet. Its primary use is on Linux and Unix systems to access shell accounts.

Do it!

A-4: Testing host functionality

Here's how	Here's why
1 Open a command prompt window	
2 Enter **ping netdc.networkplus.class**	
Observe the window	This is the classroom server. It responds, confirming that the server is definitely functional, and connectivity is working.
3 Enter **ping www.yahoo.com**	
Observe the window	This server responds. This confirms that the server is definitely functional, and Internet connectivity is working.
4 Enter **ping www.microsoft.com**	
Observe the window	There is no response because Microsoft has configured their firewall to block ping packets by default. A non-response may also mean that the server is not functioning or Internet connectivity is down.
5 Close the command prompt window	
6 Start Internet Explorer	
7 Enter **www.microsoft.com**	The Microsoft Web site appears. This confirms that the Web site is functional.
If prompted to install Silverlight, click **No thanks**	

Transport layer protocols

Explanation

TCP/IP architecture Transport layer protocols are responsible for getting data ready to move across the network. The most common task performed by Transport layer protocols is breaking an entire message down into smaller pieces called packets that can move more easily across the network. The two Transport layer protocols in the TCP/IP protocol suite are *Transmission Control Protocol* (*TCP*) and *User Datagram Protocol* (*UDP*).

Port numbers

One of the defining characteristics of Transport layer protocols is the use of *port numbers*. Each network service running on a server listens at a port number. Each Transport layer protocol has its own set of ports. When a packet is addressed to a particular port, the Transport layer protocol knows to which service to deliver the packet. The combination of an IP address and port number is referred to as a *socket*.

A port number is like an apartment number for the delivery of mail. The network ID of the IP address ensures that the packet is delivered to the correct street (network). The host ID ensures that the packet is delivered to the correct building (host). The Transport layer protocol and port number ensure that the packet is delivered to the proper apartment (service).

The following table shows well-known services and the ports they use:

Service	Port
FTP	TCP 21, 20
	20 is used for FTP data; 21 is used for FTP control
SSH	TCP 22, UDP 22
Telnet	TCP 23
SMTP	TCP 25
DNS	TCP 53, UDP 53
BOOTP and DHCP	UDP 67, 68
Trivial FTP (TFTP)	UDP 69
HTTP	TCP 80
POP3	TCP 110
NNTP	TCP 119
NTP	UDP 123
IMAP	TCP 143, UDP 143
SNMP	TCP 161, UDP 161
Secure HTTP	TCP 443

Do it!

A-5: Using port numbers

Here's how	Here's why
1 Observe the address bar	http://www.microsoft.com/en/us/default.aspx is displayed. The Web browser automatically connects you to port 80 on this server.
2 In the address bar, type **http://www.microsoft.com:21**	
Press `↵ ENTER`	The Web browser can't connect because port 21 isn't used for HTTP.
3 In the address bar, type **http://www.microsoft.com:80**	
Press `↵ ENTER`	The Web browser connects and gives you the same Web page as step 1.
4 In the address bar, type **ftp://ftp.microsoft.com**	
Press `↵ ENTER`	The Web browser automatically connects you to port 21 when using FTP.
5 In the address bar, type **ftp://ftp.microsoft.com:80**	
Press `↵ ENTER`	The Web browser can't connect because port 80 isn't used for FTP.
6 In the address bar, type **ftp://ftp.microsoft.com:21**	
Press `↵ ENTER`	The Web browser connects and gives you the same information as step 4.

TCP

Explanation

The Transmission Control Protocol (TCP) is the standard protocol used to transmit information across the Internet. It functions at the OSI Transport layer to provide acknowledged, connection-oriented communications, as well as guaranteed delivery, proper sequencing, and data integrity checks. *Connection-oriented* means that TCP creates and verifies a connection with a remote host before sending information. This verifies that the remote host exists and is willing to communicate before starting the conversation. If errors occur during transmission, TCP is responsible for retransmitting the data. File Transfer Protocol (FTP) is an example of a TCP/IP service that depends on TCP.

The establishment of a connection is a three-packet process between the source and destination host. It is often called a three-way handshake. Exhibit 5-6 shows the packets involved in the three-way handshake performed when a connection is established between Computer A and Computer B.

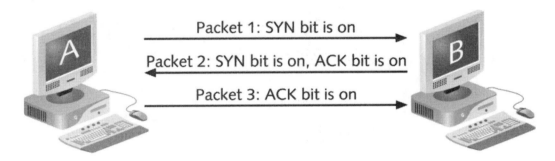

Exhibit 5-6: TCP three-way handshake

In Exhibit 5-6, you can see that Computer A initiates the connection. An option in the packet called the *SYN bit* is turned on. The SYN bit indicates that this packet is a request to negotiate a connection. This request includes parameters for the conversation such as the maximum packet size.

The response packet from Computer B to Computer A has the ACK and SYN bits turned on. The *ACK bit* is an option in a packet that indicates this packet is a response to the first packet. The SYN bit is on because this packet contains the parameters that Computer B would like to use when communicating with Computer A. If Computer B is able to use the parameters received in the first packet then those are the parameters sent in this packet. If Computer B cannot use a parameter from the first packet then it replaces that parameter with one that it can use in this packet.

The third packet is the final agreement from Computer A indicating that it has accepted the terms of the Computer B. This packet has the ACK bit turned on to indicate it is a response to the second packet.

TCP is considered *reliable* because it tracks each packet and makes sure that it arrives at its destination. If a packet is lost or damaged as part of the communication process, then the packet is transmitted again. The overall process is called a *sliding window*.

If a thousand packets are waiting to be sent as part of the communication process, not all of the packets are sent at once because it would be too difficult to track. Only a few packets are sent at a time. The number of packets is negotiated as part of the process of establishing the connection and is considered as being the size of the sliding window. For example, if the sliding window size is set to 10 packets, then only 10 packets are sent at a time. When the destination computer acknowledges receipt of the first 10 packets, then the window slides forward and another 10 packets are sent.

The sliding window cannot be moved past a packet that has not been received and acknowledged by the destination. If a packet goes missing it must be retransmitted and acknowledged before the sliding window can move past that point. A common reason why there is a pause in the middle of large downloads from the Internet is that a packet has been lost and must be retransmitted before the communication can continue.

Being reliable and connection-oriented are generally desirable qualities. Consequently, TCP is the Transport layer protocol used for most Internet services. HTTP, FTP, SMTP, POP3, and IMAP4 all use TCP.

Network Monitor

Explanation

You can capture network data using Microsoft Network Monitor, which is a simple software-based protocol analyzer. It is available for download from Microsoft. You must run it as administrator on Windows Vista computers. After you capture the data, you can then analyze it. One of the ways hackers use this information is to look for usernames and passwords. If this information is not encrypted and is sent in plain text, it is easily identified. One example of where clear text passwords are used is in anonymous FTP sessions. Likewise, you can use a protocol analyzer to identify and ultimately secure programs that send clear text passwords on the network.

```
WiFi: [ManagementBeacon] ......, (I), SSID = nic, Channel = 11
WiFi: [ManagementBeacon] ......, (I), SSID = TheNetworkWithNoNam, Channel = 11
WiFi: [ManagementBeacon] ......, (I), SSID = nic, Channel = 11
WiFi: [ManagementBeacon] ......, (I), SSID = TheNetworkWithNoNam, Channel = 11
FTP: Request from Port 57268,'USER anonymous'
FTP: Response to Port 57268, '331 Anonymous access allowed, send identity (e-mail name) as password.'
WiFi: [ManagementBeacon] ......, (I), SSID = nic, Channel = 11
WiFi: [ManagementBeacon] ......, (I), SSID = TheNetworkWithNoNam, Channel = 11
WiFi: [ManagementBeacon] ......, (I), SSID = TheNetworkWithNoNam, Channel = 11
```

Exhibit 5-7: Captured network data

As you can see in Exhibit 5-7, the user name and password are easily read from this ftp login session. If you use your e-mail address for the password in an anonymous login, this is one more piece of information a hacker can use to gain access to your account.

Do it!   **A-6: Using Network Monitor to view a TCP connection**

Here's how	Here's why
1 Minimize Internet Explorer	
2 On the Desktop, double-click **Microsoft Network Monitor 3.2**	Network Monitor is a protocol analyzer. It allows you to capture network traffic, view, and analyze it. You'll capture and view TCP connection packets in Network Monitor.
3 In the Microsoft Update Opt-in box, click **No**	To prevent Microsoft Network Monitor from using Microsoft Update to check for updates.
4 Maximize the Microsoft Network Monitor 3.2 window	
5 Click **New capture tab...**	
6 Choose **Capture, Start**	To begin capturing network traffic. You can also click the Start button (in Network Monitor) or press F5 to start a capture.
7 Switch back to Internet Explorer and go to www.yahoo.com	
8 Switch to the Microsoft Network Monitor window	
9 Choose **Capture, Stop**	To stop capturing traffic data. You can also click the Stop button or press F7 to stop a capture.
10 In the Frame Summary pane, observe the type of data recorded for each of the entries	The headings describe the type of data in each column.
11 Click the Load Filter button	(The file folder next to the History button.)
Choose **Standard Filters, TCPSynAndResets**	
12 In the Display Filter box, edit to read:	
TCP.Flags.Reset = = 1 | | TCP.Flags.Syn = = 0 OR 1	
13 Click **Apply**	

14	In the Frame Summary pane, scroll to find the iexplore.exe process entry showing your computer's IP address as the source and Yahoo as the destination	The Protocol Name for this entry should be TCP. You'll view the first packet in a TCP handshake.
	Select this packet	
15	In the Frame Details pane, expand TCP: Flags	
	Observe SrcPort and DstPort	To view the source and destination TCP ports. The source port varies, but the destination port is HTTP (80).
16	Expand Flags	To view the acknowledgement (ACK) and synchronize (SYN) flags. In this packet, the ACK flag is set to 0 and the SYN flag is set to 1.
17	Expand TCP: Options	
	Expand MaxSegmentSize	To view the packet size that is being requested.
18	In the Frame Summary pane, find the entry where the Source matches the Destination from the entry you just looked at	(It should be right below the entry you just looked at.) You'll view the second packet in a TCP handshake.
	Select that entry	The source IP address is the Web server. The destination IP address is your server.
19	In the Frame Details pane, under TCP: Flags, observe the source and destination TCP ports	The destination port is the same as the source port in the first packet. The source port is HTTP(80). Reverse of what you saw in the first packet.
20	View the acknowledgement (ACK) and synchronize (SYN) flags	Both the ACK flag and the SYN flag are set to 1.
21	Under TCP:Options, MaxSegmentSize, view the packet size that is being requested	It's the same as the first packet.
22	In the Frame Summary pane, find the next entry where the Source and the Destination match the first entry you looked at	(Again, it should be right below the entry you just looked at.)
	Observe SrcPort and DstPort	To view the source and destination TCP ports. The source port and the destination port match the first entry you looked at.

23	View the acknowledgement (ACK) and synchronize (SYN) flags	Both the ACK flag reset to 1 and the SYN flag is set to 0.
24	In the Frame Summary window, select the entry below the one you just looked at	This is an HTTP GET request. This packet is the request for the Web page.
25	In the Frame Summary window, select the entry below the one you just looked at	To view the response to the GET request. This is the information returned from the Web server based on the GET request.

UDP

Explanation

The *User Datagram Protocol* (*UDP*) was designed for connectionless, unacknowledged communications. *Connectionless* means that UDP does not attempt to negotiate terms with a remote host before sending information. UDP simply sends the information. If any terms need to be negotiated, the Application layer protocol has to do it. There is no handshake for UDP. *Unacknowledged* (sometimes called unreliable) means that UDP does not track or guarantee delivery of packets between the source and destination. UDP just sends a stream of packets without waiting for acknowledgement. There is no sliding window for UDP.

User Datagram Protocol (UDP) is not as commonly used as TCP and is used for different services. Like TCP, it also functions at the OSI Transport layer. By using IP as its underlying protocol carrier, UDP adds information about the source and destination socket identifiers. Trivial File Transfer Protocol (TFTP) is an example of a TCP/IP service that depends on UDP.

UDP is the appropriate Transport layer protocol to use when you are unconcerned about missing packets or would like to implement reliability in a special way. Streaming audio and video are in this category. If streaming audio were to pause and wait for missing packets to be sent again, then there could be long pauses in the sound. Most people prefer a small amount of static or silence be inserted for the missing packet and the rest of the audio track to continue to play. UDP does this because it does not keep track of packets that are missing or need to be re-sent. In the case of streaming audio, re-sent packets are handled by the Application layer protocol.

Connectionless communication also makes sense when the amount of data being exchanged is very small. Using three packets to set up a connection for a two-packet conversation is very inefficient. The resolution of a DNS name is a two-packet communication process and is done via UDP.

Do it!

A-7:   Using Network Monitor to capture UDP packets

Here's how	Here's why
1 Run Command Prompt as administrator	
2 Type **ipconfig /flushdns**	
Press (← ENTER)	To remove any cached DNS lookup information. This ensures that, later in the activity, a DNS lookup will be required rather than getting DNS information from cache.
3 Close the Command Prompt window	
4 Switch to Network Monitor	
5 Click **New capture**	You'll capture and view UDP packets in Network Monitor.
Click **Start**	To start capturing packets.

6 Switch to Internet Explorer	
Refresh the page with www.yahoo.com	
7 Switch to Microsoft Network Monitor 3.2	
Click **Stop**	To stop capturing packets.
8 Click the Load Filter button	(The file folder next to the History button.)
Choose **Standard Filters**, **DNSQueryName**	
9 In the Display Filter box, edit "server" to read: **"yahoo"**	
10 Click **Apply**	
11 In the Frame Summary pane, select the packet with the description "…Query for www.yahoo.com…"	You'll view the first UDP DNS packet.
In the Frame Details pane, observe the source and destination addresses	(Next to IPv4:) The source IP address is your computer. The destination IP address is the DNS server.
12 In the Frame Details pane, expand Udp	To view the source and destination UDP ports. The source UDP port varies. The destination UDP port is DNS (53)—the Domain Name Server.
13 In the Frame Details pane, expand Dns	To view the DNS-specific information.
14 In the Frame Summary pane, select the packet with the description "…Response – Success…"	It should be right below the entry you were just looking at. You'll view the second UDP DNS packet.
15 Observe the source and destination IP addresses	The source IP address is the DNS server. The destination IP address is your server.
16 In the Frame Details pane, observe the source and destination UDP ports	The source UDP port is the Domain Name Server—DNS (53). The destination UDP port is the same as the source UDP port in the previous packet.
17 Close the Microsoft Network Monitor window	Don't save any captures.
Close Internet Explorer	

TCP versus UDP

Explanation

TCP is connection-oriented and reliable. This is similar to delivering a letter by registered mail. Inside the letter each page is numbered so that it can be read in the proper order. When the message is received the sender receives notice that it arrived properly at its destination.

UDP is connectionless and unreliable. If you were to take the same message as in the previous example and place it on several postcards, take all of the postcards and dump them in the mail box separately, then the likelihood is that the recipient would be able to put them in the proper order and understand the message. However, if one postcard was missing it would be very difficult for the recipient to understand the complete message.

Do it!

A-8: Discussing TCP and UDP

Questions and answers

1 Which Transport protocol establishes a connection with the remote host before sending data?

  A   UDP

  B   TCP

  C   ARP

  D   FTP

2 Which of the following statements regarding TCP are false? (Choose all that apply.)

  A   TCP is a connection-oriented protocol.

  B   TCP uses a three-way handshake to establish a connection to the remote host.

  C   Packets lost during transit are re-sent.

  D   Packets lost during transit are not re-sent.

  E   None of the above.

3 Which Transport layer protocol is the best choice for streaming media?

  A   TCP

  B   DNS

  C   UDP

  D   HTTP

  E   ARP

Application layer protocols

Explanation

The TCP/IP architecture's Application layer accepts information from applications on the computer and sends this information to the requested service provider. In addition, there are many Application layer protocols that are only available on TCP/IP networks, each of which is associated with a client application and service. For example, FTP clients use the FTP protocol and Telnet clients use the Telnet protocol. However, some client software is capable of using more than one protocol. For example, Web browsers are capable of using HTTP to communicate with Web servers and FTP to communicate with FTP servers.

HTTP

Hypertext Transfer Protocol (*HTTP*) is the most common protocol used on the Internet today. This is the protocol used by Web browsers and Web servers. HTTP defines the commands that Web browsers can send and how Web servers are capable of responding. For example, when requesting a Web page, a Web browser sends a GET command. The server then responds by sending the requested Web page. Many commands are defined as part of the protocol.

Information can also be uploaded using the HTTP protocol. A survey form on a Web page is an example of information moving from a Web browser to a Web server. The capabilities of Web servers can also be extended using a variety of mechanisms that allow Web servers to pass data from forms to applications or scripts for processing. Some of the common mechanisms for passing data from a Web server to an application are:

- Common Gateway Interface (CGI)
- Internet Server Application Programmer Interface (ISAPI)
- Netscape Server Application Programmer Interface (NSAPI)

Note: The World Wide Web consortium (W3C) is the standards body responsible for defining the commands that are part of HTTP. To read more about the standards process visit the W3C Web site: www.w3c.org.

HTTPS connections

Secure Web servers use *SSL* (*Secure Sockets Layer*) to enable an encrypted communication channel between themselves and users' Web browsers. SSL is a public-key/private-key encryption protocol used to transmit data securely over the Internet over TCP/IP. Web sites that require SSL begin with https:// instead of http:// in the URL. When you connect using SSL, the connection itself is secure, and so is any data transferred across the connection.

Secure HTTP (*S-HTTP*) is another protocol used to secure Internet transmissions. Whereas SSL secures a connection between two computers, S-HTTP secures the individual data packets themselves.

FTP

File Transfer Protocol (*FTP*) is a simple file-sharing protocol. It includes commands for uploading and downloading files, as well as requesting directory listings from remote servers. This protocol has been around the Internet for a long time and was originally implemented on UNIX during the 1980s. The first industry-distributed document, or *Request for Comment* (*RFC*), describing FTP was created in 1985.

Web servers (using HTTP) and e-mail software (using SMTP) must encode data so it appears as text when it travels over the Internet. FTP, however, offers an alternative. FTP can transfer binary files over the Internet without the encoding and decoding overhead, making it a popular protocol for moving files over the Internet.

Note: Although there are still FTP servers running on the Internet, they number fewer than in previous years. FTP is slowly becoming obsolete due to HTTP being capable of uploading and downloading files and the inherent lack of security of FTP.

FTP is implemented in stand-alone FTP clients as well as in Web browsers. It is safe to say that most FTP users today are using Web browsers.

TFTP

Another protocol similar to FTP is Trivial File Transfer Protocol (Trivial FTP or TFTP). TFTP has fewer commands than FTP and can be used only to send and receive files. It can be used for multicasting in which a file is sent to more than one client at the same time using the UDP Transport layer protocol.

VoIP protocols

With VoIP, you can make telephone calls over a data network such as the Internet. VoIP converts the analog signals from digital back to voice at the other end so you can speak to anyone with a regular phone number. The VoIP technology uses two communication protocols to accomplish this:

- *Session Initiation Protocol* (*SIP*), which is a signaling protocol used to set up and take down Internet voice or video calls. It operates at the OSI Session layer and is independent of the transport layer, so it can use TCP or UDP.
- *Real-time Transport Protocol* (*RTP*) defines a standard packet format for delivering audio and video over the Internet. RTP can use TCP or UDP.

Do it!

A-9: Using FTP to download a file

Here's how	Here's why
1 Click **Start** and enter **ftp**	You'll use FTP to download a utility.
2 Enter the following command: **open ftp.microsoft.com**	
3 Enter **anonymous**	
4 Enter your e-mail address	
5 Enter **ls**	
6 If prompted by Windows Firewall, click **Unblock** and **Continue**	
7 Enter **cd softlib**	
8 Enter **dir**	
9 Enter **get index.txt**	This command will retrieve the file index.txt from the remote server. All retrieved files are placed in the current directory on the local machine. In this instance the current directory is C:\Users\hostadmin##\
10 Enter **bye**	
11 Use Windows Explorer to view C:\Users\hostadmin##	The index.txt file was downloaded to this directory using ftp.
12 Open **Index.txt**	
13 Close Index.txt and Windows Explorer	

Telnet

Explanation

Telnet is a terminal emulation protocol that is primarily used to remotely connect to UNIX and Linux Systems. The Telnet protocol specifies how Telnet server and Telnet clients communicate.

The most common reason to connect to a server via Telnet is to remotely manage Unix or Linux systems. All of the administration for these systems can be done through a character-based interface. This is important because Telnet does not support a *graphical user interface* (*GUI*), only text.

Telnet is similar to the concept of a mainframe and dumb terminal. The Telnet server controls the entire user environment, processes the keyboard input, and sends display commands back to the client. A Telnet client is responsible only for displaying information on the screen and passing input to the server. There can be many Telnet clients connected to a single server at one time. Each client that is connected receives its own operating environment; however, these clients are not aware that other users are logged into the system.

NTP

The Network Time Protocol (NTP) is a time synchronization system for computer clocks through the Internet network. It provides the mechanisms to synchronize time and coordinate time distribution in a large, diverse Internet, operating at rates from mundane to light wave. It uses a returnable time design in which a distributed sub network of time servers, operating in a self-organizing, hierarchical master-slave configuration, synchronize logical clocks within the sub network and to national time standards via wire or radio.

E-mail messaging protocols

SMTP

Simple Mail Transfer Protocol (*SMTP*) is used to send and receive e-mail messages between e-mail servers. It is also used by e-mail client software, such as Outlook, to send messages to the server. SMTP is never used to retrieve e-mail from a server. Other protocols control the retrieval of e-mail messages.

POP3

Post Office Protocol version 3 (*POP3*) is the most common protocol used for retrieving e-mail messages. This protocol has commands to download and delete messages from the mail server. POP3 does not support sending messages. By default, most e-mail client software using POP3 copies all messages onto the local hard drive and then erases the messages from the server. However, you can change the configuration so that messages can be left on the server. POP3 only supports a single inbox and does not support multiple folders for storage on the server.

IMAP4

Internet Message Access Protocol version 4 (*IMAP4*) is another common protocol used to retrieve e-mail messages. The abilities of IMAP4 are beyond those of POP3. For example, IMAP can download message headers, which you can use to choose which messages you want to download. In addition, IMAP4 allows for multiple folders on the server side to store messages.

Do it!

A-10: Using Telnet to verify SMTP

Here's how	Here's why
1 Open Control Panel	Telnet isn't installed by default on Windows Vista.
2 Click **Programs**	
Under Programs and Features, click **Turn Windows features on or off**	
Click **Continue**	
3 Check **Telnet Client**	
Click **OK**	
4 Close Control Panel	
5 Open a Command Prompt window	
6 Enter **telnet**	
7 Enter **set localecho**	This displays the commands that you type in the Telnet window.
8 Enter **open maila.microsoft.com 25**	
9 Enter **help**	
What commands does the mail server support?	
10 Enter **helo**	
What is the FQDN of the mail server?	
11 Enter **quit**	
12 Press (↵ *ENTER*) two times	If prompted to press a key to continue.
13 Enter **quit**	To close the Telnet utility. Leave the command prompt window open for the next activity.

Topic B: TCP/IP

This topic covers the following CompTIA Network+ 2009 exam objectives.

#	Objective
Bridge objective **1.1**	**Explain the function of common networking protocols**
	• DHCP
	• DNS
1.3	**Identify the following address formats**
	• IPv6
	• IPv4
Bridge objective **1.4**	**Given a scenario, evaluate the proper use of the following addressing technologies and addressing schemes**
	Addressing technologies:
	• Subnetting
	• Classful vs. classless (e.g. CIDR, Supernetting)
	• NAT
	• PAT
	• SNAT
	• Public vs. private
	• DHCP (static, dynamic APIPA)
	Addressing schemes:
	• Unicast
	• Multicast
	• Broadcast
Bridge objective **3.1**	**Install, configure and differentiate between common network devices**
	• NIC
	• Basic DHCP server
Bridge objective **3.2**	**Identify the functions of specialized network devices**
	• DNS server

Explanation

As discussed in a previous unit, there are two version of the Internet Protocol: IPv4 and IPv6. IPv6 is the newer version of the Internet Protocol, which offers a number of enhancements over IPv4. The most important enhancement is the increase in address size, which allows for more unique Internet addresses. Although IPv4 is currently implemented in most networks, organizations will gradually implement IPv6 over the next several years. In this topic, you'll examine both formats.

IPv4

Version 4 of the Internet Protocol (IPv4) has been the standard since September of 1981. This is the protocol that all Internet traffic was based on until recently.

Every piece of information stored in a computer can be broken down into a series of on/off conditions called bits. This type of information is called binary data because each element has only two possible values: 1 (on) and 0 (off). In binary, a byte (or octet) is a string of eight bits. An IPv4 address is made up of 32 bits of information. These 32 bits are divided into four octets. There are two main methods for depicting an IP address:

- Binary IP addresses—what the computer reads. A binary IP address has the following format: 11001010 00101101 11100001 00001111.
- Dotted-decimal IP—widely used to show IPv4 addresses. A dotted-decimal IP address has the following format: 208.206.88.56.

You write IP addresses in dotted decimal notation. With IPv4 32 bit IP addresses, you can uniquely identify up to 2^{32} addresses. However, some of those addresses are unavailable for general use. The maximum decimal value for 8 bits is 255

All IP addresses are composed of two parts: the network ID and the host ID. The *network ID* represents the network on which the computer is located, whereas the *host ID* represents a single computer on that network. No two computers on the same network can have the same host ID; however, two computers on different networks can have the same host ID.

The Internet Assigned Numbers Authority (IANA) implemented *classful* IPv4 addresses in order to differentiate between the portion of the IP address that identifies a particular network and the portion that identifies a specific host on that network. These classes of IP addresses are shown in the following table.

Class	Addresses	Description
A	1.0.0.0 - 126.0.0.0	First octet is network ID; last three octets are Host ID. Default subnet mask is 255.0.0.0.
B	128.0.0.0 - 191.255.0.0	First two octets are network ID; last three octets are Host ID. Default subnet mask is 255.255.0.0.
C	192.0.0.0 - 223.255.255.0	First three octets are network ID; last octet is Host ID. Default subnet mask is 255.255.255.0.
D	224.0.0.0 - 239.0.0.0	Multicasting addresses.
E	240.0.0.0 - 255.0.0.0	Experimental use.

Subnet masks

Subnet masks are used to identify the network ID portion of an IP address. You can use it to infer the host ID portion of the IP address. This allows additional addresses to be implemented within a given address space. The default mask for each of the classes is listed in the previous table. The following table shows two examples of how the network ID and host ID of an IP address can be calculated using the subnet mask.

IP address	Subnet mask	Host ID	Network ID
192.168.100.33	255.255.255.0	192.168.100.0	0.0.0.33
172.16.43.207	255.255.0.0	172.16.0.0	0.0.43.207

No matter how many octets are included in the network ID, they are always contiguous and start on the left. If the first and third octets are part of the network ID, the second must be as well. The following table shows examples of valid and invalid subnet masks.

Valid subnet masks	Invalid subnet masks
255.0.0.0	0.255.255.255
255.255.0.0	255.0.255.0
255.255.255.0	255.255.0.255

Reserved addresses also take up some of the available addresses. About 18 million addresses are reserved for private networks. About 16 million addresses are reserved for *multicast* addresses. The number for "this network" is also reserved. It is 0.0.0.0. The *local loopback address* is another reserved address: 127.0.0.1.

An IPv4 *broadcast address* sends information to all machines on a given subnet. The broadcast address is the last address in the range belonging to the subnet. On a Class A, B, or C subnet, the broadcast address always ends in 255. For example, on the subnet 192.168.157.0, the broadcast address would be 192.168.157.255.

CIDR

In the early 1990s it became apparent that the number of available unique IP addresses would be used up soon. Several methods were developed to cope with the need for more addresses while a new IP version was being developed and implemented.

Classless Inter-Domain Routing (*CIDR*) was implemented in 1993 to help alleviate the problem. This allows you to use variable-length subnet masking (VLSM) to create additional addresses beyond those allowed by the IPv4 classes. You can group blocks of addresses together into single routing table entries known as CIDR blocks. These addresses are managed by IANA and Regional Internet Registries (RIRs).

CIDR addresses are written in the standard 4-part dotted decimal address. This is followed by /N where N is a number from 0 to 32. The number after the slash is the prefix length. The prefix is the number of bits (starting at the left of the address) that make up the shared initial bits (which is the network portion of the address.) The default for a class B address would be /16 and for a class C address it would be /24.

NAT

Network address translation (*NAT*) is another strategy that was implemented to help alleviate the problem of insufficient IP addresses. NAT modifies network address information in the packet that it transmits from an internal network onto the Internet. This allows a single address from a router to rewrite originating IP addresses from the internal network so that they all appear to come from the router's IP address. As a result, you no longer need an Internet-valid IP address for each computer on the network. Instead, you can configure the hosts on your internal network to use private IP addresses and then assign only a single Internet-valid IP address to the router interface that connects your network to the Internet.

In addition to providing more IP addresses, NAT also helps to prevent attacks initiated by sources outside the network from reaching local hosts. This feature is part of the protection provided by NAT-enabled firewalls.

APIPA

The network 169.254.0.0 is reserved for *Automatic Private IP Addressing* (*APIPA*). Windows operating systems from Windows 2000 forward automatically generate an address in this range if they are configured to obtain an IPv4 address from a DHCP server and are unable to contact one. These addresses are not routable on the Internet.

IPv6

Internet Protocol version 6 (*IPv6*) development began in the mid-1990s. IPv6 uses 128-bit addresses, providing many more possible addresses than IPv4 provided. It provides 2^{128} addresses.

IPv6 addresses include eight 6-bit fields. They are written as eight groups of four numbers in hexadecimal notation separated by colons. You can replace a group of all zeros by two colons. Only one :: can be used per address. Leading zeros in a field can be dropped; however, except for the :: notation, all fields require at least one number. For example, fe80:0000:0884:0e09:d546:aa5b can be written as fe80::884:e09:d546:aa5b.

You indicate the network portion of the address by a slash followed by the number of bits in the address that are assigned to the network portion. If the address ends with /48, this indicates that the first 48 bits of the address are the network portion. An example of a link-local IPv6 address is fe80::884:e09:d546:aa5b.

Just like with IPv4, the loopback address is a localhost address. The IPv6 loopback address can be written as ::/128. The address fe80::/10 is equivalent to the IPv4 169.254.0.0 address.

In IPv4, the first octet of the address denotes the network's class; however, classes are no longer formally part of the IP addressing architecture, and have been replaced by CIDR. With IPv6, there are five types of addresses:

- **Link-local**—The IPv6 version of IPv4's APIPA. *Link-local addresses* are self-assigned using the Neighbor Discovery process. You can identify them using the ipconfig command. If the IPv6 address displayed for your computer starts with `fe80::` then it's a self-assigned link-local address.

- **Site-local**—The IPv6 version of an IPv4 private address. *Site-local addresses* begin with FE with C to F for the third hex digit—FEC, FED, FEE, or FEF.

- **Global unicast**—The IPv6 version of an IPv4 public address. A *global unicast address* is identified for a single interface. Global unicast addresses are routable and reachable on the IPv6 Internet. All IPv6 addresses that start with the binary values 001 (2000::/3) through 111 (E000::/3) are global addresses, with the exception of FF00::/8, which are addresses reserved for multicasts. Those bits are followed by 48 bits which designate the *global routing prefix*—the network ID used for routing. The next 16 bits designate the subnet ID. The last 64 bits are used to identify the individual network node.

- **Multicast**—Just like with IPv4, an IPv6 *multicast* sends information or services to all interfaces that are defined as members of the multicast group. The multicast address identifies a multicast group. If the first 16 bits of an IPv6 address is `ff00n`, the address is a multicast address.

- **Anycast**—Anycast is a new, unique type of address in IPv6. Anycast addresses are a cross between unicast and multicast addressing. *Anycast addresses* identify a group of interfaces, typically on separate nodes. Packets sent to an anycast address are delivered to the nearest interface as identified by the routing protocol distance measurement. In comparison, multicast addresses also identify a group of interfaces on separate nodes. However, instead of just delivering the packet to a single interface, it's delivered to all interfaces identified by the multicast address.

IPv6 doesn't use broadcast addresses; that functionality is included in multicast and anycast addresses. The all-hosts group is a multicast address used in place of a broadcast address.

IPv6 address scopes

Address scopes define regions, also known as spans. Addresses are defined as unique identifiers of an interface. The scopes are link local, site network, and global network. A device usually has a link-local and either a site-local or global address.

A network address can be assigned to a scope zone. A link local zone is made up of all network interfaces connected to a link. Addresses are unique within a zone. A zone index suffix on the address identifies the zone. The suffix follows a % character. An example is fe80::884:e09:d546:aa5b%10.

Do it!

B-1:   Comparing IPv4 and IPv6 addresses

Here's how	Here's why
1 At the command prompt, enter **ipconfig**	To display the IP configuration.
2 Record the IPv4 address and subnet mask	IPv4: _____
3 Record the IPv6 address	IPv6: _____
	You'll notice that the address begins with fe80: indicating it is a self-assigned address.
	Leave the command prompt window open for the next activity.

TCP/IP configuration parameters

Explanation

A TCP/IP address alone doesn't enable a computer to communicate on a network. Other parameters are needed to help identify the network to which the host belongs, how to reach networks to which the host doesn't belong, and how to resolve user-friendly names to computer-friendly binary addresses.

Subnet masks

A computer uses its subnet mask to determine what network it is on and whether other computers with which it is communicating are on the same network or a different network. If two computers on the same network are communicating, then they can deliver packets directly to each other. If two computers are on different networks then they must use a router to communicate. Exhibit 5-8 displays two computers that are on the same IPv4 network. Computer A has an IP address of 192.168.23.77 and a subnet mask of 255.255.255.0. Computer B has an IP address of 192.168.23.228 and a subnet mask of 255.255.255.0.

Computer A   Computer B

IP Address: 192.168.23.77   IP Address: 192.168.23.228
Subnet Mask: 255.255.255.0   Subnet Mask: 255.255.255.0

Exhibit 5-8: A simple network

Although you can look at the IP addresses of Computer A and Computer B and guess that they are on the same network, a computer can't. Instead, Computer A must use its subnet mask to find out whether it is on the same network as Computer B before communicating with Computer B.

Following are the steps that Computer A must follow before sending a message to Computer B:

1 Computer A compares its subnet mask and IP address to find its own network ID. The following table shows the calculation of the network ID for Computer A.

IP address	Subnet mask	Network ID
192.168.23.77	255.255.255.0	192.168.23.0

2 Computer A compares its subnet mask and the IP address of Computer B to find out whether they are on the same network. The following table shows the calculation of the network ID for the IP address of Computer B using the subnet mask of Computer A.

IP address	Subnet mask	Network ID
192.168.23.228	255.255.255.0	192.168.23.0

3 Both network IDs are the same, so Computer A delivers the packet directly to Computer B.

IPv4 custom subnets

To subnet a network, you take some bits from the host ID and give them to the network ID. As the manager and designer of a network, you have the freedom to do this.

An IPv4 Class B address is very large and generally needs to be subnetted to handle routing between different physical locations. To keep subnetting simple, bits are often taken from the host ID in a group of eight. This keeps the entire octet intact. The following table shows an example of subnetting an IPv4 Class B address by taking eight bits from the host ID and giving them to the network ID. Originally, the third octet was part of the host ID, but it is now part of the network ID. Using an entire octet for subnetting gives you 256 possible subnets. Traditionally, the subnets with all 1s and all 0s are discarded, leaving 254 usable subnets. Subnets of all 1s and all 0s are utilized by routers to indicate network and broadcast IDs.

	Decimal	Binary
Original network	172.16.0.0	10101100 00010000 00000000 00000000
Original subnet mask	255.255.0.0	11111111 11111111 00000000 00000000
New subnet mask	255.255.255.0	11111111 11111111 11111111 00000000
Subnet 1	172.16.0.0	10101100 00010000 00000000 00000000
Subnet 2	172.16.1.0	10101100 00010000 00000001 00000000
Subnet 3	172.16.2.0	10101100 00010000 00000010 00000000
Subnet 4	172.16.3.0	10101100 00010000 00000011 00000000
Subnet 5	172.16.4.0	10101100 00010000 00000100 00000000
Subnet 6	172.16.5.0	10101100 00010000 00000101 00000000
Subnet 7	172.16.6.0	10101100 00010000 00000110 00000000
Subnet 256	172.16.255.0	10101100 00010000 11111111 00000000

When simple subnetting is used, it is still very easy to find the network ID and host ID of an IP address because each octet is still whole. However, sometimes you need to subdivide an octet to get the number of subnets or hosts that you desire.

Complex subnetting takes less than a full octet from the host ID. The following table shows an example of subnetting a Class B network by taking three bits from the host ID. Traditionally, subnet 1 and subnet 8 are not used because all the subnet bits are set to 0 and 1, respectively. However, today, with classless routing, both subnet 1 and subnet 8 can be used. Keep in mind, however, that router compatibility should be checked before using these two subnets.

	Decimal	Binary
Original network	172.16.0.0	10101100 00010000 00000000 00000000
Original subnet mask	255.255.0.0	11111111 11111111 00000000 00000000
New subnet mask	255.255.224.0	11111111 11111111 11100000 00000000
Subnet 1	172.16.0.0	10101100 00010000 00000000 00000000
Subnet 2	172.16.32.0	10101100 00010000 00100000 00000000
Subnet 3	172.16.64.0	10101100 00010000 01000000 00000000
Subnet 4	172.16.96.0	10101100 00010000 01100000 00000000
Subnet 5	172.16.128.0	10101100 00010000 10000000 00000000
Subnet 6	172.16.160.0	10101100 00010000 10100000 00000000
Subnet 7	172.16.192.0	10101100 00010000 11000000 00000000
Subnet 8	172.16.224.0	10101100 00010000 11100000 00000000

You can calculate the number of subnets using the formula 2^n-2. In this formula n is the number of bits taken from the host ID and used for subnetting. The minus 2 is only used for traditional subnetting where the subnets of all 1s and all 0s are removed.

Host bits	Formula	Usable hosts
6	2^6-2	64–2=62
8	2^8-2	256–2=254
10	$2^{10}-2$	1024–2=1022
12	$2^{12}-2$	4096–2=4094

Supernetting

Supernetting is the opposite of subnetting. Subnetting is used to create several smaller networks from a large network, where as supernetting is used to create one large network from several smaller ones. Subnetting takes bits from the host ID and moves them to the network ID. Supernetting takes bits from the network ID and gives them to the host ID. All of the networks being combined for supernetting must be contiguous. The IP addresses from the first network to the last must be one single range with no breaks. In the first network being supernetted, the bits being taken from the network ID must be zero. In the final network being supernetted, the bits being taken must be one. Supernetting is used when a range of IP addresses larger than a Class C network is required, but a full Class B network isn't required or a reduction in routing complexity is desired.

The following table shows an example of supernetting two Class C networks into one larger network.

	Decimal	Binary
Original network 1	192.168.10.0	11000000 10101000 00001010 00000000
Original network 2	192.168.11.0	11000000 10101000 00001011 00000000
Original subnet mask	255.255.255.0	11111111 11111111 11111111 00000000
Supernetted network	192.168.10.0	11000000 10101000 00001010 00000000
New subnet mask	255.255.254.0	11111111 11111111 11111110 00000000
First host	192.168.10.1	11000000 10101000 00001010 00000001
Last host	192.168.11.254	11000000 10101000 00001011 11111110
Broadcast	192.168.11.255	11000000 10101000 00001011 11111111

IPv6 subnets

Subnetting in IPv6 follows similar rules as with IPv4. Subnet masks are denoted as fs and 0s, for example the subnet mask for a /64 network (the network address is the left 64 bits of the total 128 bits) would be ffff:ffff:ffff:ffff:0000:0000:0000:0000.

If you have an IPv6 address of:

```
fec0:0000:0000:0000:0220:edff:fe6a:0f76
```

A subnet mask of:

```
ffff:ffff:ffff:ffff:0000:0000:0000:0000
```

You get a network address of:

fec0:0000:0000:0000:0000:0000:0000:0000

You get a host address of:

0000:0000:0000:0000:**0220:edff:fe6a:0f76**

IPv6 uses subnet prefixes similar to IPv4 CIDR format:

```
IPv6-Node-Address/Prefix-Length
```

When configuring IPv6, instead of entering the hexadecimal subnet mask, you enter the subnet prefix length. For example, the IPv6 address:

```
fec0:0000:0000:0000:0220:edff:fe6a:0f76/64
```

indicates the first 64 bits of the address are used as the subnet; therefore, you enter a subnet prefix length of 64 when configuring IPv6 on your computer.

IPv6 custom subnets

Earlier in the unit, you learned that the last 64 bits of an IPv6 global unicast address represent a unique interface, while the 16 bits that precede that represent the subnet ID or *Site-Level Aggregator*. This 16-bit field allows you the flexibility to configure up to 65,535 individual subnets. For example:

- A smaller organization can set all 16 bits in the subnet ID to zero, creating a single network.

- A medium-sized organization can use all 16 bits in the subnet ID to perform the equivalent of subnetting under IPv4 by assigning a different subnet ID to each subnet, up to 65,536.

- A larger organization can use the 16 bits to create a multiple-level hierarchy of subnets, similar to what you accomplish with Variable Length Subnet Masking in IPv4. For example, you could use the first two bits to create four subnets. Then you can take the next three bits to create eight sub-subnets in some or all of the first four subnets. This leaves you with 11 more bits to create sub-sub-subnets.

Default gateway

In TCP/IP jargon, default gateway is another term for router. If a computer doesn't know how to deliver a packet, it gives the packet to the default gateway to deliver. This happens every time a computer needs to deliver a packet to a network other than its own.

A router is often a dedicated hardware device from a vendor such as Cisco, D-link, or Linksys. Other times, a router is actually a computer with multiple network cards. Operating systems such as Microsoft Windows Server 2008, Linux, and Novell Open Enterprise Server have the ability to perform as routers. (Routers can support IPv4, IPv6, or both—know which you're getting before you buy.)

The one consistent feature of routers, regardless of the manufacturer, is that they can distinguish between different networks and move (or route) packets between them. Routers can also figure out the best path to use to move a packet between different networks.

A router has an IP address on every network to which it is attached. Remember that routers keep track of networks, not computers. When a computer sends a packet to the default gateway for further delivery, the address of the router must be on the same network as the computer, as computers can only talk directly to devices on their own network. An IPv4 example of a computer using a default gateway to communicate with another computer on a different network is shown in Exhibit 5-9.

In Exhibit 5-9, Computer A is sending a packet to Computer C. Computer A uses its subnet mask to determine whether the default gateway is required. In this example, IPv4 addresses are used, but the process is the same for IPv6.

1   Computer A compares its subnet mask and IP address to find its own network ID. The following table shows the calculation of the network ID for Computer A.

IP address	Subnet mask	Network ID
192.168.23.77	255.255.255.0	192.168.23.0

2   Computer A compares its subnet mask and the IP address of Computer C to see if it is on the same network. This step does not calculate the network ID for Computer C. It only tests whether it is the same as Computer A. Computer A is not configured with the subnet mask of Computer C. So, it is impossible for Computer A to find the network ID for Computer C. The following table shows testing the network ID for the IP address of Computer C using the subnet mask of Computer A.

IP address	Subnet mask	Network ID
172.30.34.228	255.255.255.0	172.30.34.0

3   The two network IDs are different, so Computer A sends the packet to the router (default gateway) for delivery.

4   The router looks in its routing table to see if it knows where the network 172.30.34.0 is located.

5   Because the router is attached to network 172.30.34.0, it delivers the packet to Computer C. If the router were not attached to network 172.30.34.0, then it would forward it to another router until the network was reached.

Computer A

IP Address: 192.168.23.77
Subnet Mask: 255.255.255.0
Default Gateway: 192.168.23.1

IP Address: 192.168.23.1
Subnet Mask: 255.255.255.0

Router

IP Address: 172.30.34.222
Subnet Mask: 255.255.255.0

Computer C

IP Address: 172.30.34.228
Subnet Mask: 255.255.255.0

Exhibit 5-9: A routed network

In an IPv6 network, network segments are identified by using the IPv6 network prefix and prefix length.

PAT

Port Address Translation (PAT) translates TCP or UDP communications made between hosts on a private network and hosts on a public network. It allows a single public IP address to be used by many hosts on a private network, which is usually a Local Area Network or LAN.

SNAT

Source network address translation (SNAT) is the process that a router or firewall uses to rewrite source and destination addresses of IP packets as they pass through.

DNS

Domain Name System (DNS) is used to resolve host names to IP addresses and find domain controllers, as well as resources on the Internet such as Web servers and e-mail servers.

The most common use for DNS is resolving host names to IP addresses. When you access a Web site, you normally specify a fully qualified domain name (FQDN) such as www.microsoft.com in a Web browser program. FQDNs are otherwise known as Internet names and consist of two parts: a host name and a domain name. The host name is the friendly name of the computer, and the domain name is the name of the organization in which that computer is located. Domain names conform to a hierarchical naming scheme called the DNS (Domain Name System) namespace or BIND (Berkeley Internet Name Domain) because it was originally developed at the University of California at Berkeley.

DNS consists of a root domain (.) with several top-level domain names that identify the type of organization that runs the network that your computer is on. There are thousands of second-level domains existing underneath each top-level domain name to identify the name of the organization, and the host names for computers are typically listed underneath the second-level domains as shown in Exhibit 5-10.

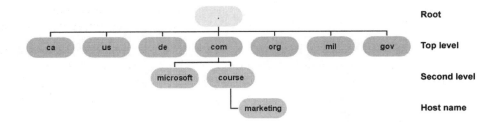

Exhibit 5-10: The DNS namespace

Because many programs such as Web browsers use FQDNs to specify other computers, there must be some method to resolve FQDNs to IP addresses such that the TCP/IP protocol can locate the destination computer by IP address.

The local %windir%\system32\drivers\etc\hosts file on a Windows computer can be used to resolve FQDNs to IP addresses. Because this file may grow too large to search efficiently, it should only contain extra or private computer names. FQDN name resolution is best achieved by contacting a DNS server that contains records associating FQDNs with IP addresses. There are several thousand DNS servers on the public Internet alone that may be used to resolve FQDNs to IP addresses.

WINS

In the past, Microsoft networks primarily used NetBIOS names to refer to other computers on a network. This works well for small network environments; however, it is cumbersome for larger networks and impossible for the Internet.

Over the past decade, however, several applications have been made for Windows that use NetBIOS names to locate other computers. As such, NetBIOS is supported on the TCP/IP protocol by default, and one may use the NetBIOS name of a computer when connecting to remote resources.

NetBIOS name resolution was performed in the past using broadcasts on the network; unfortunately these broadcasts reduce the available bandwidth. Alternatively, Windows Server 2003 can use the local %windir%\system32\drivers\etc\lmhosts file to resolve NetBIOS names to IP addresses; however, this should only contain extra or private computer names. NetBIOS name resolution is best achieved by contacting a WINS (Windows Internet Name Service) server. If WINS is configured, a WINS client registers its IP address and services with the WINS server during startup. When the WINS client is shut down, it contacts the WINS server and tells it to release the registration of its IP address and services. Also, any NetBIOS names that are resolved successfully by contacting a WINS server are stored in a *NetBIOS name cache* on the local computer to speed up future resolution.

There is a sample LMHOSTS file (called lmhosts.sam) in the %windir%\system32\drivers\etc directory that you can rename to lmhosts.

Normally, preceding a line in a script file with # marks it as a comment to be ignored by the system when executing the file. Although this holds true for the LMHOST file there are some exceptions to the rule. Preceding the following reserved words with the # symbol will not comment them out but will act as a flag for the system to take a special action.

```
#PRE
#DOM:<domain>
#INCLUDE <filename>
#BEGIN_ALTERNATE
#END_ALTERNATE
```

The #PRE tag will cause the entry to be preloaded into the NetBIOS name cache. #DOM tag will associate the entry with a specified domain affecting how the logon service functions. The #INCLUDE causes the system to locate and parse another system's LMHOSTS file, treating the contents as if they were part of the local file. The #BEGIN_ and #END_ALTERNATE reserved words cause several #INCLUDEs placed between them to be grouped together. Successful location and parsing of any one of these will cause the whole section to be seen as having succeeded. For more information on this and the structure of the LMHOSTS file in general you can view the LMHOSTS sample file on your system.

Do it!

B-2: Examining TCP/IP configuration parameters

Here's how	Here's why
1 In the Command Prompt window, identify the network and host portions of each address	
2 Close the command prompt window	
3 Open **Control Panel, Network and Internet, Network and Sharing Center**	
Under Tasks, click **Manage network connections**	
4 Right-click **Local Area Connection** and choose **Properties**	
Click **Continue**	
5 In the Local Area Connection Properties box, select **Internet Protocol Version 4 (TCP/IPv4)**	(Select the item but don't clear the checkbox.)
Click **Properties**	You are obtaining your IP information automatically from a DHCP server.
Click **Advanced**	There are tabs for IP Settings, DNS, and WINS. The IP Settings page shows you the address information is coming from DHCP. You'll look at the DHCP service next.
Activate each tab	To observe the information on each page.
Click **Cancel** twice	
6 Display properties for **Internet Protocol Version 6 (TCP/IPv6)**	You are obtaining your IP information automatically as well.
Click **Advanced**	There are tabs for IP Settings and DNS. The IP Settings page shows you the IPv6 addressing information is being generated automatically by Windows Vista.
Activate the DNS tab	To observe the information on the DNS page. It's identical to the DNS parameters for IPv4.
Click **Cancel** twice	Leave the Local Area Connection Properties dialog box open for the next activity.

Static TCP/IP parameters

Explanation All IP configuration information can be manually entered on each workstation; this is called *static IP configuration*. Unfortunately, configuring IP information manually is not efficient and is sometimes problematic. With each manual entry there is a risk of a typographical error. In addition, if the IP configuration changes, it is a very large task to visit each workstation to modify it. However, some computers require static IP addresses, such as DNS servers. The command line utility NETSH can be used to control and/or automate the allocation and changes to static IP address configuration.

Do it!

B-3:   Configuring TCP/IP parameters

Here's how	Here's why
1 In the Local Area Connection Properties box, select **Internet Protocol Version 4 (TCP/IPv4)**	(Remember to select the item; don't clear the checkbox.)
Click **Properties**	
2 Select **Use the following IP address**	
In the IP address box, enter the IPv4 address provided by your instructor	This IPv4 address will be on the classroom subnet, will be unique for your computer, and won't overlap with any IPv4 addresses the DHCP server is handing out.
Click in the Subnet mask box	The default subnet mask for class of the IPv4 address you entered is filled in automatically.
In the Default gateway box, enter the IPv4 address of the classroom's gateway	The default gateway used for Internet access in your classroom.
In the Preferred DNS server box, enter the IPv4 address of your classroom's DNS server	The DNS server used for name resolution services in your classroom.
3 Click **Advanced**	
4 Observe the information on the IP Settings tab	It displays the data you entered on the Properties page.
5 Activate the DNS tab	
6 Observe the information on the DNS tab	It displays the data you entered on the Properties page along with other options regarding DNS suffixes.
7 Click **OK**	To close the Advanced TCP/IP Settings dialog box.
8 Click **OK**	To close the Internet Protocol (TCP/IP) Properties dialog box.
9 Click **Close**	To close the Local Area Connection Properties dialog box.
10 Close Network Connections and the Network and Sharing Center	

11 Open Internet Explorer and verify
    you have Internet connectivity

12 Close Internet Explorer

DHCP and DHCPv6

Explanation

Dynamic Host Configuration Protocol (*DHCP*) is an automated mechanism to assign IP addresses to clients. There are two versions—the original DHCP, which is used for IPv4 addressing, and *Dynamic Host Configuration Protocol for IPv6* (*DHCPv6*), which is used for IPv6 addressing. A computer configured to obtain its IP configuration using DHCP or DHCPv6 will contact a DHCP or DHCPv6 server on the local network and obtain IP configuration information from it. Other TCP/IP configurations settings such as the local router or default gateway can also be handed out by a DHCP or DHCPv6 server. DHCPv6 can assign stateful IPv6 addresses or stateless configuration settings to its IPv6 clients. The DHCP Client service in Windows Vista and Windows Server 2008 supports both the original DHCP and DHCPv6.

Using DHCP to assign IP configuration to client computers on your network avoids the problem of IP information being entered incorrectly and simplifies administration. Take, for example, a 200-workstation network. If you were to manually change the IP addressing information on all of these workstations, it might take several days. With DHCP, the DHCP server can be updated with the new IP addressing information and, on the next reboot, all workstations will receive the new information.

DHCP allocates an IP address to a client computer for a fixed period of time. This temporary allocation is called a *lease*. If the client still needs the IP address, it must renegotiate the lease before it expires.

The IPv4 lease process

The overall process to lease an address is composed of four UDP messages (also called packets) exchanged during the client computer's boot process:

- DHCPDISCOVER
- DHCPOFFER
- DHCPREQUEST
- DHCPACK

Microsoft refers to this as "DORA" (Discover, Offer, Request, and Acknowledgement).

All four of these messages are broadcast messages because there are no target IP addresses involved in the communication until the client computer receives an IP address. Exhibit 5-11 shows the four messages transmitted as part of the DHCP process.

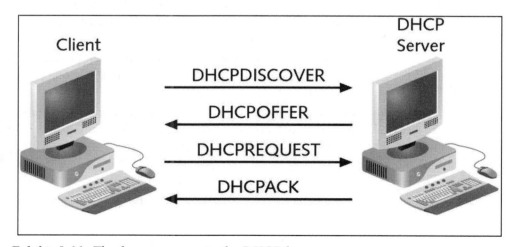

Exhibit 5-11: The four messages in the DHCP lease process

The DHCPDISCOVER message is sent from the client computer to the broadcast IP address 255.255.255.255. A broadcast address must be used because the client is not configured with the address of a DHCP server. The source IP address in the message is 0.0.0.0 because the client does not have an IP address yet. The MAC address of the client is included in address message as an identifier.

Any DHCP server that receives the DHCPDISCOVER message responds with a DHCPOFFER message. The DHCPOFFER message contains DHCP configuration information such as an IP address, subnet mask, default gateway, and lease length. The destination IP address for the message is the broadcast address 255.255.255.255. This destination IP address ensures that the client can receive the message even though it does not yet have an IP address assigned. The MAC address of the client is included in the data portion of the message as an identifier.

The DHCP client responds to the DHCPOFFER message it receives with a DHCPREQUEST message. If there are multiple DHCP servers that send a DHCPOFFER message, the client responds only to the first one. The DHCPREQUEST message contains the lease information that has been chosen by the client. This indicates to the servers that their lease offer to the client has, or has not, been chosen.

The DHCPREQUEST message is addressed to the broadcast IP address 255.255.255.255. This allows all of the DHCP servers to see the DHCPREQUEST. The servers that were not chosen see this message and place their offered addresses back into their pool of available addresses.

The chosen DHCP server sends back a DHCPACK message indicating its confirmation that the lease has been chosen and that the client is now allowed to use the lease. This message is still being sent to the broadcast IP address 255.255.255.255 because the client has not yet initialized IP with the new address. After the client receives the DHCPACK message, the client starts using the IP address and options that were in the lease.

The IPv6 lease process

One of the benefits of IPv6 is that network devices can configure themselves automatically when you connect them to a routed IPv6 network. This is called *stateless autoconfiguration*. When you first connect an IPv6 device to a network, the device performs stateless address autoconfiguration automatically and then sends a *link-local multicast router solicitation request* for its configuration parameters. The router responds to the device request with a *router advertisement packet* that contains network configuration parameters. There are flags in the router advertisement message which tell the device how to configure:

- **Managed Address Configuration Flag** (also known as the M flag)—When set to 1, this flag tells the device to use a configuration protocol such as DHCPv6 to obtain a stateful IPv6 address.
- **Other Stateful Configuration Flag** (also known as the O flag)—When set to 1, this flag instructs the host to use a configuration protocol such as DHCPv6 to obtain other TCP/IP configuration settings.

When you combine the M and O flag values a device is instructed to configure as follows:

- Both M and O flags are 0—Indicates the network doesn't have a DHCPv6 server. A device uses the router advertisement to obtain a non-link-local address and other methods, such as manual configuration, to configure other IPv6 configuration parameters. This stateless autoconfiguration is suitable for small organizations and individuals.

- Both M and O flags are 1—Indicates the devices should obtain both an IPv6 address and other configuration parameters from a DHCPv6 server. This is known as *DHCPv6 stateful addressing*.

- The M flag is 0 and the O flag is 1—Indicates the device should continue to use its stateless autoconfiguration IPv6 address, but should retrieve other configuration parameters from the DHCPv6 server. The DHCPv6 server isn't assigning stateful addresses to IPv6 hosts, but is assigning stateless configuration settings. This is known as *DHCPv6 stateless addressing*.

- The M flag 1 and the O flag is 0—Indicates the devices should obtain an IPv6 address from a DHCPv6 server, but not other configuration parameters. This combination is rarely used as IPv6 hosts usually need to be configured with other settings, such as the IPv6 addresses of a Domain Name System (DNS) server.

A DHCPv6 client listens for DHCP messages on UDP port 546; DHCPv6 servers and relay agents listen for DHCPv6 messages on UDP port 547.

Do it!   **B-4:   Discussing the DHCP lease process**

Questions and answers

1 What type of message is used during the DHCP leasing process?

   A   Unicast

   B   Multicast

   C   Broadcast ——

   D   None, it is all performed internally on the client.

2 What message is first in the DHCP lease process?

   A   DHCPACK

   B   DHCPOFFER ——

   C   DHCPDISCOVER

   D   DHCPREQUEST

3 From an IPv6 router advertisement packet, how does the IPv6 device know where to get its IPv6 address?

   m Flag

4 From an IPv6 router advertisement packet, how does the IPv6 device know where to get its IPv6 configuration parameters?   *O Flag*

5 When an IPv6 device automatically configures its IPv6 address, is it referred to as a stateful or stateless address?
   stateless

Topic C: DHCP servers

This topic covers the following CompTIA Network+ 2009 exam objective.

Bridge objective

#	Objective
3.1	**Install, configure and differentiate between common network devices** • Basic DHCP server

Installing a DHCP server

Explanation

DHCP is a standard networking service that's included with Windows Server 2008. It supports both DHCP for IPv4 and DHCPv6. However, this service isn't installed as part of a default installation. You must add it manually by using the Add Roles feature in Server Manager.

If your DHCP server is part of a domain that is running Active Directory, Windows Server 2008 must be authorized to start the DHCP service. When Windows Server 2008 attempts to start the DHCP service, it checks to see that the server is authorized. If the server is authorized, DHCP starts. If the server isn't authorized, the DHCP service shuts itself down. It then logs an error message in Event Viewer documenting the unauthorized DHCP server's attempt to start.

Within a corporation's IT department, control over network resources is always important. Control over DHCP is very important because an unauthorized DHCP server can hand out incorrect IP addressing information to hundreds of client computers very quickly. These computers are then unable to access network resources, which can be as serious as a server crashing.

Do it!

C-1: Installing a DHCP server

Here's how	Here's why
1 Click **Start** and choose **All Programs, Microsoft Virtual PC**	To start the PC emulation software. Windows Server 2008 was installed in a virtual PC during setup.
With Windows Server 2008 selected, click **Start**	To start the Windows Server 2008 PC.
2 Open **Control Panel, Network and Internet, and then Network and Sharing Center**	In Control Panel Classic View, it's just Network and Sharing Center.
Click **Manage network connections**	DHCP servers must use a static IP address. Currently your server is getting its IP address from the classroom DHCP server.
3 Right-click **Local Area Connection** and choose **Properties**	
4 Select **Internet Protocol Version 4 (TCP/IPv4)** and click **Properties**	
5 Assign your computer a manual IP address, subnet mask, default gateway, and DNS server as directed by your instructor	
6 Click **OK**	
Click **Close**	
Close Network Connections and the Network and Sharing Center	
7 Click **Start** and choose **Server Manager**	(If necessary.)
8 Select **Roles**	You might need to wait for Server Manager to collect its data.
Click **Add Roles**	
9 Click **Next**	
10 Check **DHCP Server**	
Click **Next** twice	

11	Click **Next**	To accept the default network connection this computer will use to service clients.
12	In the Preferred DNS Server IPv4 Address box, enter the IP address of the classroom server	
	Click **Validate**	
	Click **Next**	
13	Click **Next**	To skip adding WINS Server information.
14	Click **Add**	You'll create a scope containing a range of IPv4 addresses for your DHCP server to hand out.
15	In the Scope Name box, enter **Student##_Scope**	(Where ## is your assigned student number.)
16	In the Starting IP Address box, enter the beginning IPv4 address for the block your instructor has assigned you	
17	In the Ending IP Address box, enter the ending IPv4 address for the block your instructor has assigned you	
18	In the Subnet Mask box, enter the subnet mask for the classroom	
19	In the Default Gateway (optional) box, enter the IPv4 address of the classroom default gateway	
20	Observe the values in the Subnet Type list	You have a choice for Wired and Wireless.
21	Choose **Wired (lease duration will be 6 days)**	
22	Observe the Activate this scope checkbox	By default, the scope will be activated automatically.
23	Click **OK**	
24	Click **Next**	
25	Observe the DHCPv6 options	You can choose stateless or stateful mode.

26	Click **More about DHCPv6 stateless mode**	This help screen explains the two settings.
	Close Help	
27	Select **Disable DHCPv6 stateless mode for this server**	
28	Click **Next**	
29	Verify Use current credentials is selected	You'll use your netadmin## domain administrative user to authorize the DHCP server in the classroom Active Directory.
30	Click **Next**	
31	Click **Install**	
32	Click **Close**	
33	Close Server Manager	
34	Click **Start** and choose **Administrative Tools, DHCP**	
35	Expand netsrv##.networkplus.class, IPv4	A green arrow indicates DHCP for IPv4 is functional. The scope you created during installation is listed under IPv4.
36	Expand and select **IPv6**	DHCPv6 for IPv6 is functional, but you haven't configured a scope yet.

IPv6 scopes

Explanation

Just like with IPv4's DHCP, a DHCPv6 scope is a consecutive range of possible IPv6 addresses that the DHCP server can lease to clients on a subnet. With DHCPv6, you configure your scope with available IPv6 addresses by using the DHCP console utility after you've installed DHCP. The unique feature with DHCPv6 is that you specify only the prefix for your subnet. DHCPv6 then creates and leases unique IPv6 addresses within that subnet for client requests.

Do it!

C-2: Configuring an IPv6 scope

Here's how	Here's why
1 Right-click **IPv6** and choose **New Scope...**	
Click **Next**	
2 In the Name box, enter **Student##_IPv6**	
Click **Next**	
3 In the Prefix box, type **FEC0::**	You create an IPv6 address scope by simply specifying an IPv6 subnet prefix. The Windows DHCPv6 stateful server will automatically generate an IPv6 address for allocation to the client. This particular prefix (beginning with FEC0) designates a site-local address. With a site-local address, the first 10 bits are fixed at 1111 1110 11. Therefore, the valid address prefixes for all site-local addresses are FEC0::, FED0::, FEE0::, and FEF0::.
Click **Next**	
4 Click **Next**	To skip adding any exclusions.
5 Click **Next**	To accept the default lease times.
6 Click **Finish**	To create and activate your IPv6 scope.
7 Right-click the IPv4 Scope **Student##_Scope** and choose **Deactivate**	In the IPA for this unit, you'll be practicing installing and configuring DHCP. If the scopes remain on the computer, you could encounter a conflict.
Click **Yes**	
8 Right-click the IPv4 Scope **Student##_Scope** and choose **Delete**	
Click **Yes**	

9 Right-click the IPv6 Scope **Student##_IPv6** and choose **Deactivate**

   Click **Yes**

10 Right-click the IPv6 Scope **Student##_IPv6** and choose **Delete**

   Click **Yes**

11 Close DHCP

12 Open Server Manager

13 Remove the DHCP Server role

14 Restart the server when prompted

15 When prompted to press Ctrl+Alt+Delete, choose **Action**, **Ctrl+Alt+Del**

16 Log on as your domain netadmin## user with a password of **!pass1234**

17 When removal is finished, click **Close**

18 Close Server Manager

In the IPA for this unit, you'll be practicing installing and configuring DHCP. If the scopes remain on the computer, you could encounter a conflict.

3-12-12

Unit summary: Wired communication standards

Topic A   In this topic, you described the functions of the protocols in the **TCP/IP protocol suite**. You looked at the four layers of the TCP/IP architecture—**Network Interface**, **Internet**, **Transport**, and **Application**. You saw how each of these layers corresponds with the layers of the **OSI model**, and which communication protocols operate at each level.

Topic B   In this topic, you learned how to manually configure an **IPv4** and **IPv6** address on a Windows client, as well as configure that client to obtain an address automatically from a **DHCP/DHCPv6 server**. You learned the purpose of the different configuration parameters that you can set for **TCP/IP**, and saw which are required for network communication and which are optional.

Topic C   In this topic, you learned how to install and configure a **DHCP server** on Microsoft Windows Server 2008 for both IPv4 and IPv6 **client leases**. You learned how to activate **scopes**, as well as authorize the DHCP server in the **Active Directory**.

Review questions

1 Data information is sent onto the network cable using which of the following?

   A Communication protocol

   B Data packet

   C Media access method

   D Packages

2 To which TCP/IP architecture layer do the media access methods belong?

   A Application

   B Internet

   C Network Interface

   D Transport

3 To which TCP/IP architecture layer do TCP and UDP belong?

   A Application

   B Internet

   C Network Interface

   D Transport

4 To which TCP/IP architecture layer do routing protocols belong?

   A Application

   B Internet

   C Network Interface

   D Transport

5 To which TCP/IP architecture layer do e-mail and Web browser protocols belong?

    A Application

    B Internet

    C Network Interface

    D Transport

6 Which IEEE standard defines the communication protocol for Ethernet?

    A 802.3

    B 802.5

    C 802.11

    D 802.15

7 Which protocol is used to convert logical IP addresses to physical MAC addresses?

    A ARP

    B DNS

    C IMAP4

    D RIP

8 You can use the command-line utility _Ipconfig_ to retrieve a computer's IP configuration.

9 Which protocol is responsible for the logical addressing of each packet created by the transport layer?

    A IP

    B RIP

    C TCP

    D UDP

10 The ping utility is the most common use of which protocol?

    A ARP

    B ICMP/ICMPv6

    C IGMP

    D RIP

11 SSH was designed as a replacement for _Telnet_ and other insecure remote shells, which sent data (including passwords) in plaintext.

12 Which TCP/IP architecture layer makes use of ports?

    A Application

    B Internet

    C Network Interface

    D Transport

13 True or false? TCP is a connection-oriented protocol that creates and verifies a connection with a remote host before sending information.

14 Which is a simple software-based protocol analyzer?

   A The command-line utility ARP

   B The command-line utility IPCONFIG

   C The Windows Network Monitor utility

   D The Windows Network Control Panel utility

15 Which protocol do Web browsers and Web servers use most often?

   A FTP

   B HTTP

   C HTTP(S)

   D TFTP

16 Which e-mail protocol is used to send and receive e-mail messages between e-mail servers and used by e-mail client software to send messages to the server, but never used to retrieve e-mail from a server?

   A IMAP4

   B POP3

   C SMTP

17 The Internet Assigned Numbers Authority (IANA) implemented ___Class Ful___ IPv4 addresses in order to differentiate between the portion of the IP address that identifies a particular network and the portion that identifies a specific host on that network.

18 What is the default subnet mask for a Class C IP address?

   A 255.0.0.0

   B 255.255.0.0

   C 255.255.255.0

   D 0.255.255.255

19 Which is not a valid subnet mask?

   A 255.255.0.0

   B 255.247.0.0

   C 255.255.255.0

   D 255.0.255.0

20 IP address 227.43.76.109 is an example of which of the following classes of IP addresses?

   A Class A

   B Class B

   C Class C

   D Class D

21 How many octets are part of the network ID when using the subnet mask 255.255.255.0?

   A 1

   B 2

   C 3

   D 4

22 True or false? The IP address 169.254.226.4 can be routed on the Internet.

23 What was introduced to make IPv4 Internet routing more efficient?

   A Subnet masks

   B Switches

   C DHCP

   D CIDR

24 An IPv4 packet sent to all workstations on the network is called a _____.

   A Directed packet

   B Unicast

   C Multicast

   D Broadcast

25 True or false? A computer will use a default gateway if the destination IP address is on a different network.

26 Which of the following is another name for default gateway?

   A Host

   B Hub

   C Router

   D Switch

27 How many octets are in an IPv4 address?

   A 2

   B 4

   C 8

   D 16

28 How many bits are in an octet?

    A 2

    B 4

    C 8

    D 16

29 How many bits is an IPv6 address?

    A 8

    B 32

    C 64

    D 128

30 Which type of address is written in the standard 4-part dotted decimal address, followed by /N where N is a number from 0 to 32?

    A APIPA

    B CIDR

    C IPv4

    D IPv6

31 An IPv6 subnet ID is how many bits long?

    A 8

    B 16

    C 32

    D 64

32 True or false? A WINS server is necessary for address translation between IP addresses and network nodes' FQDNs.

33 After installing the DHCP Server service on a domain member server, what must be done in Active Directory before it begins delivering leased IP addresses?

    A Authorize it.

    B Reinstall Active Directory.

    C Activate it.

    D Modify the firewall rules.

34 What is the default lease length used by a wired scope created in the Windows Server 2008 DHCP Service?

    A Three hours

    B Three days

    C Six days

    D Eight days

    E 30 days

35 Which of the following are client options that can be set at the scope level? (Choose all that apply.)

A DNS

B WINS

C ROUTER

D MAC address

Independent practice activity

In this activity, you'll practice configuring TCP/IP on a client computer. You'll also practice installing the DHCP service on a Windows Server 2008 computer and creating scopes.

1 On the Microsoft Windows Vista host computer, set your Local Area Connection to obtain its IPv4 address and DNS server information automatically.

2 Use the Ipconfig utility to verify you're receiving IP addressing information from the classroom DHCP server.

3 Verify you have Internet connectivity. (You can check your Access status in Network and Sharing Center or use Internet Explorer.)

4 Enable LAN2 – PCI Card.

5 Manually configure a valid IPv4 address on the classroom subnet for this NIC. Configure the default gateway and DNS server parameters. Disable IPv6 on the connection.

6 Disable Local Area Connection.

7 Use the Ipconfig command to determine your TCP/IP information.

8 Verify you have Internet connectivity.

9 Enable Local Area Connection.

10 Use the Ipconfig command to determine your TCP/IP information. It should report TCP/IP information for both connections.

11 What's reported by the ipconfig command for each connection?

12 Disable LAN2 – PCI Card.

13 Close all open windows (except Microsoft Virtual PC if it's still open).

14 In the Windows Server 2008 Virtual PC, add the DHCP Server role.

— Use the classroom domain and DNS server and your IPv4 DNS settings.

— Don't use WINS.

— Name the scope IPv4_Student##

— Your instructor will provide you with a unique range of IPv4 addresses on the classroom subnet.

— Use the classroom subnet mask and default gateway.

— Create the scope for wired connections and activate.

— Disable DHCPv6 stateless mode. (The classroom DNS server has IPv6 disabled on its NIC and won't be able to respond to requests.)

— Use your NETWORKPLUS\netadmin## credentials to authorize the DHCP server in the classroom Active Directory.

15 Use the DHCP console to verify your DHCP scope is functional.

16 Observe the Scope Options for your IPv4_Student## Scope.

17 Which TCP/IP configuration parameters are configured for distribution to clients with an IPv4 address lease?

18 Under IPv4, select Server Options. Right-click Server Options and choose Configure Server Options. Scroll through the available options.

19 If you had added a WINS server to your network, which value would you configure in the Server Options box?

20 Close the Server Options dialog box.

21 Delete your IPv4_Student## scope and uninstall DHCP.

22 Restart the server when prompted. Log on as using your domain netadmin## account with a password of !pass1234.

23 When the removal is done, click Close.

24 When finished with this activity, save the state and close the Windows Server 2008 Virtual PC by choosing Action, Close, and Save state. Click OK.

Unit 6

Wireless networking

Unit time: 165 minutes

Complete this unit, and you'll know how to:

A Identify the hardware components needed to create a wireless connection.

B Differentiate between the various communications standards used in wireless networks.

C Install and configure a wireless network connection.

Topic A: Wireless network devices

This topic covers the following CompTIA Network+ 2009 exam objectives.

#	Objective
2.5	**Categorize WAN technology types and properties** • Wireless
3.1	**Install, configure and differentiate between common network devices** • NIC • Wireless access point
3.4	**Implement a basic wireless network** • Access point placement
4.7	**Given a scenario, troubleshoot common connectivity issues and select an appropriate solution** Logical issues • Wrong subnet mask – Wireless issues ○ Interference (bleed, environmental factors) ○ Distance ○ Bounce ○ Incorrect antenna placement

Bridge objective (2.5)
Bridge objective (3.1)
Bridge objective (3.4)
Bridge objective (4.7)

Wireless

Explanation

The term "wireless" refers to several technologies and systems that don't use cables for communication, including public radio, cellular telephones, one-way paging, satellite, infrared, and private, proprietary radio. Wireless technologies can be implemented on a small scale within a LAN or on a large scale in a WAN.

Wireless connections

Wireless connections are a popular means of linking devices, such as PCs, handheld computers, music players, and others. Wireless connections generally use one of the following:

- Infrared
- Radio
- Bluetooth

Infrared and Bluetooth create a wireless connection between two devices. Radio technology is used to form larger wireless networks.

Infrared

Infrared wireless uses pulses of invisible infrared light to transmit signals between devices. It offers relatively low-speed, line-of-sight connections between devices. Infrared light can't pass through obstructions or around corners. Connection speeds range from 9600 bps to 4 Mbps with a typical maximum range of 10-20 feet. To make connections, devices must aim their transceivers nearly directly at each other. Devices that are more than 45 degrees off to the side of a receiver are generally unable to connect.

The most popular form of infrared wireless is the Infrared Serial Data Link technology, which offers a wireless serial connection at 1.5 Mbps with a maximum range of 20 feet. An IrDA infrared port is shown in Exhibit 6-1. Laptops and PDAs with infrared ports typically implement ISDL infrared.

Exhibit 6-1: An IrDA infrared port on a laptop

Devices that use infrared include laptop and handheld computers, such as PDAs, and occasionally wireless keyboards, mice, and printers. Infrared connection technology standards are set forth by the Infrared Data Association (IrDA).

Radio

Radio-based wireless communications use signals sent over electromagnetic radio waves to transmit data between devices. Radio transmissions can pass through most nonmetallic obstructions and around corners. Thus, radio isn't a line-of-sight technology. Radio offers moderate- to high-speed local and wide area connections.

Various radio networking technologies have been developed. Currently, the most common of these include 802.11b and 802.11g. 802.11n devices are becoming increasingly available for consumers although the standard hasn't been finalized. These offer up to 10 Mbps business or home networking and Internet connectivity over modest distances. An 802.11g wireless router is shown in Exhibit 6-2.

Exhibit 6-2: An 802.11g wireless router

Radio networking technologies are sometimes called RF technologies, where RF stands for radio frequency. RF devices have antennas, but those antennas might be hidden inside the device. For example, a laptop's 802.11g wireless network adapter antenna is typically hidden within the laptop's case.

Bluetooth

Bluetooth is a short-distance (up to 10 meters) radio communications technology, developed by the Bluetooth Special Interest Group, which includes over 1,000 companies. Chief among these are Siemens, Intel, Toshiba, Motorola, and Ericsson.

Bluetooth is designed to enable devices—such as cellular telephones, PDAs, personal audio players, PC peripherals, and PCs—to discover the presence of other Bluetooth devices within range. After detected, these devices self-configure and begin communicating. With Bluetooth devices, you shouldn't have to configure any communications parameters, such as network addresses. A Bluetooth mouse is shown in Exhibit 6-3.

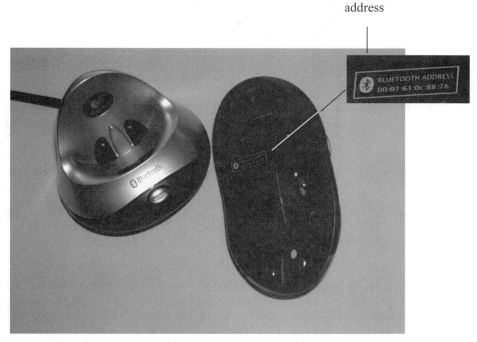

Bluetooth address

Exhibit 6-3: A Bluetooth mouse

Bluetooth devices have antennas, but those antennas are most often hidden inside the device. A cell phone that supports Bluetooth probably has an external antenna that serves the needs of both the cellular telephone communications and Bluetooth connectivity.

Wireless communications

Wireless communications and access is becoming more prevalent. It enables users to make a connection to the Internet while traveling, or to the Internet or a LAN while freely moving about their house or office. Wireless is an important technology for mobile devices and for Internet access in remote locations where other methods are not an option. For travel, users can connect to the Internet via *hot spots* (public areas in which a connection to the Internet can be established wirelessly). Wireless access also helps eliminate cable clutter in an office environment. It can be configured for a single machine or network within a building.

There are basically three types of wireless links:

- Indoor point-to-multipoint LANs
- Outdoor point-to-point links
- Outdoor point-to-multipoint links

These links all use radio signals as the connection method.

Indoor point-to-multipoint LANs

Implementing wireless access in a home or office isn't exorbitantly expensive. All that's required is a wireless network card in the computer and a WAP (wireless access point) to connect computers together or to connect to the wired LAN. A corporate wireless indoor LAN links wireless workstations to the corporate LAN backbone. You should place the WAP or wireless router in a central location within the area of the users who'll be accessing it. The closer the users are to the device, the stronger the signal, and the better the network speed. Generally, access points are distributed throughout a building to provide sufficient wireless coverage, as shown in Exhibit 6-4. If the signal from your WAP or wireless router isn't strong enough using the built-in antennas, you can add a more powerful antenna and, in some cases, a signal booster.

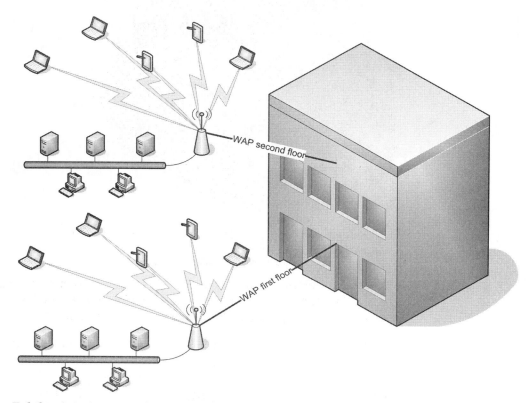

Exhibit 6-4: An example of a wireless LAN

Outdoor point-to-point links

With outdoor point-to-point links, a wireless connection connects two wired networks within different buildings. This is often referred to as *fixed-point wireless*. With fixed point wireless, a directional antenna sits on your house or office building and communicates with a second directional antenna, as shown in Exhibit 6-5. These antennas are weatherproof and connected to a special indoor-mounted WAP that uses special bridging software. Outdoor point-to-point bridges can connect wired LANs using high-gain antennas through a wireless connection of about 20 kilometers when there is a clear line of sight and there are no other obstructions for the radio signal to bounce off of.

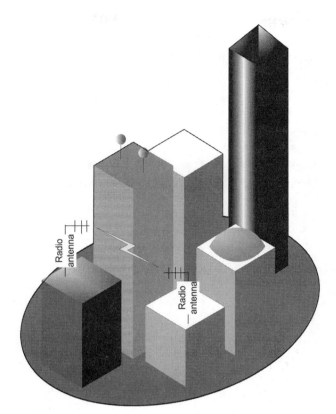

Exhibit 6-5: An example of an outdoor point-to-point WAN

Outdoor point-to-multipoint links

In an outdoor point-to-multipoint system, an omnidirectional antenna links multiple directional antennas, as shown in Exhibit 6-6. Common examples of outdoor point-to-multipoint systems include cellular phone connections and TV broadcasts.

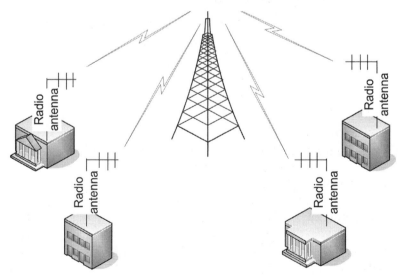

Exhibit 6-6: An example of an outdoor point-to-multipoint WAN

Wireless LAN connection components

To establish a wireless LAN, you need a network card in the computer and a wireless router or wireless access point device on the network. The router or WAP broadcasts radio signals, and the wireless network cards pick up the broadcasts.

Wireless NICs

LAN network adapters of all current types (PCI, PC card, and USB, shown in Exhibit 6-7) come in wireless versions. Wireless capability is built into many newer laptops as standard equipment and can easily be added to laptops using wireless PC Card or USB NICs. Desktops are also easily outfitted with wireless capabilities using a PCI Card or USB wireless NIC. If wireless access is available, these cards can communicate with a wireless access point—examples shown in Exhibit 6-8—allowing you to access the network without the need for cables. This is especially useful in places like libraries, where wandering around with a laptop while maintaining network access can be very convenient.

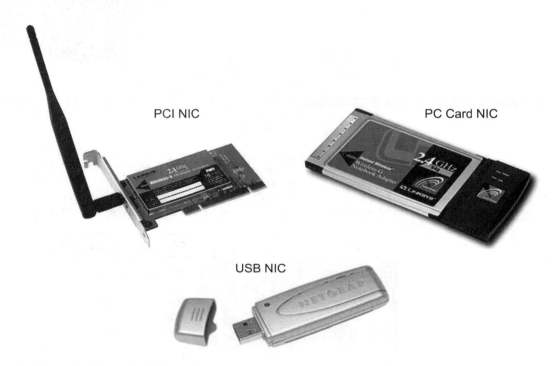

PCI NIC

PC Card NIC

USB NIC

Exhibit 6-7: Wireless NIC cards

Wireless access points

The access point contains at least one interface to connect to the existing wired network (typically called the WAN port), and transmitting equipment to connect with the wireless clients. APs often integrate other networking functions. Many include Ethernet networking ports for connecting wired devices and thus function as switches. Many include routing capabilities, and such devices most often also include firewall functions. The popular Linksys Wireless-G family of wireless routers are one such example of multi-function APs. Two different wireless access points are shown in Exhibit 6-8.

Cisco Aironet Access Point

Linksys Wireless-G 2.4 GHz router/wireless access point

Exhibit 6-8: Wireless access points

Manufacturers of wireless LAN equipment will often promote access ranges of 550 meters. As shown in the following table, as you move farther away from an access point, the data speed drops. It's important for you to realize that interference from your building's structure and environmental noise affects data throughput as well.

IEEE speed	Data speed	Distance from AP
High	4.3 Mbps	40 to 125 meters
Medium	2.6 Mbps	55 to 200 meters
Standard	1.4 Mbps	90 to 400 meters
Standard low	0.8 Mbps	115 to 550 meters

You should place your wireless LAN access points within 60 to 90 meters of the wireless clients. When determining the number and placement of your wireless access points, you need to account for obstructions in your floor plan. For example, in a large room with no walls, you conceivably could centrally place one wireless access point to service up to 200 devices. There are two methods for determining correct WAP placement—an informal site survey and a formal site survey.

- In an *informal site survey*, you temporarily set up your WAPs at the locations you're considering for permanent placement. Then you use a wireless client to test the signal strength of connections within the range that WAP will service, preferably testing right from actual client desk locations. If the connection signals are strong where you need them to be, you go back and permanently mount and install the WAPs. If not, you move the WAPs and retest.

- In a *formal site survey*, you use field-strength measuring equipment. You install a test antenna in the estimated WAP locations and then use the field-strength measuring equipment to determine the exact strength of a test signal at various points within the range the WAP will service. You move the test antenna to obtain the best possible signal for the wireless coverage area. Once you've determined the exact locations for your WAPs, you can permanently mount and install them.

Do it!

A-1: Examining wireless devices

Here's how	Here's why
1 In wireless communications, what replaces the wire?	
2 Does your PC have an infrared wireless port?	Desktop PCs typically don't have such ports, though laptops typically do.
3 Examine the infrared wireless device provided by the instructor. What issues can you surmise might arise as you use such a device?	
4 If your PC has an infrared port, turn on the infrared device and bring it within range of the PC's receiver	If your devices connect, you should see an indicator in the status bar area of the screen that the device has been detected.
5 How far can you move from the PC before you lose the infrared connection?	
6 Examine the radio wireless device provided by your instructor	
7 Does it have a visible, obvious antenna or more than one antenna?	

8 If you've used a wireless network, share your experiences with the rest of the class—for example, where you used it, if it worked well, from how far away you were able to connect, if the particular environs caused interference, and so forth

9 Examine the Bluetooth wireless device provided by your instructor

Your cellular telephone or PDA might support Bluetooth. You could examine it instead.

10 Do the Bluetooth devices have a visible, obvious antenna or more than one antenna?

11 Can you connect to other Bluetooth devices within the classroom?

12 Does your classroom have a wireless access point visible?

13 If so, where is it placed with relationship to client computers?

14 If available, use a wireless client (such as a notebook computer) to walk around the classroom and observe the signal strength reported by Windows Vista

There's an icon in the system tray that reports the signal strength for the wireless connection.

Topic B: Wireless networking standards

This topic covers the following CompTIA Network+ 2009 exam objectives.

Bridge objective

#	Objective
1.7	**Compare the characteristics of wireless communication standards**
	• 802.11 a/b/g/n
	– Speeds
	– Distance
	– Channels
	– Frequency
3.3	**Explain the advanced features of a switch**
	• Port authentication
4.7	**Given a scenario, troubleshoot common connectivity issues and select an appropriate solution**
	Logical issues
	• Wrong subnet mask
	– Wireless issues
	○ Standard mismatch (802.11 a/b/g/n)

Bridge objective (for 3.3)

Bridge objective (for 4.7)

Standards

Explanation

Since the first wireless transmissions took place over a century ago, there has been a push to manage the public airwaves responsibly. During that time, frequency bands have been divided up to accommodate the various user categories such as the military, broadcasters, and amateur radio operators. One of the issues with the current wireless technology is that it's a broadcast signal. This means a wireless device advertises its presence, making it easy for an intruder to pick up and monitor. In order to prevent this from happening, standards were developed and implemented. The WLAN solution provided by Windows clients since Windows XP is based on IEEE standards 802.1x and 802.11.

802.1x standard

The *802.1x standard* is a port-based, authentication framework for access to Ethernet networks. Although this standard is designed for wired Ethernet networks, it applies to 802.11 WLANs. This port-based network access control uses the physical characteristics of the switched LAN infrastructure to authenticate devices attached to a LAN port. It requires three roles in the authentication process:

- A device requesting access
- An authenticator
- An authentication server

802.1x allows scalability in wireless LANs by incorporating centralized authentication of wireless users or stations. The standard allows multiple authentication algorithms and is an open standard.

802.11 standard

The *IEEE 802.11 standard* specifies a technology that operates in the 2.4 through 2.5 GHz band. Wireless networks operate according to the specifications of the IEEE 802.11 standards. The IEEE 802.11 standards are defined at the Data Link layer of the Open Systems Interconnection (OSI) model. In this standard, there are two different ways to configure a network: ad-hoc and infrastructure. In the ad-hoc network, computers are brought together to form a network on the fly. The 802.11 standard also places specifications on the parameters of both the physical and medium access control (MAC) layers of the network.

The 802.11 standard defines an *access point (AP)* as a device that functions as a transparent bridge between the wireless clients and the existing wired network. The access point contains at least one interface to connect to the existing wired network, and transmitting equipment to connect with the wireless clients. It also contains IEEE 802.1D bridging software to act as a bridge between wireless and wired data-link layers.

The current and future WLAN standards under 802.11 are listed in the following table.

Standard	Description
802.11a	Ratified in 1999, 802.11a uses Orthagonal Frequency Division Multiplexing (OFDM) signaling to transmit data. OFDM offers significant performance benefits compared with the more traditional spread-spectrum systems. OFDM is a modulation technique for transmitting large amounts of digital data over radio waves. Capacity per channel is 54 Mbps with real throughput at about 31 Mbps. It operates at a frequency of 5 GHz, which supports eight overlapping channels.
802.11b	Ratified in 1999, 802.11b is one of the most popularly used 802.1x technologies. Uses Direct Sequence Spread Spectrum (DSSS). Capacity per channel is 11 Mbps with real throughput at about 6 Mbps. It operates at a frequency of 2.4 GHz, which supports three non-overlapping channels.
802.11c	Pertains to the operation of bridge connections. Was moved to the 802.1 standards set.
802.11d	Ratified in 2001, 802.11d aims to produce versions of 802.11b that are compatible with other frequencies so it can be used in countries where the 2.4 GHz band isn't available.
802.11e	Not yet ratified, 802.11e adds Quality of Service (QoS) capabilities to 802.11 networks. It uses a Time Division Multiple Access (TDMA) data signaling scheme and adds extra error correction.
802.11F	Ratified in 2003, 802.11F improves the handover mechanism in 802.11 so users can maintain a connection while roaming. It's aimed at giving network users the same roaming freedom cell phone users have.
802.11g	Ratified in 2003, 802.11g is a combination of 802.11a and 802.11b. It can use either Direct Sequence Spread Spectrum (DSSS) or Orthagonal Frequency Division Multiplexing (OFDM)) to transmit data. Capacity per channel is 54 Mbps with real throughput at about 12 Mbps. It operates at a frequency of 2.4 GHz. 802.11g is a popularly used 802.11 technology.
802.11h	Ratified in 2003, 802.11h attempts to improve on 802.11a by adding better control over radio channel selection and transmission power.
802.11i	Ratified in 2004, 802.11i deals with security. This is an entirely new standard based on the Advanced Encryption Standard (AES). This standard has a feature called Robust Security Network (RSN), which defines two security methodologies. The first is for legacy-based hardware using RC4, and the second one is for new hardware based on AES.

Standard	Description
802.11j	Ratified in 2004, 802.11j allows 802.11a and HiperLAN2 networks to coexist in the same airwaves. 802.11j made changes to the 5GHz signaling capabilities to support Japan regulatory requirements.
802.11k	A WLAN management system, currently in progress.
802.11l	This letter was skipped by the IEEE governing board to avoid confusion with 802.11i.
802.11m	This contains maintenance of documentation for the 802.11 family.
802.11n	Currently in progress, 802.11n is a 200+ Mbps standard.

Although devices that support the 802.11a standard are generally incompatible with those that support 802.11b, some devices are equipped to support either 802.11a or 802.11b. The newest approved standard, 802.11g, allows 802.11b and 802.11g devices to operate together on the same network. This standard was created specifically for backwards compatibility with the 802.11b standard. Many modern APs support multiple standards. For example, one AP might offer concurrent support for 802.11a, b, g, and n clients in addition to 100 Mbps wired network clients.

Wireless protocols

There are four major wireless protocols:

- *Wi-Fi* (*Wireless Fidelity*) is the most widely used wireless technology at present. It began as an IEEE 802.11b wireless standard that transmits data at up to 11 Mbps in the 2.4 GHz band. 802.11b is being replaced in most cases with the faster IEEE 802.11g standard, which operates at 20+ Mbps in the 2.4 GHz band. You will often see 802.11g advertised with speeds of up to 54 Mbps. 802.11b and 802.11g devices have an indoor transmission range of up to 35 meters. It's important to note that both of these standards experience interference from other common household devices such as microwave ovens, Bluetooth devices, baby monitors and cordless telephones that also operate in the 2.4 GHz band. 802.11g devices are compatible with older and slower 802.11b hardware.

- *Bluetooth* is a short-range wireless technology limited to transmission distances of about 100 meters or less, which generally confines it to connecting nodes within a single room or adjacent rooms. It operates at low speeds compared to other wireless technologies, sending data at 721 Kbps.

- *802.11a* is an improved version of the original Wi-Fi technology and is also based on the same IEEE 802 standard. It can transmit data at speeds up to 54 Mbps in the 5 GHz band. 802.11a devices have an indoor transmission range of up to 35 meters. 802.11a devices aren't compatible with 802.11b.

- *WiMAX* (IEEE 802.16 Air Interface Standard) is a point-to-multipoint broadband wireless access standard in the frequency ranges 10 to 66 GHz for licensed and 2 to 11 GHz for unlicensed communications, providing bandwidth in excess of 70 Mbps. It's an emerging wireless connection standard for long distances, as it has a theoretical maximum of 31 miles with no obstructions.

You might also hear discussion about 802.11n. 802.11n is currently in the proposal stages and is expected to be released in June of 2009. The 802.11n standard will transmit data at up to 300 Mbps in either the 5 GHz or 2.4 GHz band. It will have an indoor transmission range of up to 70 meters.

The following current, but less popular LAN technologies include wired and wireless standards:

- IEEE 1394 is a standard known mostly by its brand names, FireWire (Apple) and i.LINK (Sony). It's now used widely in the video production and graphics industry to connect digital video cameras and graphics peripherals to computers. Consumer use in the same areas is becoming more common, and IEEE 1394 has recently been used for networking some devices, particularly video systems. IEEE 1394 is a fast serial protocol that can transmit data at speeds from 100 to 400 Mbps—and up to 800 Mbps in the next version.

- USB (Universal Serial Bus) is a bidirectional serial interface that's widely used to connect peripheral devices, such as game controllers, cameras, scanners, and other input devices to computers. USB connections can be made while the equipment is running, and its high speed (USB 1.1 transmits data at 1 to 12 Mbps, and USB 2.0 transmits at up to 480 Mbps) makes it a convenient method of downloading large files. USB connections are now being used in some networks, particularly with Home Plug and Play systems.

Wi-Fi

The first IEEE standard that outlined wireless LAN specifications was IEEE 802.11, published in 1990. Most current WLAN devices operate under the 1999 IEEE 802.11b standard. This standard is also called *Wi-Fi* (*Wireless Fidelity*).

In documentation produced by Apple Computer, Inc., Wi-Fi is called AirPort. 802.11b uses a frequency range of 2.4 GHz in the radio band and has a distance range of about 100 meters. Up to 11 Mbps of data can be sent over distances ranging up to several hundred feet. The range of any specific transmitter depends on what type of obstructions its signal encounters and a clear line of sight between transmitter and receiver. 802.11b is a popular and inexpensive network solution for home and office. Unfortunately, many cordless phones also use the 2.4-GHz frequency range and might interfere with an 802.11b wireless network.

802.11b is an extension of the Ethernet protocol to wireless communication. It can handle many kinds of data. It's primarily used for TCP/IP, but it can also handle other forms of networking traffic, such as AppleTalk or PC file-sharing standards. The Wi-Fi standard is backwards compatible to earlier specifications, which are known as 802.11. This flexibility allows data to move at speeds of 1, 2, 5.5, and 11 Mbps to and from the transceivers.

Bluetooth

Another popular wireless technology is called *Bluetooth*. Bluetooth is a standard for short-range wireless communication and data synchronization between devices. This standard was developed by a group of electronics manufacturers, including Ericsson, IBM, Intel, Nokia, and Toshiba, and it's overseen by the Bluetooth Special Interest Group. The transmitters and receivers are application-specific integrated circuits (ASICs) and can transmit data at rates as high as 721 Kbps with up to three voice channels also available. Bluetooth, which has a range of only 10 meters, also works in the 2.4-GHz frequency range, is easy to configure, and is considered a viable option for short-range connections, such as connecting a PDA to a cell phone so that the PDA can connect to a remote network.

Bluetooth technology allows wireless connections between computers, printers, fax machines, and other peripherals, but it doesn't have the range to serve as a wireless connection between an access point and laptops dispersed throughout a home and yard.

Some vendors have developed Bluetooth devices with higher transmitting power, which increases the range of the technology up to 100 meters, but these higher-power devices haven't yet gained wide acceptance.

802.11a/802.11g

IEEE has two more wireless standards, 802.11a and 802.11g, which are also collectively referred to as Wi-Fi.

802.11a works in the 5.0-GHz frequency range and isn't compatible with 802.11b. It allows for a shorter range between a wireless device and an access point (50 meters compared with 100 meters for 802.11b) but is much faster than 802.11b and doesn't encounter interference from cordless phones, microwave ovens, and Bluetooth devices, as does 802.11b. If its higher cost is acceptable, 802.11a could be an option for a wireless home LAN easily capable of broadcasting high-definition DVD movies to TVs located throughout the house without worrying about bandwidth or cables. If you adopt this protocol, you must use only equipment designed specifically for 802.11a.

802.11g is another IEEE wireless standard that uses the 2.4-GHz band and has become widely available. It's backwards compatible with 802.11b but has higher throughput at 54 Mbps. (Apple Computer, Inc. calls 802.11g AirPort Extreme.) There are tri-standard modulation devices available that can use all three standards—802.11a, 802.11b, and 802.11g.

Another standard is 802.11d, which is designed to run in countries outside the United States where other 802.11 versions don't meet the legal requirements for radio band technologies.

WiMAX

WiMAX, which stands for Worldwide Interoperability for Microwave Access, provides wireless DSL and T1-level service. It's an emerging technology standard that services Wide Area and Metropolitan Area Networks, allowing wireless users with 802.16e devices to roam between current wireless hot spots. As a comparison, WiMAX wireless coverage is measured in square miles, while Wi-Fi is measured in square yards. WiMAX doesn't rely on line-of-sight for connection. WiMAX technology can be deployed in areas where physical limitations, such as no existing DSL or T1 cabling, prevent broadband access.

Do it!   **B-1:   Comparing wireless networking standards**

Questions	Answers
1 List the major wireless protocols.	
2 Which wireless standard is currently used in airports and coffee shops?	
3 Which LAN technologies include wired and wireless standards?	
4 What's the range of the original Bluetooth technology?	
5 Are 802.11b products compatible with 802.11a products?	
6 What should you consider when determining which wireless technology to use?	
7 You work for a company that supplies parts to several automobile dealerships on a daily basis. Each part is assigned an ID and that ID is bar-coded on the shelf where it's stocked. Currently, as each item is pulled for delivery, it's taken to one of the three central computers and scanned to update the inventory database. Can wireless networking benefit your organization?	

8 Match the 802.11 standard with its description.

A. 802.11a

B. 802.11b

C. 802.11F

D. 802.11g

E. 802.11i

It can use either DSSS or OFDM and operates at a frequency of 2.4 GHz.

Uses Direct Sequence Spread Spectrum (DSSS) operating at a frequency of 2.4 GHz, which supports three non-overlapping channels.

Uses the OFDM modulation technique for transmitting large amounts of digital data over radio waves. It operates at a frequency of 5 GHz, which supports eight overlapping channels.

A standard based on the Advanced Encryption Standard (AES). It includes a feature called Robust Security Network (RSN), which defines two security methodologies: the first is for legacy-based hardware using RC4 and the second one is for new hardware based on AES.

Allows users to maintain a connection while roaming.

Topic C: Wireless configuration

This topic covers the following CompTIA Network+ 2009 exam objectives.

#	Objective
Bridge objective **1.7**	**Compare the characteristics of wireless communication standards**
	• Authentication and encryption
	– WPA
	– WEP
	– RADIUS
	– TKIP
Bridge objective **3.1**	**Install, configure and differentiate between common network devices**
	• NIC
	• Wireless access point
Bridge objective **3.4**	**Implement a basic wireless network**
	• Install client
	• Install access point
	– Configure appropriate encryption
	– Configure channels and frequencies
	– Set ESSID and beacon
	• Verify installation
Bridge objective **4.7**	**Given a scenario, troubleshoot common connectivity issues and select an appropriate solution**
	Logical issues
	• Wrong subnet mask
	– Wireless issues
	○ Incorrect encryption
	○ Incorrect channel
	○ Incorrect frequency
	○ ESSID mismatch
Bridge objective **6.4**	**Explain methods of user authentication**
	AAA
	• RADIUS
	Network access control
	• 802.1x

WLAN security risks

Explanation

Given all of the benefits, the security drawbacks with WLANs would need to be fairly severe to undermine their appeal. Wireless devices present a whole new set of threats that network administrators might be unaware of. The most obvious risks concerning wireless networks are theft and rogue devices. Most cell phones, text pagers, PDAs, and wireless network cards are small enough they can be easily lost or stolen. Because they are simple to conceal and contain valuable information about a company, they have become favorite targets of intruders. Wireless LANs can be subject to session hijacking and man-in-the-middle attacks. Additional risks remain because anyone can purchase an access point and set it up.

Wireless access points, when set up right out of the box, have no security configured. They broadcast their presence—in essence saying, "Hey, my name is xxx, here I am!" The free availability of 802.11 network audit tools, such as Airsnort and NetStumbler, means that breaking into wireless networks configured with weak security is quite easy. These tools can be used to check wireless security by identifying unauthorized clients or access points, as well as verifying encryption usage. There are tools available, however, in the form of management software. To eliminate existing 802.11 shortcomings and to help improve the image of wireless technology on the market, the *Institute of Electronic and Electric Engineers* (*IEEE*) together with *Wireless Ethernet Compatibility Alliance* (*WECA*) proposed standards for significantly improved user authentication and media access control mechanisms.

Additional risks associated with wireless networks include:

- 802.1x transmissions generate detectable radio-frequency traffic in all directions. Persons wishing to intercept the data transmitted over the network might use many solutions to increase the distance over which detection is possible, including the use of metal tubes such as a Pringles or a large tomato juice can.

- Without the use of an encryption standard of some type, data is passed in clear text form. Even though technologies such as Wired Equivalent Privacy WEP encrypt the data, they still lack good security and a determined listener can easily obtain enough traffic data in order to calculate the encryption key in use.

- The authentication mechanism is one-way, so it's easy for an intruder to wait until authentication is completed and then generate a signal to the client that tricks the client into thinking it has been disconnected from the access point. Meanwhile, the intruder begins to send data traffic to the server pretending to be the original client.

- The client connection request is a one-way open broadcast. This gives an intruder the opportunity to act as an access point to the client, and act as a client to the real network access point. This allows an intruder to watch all data transactions between the client and access point, then modify, insert, or delete packets at will.

- A popular pastime is wardriving. *Wardriving* involves driving around with a laptop system configured to listen for open wireless access points. Several Web sites provide detailed information locating unsecured networks. These sites provide locations, sometimes on city maps for the convenience of others looking for open access links to the Internet. This is an attractive method to not only capture data from networks, but a way to connect to someone else's network, use their bandwidth, and pay nothing for it.

- *War chalking* is the process of marking buildings, curbs, and other landmarks indicating the presence of an available access point and its connection details by utilizing a set of symbols and shorthand.

WLAN security components

There are four components to security on a wireless network:

- Access control
- Encryption
- Authentication
- Isolation

Access control

You can control which clients can access your AP through various techniques. The simplest, and least effective, is to simply turn off SSID broadcasts. This "hides" the presence of your AP. However, the SSID is also included in routine client-to-AP traffic. Thus, it's easy for appropriately configured devices to detect SSIDs that aren't explicitly broadcast.

A stronger means of access control is to enable a MAC filter on your AP. The MAC address is the hardware-level address of a client's network adapter. On most APs, you can enter a list of permitted MACs, or blocked MACs, to limit connections. This method prevents access to resources on your network, but it's very awkward to implement because each WAP must be configured with the MAC address of each wireless network card. It's also not satisfactory because your data is still vulnerable to being read with a packet sniffer. A packet sniffer could view your MAC address and then configure his or her computer to use the same MAC address after you turn yours off, effectively impersonating you on the network.

As with the SSID, valid MAC addresses are transmitted across the wireless network. Thus, a malicious user could detect a valid MAC address and then configure their computer to impersonate that MAC address and thus gain access to your AP.

Encryption

You can encrypt communications between your AP and clients. Various techniques exist, with some more secure than others. To make a connection, clients must use the same encryption scheme and possess the appropriate encryption key. Once connected, a static or dynamically-changing key provides on-going encryption.

In theory, encryption blocks unapproved connections to your AP. Additionally, as long as the encryption scheme is sufficiently strong, your data streams are kept private from eavesdroppers. As you will see, not all wireless encryption systems are sufficiently robust to actually provide these protections.

Authentication

Through RADIUS or other systems, you can enable client authentication over your wireless network. Using a system essentially like the user name and password you use when you log on, your AP could authenticate the identity of wireless networking clients.

Authentication provides much stronger access control protection than SSID hiding or MAC filtering. You should still use encryption with authentication. Without it, eavesdroppers could access the data that legitimate clients transmit once those clients have connected to the AP.

Authentication typically requires the use of additional software or hardware devices, such as a RADIUS server.

Isolation

Isolation is a means of segregating network traffic. There are two types: wireless client isolation and network isolation.

With wireless client isolation, also called AP isolation, wireless clients are put onto individual VLANs so that they cannot access each other. This is commonly used in public wireless networks to prevent one user from accessing another user's computer. Imagine the risk you face in a library or coffee shop where another user might attempt to access your shared folders or even mount brute force attacks on your PC over the Wi-Fi hotspot network.

You might also want to provide network isolation. For example, you might want to permit wireless clients to access the Internet and your corporate mail server, which is on your wired network. However, you might also want to prevent wireless clients from accessing other wired nodes, such as your file servers.

Some APs offer network isolation through custom routing configurations. You can also enable such isolation through your general network design and firewall configuration.

Transmission encryption

You should enable transmission encryption on your wireless routers unless you have a very good reason not to. Transmission encryption both limits which clients can connect to your AP and protects data from eavesdropping during transmissions.

Products certified by the Wi-Fi Alliance as Wi-Fi compatible must support at least the WPA Personal level of encryption. As of this writing, products don't have to support the 802.11i standard, but the requirement is soon to take effect.

Encryption method	Description
WEP	Wired Equivalent Privacy (WEP) was built into the 802.11 standards for wireless connectivity that govern how data can be encrypted while in transit on the wireless network. It uses a 64-bit or 128-bit symmetric encryption cipher. For WEP to work, a key is configured on both the WAP and the client. This key is used to encrypt the data transmitted between the WAP and the client. There are no standards for how the WEP key is to be placed on the clients and the WAP. Most implementations require you to type in the key manually on each client and the WAP.
	Although WEP is an easy way to prevent casual hackers from viewing the traffic transmitted on your wireless LAN, this method is the least secure encryption technique. WEP has known design flaws that make it relatively easy to crack. However, it is the only viable option for 802.11b and other older wireless clients.
WPA Personal	Wi-Fi Protected Access (WPA) was developed to overcome the weaknesses in WEP. It uses the RC4 symmetric cipher with a 128-bit key. WPA Personal uses a "pre-shared key" (PSK), which simply means you must enter a passphrase onto both the AP and clients.
	The actual encryption key is built from this passphrase and various other data, such as the sending node's MAC address. With the Temporal Key Integrity Protocol (TKIP) option, the full encryption key changes for each packet.
	WPA authorizes and identifies users based on a secret key that changes automatically at a regular interval. WPA uses TKIP (Temporal Key Integrity Protocol) to change the temporal key every 10,000 packets. This insures much greater security than the standard WEP.

Encryption method	Description
WPA2	WPA2 builds upon WPA by adding more features from the 802.11i standard. Notably, WPA2 uses Advanced Encryption System (AES) cipher for stronger encryption.
WPA Enterprise	Works in conjunction with an 802.1X authentication server, which distributes unique keys to each individual. Communications between the client and AP are encrypted using the individual's key.
RADIUS	Remote Access Dial-in User Service (RADIUS) uses a specialized server for authentication and WEP for data encryption, as shown in Exhibit 6-9. The authentication server can include keys as part of the accept message that's sent back to the WAP. In addition, clients are usually able to request a key change. This ability ensures that keys are changed regularly to limit the ability of hackers to view information on the wireless network.
802.11i	802.11i defines security mechanisms for wireless networks. As of this writing, 802.11i compatible devices are relatively rare. However, the popularity of this new technology will grow as more people use wireless as their primary means of connecting to a network.

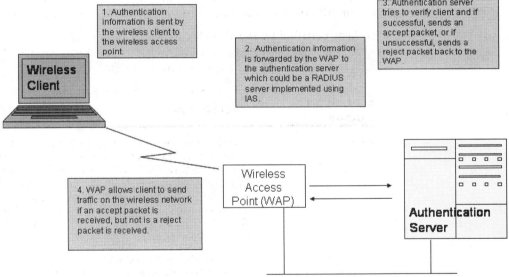

Exhibit 6-9: 802.1x standard protocol authentication process

Do it!

C-1: Identifying the technology used to implement WLANs

Questions and answers

1 What are the two technologies you can use to secure your wireless networks?

2 You've recently been hired as a consultant to evaluate Outlander Spices' wireless network security. What items should you check in evaluating their security practices?

Wireless access point configuration

Explanation

After you have connected your wireless access point to your wired network, you need to configure it. When setting up your AP, you assign a service set identifier (SSID), which is essentially a name for your wireless network. It is possible, and sometimes likely, that multiple wireless networks will be accessible from a given location. In such cases, clients use the SSID to distinguish between WLANs and connect to a particular network.

An AP typically broadcasts the SSID. In this way, clients can discover the presence of a nearby AP. Such broadcasts identify the security mechanisms in place to enable clients to auto-configure connections.

Securing your AP

Out of the box, your wireless access point isn't secure. Some configuration tasks you should complete to make your AP more secure include:

- Setting the most secure transmission encryption method compatible with your clients—Choices might include WEP, WPA Personal, WPA2, WPA Enterprise, RADIUS, and 802.11i.
- Changing access point default administration passwords—Many devices right out of the box don't have a password set on the Administrator account. Programs like AirSnort identify the manufacturer based on the MAC address, so if you only change the SSID, chances are that an informed hacker can easily gain access.
- Changing default Service Set Identifiers (SSIDs)—Don't change the SSID to reflect your company's main names, divisions, products, or address. This makes you an easy target. If an SSID name is enticing enough, it might attract hackers.
- Disabling SSID broadcasts—Broadcast SSID is enabled by default. When you disable this feature, an SSID must be configured in the client to match the SSID of the access point.
- Separating the wireless network from the wired network—Consider using an additional level of authentication, such as RADIUS, before you permit an association with your access points. RADIUS (Remote Authentication Dial In User Service) is an authentication, authorization, and accounting protocol for network access. The wireless clients can be separated so the connections not only use RADIUS authentication, but are also logged.
- Putting the wireless network in an Internet-access only zone or a Demilitarized Zone (DMZ)—Place your wireless access points in a DMZ and have your wireless users tunnel into your network using a VPN. This requires extra effort on your part to set up a VLAN for your DMZ, but this solution adds a layer of encryption and authentication that makes your wireless network secure enough for sensitive data.
- Disabling DHCP within the WLAN to keep a tighter control over users—Assign static IP addresses to your wireless clients. This creates more administrative overhead to manage, but it makes it harder to access your network.
- Enabling MAC address filtering on access points to limit unauthorized wireless NICs—Many access points allow you to control access based on the MAC address of the NIC attempting to associate with it. If the MAC address of the wireless client's NIC isn't in the access point's table, access is denied. Although there are ways of spoofing a MAC address, it takes an additional level of sophistication.

- Enabling 802.1x—802.1x is the recommended method of authentication and encryption for enhanced security on computers running versions of Windows later than Windows XP. The use of 802.1x offers an effective solution for authenticating and controlling user traffic to a protected network, as well as dynamically varying encryption keys. 802.1x ties EAP to both the wired and wireless LAN media and supports multiple authentication methods, such as token cards, Kerberos, one-time passwords, certificates, and public key authentication. You configure 802.1x encryption from the IEEE 802.1x tab of the policy setting's Properties dialog box.

A network administrator should periodically survey their site using a tool such as NetStumbler or AirSnort, to see if any rogue access points are installed on the network. In addition, they can take a notebook equipped with a wireless sniffer installed and an external antenna outside the office building to check to see what information inside the building can be accessed by someone parked in the parking lot or across the street.

Do it!

C-2: Configuring a wireless access point (instructor demo)

Here's how	Here's why
1 Open Internet Explorer and enter the IP address of your WAP	You are prompted for administrator credentials on the WAP.
2 Enter the appropriate user name and password for your WAP and click **OK**	
3 Activate the **Wireless Settings** tab	
In the SSID box, edit default to read **123ABC567**	Remember, one of the security guidelines for creating a more secure SSID is to not reflect your company's main names, divisions, products, or address.
For SSID broadcast, select **Disabled**	
For Security, select **WEP** and record the WEP key	WEP key: _____
Check **Apply**	The device restarts itself.
4 Activate the **Tools** tab	
In the New password and Confirm password boxes, enter **!pass4321**	
Check **Apply**	

5 Activate the **Advanced** tab

Select **MAC filters**

Choose **Only allow computers with MAC address listed below to access the network**

In the Name box enter your computer's name

In the MAC address box, enter your computer's MAC address

Check **Apply**

6 Close Internet Explorer

Wireless clients

Explanation

When you implement an authenticating server, such as RADIUS, the wireless client must submit its credentials with the authenticating server before wireless network access is established. When the client computer is in range of the wireless AP, it tries to connect to the WLAN that is active on the wireless AP. If the wireless AP is configured to allow only secured or 802.1x authenticated connections, the wireless AP issues a challenge to the client. The wireless AP then sets up a restricted channel that allows the client to communicate only with the RADIUS server. The RADIUS server accepts a connection only from a trusted wireless AP, or one that has been configured as a RADIUS client on the Microsoft Internet Authentication Service (IAS) server and provides the shared secret for that RADIUS client. The RADIUS server validates the client credentials against the directory. If the client is successfully authenticated, the RADIUS server decides whether to authorize the client to use the WLAN. If the client is granted access, the RADIUS server transmits the client master key to the wireless AP. The client and wireless AP now share common key information they can use to encrypt and decrypt the WLAN traffic passing between them. How you configure Windows clients to participate in this process depends on the operating system.

Windows Vista and Windows XP wireless clients

Wireless Auto Configuration dynamically selects the wireless network to which a connection attempt is made, based on configured preferences or default settings. Computers running Windows Vista and Windows XP support *Wireless Zero Configuration*, which enables computers to automatically connect to available wireless networks. Windows Vista and Windows XP client computers can choose from available wireless networks and connect automatically without user action by default. Wireless Zero Configuration automatically configures items such as TCP/IP settings, DNS server addresses, and IAS server addresses. Wireless Zero Configuration includes support for 802.1x authentication and encryption. The default preferences for Wireless Zero Configuration using IEEE 802.1x authentication include:

- Infrastructure before ad hoc mode, and computer authentication before user authentication.
- WEP authentication attempts to perform an IEEE 802.11 shared key authentication if the network adapter has been preconfigured with a WEP shared key; otherwise, the network adapter reverts to the open system authentication.

Although the IEEE 802.1x security enhancements are available in Windows Vista and Windows XP versions, the network adapters and access points must also be compatible with this standard for deployment.

You can change the default settings to allow guest access, which isn't enabled by default. You shouldn't turn on guest access on a laptop using Wireless Zero Configuration. An unauthorized user could establish an ad hoc connection to the laptop and gain access to confidential information on the laptop.

Windows 2000 Professional wireless clients

Computers running Windows 2000 Professional don't support Wireless Zero Configuration. You can configure a wireless network card for connection using EAP-TLS or PEAP authentication just as you can when configuring Windows Vista and Windows XP computers. Only Windows Vista and Windows XP computers natively support IEEE 802.1x authentication. Microsoft provides an 802.1x Authentication Client download that allows Windows 2000 computers to use the 802.1x standard. This download can be found at:

http://www.microsoft.com/windows2000/server/evaluation/► news/bulletins/8021xclient.asp.

Windows CE wireless clients

Palm-top computers running Windows CE .NET include Wireless Zero Configuration and similar manual configuration options to those found on Windows Vista and Windows XP. They support 802.11a and *Native Wireless Fidelity* (*Wi-Fi*). You can configure older Windows CE palm-top computers for wireless networking. The settings and configuration are similar to those for Windows 2000 Professional.

Do it!

C-3: Configuring a wireless client (instructor demo)

Here's how	Here's why
1 On the computer with a wireless NIC, click **Start** and choose **Control Panel**, **Network and Internet**	You'll configure the client to connect using the settings on the wireless access point.
Click **Network and Sharing Center**	
Under Tasks, click **Manage wireless networks**	
2 Click **Add**	
Click **Manually create a network profile**	Because you disabled broadcast of the SSID, you must manually configure the connection.
3 In the Network name box, enter **123ABC567**	
In the Security type box, select **WEP**	
Select **Manually assign a network key**	
4 In the Security Key/Passphrase box, enter the WEP key you recorded in the previous activity	
5 Check **Connect even if the network is not broadcasting**	
Click **Next**	
6 Click **Connect to...**	
Select **123ABC567**	This must match the SSID of the WAP you want to connect to.
Click **Connect**	
7 In the SSID name box, enter **123ABC567**	
8 In the Security key or passphrase box, enter the WEP key you recorded in the previous activity	
9 Click **Connect**	
10 Close all open windows	

Unit summary: Wireless networking

Topic A
In this topic, you looked at the three technologies used to create wireless connections between devices: **infrared**, **radio**, and **Bluetooth**. You identified the hardware components needed to create a wireless network connection via radio signals—a **wireless access point** and a **wireless network interface card**. Also, you examined the three basic types of wireless network links: **indoor point-to-multipoint LANs**, **outdoor point-to-point links**, and **outdoor point-to-multipoint links**. You learned how to determine the proper placement of an **access point** in your network to ensure acceptable signal strength for your wireless client computers.

Topic B
In this topic, you learned about the **IEEE 802.11 standards** that govern wireless network communications. You examined the protocols used for wireless communications: **Wi-Fi**, **Bluetooth**, **802.11a**, and **WiMAX**, as well as two LAN protocol standards that have both wired and wireless components: **IEEE 1394** and **USB**.

Topic C
In this topic, you learned how to create a wireless network connection between a client and an access point. You also learned how to secure the communication using the four components critical to security on a wireless network: **access control**, **encryption**, **authentication**, and **isolation**.

Review questions

1 Which wireless technology is used to create a connection between two devices? (Select all that apply.)

A Bluetooth

B Infrared

C Radio

D Wi-Fi

E WiMAX

2 Which connection type uses two directional antennas to make the wireless link?

A Indoor point-to-multipoint LANs

B Outdoor point-to-point links

C Outdoor point-to-multipoint links

D Wi-Fi

E WiMAX

3 The interface on the access point used to connect to the existing wired network is typically called what?

A Antenna

B Transmitter

C WAN port

D Wireless NIC

4 You should place your wireless LAN access points within how many meters of the wireless clients?

 A 40 to 125

 B 55 to 200

 C 60 to 90

 D 90 to 400

 E 115 to 550

5 To obtain the IEEE speed designated as high, clients are within how many meters of the AP?

 A 40 to 125

 B 55 to 200

 C 60 to 90

 D 90 to 400

 E 115 to 550

6 In a(n) _____ site survey, you temporarily set up your WAPs at the locations you're considering for permanent placement.

7 The 802.1x standard requires which roles in the authentication process? (Select all that apply.)

 A Authentication server

 B Authenticator

 C Encryption algorithm

 D Requesting access device

8 Which of the following is the most widely used wireless technology at present?

 A 802.11a

 B Bluetooth

 C Wi-Fi

 D WiMAX

9 True or false? 802.11b, 802.11a, and 802.11g are all considered Wi-Fi.

10 Ratified in 2003, which standard is a combination of 802.11a and 802.11b?

  A 802.11c

  B 802.11g

  C 802.11h

  D 802.11n

11 Of the four components to security on a wireless network, to which one does a RADIUS server belong?

  A Access control

  B Authentication

  C Encryption

  D Isolation

12 War _____ is the process of marking buildings, curbs, and other landmarks indicating the presence of an available access point and its connection details by utilizing a set of symbols and shorthand.

13 Which encryption method uses Advanced Encryption System (AES) cipher for stronger encryption?

  A 802.11i

  B WEP

  C WPA Personal

  D WPA2

14 An AP typically broadcasts its _____ so clients can discover its presence.

15 True or false? Wireless Zero Configuration enables Windows Vista and Windows XP computers to automatically connect to available wireless networks.

16 True or false? Windows 2000 Professional clients have no way of supporting IEEE 802.1x authentication.

Independent practice activity

In this activity, you'll practice adding a wireless access point and client to your network. You might need to work with one or more other students depending on the number of available wireless routers.

1 Remove the network cable from your secondary NIC. (This is the wired NIC card that's currently disabled.)

2 Connect the network cable to your wireless router.

3 Connect the power to the wireless router.

4 Check the router documentation for how to access the configuration utility.

5 Change the SSID name to your lab number followed by your first name. (For example, 06Jane.) Most often you use an Internet browser to connect to an IP address such as 192.168.1.1.

6 Following the directions in the wireless router documentation, configure WPA or WEP.

7 Install a wireless network interface card on your computer. If you don't have an empty PCI slot, you can remove your secondary wired NIC card and install the wireless card.

8 Create a connection to your WAP. (There is a DHCP server in the classroom that you should be able to use to assign IP addressing information to the wireless NIC.) Configure WPA or WEP on the connection to match what you just set in the wireless router.

9 Verify you have Internet connectivity.

10 Uninstall the wireless NIC from your computer. If necessary, reinstall your wired NIC.

11 Unplug the network cable from the wireless router. Plug the network cable back into your secondary NIC card.

Unit 7

Security threats and mitigation

Unit time: 135 minutes

Complete this unit, and you'll know how to:

A Describe and explain common security threats.

B Explain ways to mitigate security threats.

Topic A: Security threats

This topic covers the following CompTIA Network+ 2009 exam objectives.

Bridge objective

#	Objective
5.2	**Explain the purpose of network scanners**
	• Port scanners
6.6	**Identify common security threats and mitigation techniques**
	• DoS
	• Viruses
	• Worms
	• Attackers
	• Man in the middle
	• Smurf
	• Rogue access points
	• Social engineering (phishing)

Explanation

The goals of network security are integrity, confidentiality, and availability. Threats to even the most secure systems' data challenge administrators as well as users every day. The cost of lost assets must be balanced against the cost of securing the network; you must decide how much risk your company is willing to take.

Compromised data integrity typically costs an organization a lot in terms of time and money in order to correct the consequences of attacks. Consequences to the organization of compromised data confidentiality aren't always immediate, but they are usually costly. Application availability can be compromised by network outages, causing organizations to lose millions of dollars in just a few hours.

There are four primary causes for compromised security:

- Technology weaknesses
- Configuration weaknesses
- Policy weaknesses
- Human error or malice

Technology weaknesses

Computer and network technologies have intrinsic security weaknesses in the following areas:

- TCP/IP—Designed as an open standard to facilitate communications. Due to its wide usage, there are plenty of experts and expert tools that can compromise this open technology.
- Operating systems—UNIX, Linux, and Microsoft Windows, for example, need the latest patches, updates, and upgrades applied to protect users.
- Network equipment—Routers, firewalls, and switches must be protected through the use of password protection, authentication, routing protocols, and firewalls.

Configuration weaknesses

Security breaches of even the most secure technology are often caused by one of the following configuration weaknesses:

- Unsecured accounts—User account information transmitted unsecurely across the network, exposing usernames and passwords to programs used to monitor network activity, such as packet sniffers, which can capture and analyze the data within IP packets on an Ethernet network or dial-up connection.

- System accounts with weak passwords—Lack of strong password policies allows users to create passwords that can be easily guessed or cracked.

- Misconfigured Internet services—If Java and JavaScript are enabled in Web browsers, they are subject to hostile Java applets. You should not store high-security data on a Web server; you should store data such as social security numbers and credit card numbers behind a firewall that can only be accessed through user authentication and authorization.

- Unsecured default settings—Many products have default settings that contain security holes.

- Misconfigured network equipment—Misconfiguration of network devices can cause significant security problems. For example, misconfigured access control lists, routing protocols, or Simple Network Management Protocol (SNMP) community strings can open up large security holes.

- Trojan horse programs—These programs contain destructive code but appear to be harmless; however, they are enemies in disguise. They can delete data, mail copies of themselves to e-mail address lists, and open up other computers for attack.

- Viruses—This has grown into possibly the single largest threat to network security . Viruses replicate themselves and infect computers when triggered by a specific event.

Human error and malice

Human error and malice constitute a significant percentage of security breaches. Even well trained and conscientious users can cause great harm to security systems, often without knowing it.

Users can unwittingly contribute to security breaches in several ways:

- Accident—The mistaken destruction, modification, disclosure, or incorrect classification of information.

- Ignorance—Inadequate security awareness, lack of security guidelines, lack of proper documentation, and lack of knowledge.

- Workload—Too many or too few system administrators.

Conversely, ill-willed employees or professional hackers and criminals can access valuable assets through:

- Dishonesty—Fraud, theft, embezzlement, and the sale of confidential corporate information.
- Impersonation—Attackers might impersonate employees over the phone in an attempt to persuade users or administrators to give out usernames, passwords, dial-in information, and so on.
- Disgruntled employees—Employees who were fired, laid off, or given a reprimand might infect the network with a virus or delete files. Many times these people know the network and the value of the information on it, which can make them a huge security threat.
- Snoops—Individuals who take part in corporate espionage by gaining unauthorized access to confidential data and providing this information to competitors.
- Denial-of-service attacks—These attacks swamp network equipment, such as Web servers or routers, with useless service requests, which can cause systems to slow down or even crash.
- Identity theft—If an attacker gains access to an employee's personal information, they can use that information to commit fraud. It often takes the form of financial abuse, but can also be used to obtain accounts that are then used to perform network attacks.

Viruses, worms, and Trojan horses

Viruses are one of the biggest threats to network security. Network technicians need to keep a constant lookout for them and prevent their spread. They are designed to replicate themselves and infect computers when triggered by a specific event. The effect of some viruses is minimal and only an inconvenience, but others are more destructive and cause major problems, such as deleting files or slowing down entire systems.

Worms

Worms are programs that replicate themselves over the network without a user's intervention. A worm attaches itself to a file or a packet on the network and travels of its own accord. It can copy itself to multiple computers, bringing the entire network to its knees. One method worms use to spread themselves is to send themselves to everyone in a user's e-mail address book. The intent of a worm infiltration is to cause a malicious attack, which often uses up computer resources to the point that the system, or even the entire network, can no longer function or is shut down.

Trojans

Trojan horses are delivery vehicles for destructive code. They appear to be harmless programs but can be incredibly destructive. They can delete data, mail copies of themselves to e-mail address lists, and open up other computers for attack. Trojans are often distributed via spam or through a compromised Web site.

A *logic bomb* is hidden code within a program designed to run when some condition is met. For example, the code might run on a particular date. Or, perhaps the bomb's author sets some sort of condition that would be met after he or she is fired, at which time the code would run. Because a logic bomb is contained within another presumably useful program, it is considered a type of trojan.

Zombies and botnets

In many cases, the goal of malware is to turn compromised systems into "zombies," sometimes called "bots." At a signal from the malware author, these zombies are made to attack some computer or group of computers. For example, in a Distributed Denial of Service (DDoS) attack, a collection of zombies overwhelms a system with bogus requests. A collection of zombies is sometimes called a botnet, though that term is also used to describe collections of uninfected computers working together to perform a distributed computing task.

Rootkits

A *rootkit* is software that grants full system control to the user. The term comes from the UNIX/Linux environment, where the highest level of system administrator is the user called root. Viruses, worms, and so forth sometimes act as rootkits, granting the malware author full access to the compromised system.

Rootkits are a specific example of a type of program that seeks privilege escalation. Many forms of malware seek to gain higher privileges in order modify user or system files. Users themselves attempt a privilege escalation attack when they try to log on using someone else's account.

Do it!

A-1: Identifying common security threats

Questions and answers

1 Which of the following computer and network technologies have intrinsic security weaknesses?

  A   TCP/IP

  B   Operating systems

  C   Network equipment

  D   All of the above

2 What is a crime called in which one person masquerades under the identity of another?

  A   Identity theft

  B   Confidentiality

  C   Integrity

  D   All of the above

3 Which of the following is not a primary cause of network security threats?

  A   Encryption algorithm

  B   Technology weaknesses

  C   Policy weaknesses

  D   Configuration weaknesses

  E   Human error

4 True or false? Trojan horses are destructive programs that masquerade as benign applications.

5 Which of the following is not considered a configuration weakness?

  A   Unsecured accounts

  B   Misconfigured Internet services

  C   Viruses

  D   Human ignorance

6 Compare and contrast trojans and logic bombs.

7 Is every program that attempts privilege escalation a rootkit?

8 What does it mean to say your system is part of a botnet?

Social engineering

Explanation

Social engineering is the equivalent of hacking vulnerabilities in computer systems to gain access—except it occurs in the world of people. Social engineering exploits trust in the real world between people to gain information that attackers can then use to gain access to computer systems. These trust exploits usually, though not always, involve a verbal trick, a hoax, or a believable lie.

Goals of social engineering techniques include fraud, network intrusion, industrial espionage, identity theft, or a desire to disrupt a system or network.

Targets for social engineering techniques tend to be larger organizations where it is common for employees who have never actually met to have communications and those that have information desired by attackers: industrial/military secrets, personal information about targeted individuals, and resources such as long-distance or network access.

Social engineering techniques are often used when the attacker cannot find a way to penetrate the victim's systems using other means. For example, when a strong perimeter security and encryption foil an attacker's efforts to penetrate the network, social engineering might be the only avenue left. A slip of words is all the attacker needs to gain access to your well-defended systems.

Shoulder surfing

Shoulder surfing is a social engineering attack in which someone attempts to observe secret information "over your shoulder." Imagine someone standing behind you as you log onto your workstation. By watching your fingers, there's a chance they can determine your password, and then later log on as you.

Dumpster diving

Digging useful information out of an organization's trash bin is another form of attack, one that makes use of the implicit trust that people have that once something is in the trash, it's gone forever. Experience shows that this is a very bad assumption, as *dumpster diving* is an incredible source of information for those who need to penetrate an organization in order to learn its secrets. The following table lists the useful information that can be obtained from trash bins:

Item	Description
Internal phone directories	Provide names and numbers of people to target and impersonate—many usernames are based on legal names.
Organizational charts	Provide information about people who are in positions of authority within the organization.
Policy manuals	Indicate how secure (or insecure) the company really is.
Calendars	Identify which employees are out of town at a particular time.
Outdated hardware	Provide all sorts of useful information; for example, hard drives that might be discarded.
System manuals, network diagrams, and other sources of technical information	Include the exact information that attackers might seek, including the IP addresses of key assets, network topologies, locations of firewalls and intrusion detection systems, operating systems, applications in use, and more.

Online attacks

Online attacks use instant-messenger-chat and e-mail venues to exploit trust relationships. Similar to the trojan attacks, attackers might try to induce their victims to execute a piece of code by convincing them that they need it or because it is something interesting, such as a game. While users are online, they tend to be more aware of hackers, and are careful about revealing personal information in chat sessions and e-mail. By getting a user to install the program from such a link as described here, the attacker's code tricks the user into reentering a username and password into a pop-up window.

Social engineering countermeasures

There are a number of steps that organizations can take to protect themselves against social-engineering attacks. At the heart of all of these countermeasures is a solid organizational policy that dictates expected behaviors and communicates security needs to every person in the company.

1   Take proper care of trash and other discarded items.

- For all types of sensitive information on paper, use a paper shredder or locked recycle box instead of a trash can.

- Ensure that all magnetic media is bulk erased before it is discarded.

- Keep trash dumpsters in secured areas so that no one has access to their contents.

2   User education and awareness training are critical. Ensure that all system users have periodic training about network security.

- Make employees aware of social engineering scams and how they work.

- Inform users about your organization's password policy (for example, never give your password out to anybody at all, by any means at all).

- Give recognition to people who have avoided making mistakes or caught real mistakes in a situation that might have been a social-engineering attack.

- Ensure that people know what to do in the event they spot a social-engineering attack.

Phishing

Another method hackers use to obtain personal information is through *phishing*. This is done by the hacker sending an e-mail that appears to be from a trusted sender such as a credit card company, PayPal, the IRS, or eBay. The message directs the recipient to a Web site that looks like the company's site they are impersonating. The hacker can then record the user's logon information when they visit the site in the e-mail. Sometimes the user does briefly pass through the legitimate site on the way to the hacker's site.

At the hacker's site the user is asked for personal information, usually in the guise of verifying or updating their information. The information requested often includes social security numbers, credit card information, name, address, and so forth.

The phishing attack is usually sent by e-mail to make it appear valid, but sometimes it comes via instant message or phone. Most companies do not send e-mail to users to gather such information, especially since phishing has become such a problem.

Clues

Sometimes there are obvious clues that you received a fraudulent message. This includes poor grammar, typos, and misspellings. Most of the sites that have been impersonated no longer include their logo in official messages. This is because the logo is often used by the hacker as the link users click to get to their impersonated site. Since most phishing messages still include logos, this is another clue that it is not a legitimate message from the company.

Countermeasures

Browsers have implemented measures to protect users from phishing scams. Internet Explorer 7 includes a Phishing Filter to automatically check the sites you visit. It first checks the site against its list of legitimate sites. Then it examines the site for typical characteristics found on a phishing site. If you want, you can also send the address of a site to Microsoft to be checked out further against an updated list of phishing sites.

If Internet Explorer determines that it believes you are visiting a phishing site, an information message is displayed, and your browser is redirected to a warning page. You can then continue on to the site or close the page.

Other browsers such as Firefox and Opera have also implemented protection against phishing. Some of the methods they use are comparing the URL to white-listed sites, sites that are legitimate, and to black-listed sites, those that are known phishing sites.

Some sites have also implemented measures to protect users from visiting impersonated versions of their sites. One such method is to have a user select an image that is displayed when they log on. If their selected image is not displayed, then the user should not log on since that is a clue that they are not visiting the official site.

Do it!   **A-2:   Discussing social engineering**

Questions and answers

1 Which of the following are the best ways to protect your organization from revealing sensitive information to dumpster divers?

    A   Use a paper shredder or locked recycle box.

    B   Teach employees to construct strong passwords.

    C   Add a firewall.

    D   Keep trash dumpsters in secured areas.

2 How can you secure system users from social attacks?

3 Give examples of shoulder surfing in the context of both corporate and individual security.

Denial of Service attacks

Explanation

Denial of Service (DoS) attacks consume or disable resources so that services to users are interrupted. Rather than destroying or stealing data, a DoS attack is designed to disrupt daily standard operation. This can lead to loss of reputation and loss of revenue for the victim.

DoS attacks are conducted in a variety of ways by using a variety of methods. Many of the attack tools are easy to use, making the attacks easy to implement. Some of the attack modes cause the user's application or operating system to crash. Others clog Web server connections with illegitimate traffic or consume disk space, buffers, or queues, making server response time slow or causing the server to be unable to respond to valid user requests. Another attack attempts to log on to the server multiple times until the account is locked due to too many incorrect logon attempts. An attacker might also cause a DNS server to crash by sending so many DNS lookup requests that the server runs out of memory and crashes, causing Web pages within the domain to be inaccessible.

SYN flood attacks

As you learned earlier in the course, a normal TCP connection is created using a three-way handshake. The SYN flag, a synchronize control flag, is sent from the client to the server. The session is acknowledged by the server with a packet containing the SYN flag and an ACK, an acknowledgement flag, known as a SYN/ACK packet. The client then responds back to the server with an ACK packet to complete the session so that the hosts can exchange data. The process is illustrated in Exhibit 7-1.

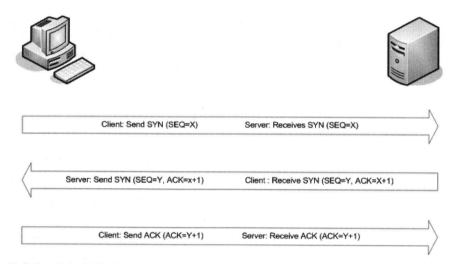

Client: Send SYN (SEQ=X)   Server: Receives SYN (SEQ=X)

Server: Send SYN (SEQ=Y, ACK=x+1)   Client : Receive SYN (SEQ=Y, ACK=X+1)

Client: Send ACK (ACK=Y+1)   Server: Receive ACK (ACK=Y+1)

Exhibit 7-1: TCP 3-way handshake

SYN flood attacks flood a server with half-open TCP connections which prevent valid users from being able to access the server. If the client doesn't send the ACK packet back to the server, the connection can't be completed. The server waits a bit for the client to try again before it removes the incomplete connection from memory. Most servers can handle establishing only a few connections at a time because they usually are established very quickly. If the server is flooded with half-open connections, no more connections can be established until all of the memory has been cleared.

An attacker uses a spoofed address source to flood the connections queue with SYN packets. Because the SYN/ACK packet can't reach the spoofed address, the ACK packet is never returned to the server. Legitimate users are prevented from accessing the server until the half-open connections time out.

Firewalls often include features that help avoid the problems caused by SYN flood attacks. For example, a firewall can withhold or insert packets in the data stream as needed to stop SYN flood attacks. The firewall can also immediately respond to the server SYN/ACK packet with an ACK using the spoofed client IP address, which enables the server to remove the session from the half-open connection queue. A legitimate connection responds with its own ACK packet from the client shortly after this, and the firewall forwards it on to the server. An illegitimate half-open connection sends no ACK from the client. The firewall sends a reset (RST) packet to kill the TCP session if no ACK is received from the client. This is illustrated in Exhibit 7-2.

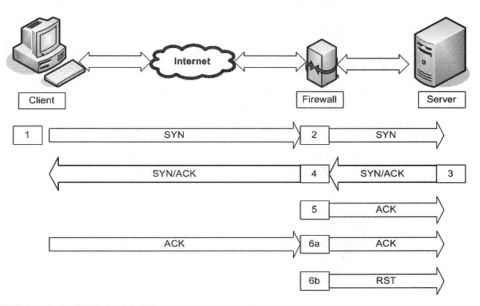

Exhibit 7-2: SYN flood defense

Other defensive measures can be taken to prevent SYN flood attacks. These include:

- Increasing the half-open connection queue size on the server.
- Decreasing the time-out period for the queue, thereby limiting the amount of half-open connections from a single address.
- Implementing an intrusion detection system that detects SYN flood attacks.
- Use Regedit to configure the SynAttackProtect to a value of 1. The Tcp MaxConnectResponseRetransmissions value needs to be set to at least 2 on the server.

Smurf attacks

A smurf attack overwhelms a host by flooding it with ICMP packets. It uses a third-party network to do so. A ping is sent by the hacker to the broadcast address of the intermediary network. The IP address for the packet source fakes to be from the victim system. Every host on the subnet replies to the broadcasted ping request on the victim's address. Without knowing it, the hosts on the third-party network inundate the victim with ping packets. The hacker achieves two results using a smurf attack: it overwhelms the system that receives the echo packet flood as well as saturates the victim's Internet connection with fraudulent traffic, which prevents valid traffic from getting through.

To prevent smurf attacks, you can configure routers to drop ICMP packets that originate outside of the network and have an internal broadcast or multicast destination address. You can also configure hosts to ignore echo requests targeted at their subnet broadcast address.

Ping of death attacks

Operating systems have been updated so that ping of death attacks are no longer much of a threat, but at one time they were successfully used to crash systems. AN IP packet has a maximum size of 65,535 bytes. By sending a 65,536 byte fragmented ping packet, when the packet is reassembled, it causes a buffer overflow which can crash a system.

Do it!

A-3: Discussing DoS attacks

Questions and answers
1 How does a SYN attack inhibit services?
2 How can you defend your systems from smurf attacks?

Distributed Denial of Service attacks

Explanation

A network attack in which the attacker manipulates several hosts to perform a DoS attack is known as a *Distributed Denial of Service (DDoS) attack*. This usually causes the target to be inaccessible for a time. It also results in revenue and reliability losses for the victim.

DDoS attacks use automated tools which make them easy to execute. They are often used to attack government and business Internet sites.

A DDoS assault requires that the hacker first finds a computer to use as the handler. The compromised system is usually one with lots of disk space and a fast Internet connection. The hacker uses this computer to upload their chosen attack toolkit. The hacker needs to remain undetected, so often chooses a host with many user accounts or one with a careless administrator to use as the handler.

The next step after the handler has been set up is to use automated scripts to scan large areas of IP address space to locate targets to use as zombies or agents. The scripts often make use of known weaknesses in Windows operating systems. The zombie software is loaded onto these systems transparently to the system user. The hacker typically creates hundreds or thousands of zombies to launch the DDoS attack. A collection of zombies is sometimes called a botnet. Home PCs that aren't adequately protected and that use DSL or cable connections which are always on are often targeted as zombies.

The attack is usually launched through Internet Relay Chat (IRC) connections. The compromised host is automatically logged on to an IRC channel. The host waits passively for the order to attack from the handler system. At the time of the attack, a command is delivered from the handle system to the zombies connected to the IRC channel. The zombies are instructed remotely to flood the victim's network. All of this happens without the owner of the machine ever knowing that their system was compromised.

There are several steps you can take to prevent your system from being compromised by DDoS attacks. Clients and servers should install all security patches issued by software vendors. Personal firewalls should be configured on PCs along with antivirus software that regularly scans hard disks. E-mail servers should also have antivirus software installed. Firewalls and routers should be configured in the following ways:

- Filter packets entering the network with a broadcast address for the destination.
- Directed broadcasts on internal routers should be turned off.
- For any source address that is not permitted on the Internet, the packet should be blocked.
- Any port or protocol not used for Internet connections on your network should be blocked.
- Packets with a source address that originates inside your network should be blocked from entering the network.
- Packets with counterfeit source addresses should be blocked from leaving your network.

Port scanners

A *port scanner* is a piece of software that is designed to scan network computers to find any open ports. When attackers use port scanners, they're searching for a vulnerability that they can exploit to gain access to the computer. When network technicians and security experts use a port scanner, they're trying to determine where their weaknesses are so they can harden their systems to protect them from attack.

There are a variety of port scanners available for you to use to assess a system's vulnerabilities. Many port scanners are free; just be sure to use one from a reputable software vendor. How you run the port scanner will depend on the specific port scanner you decide to use. Follow the vendor's instructions to complete a port scan.

Do it!

A-4: Assessing your vulnerability to DDoS attacks

Here's how	Here's why
1 Start the Windows Server 2008 virtual PC	You should be logged on to as the domain user netadmin##.
2 Open Internet Explorer	You will use DDoSPing to scan for zombies on your network.
3 Go to **foundstone.com**	DDoSPing is a utility that scans for common DDoS programs. It will detect Trinoo, Stacheldraht, and Tribe Flood Network programs on the computer.
In the Microsoft Phishing Filter, select **Ask me later** and click **OK**	
4 Click **Install**	To install Adobe Flash Player Installer.
5 Click **Resources** Click **Free Tools**	
6 Under Scanning Tools, click **DDoSPing™**	Scroll down.
7 Click **Download this Tool Now**	
8 Read the Terms of Use and download the tool	
9 Click **Save** Save the file to the Net Admin##\Downloads folder	
10 Click **Open Folder**	

11 Right-click **ddosping** and
choose **Extract All...**

Click **Extract**

12 In the Net Admin##\Downloads\ddosping folder,
double-click **ddosping**

13 Click **Run**

14 Observe the Target IP address
range

By default, the DDoSPing utility scans the IP
subnet your computer is on. Make note of this
range. You'll need it in the next activity:

Start IP: _____

End IP: _____

15 Move the Transmission speed
control setting to **Max**

16 Click **Start**

The scan runs quickly and should complete in a
few seconds. The message "Program stopped:"
followed by the date and time indicates that the
scan was completed.

A scan of this type is often detected by a
network administrator and might violate
computer use policies if permission has not been
granted to perform the scan.

17 Examine the Infected Hosts and
Status boxes

Any host infected with a zombie is listed. If no
hosts are listed, no zombies were found. The
Status box will indicate whether any zombies
were detected.

18 Close all open windows *except* the
Internet Explorer window with
Foundstone Free Tools

Man-in-the-middle attacks

To conduct a man-in-the-middle attack, the attacker positions himself between the two hosts that are communicating with each other. The attacker then listens in on the session. Each of the hosts believes that they are communicating only with each other. However, they are actually communicating with the attacker.

Man-in-the-middle attacks can be used for several types of attacks. They can be used for DoS attacks, for corrupting transmitted data, or analysis of the traffic to gather information about the network. Other attacks include:

Attack	Description
Web spoofing	The attacker puts a Web server between the victim's Web browser and a legitimate server. The attacker monitors and records the victim's online activity. The attacker can also modify the content viewed by the victim.
Information theft	The attacker passively records data passing between hosts to gather sensitive information such as usernames and passwords or even industrial secrets.
TCP session hijacking	The attacker between the two hosts takes over the role of one of the hosts and assumes full control of the TCP session.

Anyone with access to network packets that travel between hosts can conduct a man-in-the-middle attack. Some of the methods used to do so include:

Attack method	Description
ARP poisoning	Can be conducted using programs such as Dsniff, Hunt, ARPoison, Ettercap, or Parasite that allow the attacker to monitor and modify a TCP session. The attacker needs to be on the same Ethernet segment as the victim or as the host.
ICMP redirect	Attacker instructs a router to forward packets with a destination of the victim to instead go through the attacker's system. It uses ICMP redirect packets to bring about this attack. The attacker can monitor and modify packets before sending them to their destination. To prevent these attacks, routers should be configured to ignore ICMP redirect packets.
DNS poisoning	Traffic is redirected by the attacker by modifying the victim's DNS cache with the wrong hostname to IP address mappings.

Spoofing

Impersonating someone else is known as *spoofing*. Presenting credentials that don't belong to you in order to gain access to a system is spoofing the system. There are several types of spoofing, including:

- IP address spoofing
- ARP poisoning
- Web spoofing
- DNS spoofing

IP address spoofing

TCP/IP packets generated by the attacker using the source address of a trusted host are used to gain access to a victim through IP address spoofing. Using this trickery, the attacker is able to bypass filters on routers and firewalls to gain network access.

The steps to stage an IP spoofing attack are:

1. Identify a target to be the attack victim and a machine trusted by the victim. The trusted machine's ability to communicate is disabled by the attacker using SYN flooding.

2. Using a sniffer, sampling packets, or some other method, the attacker determines the sequence numbers used by the victim in the communication. The source IP address of the trusted host is spoofed by the attacker and used to send their own packets to the victim.

3. The spoofed packets are accepted and responded to by the victim. Even though the packets are routed to the trusted host, they are unable to be processed by the trusted host due to the SYN flood attack.

4. The attacker guesses the content of the victim's response and creates a response using the spoofed source address and guesses at what the appropriate sequence number should be.

One way to prevent IP spoofing is to disable source routing on internal routers. You can also filter out packets from outside the network that have a local network source address.

Do it!

A-5:   Port scanning

Here's how	Here's why
1 In Internet Explorer, under Scanning Tools, click **SuperScan™**	You will use SuperScan, which is a connection-based TCP port scanner, pinger, and hostname resolver, to scan IP addresses.
2 Download the tool	
3 Click **Save**	
Save the file to the Net Admin##\Downloads folder	
4 Click **Open Folder**	
5 Right-click **superscan4** and choose **Extract All...**	
Click **Extract**	
6 Right-click **SuperScan4** and choose **Run as administrator**	
Click **Run** and click **Allow**	
7 Enter your Start IP address for your network	(You recorded this range in the previous activity.)
Press (TAB)	The end IP address is automatically entered for the subnet based on the IP address you entered.
8 Click the arrow button next to the IP address range	To add the starting and ending IP addresses to the scanned range.
9 Click the blue Start arrow	It is located at the bottom left corner of the SuperScan 4.0 window.
	Again, a scan of this type is often detected by a network administrator and might violate computer use policies if permission has not been granted to perform the scan.
10 Review the results in HTML	The IP address of the host performing the scan isn't included in the list because no ports are open on the host performing the scan. By default, hosts without open ports are not listed.
	The ports that are open on the system are of great use to attackers.

11   What information is displayed in
     the scan results?

12   Close all open windows

Topic B: Threat mitigation

This topic covers the following CompTIA Network+ 2009 exam objectives.

Bridge objective

#	Objective
4.2	**Identify types of configuration management documentation** • Wiring schematics • Physical and logical network diagrams • Baselines • Policies, procedures and configurations • Regulations
6.6	**Identify common security threats and mitigation techniques** • Policies and procedures • User training

Security policies

Explanation

Every organization should have a well-defined *security policy*, as well as a human resources policy that outlines and defines the organization's commitment to information security. Working together, the Information Technology staff and senior management create the security policy. It defines rules and practices the organization puts in place to manage and protect information within the organization.

The security policy document defines the security program's policy goals and who is responsible for making sure those goals are achieved. Within the security policy there should be sections covering:

- Acceptable use
- Due care
- Privacy
- Separation of duties
- Need-to-know information
- Password management
- Account expiration
- Service level agreements
- How to destroy or dispose of equipment, media, and printed documents

A sample security policy is shown in Exhibit 7-3.

XYZ, Inc. Security Policy

Each individual employee of XYZ, Inc. has the responsibility to protect informational assets of the organization along with all intellectual property of the organization. The assets need to be protected to reduce potential negative impact on XYZ's clients. Security of information is critical and should be integrated into all facets of XYZ's operations.

To ensure that these objectives are met, polices and procedures have been developed to assure secure practices are used at XYZ. Information security is a high priority at XYZ and detailed procedures have been developed to secure the information.

XYZ is required to abide by specific privacy laws and regulations defined by state and federal laws. Failure to abide by these regulations might result in fines, legal actions, audits, and customer confidence could be affected; this could result in direct financial losses to the organization. Every employee of XYZ therefore must be responsible to all pertinent laws and regulations.

Exhibit 7-3: Sample Security Policy

Acceptable use

Acceptable-use policies define how an organization's computer equipment and network resources can be used. The main goal is to protect the organization's information and to limit the potential liabilities and legal action against the organization or its users. It also might address the productivity of users as it relates to Internet use.

The misuse of computer resources and its impact on business activity can affect the productivity of an organization and its users. Many people use the organization's Internet connection for personal use, and it is important that they not use it to access resources that might reflect poorly on the organization. The time used for personal Internet use can have a big impact on productivity and lead to loss of revenue for the organization. Organization information might be compromised if users share sensitive information with external parties or access sexually explicit or socially unacceptable Web pages. An organization could be held legally responsible for agreements made by a user made with an e-mail address from the organization.

The acceptable-use policy needs to identify whether specific actions are appropriate use of company resources and time. An organization should require employees to read and sign the policy when they are hired, and the organization should keep a copy of the signed document in the employee's HR file. If there is reason to believe that a violation has occurred, this document will help absolve the organization of responsibility in the matter. The measures for enforcing the policy also need to be documented so that all employees are aware of the consequences of their actions.

Due care

The exercise of judgment or care that someone would exercise in a given circumstance is known as *due care* or *due diligence*. It identifies the risks to the organization and assesses those risks and the measures employees need to take to ensure the security of the organization's information.

If a major security incident occurred within the organization, the organization might be sued by the customers, business partners, shareholders, and others who were negatively impacted by the incident. Creating and abiding by a strong security policy helps an organization prove that due care was exercised which can help protect the organization from legal actions against it.

Privacy

Security policies also need to address the privacy and protection of customer and supplier information. Trust between the organization and external entities can be strengthened when both parties know that the information is secure. Because this information could be highly sensitive, it is imperative that the organization show its respect for the external entities' information. This information might include contracts, sales documents, financial data, or personally identifiable information. If the information is compromised, the entities might not only lose their trust in an organization, but they might also take legal action against the organization for the exposure of their information.

Separation of duties

In any situation where too much of a process falls to one person, there is the potential for abuse. If the function is too valuable to do without, as is the case with an organization's information assets, then it is imperative that no one person is given the power to abuse the trust others place in the information's security.

No one in the organization should be irreplaceable, because eventually the person likely will be replaced, and the smoother the transition, the better. Sometimes employees purposely poorly document their work so that it will be harder to replace them. The company might face a dilemma: pay this person what they demand, or face possible problems when the person leaves. The best strategy is to make sure the next person does not leave you in such a predicament.

Another reason to separate duties is that if the person with all of the knowledge suddenly leaves the company or dies in a tragic accident, then all of their knowledge is gone with the person. This would require that someone else quickly be put in place, possibly without adequate training, leaving the information vulnerable to attack while the new person learns the role.

By distributing security tasks throughout the IT staff and documenting all procedures, this can help alleviate such issues. If someone leaves the company, then other people know how to handle the security concerns. Also, by sharing the tasks, no one person has all of the power, so there is less chance of abusing control.

The security function should be separated into multiple elements. Each of those elements is part of making the whole security structure work. Each of the elements is assigned to a different person or group of persons. This helps alleviate abuse of power and assures that you have someone in place if one person suddenly becomes unavailable.

Need to know

In the case of very sensitive information, only those who absolutely must have access to the data should have it. This is referred to as being need-to-know information. The goal is to make unauthorized access highly unlikely to occur without unduly hassling users who have authorized access.

Giving employees on the Information Technology team just enough permissions to perform their duties is an example of where this might come into play. This *least privilege* basis of access prevents an employee from putting the company at risk. Users should be given permission to access only the information they need to access. For example, not every employee needs access to the organization's marketing plan, and certainly most employees don't need access to HR or IT databases. Those employees who do need access to that information need to be given explicit access.

Password management

Implementing a strong password policy is an important part of your organization's security policies. The policy must be clear to the users so that they can adhere to it and create strong passwords. Passwords are used on workstations, networks, Web sites, and even on entry doors. The risk of mismanaged passwords needs to be addressed with good password policies.

Sometimes organizations underestimate the need for password management policy complexities. When this happens, the company's information and network assets are at risk. Policies should address several attributes including:

- Minimum password length
- Required characters (minimum number of alphabetic, numeric, and/or special characters)
- Password reset interval (how long the password is good for before changing the password)
- Re-use of passwords including variations on existing passwords

The policy should also address users' handling of their passwords. The policy should state the consequences for revealing a password to someone, under what circumstances it can be done, and what to do after it has been revealed. For example, if an IT technician needs the password to troubleshoot a user's e-mail problem, then using a secure method, the user can give the technician the password; when the technician is finished, the user needs to immediately change the password.

When feasible, domain password policies should be set in Active Directory using Group Policy. The network team should routinely check for weak passwords. They can use password cracking tools to locate any weak passwords. If any are found, the user should be notified immediately and measures should be taken to educate the user on how to create a strong password and to reset the weak password.

Account expiration

Unneeded user accounts must be deleted or at the least disabled. Some systems enable you to automatically disable unused accounts. For example, if a user doesn't log on for 30 days, their account is automatically disabled. You should implement such a feature, if available. Or, you should routinely scan for unused accounts, especially those associated with former staff.

Obviously, your expiration period will need to take into account vacations, holidays, sabbaticals, maternity leave, and so forth. However, it is not uncommon for accounts to be disabled (but not deleted) during extended leaves.

Service-level agreements

A contract documenting the service level between a service provider and the end user is known as a *service-level agreement* (*SLA*). This binding document specifies the service levels for support. It should also document any penalties for the service level not being met by the provider. Disaster recovery plans also need to be documented within the SLA.

In addition, there need to be contingency plans to be implemented in case the provider is unable to meet their obligations. This might happen if the entire area is in the midst of a weather-related event preventing local service providers from being able to respond. Initial recovery period plans for ensuring business continuity should be covered as well.

Disposal and destruction

It is just as important to secure discarded and unused documents and equipment as it is to secure them while they are in use. Simply deleting files or reformatting disks doesn't eradicate all of the information necessarily.

Magnetic media should be degaussed, which demagnetizes the media and thus makes anything on the media unreadable. An alternative approach is to overwrite all of the data with zeros which is referred to as *zeroization*. If neither of this is enough to ensure the safety of the organization's information, you can physically destroy the media by breaking the media apart and making it unusable. Sometimes all of these techniques are used together to ensure that nobody will ever have a chance at reading the media ever again.

Hard copies of important information also need to be destroyed. Documents should be placed in locked recycle bins and then shredded or burned, or both. Document shredding companies can be hired to do the shredding. A bonded and insured technician shreds the documents on-site under the supervision of someone from the organization into the smallest possible size so that the documents have no chance of being pieced back together.

Not all data deserves the same level of protection. Some data is simply not that critical or secret. Likewise, not all obsolete data and equipment deserves the same disposal treatment. You should classify data and equipment according to their protection and disposal needs.

Those items that contain sensitive or secret information warrant more thorough destruction practices. For example, you might be able to get away with simply erasing less sensitive information from a hard drive. But you would need to physically destroy obsolete hard drives containing your company's financial records. Handling disposal according to your classifications can save money, and ensure that you have the resources to properly dispose of the most sensitive items.

Do it!   **B-1:   Creating a security policy**

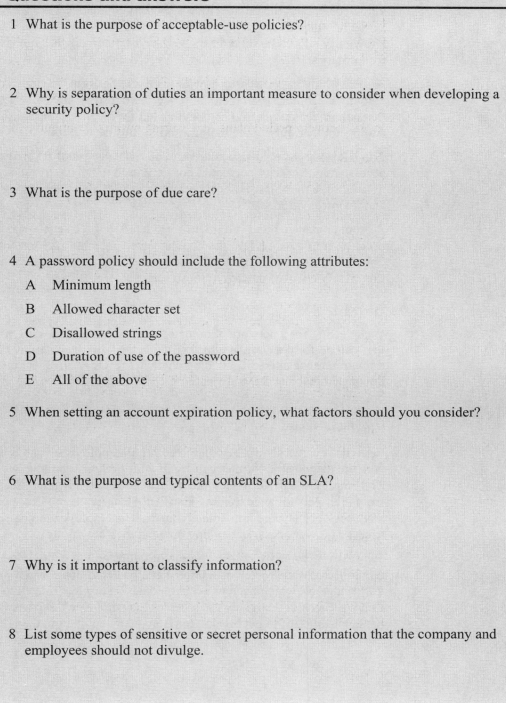

Questions and answers

1 What is the purpose of acceptable-use policies?

2 Why is separation of duties an important measure to consider when developing a security policy?

3 What is the purpose of due care?

4 A password policy should include the following attributes:

   A   Minimum length

   B   Allowed character set

   C   Disallowed strings

   D   Duration of use of the password

   E   All of the above

5 When setting an account expiration policy, what factors should you consider?

6 What is the purpose and typical contents of an SLA?

7 Why is it important to classify information?

8 List some types of sensitive or secret personal information that the company and employees should not divulge.

Human resources policy

Explanation

Redundant knowledge is as important as redundant hardware. If staffing places all of the knowledge about the organization's security policies in one person's hands, and something happens to that person, then nobody else will know what to do. The knowledge should be shared by several staff members through cross-training of the technology staff.

Another thing to consider is how to manually perform the duties that are usually automated. If there is an incident rendering hardware unavailable, whenever possible, manual procedures should be documented for business continuity. This might mean adding another duty to technology staffs' jobs descriptions.

The HR policy should also address issues such as use of ID badges, keys, and restricted access areas. Security personnel not only need to adhere to such policies, but be able to help enforce those issues on other employees to ensure the security of the organization and its information.

Personnel management should be considered in three separate aspects. The hiring process, employee review and maintenance, and employee termination all should be documented in the HR policy. The employee's status on the security team should be thoroughly checked at each of those stages.

Hiring

When hiring for a network administrator or security team staff position, it is imperative that you perform a complete background check on the potential candidate. This includes doing reference checks (including character references), checking with past employers, doing criminal checks, and verifying certifications and degrees the candidate claims to possess.

Employee review and maintenance

Periodic reviews should be conducted for all employees. This is especially true of those who are responsible for the security of your organization's network and information. The employee's performance can be evaluated and any potential security risks arising from their performance can be identified. Security clearances should be evaluated and any necessary change immediately made. The employee might need higher security access or lower access depending on what they are doing.

Job rotation, time off, and separation of duties policies should be implemented for employees. At the review meetings it can be determined which jobs the employee has knowledge of, which need to be learned, and if any skills need to be refreshed. Another thing to check at the reviews is whether the employee has been using their vacation or personal-time-off to get breaks from the job as outlined in the HR policies.

Post-employment

The HR policy should document the procedures to be taken when an employee's employment is terminated with the organization. Part of the process should be an exit interview with an HR staff member. This meeting should be done in a friendly, professional manner.

Angry employees might act out against the company and could threaten the security of the network and of the information within the organization. For this reason, security badges, keys, and other access devices should be retrieved from any employee ending employment with the organization. After the exit interview a manager, security guard, or HR representative should escort the employee to clean out their personal belongings and escort them from the premises.

All of the employee's accounts should be disabled at this time as well. Any shared passwords need to be changed immediately.

Code of ethics

The code of ethics helps define the organization's information security policies. The code of ethics policy requests that all personnel are responsible, act legally, and are honest; these actions help protect the organization. The code of ethics should also document aspects of conduct such as employees providing proficient service to all persons they come into contact with within their professional duties when representing the organization. Being ethical in the performance of their duties, the employees help prove the reliability of the organization to customers, suppliers, and other employees.

Do it! **B-2:   Creating a human resources policy**

Questions and answers

1   Why should periodic reviews be part of a human resource policy?

2   How does job rotation help minimize security risks?

3   What is a benefit of separation of duties?

4   Why would forcing staff members to take a vacation benefit an organization, particularly from a security standpoint?

5   Identify the tasks your human resource policy should address when an employee is terminated.

6   Explain why a code of ethics in a human resource policy can help maintain information security.

Incident response policy

Explanation

A security breach or disaster should be dealt with following the details in the *incident response policy*. An incident is an event that adversely affects the network. Incidents might include viruses, system failure, unauthorized access, or service disruption. It also includes any attempt to violate the organization's security policies.

There can be numerous legal consequences depending on the way that people and automatic processes respond to an incident. Client information must be handled with due care so as not to compromise confidential information. An incident that isn't quickly brought under control can quickly turn expensive and complicated. A rise in incident occurrences can be sometimes linked to incompetent handling of an initial incident.

By developing and implementing a solid incident response plan, the organization cuts down on the probability that incidents will not be handled properly. A solidly formed incident response plan helps the organization exercise due care.

A solid incident response policy addresses six areas:

1 Preparation
2 Detection
3 Containment
4 Eradication
5 Recovery
6 Follow-up

Preparation

It is important that you have steps in place to cope with an incident before it occurs. Resources need to be made available to quickly and efficiently respond to an incident.

It is equally important to balance easy access to system resources with effective system controls that help prevent an incident. Having resources in place to balance these two diverse conditions is part of the preparation phase. Resources used to respond to an incident need to be resistant to attacks as well.

The preparation step of the incident response document needs to identify the steps to be taken by the incident response team members and under the circumstances that the steps should be taken. A detailed contact list of the team members and the information that needs to be shared with each team member needs to be included in the document.

Acceptable risks should be documented in the preparation step. It also should identify the dedicated hardware and software to be used for analysis and forensics of the incident. All incident response team members need to be trained in handling incidents.

Doing due diligence as part of the preparation phase will help the organization carry on if an incident occurs. A documented contingency plan will help the organization get through the trying time a data disaster brings. Determining tolerable risk levels will also help the organization plan for a successful incident response if the time comes when it must be implemented.

Detection

The first action the incident response team needs to take when an incident occurs is to assess the state of affairs and then try to figure out what might have caused the incident. Next, the team needs to estimate the scope of the incident to help them figure out how to deal with the incident. The team needs to ask questions and document responses to questions such as:

- How many systems were impacted?
- How many networks were impacted?
- How far did the intruder get into the internal network?
- What level of privileges was accessed?
- What information and/or systems are at risk?
- How many paths of attack were available?
- Who has knowledge of the incident?
- How extensive is the vulnerability?

The response team needs to document information about the incident. The document needs to be shared with the Chief Information Officer, any personnel affected by the incident, the public relations department, the rest of the incident response team, the legal department, and if appropriate any law enforcement or government agencies. The incident response policy should identify what needs to be reported. This might include fundamental details about the incident that need to be included in the report, the incident type, the resources being used to deal with the incident, the source of the incident, consequences of the incident, and the sensitivity of any compromised data. The policy also should specify when and how the information about the incident is shared.

Containment

For each incident that occurs, you will need to determine the containment techniques to implement. In some cases you might need to shut down a system to prevent further damage from occurring. A piece of hardware or a file system might need to be taken off-line. You might need to alter firewall filtering rules. Login accounts might need to be suspended until the incident is under control. File transfers should be disabled as well.

Monitoring levels should be increased. After an intruder has gained access to your network, it is even more important to keep an eye on what is happening. This will help determine how deeply into the network the intruder has penetrated.

If the incident is the result of a malicious attack, any compromised equipment or data should not be used until the incident has been resolved. The response team should alert the appropriate people to analyze the incident. Information gathered at this point in the process can be used to identify the perpetrator and to help prevent additional attacks.

Eradication

After the incident has been contained, the incident response team needs to eradicate whatever caused the incident. If the incident was related to viruses or malicious code, the affected files need to be cleaned or deleted. If you need to restore data to drives, verify first that the backups are free of viruses and malicious code.

Recovery

After the incident has been eradicated from the network or system that was compromised, the recovery step of the process can occur. The incident response policy should document where new equipment should be ordered from if any equipment was damaged or compromised. Procedures should be documented and worked out with suppliers for quick replacement of equipment. Arrangements might be put in place for the organization to obtain borrowed or vendor-sponsored equipment if mission critical equipment was affected so that the organization can function as close to normally as possible during recovery.

If the file system was affected, you should consider doing a full system restore. This is time consuming, but is the best assurance that the network is back to its normal state. Data should be restored from the most recent full back-up after you have made sure that it is free of any viruses or malicious code. If you use a RAID system, you can attempt to recover data from the redundant drives.

Passwords should be changed after an incident. It is difficult to determine whether an attacker was able to get a hold of passwords, thus compromising them.

Follow-up

Your incident response policy should include a follow-up step to help the recovery team learn from what happened. The entire process should be documented; this can justify the expense the organization incurs in implementing the security policy and for the incident response team. The incident response documents can be used as training material for new recovery team members. The documentation can also be used for any legal proceedings that result from the incident.

Do it!   **B-3:   Creating an incident response and reporting policy**

Questions and answers

1 What are some of the actions that should be part of the incident response preparation phase?

2 Which step comes first, Containment or Eradication? Why?

3 Identify containment methods that might need to be considered during an incident response.

4 What needs to be done during the recovery phase?

5 What are the benefits of completing the follow-up phase?

Change management

Explanation   Whenever a network change is made, a set of procedures called change management is followed. These procedures are developed by the network staff. All changes to the IT infrastructure need to be documented.

The change management process is initiated with a request for change (RFC) document. This records the change, the category that the change falls into, and any other items the change might impact.

Next, the RFC is sent through an approval process where it is reviewed. A priority is set, and it is assigned to whoever will make the change. If it is determined that the change is not to be made, this decision is documented. Depending on the scope of the RFC it will be evaluated by an IT manager or by a change advisory board (CAB). CABs are formed with representatives from various departments affected by the change, possibly including HR. All of the discussions related to the RFC are documented.

The RFC is scheduled and a proposed completion time is set. The change is then planned, developed, tested and implemented by the person or team to which the RFC was assigned. All of this is documented in the RFC log.

The change is complete when both the change owner and the requester verify that the change has been successfully implemented.

The RFC is reviewed by all parties involved, and the change is closed.

Achieving security through consistency

Develop a change management process around your network. Whenever there are network upgrades, whether patches, the addition of new users, or updating a firewall, you should document the process and procedures. If you are thorough in documenting the process, you limit your security risks. When you add new users to the network, do you always do the same thing? What if you forget a step? Is your security breached? Be methodical and follow a written process.

Configuration management documentation

Even before you begin to plan changes to a network, you must consult your organization's change management documentation, which can include any of the types in the following table.

Type	Used to document
Wiring schematics	The location of network wiring throughout the organization. Schematics provide a detailed map of wire locations that you can use to troubleshoot and repair physical wiring problems or make changes to the wiring layout if you need to expand or reconfigure the physical network layout.
Physical network diagram	The location of client computers, servers, network printers, routers, switches, firewall, wireless access points, and other devices and hardware in the network. You can easily see where these devices are in relation to one another, and which network assets you currently have deployed.
Logical network diagram	IP addressing and subnet information. You use this information to ensure that all devices have the correct addressing information and troubleshoot connectivity problems.
Baseline	Performance statistics for computers and other devices in the network. You record a device's baseline performance when you add it to the network. You can then compare its performance on any given day to the baseline you've saved to help determine if the device is operating properly.
Policies, procedures, and configurations	An organization's policies and procedures as they relate to the IT department and the network implementation.
Regulations	Any state or federal regulations that affect an organization's IT implementation, including local wiring and electrical regulations, and any HR regulations that govern users' work on computers and the network.

In addition to architecture documentation, each individual system should have a separate document that describes its initial state and all subsequent changes. This includes configuration information, a list of patches applied, backup records, and even details about suspected breaches. Printouts of hash results and system dates of critical system files may be pasted into this book.

System maintenance can be made much smoother with a comprehensive change document. For instance, when a patch is available for an operating system, it typically only applies in certain situations. Manually investigating the applicability of a patch on every possible target system can be very time consuming; however, if logs are available for reference, the process is much quicker and more accurate.

Do it!   **B-4:   Implementing change management**

Here's how	Here's why
1 Use Internet Explorer to access **www.sunviewsoftware.com/solutions/chgmgmt.aspx**	
In the Microsoft Phishing Filter, select **Ask me later**	You will examine an example of change management software.
2 Click **Product Tour**	
3 Activate the **Change Management** tab	To examine the Change Management product.
Read through the information	To see examples of the types of information captured in the management software, click the thumbnail pictures on the right side of the window. Click Close to return to the Online Tour page.
4 Active the **CMDB** tab	To see examples of software you can use to document network assets. Examine the pictures on the right.
5 How would you use these products to manage changes?	
6 Close Internet Explorer	
7 Close and save the state Microsoft Virtual PC	

Education

Explanation

Educating staff about security risks is a cost-effective investment in the organization's protection of information assets. Network administrators and end users all need to be educated about systems and security to create an environment that prevents accidental loss of data. Knowledge about the security procedures in place within the organization enables all network users to be part of the organization's security team. It also might enable a regular user to spot a potential security issue or even a security violation.

As long as they are properly secured, making security policy resources and references available to all employees of the organization provides access to information that might not have been covered during formal training sessions. If the resources and references aren't properly secured, an attacker could have access to the policies that would provide them with information on how by bypass security blocks.

The training should be customized to provide the level of knowledge needed by different groups of users. A big-picture level of knowledge of security policies is appropriate for end users. A detailed level of knowledge is required for administrative users. An exhaustive level of knowledge is required for employees that are in charge of security within the organization, including detailed knowledge of all policies and procedures.

Communication

One of the things users should learn in their training about security is what information can be shared and who they can share that information with. They also need to know what information should never be shared, such as user names and passwords.

If a technician needs to help the user troubleshoot a problem, and needs access to the user's username and password, the user should be taught the importance of immediately changing his or her password upon completion of the work. They should also learn that the technician needs to show proof of identify in order to prevent someone posing as a technician from gaining system access. The user should be taught that it is important if possible to stay with the technician while they are working on the system to make sure that the technician isn't looking through data on the user's computer or on the network.

The training should also include information about social engineering threats including how they are conducted and what kinds of information attackers usually are seeking in such an attack. In addition, user training should cover the types of information that might inadvertently be revealed through casual conversation that could be of use to an attacker in guessing a username or password.

User awareness

All personnel should have security training so that they know what measures they should take to help ensure the security of the organization's information. The training should be based on and reflect the policy objectives of the organization.

The following items should be included in user security training:

- The reason for the training
- Security contacts for the organization
- Who to contact if they suspect or encounter a security incident
- The actions to take if they suspect or encounter a security incident
- Policies regarding the use of system accounts
- Polices related to access and control of system media
- Approved techniques for sanitizing (degaussing, overwriting, or destruction) media and hard copies
- How to maintain the security of system accounts (including sharing of passwords)
- Policies regarding installation, removal, and use of applications, databases, and data
- Policies regarding use of the Internet, the Web, and e-mail

To reinforce formal training, users can be kept aware of the information presented in the training sessions. You can remind users of the security policies through such means as logon banners, system access forms, and departmental bulletins.

B-5: Identifying the need for user education and training

Questions and answers

1 How important is it that end-users are educated about security issues?

2 How can training about security help users keep information secure?

3 List some of the topics that should be covered in end-user targeted security training.

4 Identify some of the ways users might be reminded periodically of the information learned in formal security training.

Types of training

Explanation
There are a variety of ways personnel can be trained. Some training might be delivered on-the-job, as part of a classroom experience, or taken in an on-line training format. Some information might be delivered best in one way over another. Some personnel might find one format more beneficial to their learning style than other formats.

On-the-job training

Nobody wants to have to deal with a security incident, but when one does occur, you should take advantage of the experience to learn all you can about it. You need to know how to detect the incident, how to respond, how to clean it up, and how to recover from it. The next time a similar incident occurs, you'll have learned how to deal with it.

Documenting the steps taken in response to the incident serves as training as well. The act of recording this information helps reinforce it, and you have the information in case it happens again. It can also be used as an example in other training, such as classroom or online training sessions.

An advantage of this type of training is that it lets new personnel get hands on experience in dealing with incidents. However, without having some other training, it will be difficult for them to be effective in many cases.

Classroom training

A course such as the one you are taking right now is a good investment in training administrative personnel in how to keep the network secure. A course based on incidences that have occurred within your organization is also beneficial. It can be difficult to fit such classroom training into a busy IT person's schedule, but the time and investment will pay off with personnel knowing how to secure the network and how to react when an incident does occur.

An advantage of classroom training is that students can share their personal experiences. Especially if it is a public class with students from various organizations, one or more students might have experienced a security incident and could share how they dealt with it.

Online resources

Because it can be difficult to gather personnel together to deliver classroom training, online delivery of training is an effective training method. Policy and procedure training can also be delivered online.

You might have someone create training documents and store them on a company's network to which users and/or IT personnel have access. You could also consider storing the organization's security and disaster recovery policies and procedures on an internal Web site or intranet site. To make sure that all personnel who need to review these documents have done so, you could create questions based on the documents that students have to turn in to management. The sites can include text as well as multi-media content, such as audio and video files.

You could also enroll personnel in on-line courses created and presented by training organizations. Many of these courses are facilitated by on-line instructors and in some cases students can earn continuing-education credits by taking the courses.

IT personnel should also use resources on the Internet, such as knowledge bases and manufacturer's support Web sites to help troubleshoot problems and obtain software updates and fixes.

Do it!

B-6: Identifying education opportunities and methods

Questions and answers

1 List advantages of on-the-job, classroom, and online training.

2 List disadvantages of on-the-job, classroom, and online training.

3 Which type of training would work best in your organization? Why?

Unit summary: Security threats and mitigation

Topic A   In this topic, you learned about common security threats, such as **DoS**, **viruses**, **worms**, **man in the middle**, and **phishing**. You learned what these attacks are and how devastating they can be to a network.

Topic B   In this topic, you learned how to mitigate security threats. You learned about **security policies** and **incident response policies**. You then learned about educating users and providing them with important security information.

Review questions

1   Rather than destroying or stealing data, a _____DoS_____ attack is designed to disrupt daily standard operation.

2   _____Syn_____ attacks flood a server with half open TCP connections which prevent users from being able to access the server.

3   A smurf attack overwhelms a host by flooding it with _____Icmp_____ packets.

4   The target systems in a DDoS attack use _____Zombies_____ which are later woken up to launch the attack.

5   Man-in-the-middle attacks can be used for what types of attacks? Tcp Hijacking

6   _____Appreptable use_____ policies address the use of computer equipment and network resources for personal use or use that doesn't benefit the organization.

7   _____Due diligence_____ means that reasonable precautions are being taken which indicates that the organization is being responsible.

8   Least privilege refers to employees having only information that they _____. Need to know

9   Why is it necessary to have a disposal and destruction of computer equipment policy? security of info

10 How does the code of ethics in a human resources policy relate to computer security? How users Act

11 *Incident Response Policy*
    _____ policies detail how a security break or disaster is dealt with.

12 *Change management*
    _____ policies describe the set of procedures followed whenever a network change is made.

13 True or false? It is important when training users to alert them to ways that attackers attempt to gather personally identifiable information and information about the organization's network.

14 List some of the items a dumpster diver seeks.

15 A *Trojan Horse* _____ is a program that poses as something else, causing the user to 'willingly' inflict the attack on himself or herself.

16 List at least three primary causes for compromised security.
   configuration   mal Functions

17 Why can't computer equipment just be thrown in with the regular trash?
   same as #9

Independent practice activity

In this activity, you will do the following:

1 Identify the tools you need to launch protocol-based attacks in the lab.

2 Identify the tools you need to identify the attacks and prevent them from recurring.

3 Using a paper and pencil, create a physical diagram of the network. Use simple diagrams to document computers and other devices. Ask for assistance as necessary to determine which devices are on the network that might not be readily visible to you.

4 Using the physical diagram as your starting point, create a logical network diagram of the network in the classroom or lab. Ask for assistance as necessary to find any relevant addressing information.

Unit 8

Security practices

Unit time: 180 minutes

Complete this unit, and you'll know how to:

A Secure an operating system.

B Secure network devices.

Topic A: Operating systems

This topic covers the following CompTIA Network+ 2009 exam objectives.

Bridge objective

#	Objective
6.1	**Explain the function of hardware and software security devices**
	• Host based firewall
6.6	**Identify common security threats and mitigation techniques**
	• Mitigation techniques
	• Patches and updates

Antivirus software

Explanation

To stop viruses and worms, you should install antivirus software on individual computers, servers, and other network devices, such as firewalls. Most antivirus software runs a *real-time antivirus scanner*. A real-time antivirus scanner is software that's designed to scan every file accessed on a computer so it can catch viruses and worms before they can infect a computer. This software runs each time a computer is turned on.

Using a real-time scanner helps antivirus software stop infections from different sources, including a Web browser, e-mail attachment, storage media, or local area network.

Most antivirus software works by using a checksum, a value that is calculated by applying a mathematical formula to data. When the data is transmitted, the checksum is recalculated. If the checksums don't match, the data has been altered, possibly by a virus or worm. The process of calculating and recording checksums to protect against viruses and worms is called *inoculation*.

Definition files

Antivirus software must be updated to stay abreast of new viruses and worms. The software can find only threats that it knows to look for; therefore, the antivirus software manufacturer constantly provides updates, called *virus definitions*, to the software as new viruses and worms are discovered. It's important to use antivirus software that automatically checks and updates its virus definitions from the manufacturer's Web site. Having outdated virus definitions is the number one cause of virus or worm infection.

Antivirus products

The following table lists several antivirus software products and their manufacturers' Web sites. Most of these sites offer detailed information about common viruses and worms. They even offer removal tools you can download for free that you can use to remove worms and viruses from infected computers.

Software	Web site address
Norton AntiVirus by Symantec, Inc.	www.symantec.com
ESET Smart Security	www.eset.com
McAfee VirusScan by McAfee Associates, Inc.	www.mcafee.com
ESafe by Aladdin Knowledge Systems, Ltd	www.esafe.com
F-Prot by FRISK Software International	www.f-prot.com
PC-cillin by Trend Micro (for home use)	www.trendmicro.com
NeaTSuite by Trend Micro (for networks)	
avast! by ALWIL Software	www.avast.com

E-mail servers should also have antivirus software installed to protect computers on your local area network. Microsoft Forefront is an example of network antivirus software that scans all inbound and outbound e-mail, filters e-mail based on attachment type, and blocks spam.

Do it!

A-1: Installing antivirus software

Here's how	Here's why
1 On the Windows Vista computer, use Internet Explorer to download the Professional version of avast! from the avast.com Web site Save the executable file to your desktop	You're logged on to as the domain user hostadmin##.
2 Follow the prompts complete a Typical install of the software	
3 When prompted to perform a boot time scan of your computer, click **Yes**	
4 Restart your computer	Your computer scans when you reboot. Note the name and location of the report file: _____ When the scan is complete, avast! briefly displays a summary report of files scanned and infections found.
5 Log on back on to the domain as **hostadmin##**	
6 Click the avast! On-Access Scanner icon in the system tray Scroll through the list of information being protected	It's the blue icon with an "a" on it. The status should be Active.
Click **OK**	To close the avast! window.

Spyware

Explanation

Spyware is software that is installed on a system without your knowledge. It can cause a lot of problems for the user, including gathering personal or other sensitive information. Spyware can also change the computer's configuration. For example, it might change the home page in a browser. In addition, it often displays advertisements, which has earned this type of spyware the name *adware*. All of this can slow down a computer's performance.

Spyware is often installed when you are installing another application, especially free applications that you download from the Internet. For this reason, you need to be sure that you know exactly what you are installing. In some cases, the license agreement and privacy statement state that the spyware will be installed, but most people tend not to read those documents very closely. Spyware is often found on peer-to-peer and file-sharing networks. Spyware can also integrate itself into Internet Explorer, causing frequent browser crashes.

Windows Vista and Windows Server 2008 include built-in anti-spyware software called *Windows Defender*. This real-time protection software makes recommendations to the user when it detects spyware. In addition to the real-time protection, you can also schedule it to perform scans.

When Windows Defender detects spyware on your computer, it displays information about the threat, including the location on your computer, a rating of the risk it poses to you and your information, and its recommendation as to what action you should take. The alert levels include:

Alert level	Description
Severe	Especially malicious programs that will affect the privacy and security of your computer and could even damage your system.
High	Spyware programs that might affect the privacy and security of your computer and could damage your system. The changes the program makes to your computer are usually done without your consent.
Medium	Spyware programs that could potentially gather personal information or make system changes and have a negative impact on your computer's performance. The software will not be automatically deleted. You will need to evaluate the way the software operates and determine whether it poses a threat to your system. If the publisher of the software is unfamiliar to you or is an untrusted publisher, you should block or remove the software.
Low	This software was typically installed with your knowledge, but still might collect information or change the configuration of the computer. If the software was installed without your knowledge, review the alert details and determine whether you want to remove it.
Not yet classified	These programs typically do no harm unless they were installed without your knowledge. If you don't recognize the publisher or the software, evaluate the alert details to determine your course of action.

If clients are running Windows XP with SP2 installed or you have Windows Server 2003 with SP1 installed, you can download Windows Defender from Microsoft and install it on those systems to protect them. Windows Defender comes with Windows Server 2008.

Do it!   ## A-2:   Scanning your system for spyware

Here's how	Here's why
1 In Windows Vista, open Windows Security Center	(It's in Control Panel.)
2 In the left pane, click **Windows Defender**	
3 Click **Tools**	
Under Settings, click **Options**	
4 Verify "Automatically scan my computer (recommended)" is checked	
If necessary, check **Check for updated definitions before scanning**	
If necessary, check **Apply default actions to items detected during a scan**	
5 Display the "High alert items" list	The default setting is to perform the action based on the definition for the items detected.
Close the "High alert items" list	
6 If you made changes, click **Save** and then click **Continue**	To save your changes and close the Options window.
If the settings were already set, click **Cancel**	
7 Click **Scan**	To perform a quick scan. If you want to do a full scan, you'll need to go into Options and set the Type to "Full system scan" and then schedule a scan.
8 After the scan is complete, click the Help button	The Help button is a blue circle containing a white question mark.
If prompted, click **Yes**	To allow Windows Help and Support to search online for updated content.
Under the heading Getting started, click **Understanding Windows Defender alert levels**	
9 Review the alert levels	The chart indicates the actions that are taken when items for each alert level are detected.

10 Close Help and Windows
    Defender but leave Windows
    Security Center open

11 Are all examples of spyware also
    adware?

Securing the operating system

Explanation

Hardening is the process of modifying an operating system's default configuration to make it more secure from outside threats. This process might include removing unnecessary programs and services, setting access privileges, and applying hotfixes, patches, and updates to limit operating system vulnerability.

Security-related problems are often identified only after the OS has been released. Even after the problems have been identified and fixes issued, it still takes time to become aware of the problem, obtain the necessary patches, and install them. The gap between the identification of the problem and the installation of fixes gives potential intruders an opportunity to exploit the security breach and launch related attacks on the system. Typically Windows has more security vulnerabilities than other operating systems, such as Apple Macintosh and Unix/Linux.

To control such risks, network administrators and technicians should keep track of security-related announcements that apply to their systems. Depending on how critical the exposure is, the administrator might choose to disable the affected software until the hotfix, patch, or update can be applied to deal with the risk. Permanent fixes from vendors should be tested and then applied as they are made available.

Hotfixes

Hotfixes fix errors in the operating system code. These errors are discovered after the operating system has been released. The hotfixes often replace specific files with revised versions.

Patches

Patches are temporary or quick fixes. They are designed to fix security vulnerabilities. Patches can also be used to fix compatibility or operating issues.

Updates

Updates enhance the operating system and some of its features. In addition, updates are issued to improve computer security. They also are used to improve the ease of use and to add functionality. Updates can also improve the performance of the operating system on your computer.

Service packs

Periodically Microsoft releases service packs for operating systems. They contain a collection of updates as a single installation. A service pack is usually issued when a certain number of individual updates is reached. Usually service packs contain updates, but they might also contain new features.

As an example, Windows Vista Service Pack 1 (SP1) contains all of the updates that were issued during the first year of Vista's release. It makes the system more efficient and reliable, but doesn't add any new features.

Some service packs require that previous updates were installed. Others include all of the updates in the latest service pack so that you don't need to install other updates first.

In some cases the service pack will be installed as part of the Automatic Update process. For some other operating systems and applications, you will need to manually install the service pack. Refer to the documentation available with the service pack to determine how it will be installed.

Was it installed?

To determine whether a Windows service pack has been installed on a computer, you need to look at the information in the System Information window. You access this information by clicking Start, right-clicking on Computer, and then choosing Properties. The window that's displayed is the System window. In the Windows edition portion of the window it will indicate if the service pack has been installed.

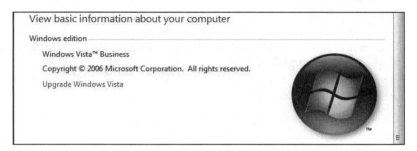

Exhibit 8-1: Windows edition information including service pack.

Windows Update

In the Windows Security Center in Windows Vista and Windows Server 2008, you can enable Windows Update. This is turned on by default. When you enable Windows Update and new updates are available from Microsoft, the Windows operating system typically downloads new updates to your computer and then installs them. This installs updates for the Windows operating system plus Microsoft applications such as Microsoft Office.

To enable automatic updates in Windows Vista and Windows Server 2008, open Control Panel and click Security. In the Security window you can then configure Windows Update.

If you want to test the hotfixes, patches, and updates before they are installed, be sure to turn off automatic updating on the computers. You can then download them manually to a test environment and evaluate them before installing them on the rest of the computers in your environment. In large environments, you typically implement a Windows Server Update Services (WSUS) server to update all Windows computers on your network. You can use WSUS to prevent Windows computers from installing any downloaded updates until you approve them.

The default setting in both Windows Vista and Windows Server 2008 is to automatically download and install the updates at 3 AM every day. You can instead configure computers to download the updates and then prompt you to install them. You can also have the computer check for updates and then prompt you to download and install them. The final option is to disable the Automatic Updates feature.

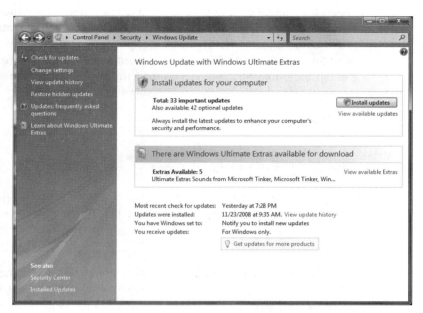

Exhibit 8-2: The Choose how Windows can install updates options

There are three categories of updates that are available through Windows Update. The Important and Recommended updates are automatically downloaded and installed by default. Windows Vista and Windows Server 2008 do not automatically download and install optional updates. Instead, you must manually download and install these updates. Important updates address security and reliability issues. Recommended updates typically deal with enhanced computer experience. Optional updates address driver issues and other software besides the operating system.

Automatic Update failures

If Windows Update reports that it failed to install an update, you can manually download and install the update directly from Microsoft's Downloads site. The update should reference a Microsoft Knowledge Base article, such as KB947562. Use this number to find the update on Microsoft's site.

Do it!

A-3: Updating the operating system

Here's how	Here's why
1 In Windows Security Center, click **Windows Update**	
Click **Change settings**	
Select **Download updates but let me choose whether to install them**	
2 Click **OK**, and click **Continue**	To allow Security Center to continue. Your computer connects to Microsoft's Web site and searches for updates.

3 If necessary, install updated Windows Update software

Windows Update will close and re-open, and then it will check for updates automatically.

4 In Windows Update, click **View available updates**

A list of updates available for installation is displayed. You can check or uncheck which updates will be installed.

5 With all updates checked, click **Install**

If prompted, accept any license terms

If prompted, in the User Account Control box, click **Continue**

The selected updates are downloaded and then installed. The progress bar in the Windows Update window keeps you informed about the progress of the task.

When prompted, click **Restart now**

(The Windows Server 2008 virtual machine should be closed.) To reboot the computer. Some updates require rebooting.

6 Log back on to the domain as hostadmin## and open Security Center

7 Click **Windows Update**

Sometimes a reboot must be done before additional updates are installed. If so, continue installing updates after the reboot.

8 If Windows Update doesn't report it is up to date, click **Check for updates**

In the left pane of the window.

9 If any updates are found, install them

To install any updates available since the last updates were downloaded and installed.

If prompted, reboot and log back on

10 Continue checking for and installing updates until Windows reports it is up to date

The Windows Update window should be open for the next activity.

Patch management

Explanation

You can review the updates that have been installed on your computer. In the Windows Update window, click View update history. You now see a list of all updates installed. The listing includes the name of the update, whether it was successfully installed, the type of update, and the date it was installed.

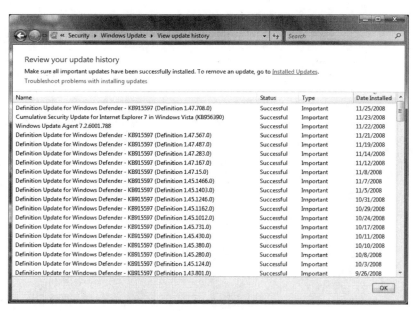

Exhibit 8-3: The Update history list

You can also remove updates by clicking the Installed Updates link on the Review your update history page. Not all updates can be uninstalled. If they can be, after you select the update, Windows Vista displays Uninstall in the toolbar. You can then click Uninstall to remove the update. You should uninstall an update only if you encountered a problem after the update was installed. If another update is issued that will fix the problem, Windows Update will take care of this for you though.

Do it!

A-4: Managing software patches

Here's how	Here's why
1 From the Windows Update window, click **View update history**	If necessary, reopen Windows Update.
2 Review the list of updates that were installed	All of the updates should have a Successful Status. The updates might be Recommended, Optional, or Important.
3 Click **Installed Updates**	This link is in the text at the top of the page.
4 Select various updates and watch to see which ones display the Uninstall icon on the toolbar	Don't click the Uninstall button. Some updates can't be uninstalled.
5 Close all open windows	

Other updates

Explanation   While patch management for operating systems (especially Windows) is the bulk of the updating you'll need to stay on top of, other network devices such as routers might also need periodic updates. How you perform the updates will depend on the type of device and the manufacturer. Be sure to consult the appropriate documentation before beginning the update.

Firmware

Like operating system weaknesses, firmware weaknesses are built-in vulnerabilities. Usually, these result from mistakes or oversights by equipment designers rather than being purposeful "back doors." The problems come to light after the device is released and many users have a chance to fully use and stress its capabilities. Most vendors quickly release firmware or software updates to fix such problems.

Higher-functioning devices such as routers are in essence specialized computers. These devices run their own custom operating system software, which is inextricably intertwined with the management functions of the device. Cisco's IOS (Internetwork Operating System) is an example of such software.

BIOS updates

The BIOS that comes in your computer usually doesn't need to be updated. However, in some cases you might need to upgrade your BIOS. Your computer manufacturer will know whether device problems are caused by BIOS problems. Also, if new technology becomes available that isn't supported by the current BIOS, the computer manufacturer might release a new version of the BIOS that includes support for it. BIOS manufacturers don't supply consumers with updates. They are released to the computer manufacturers who built the BIOS into the computers.

You can find the version of BIOS installed in your system by using the System Information tool.

To determine the version of BIOS installed in your computer:

1   Click Start and choose All Programs, Accessories, Run. In the Run dialog box enter msinfo32.

2   With System Summary selected in the System Information window, record the value listed in the BIOS Version/Date field. This field lists BIOS version data, which you can use to determine if a newer version is available on your PC maker's Web site.

3   If it's present, record the value listed in the SMBIOS Version field. The SMBIOS is used by PC inventorying programs to collect data about your computer. SMBIOS updates are usually included with BIOS updates. Not all PCs include SMBIOS, however—particularly older computers.

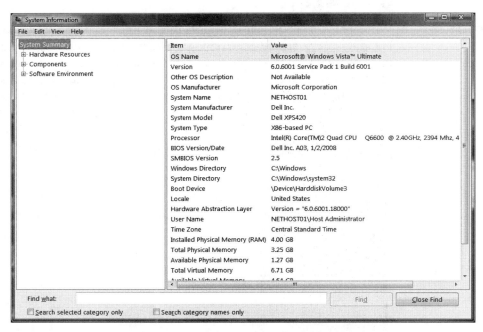

Exhibit 8-4: The System Information utility displays the BIOS version

Do it!

A-5: Determining BIOS version

Here's how	Here's why
1 In Windows Vista, click **Start** and in the Search box type **msinfo32**	
Press (↵ ENTER)	To display the System Information window.
2 Record your BIOS and SMBIOS information	Manufacturer: Version: Date: SMBIOS Version:
3 Close System Information	
4 Visit your PC manufacturer's Web site and determine if a newer version of the BIOS is available	
5 Is a newer BIOS version available?	
6 Close all open windows	

Windows Firewall

Explanation

Windows Firewall is a host-based software firewall that's turned on by default in Windows Vista and Windows Server 2008. However, if a third-party firewall is installed on the computer, the Windows Firewall is turned off. If a user is experiencing problems sending or receiving data, the problem could be that the current firewall settings are preventing the communication from passing through. You might need to allow a specific type of communication—that's prohibited by default—to pass through the firewall. When you need to configure Windows Firewall, open the Security Center then click Windows Firewall to open the Windows Firewall dialog box, as shown in Exhibit 8-5.

Exhibit 8-5: The Windows Firewall dialog box

You can use this dialog box to turn the firewall on and off, and you can click Change Settings and then use the Exceptions tab to allow or deny specific types of network communication based on application or TCP/UDP port. The settings on the Advanced tab let you configure firewall protection for multiple network connections.

To manage the log file and configure Internet Control Message Protocol (ICMP) settings, open the Windows Firewall with Advanced Security console from Administrative Tools.

Do it!

A-6: Configuring Windows Firewall

Here's how	Here's why
1 In Windows Vista, open the Windows Security Center	
2 In the left pane, click **Windows Firewall**	To open the Windows Firewall window.
3 Click **Change settings**	
Click **Continue**	
Activate the **Exceptions** tab	This is where you select the programs or ports you want to create exceptions for.
4 Activate the **Advanced** tab	Here you can specify which network connections you want to use Windows Firewall.
5 Click **Cancel**	
6 Close all open windows	

Topic B: Devices

This topic covers the following CompTIA Network+ 2009 exam objectives.

#	Objective
Bridge objective **6.1**	**Explain the function of hardware and software security devices**
	• Network based firewall
	• IDS
	• IPS
	• VPN concentrator
Bridge objective **6.2**	**Explain common features of a firewall**
	• Application layer vs. network layer
	• Stateful vs. stateless
	• Scanning services
	• Content filtering
	• Signature identification
	• Zones
Bridge objective **6.3**	**Explain the methods of network access security**
	• Filtering:
	• ACL
	• MAC filtering
	• IP filtering
Bridge objective **6.5**	**Explain issues that affect device security**
	• Physical security
	• Restricting local and remote access
	• Secure methods vs. unsecure methods
	• SSH, HTTPS, SNMPv3, SFTP, SCP
	• TELNET, HTTP, FTP, RSH, RCP, SNMPv1/2

Firewalls and proxy servers

Explanation

A *firewall* is a device that controls traffic between networks, typically between a public network and private internal network. Firewalls examine the contents of network traffic and permit or block transmission based on rules.

At their core, all firewalls protect networks using some combination of the following techniques:

- Network address translation (NAT)
- Basic packet filtering
- Stateful packet inspection (SPI)
- Access control lists (ACL)

Basic firewalls use only one technique, usually NAT, but firewalls that are more comprehensive use all of the techniques combined. Of course, as you add features, complexity and cost increase. Depending on the features you need, you can get firewalls that operate at various levels of the TCP/IP protocol stack:

- *Network layer firewalls*, also called packet filters, operate at layer 3 (IP addresses). Stateless packet filters examine IP addresses and ports to determine if a packet should be passed. Stateful packet filters monitor outbound and inbound traffic, by watching addresses, ports, and connection data. Stateful packet filters can determine if a packet is part of an existing communication stream or a new stream.

- *Application layer firewalls* "understand" the data contained in packets and thus can enforce more complex rules. For example, an application layer firewall might determine that an inbound packet is carrying an HTTP (Web) request and is going to a permitted address and port. Such a packet would be transmitted. Packets carrying other protocols or going to other addresses might be blocked.

Proxy servers

A *proxy server* is a type of firewall that services requests on behalf of clients. With a proxy server, a client's request is not actually sent to the remote host. Instead, it goes to the proxy server, which then sends the request to the remote host on behalf of the client. Before sending the packet, the proxy server replaces the original sender's address and other identifying information with its own. When the response arrives, the proxy server looks up the original client's information, updates the incoming packet, and forwards it to the client.

By these actions, a proxy server masks internal IP addresses like a NAT device. It also blocks unwanted inbound traffic—there will be no corresponding outbound connection data in its tables so the packets will be dropped. Many proxy servers also provide caching functions. The contents of popular Web pages, for example, could be saved on the proxy server and served from there rather than by sending requests out across a wide area network link.

Internet content filters

Arguably, an Internet content filter could be described as a form of firewall or proxy. Content filters, also called Web filtering or even censorware, are software that examines HTTP (Web) traffic, blocking access to sites deemed by the software to be inappropriate. Some ISPs include content filtering in their service offerings, typically as an add-on and often at a monthly fee. You can also purchase applications, such as NetNanny (ContentWatch) or CYBERsitter (Solid Oak Software), to install on your own computer.

Do it!   **B-1:   Examining firewalls and proxy servers**

Questions and answers

1 Describe the primary difference between a proxy server and application layer firewall.

2 True or false? Firewalls operate at layer 2 of the protocol stack.

3 Does your company use a firewall and if so, what features does it offer that encouraged your company to select it versus another firewall solution?

4 Does your company use a proxy server and if so, do you use it for caching WWW requests, filtering content, or masking internal IP addresses?

5 Describe the pros and cons of using Internet content filter software.

Security zones

Any network that is connected (directly or indirectly) to your organization, but is not controlled by your organization, represents a risk. To alleviate these risks, security professionals create *security zones* which divide the network into areas of similar levels of security (trusted, semi-trusted, and untrusted). You create the security zones by putting all your publicly accessed servers in one zone and restricted-access servers in another, then separating both from an external network like the Internet using firewalls.

The three main zones into which networks are commonly divided are the intranet, perimeter network, and extranet.

Intranet

The *intranet* is the organization's private network; this network is fully controlled by the company and is trusted. The intranet typically contains confidential or proprietary information relevant to the company and, consequently, restricts access to internal employees only. The private internal LAN(s) are protected from other security zones by one or more firewalls, which restrict incoming traffic from both the public and DMZ zones.

As an additional safeguard to prevent intrusion, intranets use private address spaces. These IP addresses are reserved for private use by any internal network and are not routable on the Internet. The following address ranges are reserved:

- Class A   10.0.0.0 – 10.255.255.255
- Class B   172.16.0.0 – 172.31.255.255
- Class C   192.168.0.0 – 192.168.255.255   *on Test*

Additional security measures include:

- Installing anti-virus software
- Removing unnecessary services from mission-critical servers
- Auditing the critical systems configurations and resources
- Subnetting to divide the intranet into distinct segments and isolating unrelated traffic

Perimeter network

You have various options for connecting your network to a public, insecure network such as the Internet. The topology you choose will have a profound impact on the security of your network and its hosts.

Small networks, such as those in users' homes or at small businesses, will often be directly connected to the Internet over a connection provided by an ISP. Such connections should always be secured through the use of a firewall. A typical configuration involves a cable or DSL connection and a hardware-based firewall built into a router, which might include wired or wireless internal network connections.

In such topologies, connections are permitted from inside the network to points on the Internet. However, unsolicited connections from the Internet to nodes on the internal network are blocked. Of course, you could permit some connections to the internal network by opening selected ports. But that is rarely needed.

Larger networks, or when access to internal systems is regularly needed, often use a different topology. These systems often employ a perimeter network, kept separate from the intranet. A perimeter network is also known as a *demilitarized zone* (DMZ).

DMZ configurations

A DMZ is an area between the private network (intranet) and a public network (extranet) such as the Internet. A DMZ isn't a direct part of either network but is instead an additional network between the two networks.

Computers in the DMZ are accessible to nodes on both the Internet and intranet. Typically, computers within the DMZ have limited access to nodes on the intranet. However, direct connections between the Internet and nodes on the internal network are blocked.

You can set up a DMZ in several ways:

- Screened host
- Bastion host
- Three-homed firewall
- Back-to-back firewall
- Dead zone

Screened host

With a screened host, a router is used to filter all traffic to the private intranet but also to allow full access to the computer in the DMZ. The router is solely responsible for protecting the private network (see Exhibit 8-6). The IP address of the DMZ host is entered in the router configuration. This IP address is allowed full Internet access, but other computers on the network are protected behind the firewall provided by the router. The disadvantage of this setup is that sometimes a router firewall can fail and allow traffic through to the intranet.

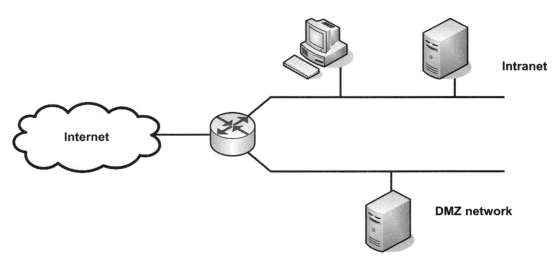

Exhibit 8-6: A screened host DMZ

In addition to using a router to protect a network, an administrator can also use subnets and subnet masks to protect the private network from a screened host. If the screened host is on one subnet and all other computers on the private intranet are on another subnet, if the screened host is penetrated, the intranet on another subnet is less likely to be compromised.

Bastion host

Another DMZ configuration is the bastion host. The word *bastion* means a protruding part of a fortified wall or rampart. Bastion hosts are computers that stand outside the protected network and are exposed to an attack by using two network cards, one for the DMZ and one for the intranet, as shown in Exhibit 8-7. Network communication isn't allowed between the two network cards in the bastion host server, or, if it is allowed, the bastion host must be the proxy server to the network. With this configuration, only one host, the bastion host, can be directly accessed from the public network. Bastion hosts are also known as *dual-homed hosts* or *dual-homed firewalls*.

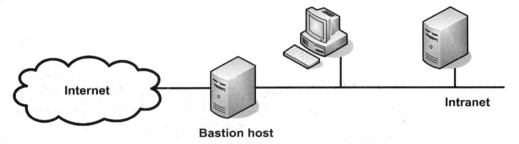

Exhibit 8-7: Bastion host

Three-homed firewall

If there are several computers in the DMZ, such as a Web server, a DNS server, and an FTP server, you can use a *three-homed firewall* (see Exhibit 8-8). In such a configuration, the entry point to the DMZ requires three network cards. One network card is connected to the Internet, one to the DMZ network (or perimeter network), and the final network card to the intranet. Firewall software, such as Microsoft Internet Security and Acceleration Server, is required to control traffic on the server or group of servers that have these three network cards installed. Traffic is never allowed to flow directly from the Internet to the private intranet without filtering through the DMZ.

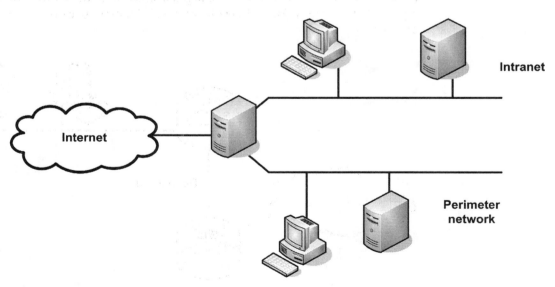

Exhibit 8-8: A three-homed firewall

Back-to-back firewall

The *back-to-back firewall* configuration offers some of the best protection for networks. In this design, the DMZ network is located between two firewalls, as shown in Exhibit 8-9. The two firewalls between the Internet and the DMZ and the DMZ and the intranet each have two network cards. In addition, the server within the DMZ has two network cards. Although this design offers exceptional protection, it's also expensive and complicated to implement. Therefore, only those companies that require the highest level of security generally use it.

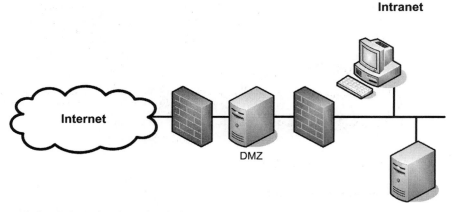

Exhibit 8-9: A back-to-back firewall

Dead zone

A *dead zone* is a network between two routers that uses another network protocol other than TCP/IP. If the DMZ is using some other protocol, such as IPX/SPX, this network between the two routers is a dead zone. This is the most secure of all DMZ configurations, but it comes with a price. Network protocol switching must happen at each router for communication to take place among the networks. This configuration is especially resistant to Ping of Death and SYN flooding, because these attacks depend on TCP/IP.

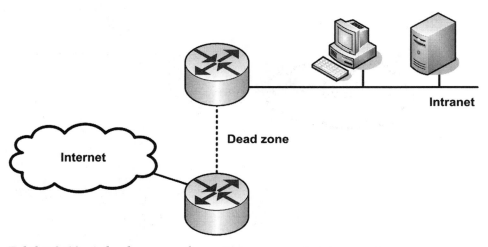

Exhibit 8-10: A dead zone configuration

Traffic filtering

You can set up filtering rules that control the flow of packets between the three zones: intranet, perimeter network, and extranet. You would configure such rules in your firewalls and routers. Unwanted packets could be dropped, or you could configure intrusion detection alarms—console notifications, e-mails, log entries, and so forth.

Filter outgoing traffic

You might filter outgoing traffic that originates from a DMZ computer. Doing so would prevent an attack in which a hacker configures a DMZ computer to initiate communications with his or her host. It would also keep your DMZ computers from being used as traffic-generating agents in distributed denial-of-service (DDoS) attacks.

However, you might have legitimate reasons for your DMZ computers to initiate communications with remote hosts. For example, the mail server in your DMZ might periodically contact a remote mail host to download mail messages. Your local DNS server will likely initiate contacts to higher-level DNS servers in order to keep tables up to date. Make sure you know all the legitimate data flows in use before configuring a firewall rule that might drop critical data packets.

Filter incoming traffic

You might filter incoming traffic. For instance, at the interface between your DMZ and intranet, you would want to block all traffic with a source network address other than that of your DMZ. Such traffic is likely spoofed traffic associated with an attack.

You will also likely configure the firewall between your DMZ and the extranet to filter some types of incoming traffic. For example, you might permit only inbound connections to your mail servers while dropping all other uninitiated inbound traffic.

Do it!

B-2: Comparing firewall-based secure topologies

Questions and answers

1 How does a NAT differ from a DMZ?

2 A computer that resides in a DMZ and hosts Web, mail, DNS, and/or FTP services is called a _____ _____.

3 Some of the features of a DMZ are:

A It is a network segment between two routers.

B Its servers are publicly accessible.

C Its servers have lower security requirements than other internal servers.

D It commonly contains bastion, public Web, FTP, DNS, and RADIUS servers.

E All of the above.

Network Access Control

Explanation

Computers on your network should adhere to your corporate security policy. For example, let's say your policy dictates that all computers on your network run an up-to-date antivirus program. How do you know that the antivirus definitions are actually current? Is the computer running a firewall? Is the operating system up-to-date?

Consider what might happen if a laptop that has been disconnected from your network has become infected with a virus, and is then reconnected to your network. All of your systems might be vulnerable to attacks from this laptop.

Network Access Control (NAC) is the means to ensure that computers comply with your policies. NAC is a process or architecture through which computers are verified to be in compliance, and brought into compliance if they fall short, before they are permitted access to the network.

Microsoft's implementation of NAC is called Network Access Protection (NAP). It is a new feature of Windows Server 2008. Cisco offers the Network Admission Control architecture, and the Trusted Computing Group's Trusted Network Connect (TNC) system are other implementations of NAC.

Vendors, such as Microsoft, Juniper, IBM, Computer Associates, and Cisco, offer NAC components. These tools work together to support an overall NAC architecture. For example, IBM's Tivoli network management system might be the central reporting and management console for other NAC components, such as an antivirus scanner from Computer Associates.

Do it!

B-3: Identifying the benefits of NAC

Questions and answers
1 Why might you want to implement NAC on your network?
2 Is NAC a product you buy?

Virtual private network

Explanation

A *virtual private network* (*VPN*) is a private communications network transmitted across a public, typically insecure, network connection. With a VPN, a company can extend a virtual LAN segment to employees working from home by transmitting data securely across the Internet. A VPN represents a means of providing secure communications across the extranet zone.

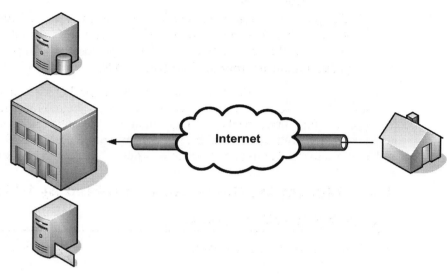

Exhibit 8-11: A typical VPN using Point of Presence (POP)

With a VPN, TCP/IP communications are encrypted and then packaged within another TCP/IP packet stream. The VPN hardware or software can either encrypt just the underlying data in a packet or the entire packet itself before wrapping it in another IP packet for delivery. If a packet on the public network is intercepted along the way, the encrypted contents cannot be read by a hacker. Such encryption of data or packets is typically implemented by using Internet Protocol Security (IPsec). *VPN concentrators* offer high-performance remote VPN access to the local network for anywhere from 100 to thousands of remote employees.

IPsec encryption

IPsec was initially developed for Internet Protocol version 6 (IPv6), but many current IPv4 devices support it as well. IPsec enables two types of encryption. With *transport encryption*, the underlying data in a packet is encrypted and placed within a new packet on the public network. With *tunnel encryption*, the entire packet including its header are encrypted and then placed in the public network's packet.

The following steps illustrate the process:

1   A remote user opens a VPN connection between his computer and his office network. The office network and the user's computer (or their respective VPN gateways) execute a handshake and establish a secure connection by exchanging private keys.

2   The user then makes a request for a particular file.

3   Assuming that the user has sufficient rights, the network begins to send the file to the user by first breaking the file into packets.

- If the VPN is using transport encryption, then the packet's data is encrypted, and the packets are sent on their way.

- If the system is using tunneling encryption, then each packet is encrypted and placed inside another IP envelope with a new address arranged for by the VPN gateways.

4   The packets are sent along the Internet until they are received at the user's VPN device, where the encryption is removed and the file is rebuilt. If the VPN is using tunneling encryption, the peer VPN gateway forwards the decrypted packets to the appropriate host on its LAN.

With IPsec in place, a VPN can virtually eliminate packet sniffing and identity spoofing. This is because only the sending and receiving computers hold the keys to encrypt and decrypt the packets being sent across the public network. Anyone sniffing the packets would have no idea of their content and might not even be able to determine the source and destination of the request.

Do it!

B-4:   Identifying the security enabled by VPNs

Questions and answers

1   What could you use a VPN for?

2   Which encryption method encrypts the entire packet including its header before packaging it into the public network's packet stream?

A   CHAP

B   IPsec

C   Tunneling

D   Transport

3   Do you have to use IPsec to enable a VPN?

Security issues

Explanation

Your network devices present a tempting target for hackers. If they gain virtual or physical access to your device, they could disrupt your network or even gain access to the data flowing over it. Devices present the following general vulnerability points:

- Built-in management interfaces
- Physical attack susceptibility

Built-in management interfaces

Devices such as switches, routers, and firewalls, include management interfaces so that you can monitor or configure them without physically visiting the device. You might use a Web browser, TELNET application, or SNMP console to connect to and manage these devices. Such interfaces are a crucial feature for many of these devices. However, they're also an opportunity for attacks. Attackers attempt to log in, using default account credentials, in order to gain escalated permissions and take control of your device.

Security problems with switches

Switch hijacking occurs when an unauthorized person is able to obtain administrator privileges of a switch and modify its configuration. Once a switch has been compromised, the hacker can do a variety of things, such as changing the administrator password on the switch, turning off ports to critical systems, reconfiguring VLANs to allow one or more systems to talk to systems they shouldn't, or they might configure the switch to bypass the firewall altogether. There are two common ways to obtain unauthorized access to a switch: trying default passwords, which might not have been changed, and sniffing the network to get the administrator password via SNMP or TELNET.

Almost all switches come with multiple accounts with default passwords, and in some cases, no password at all. While most administrators know enough to change the administrator password for the TELNET and serial console accounts, sometimes people don't know to change the SNMP (Simple Network Management Protocol) strings that provide remote access to the switch. If the default SNMP strings are not changed or disabled, hackers might be able to obtain a great deal of information about the network or even gain total control of the switch. The Internet is full of sites that list the various switch types, their administrator accounts, SNMP connection strings, and passwords.

If the default password(s) do not work, the switch can still be compromised if a hacker is sniffing the network using a protocol analyzer while an administrator is logging on to the switch. Contrary to popular belief, it's very possible to sniff the network when on some switches. This means that even if you change the administrator password(s) and the SNMP strings, you might still be vulnerable to switch hijacking.

The easiest way to sniff a switched network is to use a software tool called "dsniff," which tricks the switch into sending packets destined to other systems to the sniffer. Dsniff not only captures packets on switched networks, but also has the functionality to automatically decode passwords from insecure protocols such as TELNET, HTTP, and SNMP, which are commonly used to manage switches.

Secure and unsecure connection methods

Some methods for communicating with network devices and computers are more secure than others. Several common protocol and their levels of security are discussed in the following table.

Protocol	Description
Telnet	A utility that enables a host to connect and run a session on another host through remote terminal emulation. It uses TCP for acknowledgement. Telnet isn't a very secure communication method.
HTTP, HTTPS, SHTTP	Hypertext Transfer Protocol is the standard for transferring data been Web servers and Web browsers. HTTPS uses Secure Sockets Layer (SSL) to encrypt TCP/IP communications. Transport Layer Security (TLS) replaces SSL in newer implementations. Both SSL and TLS encrypt packets for Transport layer protocols. Files exchanged using Secure HTTP are either encrypted or contain a digital certificate, or both.
FTP, SFTP, TFTP	File Transfer Protocol is used to support unencrypted authentication and file transfer between similar or dissimilar systems. Secure FTP is used for secure, encrypted file transfers. Secure FTP is officially FTP over SSH. Trivial FTP uses UDP for less overhead and thus is faster than FTP. On the other hand, TFTP is less reliable than FTP. TFTP doesn't enable you to list the contents of a directory. TFTP is also less secure than FTP.
SNMP	Simple Network Management Protocol collects management statistics and trap error events information between TCP/IP hosts using UDP. It enables remote device control and management of parameters.
SSH and SCP	Secure Shell (SSH) enables users to securely access a remote computer. All passwords and data are encrypted. A digital certificate is used for authentication. Secure Copy (SCP) uses SSH for data encryption and authentication when copying data between computers.
RSH and RCP	Remote Shell is a Unix command used to execute commands as another user or on a remote device or computer. Data is not encrypted as it's sent across the network. Remote Copy is another Unix command that you can use to copy files from one host to another. Like RCP, it sends information unencrypted across the network.

Physical attack susceptibility

Devices are susceptible to attack whenever someone gains physical access. The range of possible attacks is nearly limitless. Someone could simply steal your router, server, or switch. They might do so in the case of a server or external storage device so that they could work to bypass data security controls at their leisure.

In the case of networking appliances, hackers are more likely to attempt to reconfigure the device to block traffic or permit unwanted communications. Another form of physical susceptibility involves access to your communications medium. Such problems can lead to eavesdropping or even network hijacking.

Network hijacking

If a hacker has physical access to your network, he or she can mount attacks that could disrupt or reroute your communications. Consider what would happen if a hacker were able to put their own router onto your network. The server could be configured to send packets to the wrong destinations or cause packets to simply be lost along the way.

This might sound far-fetched, but it has happened on the Internet. The *BGP (Border Gateway Protocol)* is susceptible to an attack known as prefix hijacking. In this scheme, a rogue router is placed on the network with a modified routing table. The table is configured to report that the router can service various network routes. When packets are sent via that router, they are either dropped or sent to the wrong locations.

With bus topology networks, stations are attached to the backbone via *vampire taps*, also called piercing taps. These devices clamp around the network cable, pierce its insulation, and make contact with the conductors within. Vampire taps are rarely used in modern networks. If you use an older style bus network, or if you use broadband copper backbones to span long distances, your network could be susceptible to physical attack by someone attaching a vampire tap to your network cable.

Fiber taps are devices that work in a somewhat similar fashion. In normal operations, the light flowing down a fiber reflects completely within the fiber with none escaping through the walls of the fiber strand. However, at sharp bends in the strand, some light can escape. Fiber taps can take advantage of this by capturing that light to give an attacker access to your network transmissions. Such taps are often easy to detect due to the attenuation they introduce into the line.

Another such problem would be Wi-Fi Hijacking. In this scheme, a hacker configures his or her computer to present itself as a wireless router. So, you're at the coffee shop and think you're connecting to the shop's router when in fact you're connecting to the hacker's computer. He then has the option to intercept your communications or even access your computer's files.

Do it!   **B-5:   Identifying inherent weaknesses in network devices**

Questions and answers

1   What is switch hijacking?

2   What are some malicious acts someone could perform if he or she had physical access to your network's communication medium?

3   What are the default administrator user names and passwords for Linksys and DLink brand routers? (Hint: Use your favorite search engine if you don't already know the answer.)

Overcoming device weaknesses

Network and security administrators need to be aware of the vulnerabilities of their hardware and software systems. If you work in such a role, you will need to take specific actions to limit your risk of attacks. These include:

- Changing default passwords
- Disabling features, protocols, and options you do not need
- Applying firmware and software updates regularly
- Monitoring physical and virtual access to your network and devices

Change default passwords

Always set strong passwords on network devices. Passwords should be seemingly random strings of letters, numbers, and punctuation characters. Use long passwords of more than eight characters if supported by your device.

A device might offer multiple accounts, such as one for TELNET access and another for browser-based access. Make sure that you change default passwords and user IDs for all access methods.

Many switches and routers use TELNET or HTTP—both being open text protocols— for management. Wi-Fi routers sometimes permit management access over both wired and wireless interfaces.

You need to limit the chances that your management passwords will be discovered. You should perform management of devices via a serial port connection or by using a secure shell (SSH) or another encrypted communications channel if available. For wireless devices, when possible, perform management functions over wired connections only.

Disable features, protocols, and options you do not need

When installing or reconfiguring a device, turn off options and protocols that you do not need and won't use. For example, unless you absolutely need to enable a LAN client to reconfigure your Internet router, you should turn off UPnP (Universal Plug and Play). There are known vulnerabilities in UPnP.

For wireless devices, disable access to management functions via wireless connections. For wired devices, turn off protocols (such as SNMP or TELNET) that you won't be using for management.

Apply firmware and software updates regularly

You must stay alert for notices of new updates and then take action quickly to prevent problems. If your software vendor provides regular notices of updates, for example via e-mail or RSS, make sure to subscribe and read the notices regularly. Then, as they become available, you should quickly test and then install firmware and OS updates.

Monitor physical and virtual access to your network and devices

Cameras and key-card entry systems provide a way to monitor physical access to network devices. However, simple awareness might be the key to catching someone trying to access your network media.

Network monitoring software will enable you to monitor access to servers. You will need to rely on device logs to monitor access to non-server devices. If supported, you should collect such logs regularly to a central console for archiving and examination.

Do it!   **B-6:   Examining the ways to overcome device threats**

Questions and answers

1 List the four tasks you should undertake to overcome device threats:

2 What is the advantage of disabling features or services you don't need?

3 Should you immediately apply firmware and other device software updates?

Intrusion detection and prevention

Explanation   Intrusion detection is the process of detecting and possibly reacting to an attack on your network or hosts. Intrusion detection systems (IDS) monitor key network points, network devices, and important hosts for anomalous activity. For example, a pattern or volume of network traffic might indicate an attack on your network.

Intrusion detection and monitoring systems can generally be classified as follows.

Classification	Description
Anomaly-based	IDS compares the current state of your system to a baseline, looking for differences that would signal an attack or compromised system.
Behavior-based	The IDS monitors your system for behaviors that would be typical of a compromised system. For example, if a client workstation begins sending a large volume of e-mail messages, the IDS may flag that as indicative of a system infected with a virus, which is sending itself to unsuspecting users.
Signature-based	The IDS monitors your system based on signatures, much like antivirus scanners use virus definitions to look for infected files.

Once an activity is identified as malicious, the IDS can take either passive actions (logging, sending alerts, and so forth) or reactive actions (dropping packets, ending user sessions, stopping applications, and so forth). A reactive IDS is often called an intrusion prevention system (IPS).

Network intrusion detection systems (NIDS) are devices or systems designed to monitor network traffic on a segment or at a network entry point, such as a firewall. NIDS monitor network traffic volumes and watch for malicious traffic and suspicious patterns. Depending on where you located a NIDS, it can monitor some or all of your network. A reactive NIDS is sometimes called a NIPS (network intrusion prevention system).

Host intrusion detection systems (HIDS) are typically software-based systems for monitoring the health and security of a particular host. HIDS monitor operating system files for unauthorized changes, watch for unusual usage patterns, or failed logon requests.

When analyzing an event, an IDS can make one of four possible determinations.

Determination	Description
True negative	A true negative determination indicates that the IDS has correctly identified the event as a normal, non-threatening action. In other words, the IDS correctly determined that normal network or system activities occurred.
True positive	A true positive indicates that the IDS has correctly identified an attack or breach of security.
False positive	A false positive means that the IDS has incorrectly identified normal or benign activity as being a sign of an attack or breach. The pattern of activity has fooled the IDS into thinking malicious acts are being carried out when in fact normal user activity is occurring.
False negative	A false negative is the worst situation: the IDS has misidentified an attack or breach as normal or benign activity. In the case of a false negative, your network or host is under attack, and the IDS is not detecting this situation.

The administrator of an IDS will typically spend considerable time at first tuning the system to correctly identify the many events the system will monitor. As time goes on, if he or she correctly tunes the system, fewer false positive and negative readings will be made. During the initial tuning time, you will need to be diligent to not only tune the IDS but to follow up each potential attack to be sure your system is not actually being breached.

Do it!

B-7: Discussing IDS characteristics

Questions and answers

1 Considering a network protected by a firewall, why would you want to implement an IDS (either NIDS or HIDS)?

2 You want to detect and thwart attacks against the server in your perimeter network. Would you implement a NIDS, NIPS, or HIDS?

3 Describe a false positive event example.

4 Describe a false negative event example.

5 Which of the IDS classifications—anomaly-based, behavior-based, and signature-based—requires the least on-going interaction by a network administrator? Does that make it the best system?

NIDS

Explanation
NIDS, network intrusion detection systems, are typically dedicated devices or single purpose hosts running specialized software. A NIDS often uses two network interfaces. One is placed in promiscuous mode, meaning that it reads all packets that pass by rather than reading only those for its specific MAC address. This interface analyzes the network traffic to look for patterns of suspicious behavior. This interface does not have a network address and cannot be used for normal networking activities.

The second network interface connects to the network so that the NIDS can send alerts, interface with management ports on network devices, and so forth. Through this port, you can also remotely administer the NIDS, if it supports such actions.

Network location

Where you place a NIDS determines what portion of your network it can monitor. This does not imply that you should choose the location to maximize the extent of coverage. Instead, you should locate a NIDS where it can monitor the most crucial or valuable network resources. For example, you might put a NIDS on the segment on which your primary corporate servers are also located. Other typical locations for NIDS include on your perimeter network segment or integrated with your firewall to monitor incoming traffic.

Indicators of malicious activity

NIDS can be configured to watch for various anomalous conditions which might indicate an attack. These include:

- String signatures—the NIDS watches for text within the packet's payload which matches specific patterns. For example, this might include watching for strings that contain command-line entries that might compromise a password file. String signatures are system-dependent and are also subject to change as new vulnerabilities are discovered and exploited.
- Port signatures—the NIDS monitors connections to specific ports on selected hosts. For example, you might configure a NIDS to monitor for attempted connections to TCP port 23, which is the TELNET service port number. Such attempts might represent an attempted attack.
- Header signatures—the NIDS watches for specific patterns of header fields that are either known to be dangerous or are simply illogical (possibly representing a new type of attack).

For such signature-based monitoring, you must regularly update the NIDS. For example, you might need to enter new string signatures, update monitored ports, and so forth. Some commercial systems offer subscription services to make such updates simple or automatic. (However, such subscriptions would not include port signatures as those are dependent on your specific network configuration.)

Not all malicious activity is indicated by the contents of the packets analyzed by the NIDS. A large quantity of packets targeting a specific host or coming from a single address might indicate a denial of service attack. Profile-based detection builds a statistical profile of normal activity and considers activities that fall outside that profile to be potential attacks. Successful profile-based detection does not depend on up-to-date signature files.

Active reaction options

A NIDS can take various actions to respond to an indicator of malicious activity.

- TCP reset—The NIDS sends a TCP reset packet to the victim host, which terminates all current sessions. In many cases, this will halt an attack that is in progress. TCP resets do not block the initial packet sent to the victim, which means they are not effective in halting all forms of attack.

- Shunning—Also called blocking, shunning involves automatically dropping packets from the attacker. Typically, the NIDS would connect to the firewall and create a temporary rule that would drop all packets coming in from the attacker.

- Antivirus scanning and cleaning—Some NIDS examine packet contents to detect virus-infected payloads. When appropriately configured, these NIDS can also attempt to remove the virus from the payload before transmitting the packets.

Passive reaction options

In addition to active responses, a NIDS can also take these passive actions during an attack:

- IP session logging—The NIDS logs some or all of the traffic between the attacker and victim hosts for later forensics and investigations.

- Alerts—The NIDS can send various alerts, including console messages, e-mails, pager messages, and so forth to in essence request human intervention.

NIDS examples

Examples of commercial NIDS include Cisco's IOS NIDS (www.cisco.com) and Computer Associates' eTrust Intrusion Detection (www.ca.com). Examples of free or open source NIDS include Snort (www.snort.org) and Untangle (www.untangle.com).

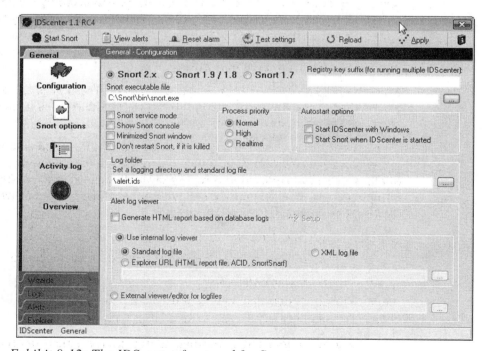

Exhibit 8-12: The IDScenter front-end for Snort

HIDS

Host-based intrusion detection systems are software that runs on a host computer, monitoring that system for signs of attack. A HIDS typically relies on operating system logging features to gather the data it analyzes. By relying on the OS to gather data, the HIDS places less of a resource burden on the host than if it added its own monitoring functions to those already included in the operating system.

HIDS monitor only the host on which they are installed. However, many HIDS products enable you to install agents on various hosts, each of which sends reports of events to a central monitoring server. In this way, you can create a centrally managed network-wide infrastructure of HIDS monitors.

HIDS operation

A HIDS will use one or more of these techniques to watch for suspicious activity:

- Auditing of system, event, and security logs
- Monitoring of files to watch for modifications
- Monitoring application, system process, and resource requests
- Monitoring of incoming packets from the network interface

Logs

HIDS monitor log entries looking for patterns that match attack signatures. As with NIDS signatures, you must keep your HIDS software up-to-date with current signatures to detect ever-evolving forms of attack.

File modifications

HIDS monitor operating system and application executable files, watching for changes that might indicate an attack. Typically, a HIDS will do so by recalculating file checksums, which are hashes of the file's contents, and comparing the new checksums with archived checksum values.

Application and resource monitoring

Modern HIDS products monitor requests for system resources and applications. For example, they can watch for attempts to access restricted files or user attempts to take administrative actions or elevate their privilege levels.

To perform such monitoring, HIDS must be tightly integrated with the operating system. Such products must be able to intercept software requests at the driver and kernel level. You will need to carefully evaluate such software to be confident that it will effectively monitor your system without interfering with normal operations or slowing performance unacceptably.

OS-integrated HIDS have the advantage that they can:

- Prevent files from being modified, deleted, or even opened.
- Prevent registry changes.
- Prevent system services from being stopped or modified.
- Prevent changes to user-level configuration settings.
- Prevent users from performing administrative actions or escalating their permission levels.

HIDS that provide log, file, application, and resource monitoring do so through agents. Host-based agents are essentially services (or daemons) that you install atop the operating system.

Network traffic monitoring

HIDS can monitor packets as they arrive before they are processed by the operating system. They can also monitor connection requests. In either case, the HIDS can detect a malicious network action before the operating system receives the communication and then block the connection. HIDS provide network monitoring capabilities through host wrappers, which are in essence a type of personal firewall.

HIDS advantages

HIDS monitoring offers a number of advantages over NIDS monitors. These include:

- HIDS can verify that an attack failed or was successful by analyzing logs, comparing checksums, and so forth.
- HIDS monitor individual user actions and thus can identify the exact user account and location being used by an attacker. HIDS can also take immediate actions to stop such actions.
- HIDS can monitor attacks in which the attacker has direct physical access to the system.
- HIDS do not rely on a particular network location, topology, or network device. Thus, they can be easier to set up than a NIDS.

In general, however, NIDS and HIDS products are complimentary. You will likely find advantages to using both to protect your networked systems.

HIDS examples

Examples of commercial HIDS include: Computer Associates' Host-based Intrusion Detection System (CA HIPS, www.ca.com), IBM Internet Security Systems' Proventia IPS (www.iss.net), and McAfee's Entercept (www.mcafee.com).

OSSEC (www.ossec.net) is an open source HIDS product. While components are available for Linux, Windows, Macintosh, and other operating systems, OSSEC requires one Linux server to act as the central management and reporting console.

WinSNORT (www.winsnort.com) is free HIDS system which implements the SNORT intrusion detection application on a Windows system. It relies on various third-party add-on products, including WinPcap, MySQL, PHP, and the Apache Web server.

Tripwire is sometimes described as a HIDS solution, and is available in both open source (http://sourceforge.net/projects/tripwire/) and commercial (www.tripwire.com) versions. However, it is primarily a configuration-change monitoring product. In other words, it will monitor systems for configuration changes but not necessarily perform other HIDS operations, such as monitoring log files, detecting attacks, and so forth.

Do it!

B-8:   Comparing HIDS and NIDS

Questions and answers

1 Considering the following diagram, what portion of the network would be protected by the NIDS?

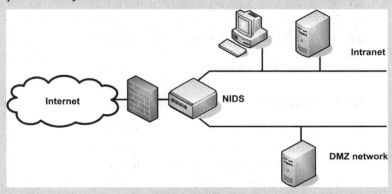

2 Considering the diagram in the previous step, would the NIDS detect internal or external attacks?

3 Is the location of the NIDS in the preceding diagram optimal?

4 Would the server on the perimeter network in this example be better protected by a HIDS than the NIDS as shown?

Physical access control

Explanation The data on the network needs to be secured using network access controls. The facility housing the network also needs access control. Physical access security protects the data, the employees, power sources, utility lines, the equipment, and the building. This control comes in the form of security guards, ID badges, security cameras, lighting, locks, fences, and other physical barriers. Failure of any of these barriers can result in a breach that compromises the organization's information.

The level and amount of physical access controls should be in direct proportion to the importance of the information and assets you are trying to protect. For example, a government organization with top secret information is going to need much stricter security controls than the local baseball team league headquarters.

Physical tokens

A *physical token*, also known as a hardware token or cryptographic token, can be required in order to access a computer. This might take the form of a smart card and a reader or a USB token. Both of these tokens contain a microcontroller and operating system, a security application, and a secured storage area. The device stores a cryptographic key which might be a digital signature or biometric data.

These sometimes contain a method for the user to enter additional information such as an account number. They can be used in *single sign-on* environments. Single sign-on lets the user log on once to gain access to multiple systems without being required to log on each time another system is accessed. Because single sign-on gives the user access to so many resources, it is imperative that strong authentication be used. Using a physical token along with a username and password helps provide strong authentication.

Locks

Locks are the most common physical access control method. The lock is a good first line of defense against break-ins. An attacker needs the key or a set of lock picks to gain access through a locked door or locked device.

Most homes, many office doors, and small business offices usually use a *preset lock*. These are opened or closed with a metal key or by turning or pressing a button in the center of the lock. These are not very secure because keys can be duplicated, lost, or stolen, and such locks are easily picked with a set of picks. An example of a preset lock is shown in Exhibit 8-13.

Exhibit 8-13: A preset lock

A deadbolt can be added. Instead of using spring pressure, it uses the weight of the bolt. These are more secure than a standard preset lock. Some are installed in a vertical position at the top of the door rather than the typical placement at the side of the door. Vertical placement makes the lock more difficult to pry open.

A more secure type of lock is a *cipher lock*. These are electronic, programmable locks. They use either a keypad or a card reader. These more expensive locking devices provide better security than a standard preset or deadbolt lock. There is no need for everyone requiring access to the building or room to have a key; they just need to know the combination to enter to open the lock. Some cipher locks allow you to set unique codes for each individual. Some also include a key to override entering the cipher. Some examples of cipher locks are shown in Exhibit 8-14.

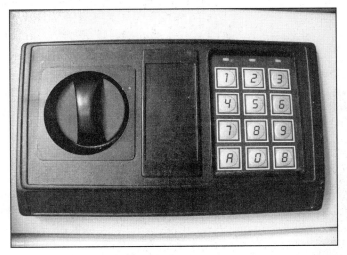

Exhibit 8-14: A cipher lock

The risk of one of these locks is that the person might write down the combination which might be found by an intruder. A cipher lock card reader's main risk is that the user might lose his or her card to an intruder. The card often doubles as the user's ID badge for the organization. Some of the features that make cipher locks better options than preset locks include:

Feature	Description
Door delay	An alarm is triggered if the door is held open or propped open after a preconfigured time.
Key override	A special code can be set for use in emergencies or for management needs.
Master key ring	A function that enables management to change access codes or other features.
Hostage alarm	If the user is being forced to enter their PIN into the cipher lock, they can enter a special code that notifies security or law enforcement of the attempted break-in.

Locks can also be used to secure devices. These *device locks* are often a cable of vinyl coated steel that attaches the device to a stationary object. There are also switch controls to cover the power switch on the device, *slot locks* to cover open expansion slots in a device, and *port locks* to block access to drives or ports. *Cable traps* prevent the cable from being removed.

Man-trap

A *man-trap* is a set of doors that are interlocked. When one door is opened, the other door can't be opened. Using this security method provides secure access control. It is usually configured as two doors at one entrance with a space between them. You can also configure it so that when one entrance is being used, another entrance can't be used.

Fences

A fence around the facility is a good deterrent to casual entry. The local zoning laws might preclude installation of fencing, the height of installed fences, and the type of fencing allowed. Security fences range from simple chain link fencing to razor-wire-topped eight-foot fences. You will need to do a cost analysis to determine whether the expense of installing the fence is worth the security it would provide for the perimeter of your facility.

Lights

A well lit area around your facility will make employees feel more secure and will deter intruders. It is recommended that key areas have illumination at least eight feet up and two feet out. You might want full illumination. You can install flood lights, street lights, or spot lights depending on the location of the light and the needs of the organization.

Do it!   **B-9:   Identifying the risks associated with physical access to systems**

Here's how	Here's why
1 Determine the cost of various types of door locks	Use your favorite search engine to locate and price locks.
2 Compare the cost of the lock to the cost of the potential loss of data	In most cases, the cost can easily be justified.
3 Determine whether fencing is allowed by the zoning laws where your organization does business. Determine the types of fencing allowed and if there are any ordinances regarding lighting in your area.	
4 If you are required to carry or wear a security ID badge at your workplace, examine the badge and the policies that describe its use. How could you improve the security that the ID badge enables?	

Surveillance

Explanation

Surveillance is another important part of physical security. A security guard is a good deterrent to intruders. Guards might be stationed at a fixed location, or they might patrol the facility. A fully-trained guard will know the procedures to follow and the actions to take if an emergency occurs.

Guard dogs are also effective deterrents to intrusion. A trained guard dog knows how to take down an intruder and hold them until human help arrives. Just their very presence is a deterrent to casual intrusion, and their barking alerts others of the potential threat that they sense. Guard dogs are usually used along with security guards.

In addition to guards and dogs, further surveillance with cameras is often used. These cameras are connected to one or more monitors and usually are recorded as well for later review. Cameras should be placed both inside and outside the facility.

Logging

When users log on to the network you can create a log file of their activity. When the server is shut down, you can create a log file with the reason for the shutdown. When intrusion detection software detects an intruder, it writes it to a log file. There are many network log files for various events.

In the physical security of the facility, you can also have logs. When a card reader cipher lock is used, it can create a log file of who enters the building, since the card identifies the user. When visitors come to your building, they can be required to sign into a log book at the front desk. Security guards are often required to create a log that states that everything was okay on their last tour of sentry duty.

These various logs can be used to identify potential suspects when an incident occurs. They can also help identify potential threats if anomalies are noted in any of the logs.

Do it!

B-10: Examining logging and surveillance best practices

Here's how	Here's why
1 Determine the cost of hiring a security guard with a guard dog	
2 What logging needs to be done at your organization regarding physical security?	

Unit summary: Security practices

Topic A   In this topic, you examined core system maintenance. First, you used Windows Update to **apply patches** and **hot fixes**. You also installed any **service packs** your operating system required to bring it up-to-date. Then, you determined whether your **BIOS** needed to be updated. Finally, you examined **Windows Firewall** configuration.

Topic B   In this topic, you learned how to secure network devices. You learned about **network-based firewalls** and how they're used to protect the internal network. You learned about the different types of firewalls and which firewall configurations offer the most security. You then learned about **Intrusion Detection Systems (IDS)** and **Intrusion Prevention Systems (IPS)**. Finally you learned about physically securing your systems using **locks** and **surveillance**.

Review questions

1 What is meant by operating system hardening? *Properly patched*

2 _____ are designed to fix security vulnerabilities.
  A Hotfixes *-Fixing Application*
  B Patches
  C Updates
  D BIOS updates

3 How can you remove an update from Windows Vista?
  unistall   un install

4 Where do you need to look to determine whether a service pack has been installed?
  Properties

5 Why might you filter outgoing traffic between your DMZ and the Internet?
  Do not want for Bot or Bot Network

6 Define bastion host.
  2 network cards

7 The three main zones into which you can divide a network are the *intranet*, *Internet*, and *Extra net*

8 Name at least two actions you should take to limit risk of attacks on your network devices (switches, routers, and so forth).

Set-up security | Hardening / updated

9 You're configuring your network switch to improve its security. You have changed the default password for the unit's Web interface. What else should you configure to be sure all management interfaces have been locked down?

Lock or Telenet, Cisco

10 How does antivirus software recognize new viruses and worms?

Page 8-2

11 What is the Windows Vista built-in spyware protection function called?

Defenders

Independent practice activity

During the activities in this unit, you secured the client operating system. In this activity, you will use the same principles to secure your server.

1 Start your Windows Server 2008 virtual machine. Open Windows Update. Turn on automatic updating, if necessary. Determine if there are any updates available for your server operating system. (If prompted, install new Windows Update software.)

2 Install the updates including patches, hotfixes, updates, and service packs to the server. If prompted, restart Windows Server 2008 and log back in as netadmin##.

3 Determine whether the server's BIOS is up to date.

4 Using resources on the Web, determine the cost of a surveillance system composed of:

- 4 cameras at each outside entrance
- A camera at the front lobby
- A camera at the door to the server room
- A camera at the accounting office

5 Close all open windows. Save state and close Windows Server 2008 virtual machine.

Unit 9

Network access control

Unit time: 240 minutes

Complete this unit, and you'll know how to:

A Explain network authentication methods.

B Explain the basic concepts behind public key infrastructure.

C Explain the methods of remote access security.

D Explain the methods to secure a wireless network.

Topic A: Authentication

This topic covers the following CompTIA Network+ 2009 exam objectives.

#	Objective
6.3	**Explain the methods of network access security**
	• Remote Access
	• PPPoE
6.4	**Explain methods of user authentication**
	• Kerberos
	• AAA
	• CHAP
	• MS-CHAP
	• EAP

Bridge objective (next to 6.3)

Bridge objective (next to 6.4)

Authentication

Explanation

Security of system resources generally follows a three-step process of authentication, authorization, and accounting (AAA).

Step	Description
Authentication	Positive identification of the entity, either a person or a system, that wants to access information or services that have been secured. This could be done through a user name and password, smartcard, or even a fingerprint scan. At the end of this stage, you know that either the user is who he or she claims to be, or is an imposter.
Authorization	A predetermined level of access is granted to the entity so that it can access the resource.
Accounting	The stage that involves tracking the user's actions. It could include determining how long he or she is connected, what systems were accessed, how much data was transferred, and so forth. While such information is great if you plan to bill users based on usage, it's also helpful in determining if you have sufficient bandwidth, optimal connectivity, and so forth.

Usernames and passwords

Throughout the ages secret codes have been used for access to things and locations that only those with the secret code can get into. The secret code can be very simple and easily guessed or extremely complicated. In the computing environment these secret codes are the passwords we use to gain access to files and systems.

Usernames and passwords

Your *username* uniquely identifies you to a computer or network system when you log in. The username you are given is often very simple and might even be based on your name; other times, it is a complex string of characters that you need to memorize. When your username is combined with a password, it authenticates you.

Your *password* is your secret code. In some cases, it can be very simple, although this is not a good practice because someone else could easily guess your password. Most times, you will be required to create a complex password that consists of letters, numbers, and possibly special characters. Usually a minimum password length is also required.

Both the username and password should be kept confidential. If someone knows your username a potential hacker has half of the information to impersonate you and make use of the rights you have been granted to resources.

Password protection

Weak passwords are a major problem. Hackers have tools that help them more quickly retrieve passwords from a compromised system. Users need to create stronger passwords and protect them diligently, and administrators need to use every tool available to them to protect password files.

Some steps to protect passwords include:

- Memorizing passwords rather than writing them down.
- Using a different password for every account that requires a password.
- Creating a password at least eight characters long. Longer passwords are harder to crack.
- Using a mixture of upper- and lower-case letters, numbers, and special characters when creating a password.
- Changing passwords frequently.
- Avoiding using the same password again within a year.

Strong password creation

When you create a password you need to balance the ability to remember the password with the complexity of the password. If the password is so complex that the only way to remember it is to write it down, then you are sacrificing the security of the password.

The way some people create passwords is to take the first letter of a song title, book title, or phrase and use it as the basis of a password. This is often referred to as a *pass phrase*. They make some of the letters upper-case and some lower-case, then add numbers and special characters to make it more secure. This has the benefit of giving you something that is easily remembered along with the more secure password created with numbers and special characters.

Be sure not to include any personal information such as your name or your pet's name. Also, you shouldn't use any word that can be found in the dictionary since hackers routinely perform dictionary-based attacks.

Multiple passwords

If you have multiple passwords to remember for different systems and Web sites, it can be difficult to remember all of the username and password combinations. One way to record them is to use a password management tool, which is a program in which you store your passwords in an encrypted format. You just need to remember a single password to access the file. Some of the password management tools will create complex passwords for you using rules that you define.

Authentication factors

There are several factors that can be used to authenticate you to the system when you log on. These are:

- Something you know
- Something you have
- Something you are

One-factor authentication

One-factor authentication typically consists of only something you know—your username and password. When you log in to your Windows computer using the logon box, you are using one-factor authentication. Even if you had to log in a second time to gain access, you are still using one-factor authentication. This is your username and password combination. This is not a very secure type of authentication compared to two or three-factor authentication.

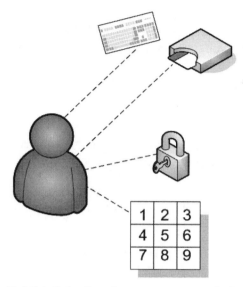

Exhibit 9-1: One factor systems include username/password, keycards, locks and keys, and PIN pads

If you use only something you have or only something you are, that is also one-factor authentication. Any time you use just one type of authentication, you are using one-factor, also known as single-factor, authentication.

If you use only a fingerprint sensor or a card reader, that is also one-factor authentication. If you combine the fingerprint sensor with a password, that would be two-factor authentication. If you combine a card reader with something else such as a fingerprint scan or password, that would also be considered two-factor authentication.

Opening a door with a PIN pad would also be considered one-factor authentication. However, if you first needed to swipe a card through a reader before entering your PIN, that would be considered two-factor authentication.

A token which generates new passwords every few seconds is another form of one-factor authentication. In this case, it is not being combined with anything that you know.

Two-factor authentication

Two-factor authentication consists of something you know plus either "something you have" or "something you are."

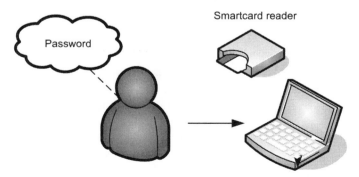

Exhibit 9-2: A smart-card plus password is a form of two-factor authentication

For something you know plus something you have, something you have is a token of some sort, such as a card that you swipe through a reader. One example of this is an ATM card. When you go to the bank's ATM machine, you use the ATM card along with something you know—your personal identification number (PIN).

For something you know plus something you are, the something you are includes things like your fingerprint, a voice print, a retinal scan, or something else unique on your body that can be measured. Combined with a password or PIN, this is another example of two-factor authentication.

A token that creates new passwords every few seconds that is combined with a PIN to access the passwords is another example of two-factor authentication.

Three-factor authentication

Three-factor authentication uses something you know, something you have, and something you are. In addition to having a token such as a card and a PIN, you also use a biometric scan of your fingerprint, voice, retina, or other uniquely distinguishing body feature to provide a third authentication factor in order to gain access to the system.

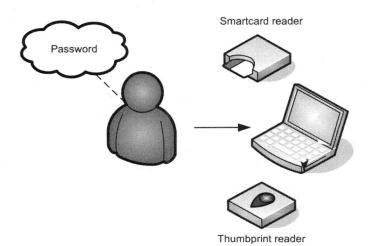

Exhibit 9-3: Add a biometric reader to create a three-factor authentication system

Do it!   **A-1:   Comparing one, two, and three-factor authentication**

> **Questions and answers**
>
> 1 List the three types of authentication factors.
>
> 2 List two types of one-factor authentication.
>
> 3 What is combined to create two-factor authentication?   Biometric smartcard Token
>
> 4 Three-factor authentication makes use of what types of authentication methods?

Authentication protocols

In a Windows environment, two primary authentication protocols are commonly used:

- Kerberos version 5 (Kerberos v5)
- NT LAN Manager (NTLM)

Kerberos v5

Kerberos v5 is the primary authentication protocol used in Active Directory Domain Services environments. Microsoft operating systems that support Kerberos v5 include:

- Windows 2000
- Windows XP
- Windows Server 2003
- Windows Vista
- Windows Server 2008

NTLM

NTLM is a challenge-response protocol that's used with operating systems running Windows NT 4.0 or earlier. Common examples of when NTLM authentication is used include:

- When a Windows Server 2003/2008 system attempts to authenticate to a Windows NT 4.0 domain controller.
- When a Windows NT 4.0 Workstation system attempts to authenticate to a Windows 2000 Server or Windows Server 2003/2008 domain controller.

LM

The Windows Vista password is stored as an NTLM hash. Prior to Windows Vista, Windows passwords were also stored as a LANMAN hash or LM hash. In Windows Vista, you can store it as an LM hash if you need to connect to an older computer or device which doesn't support NTLM or Kerberos authentication. In order to do so in Windows Vista, you have to enable support for storing LM hashes.

LM hashes are easily cracked using brute force attacks, so it isn't recommended that you store these hashes unless absolutely necessary. It starts by converting all characters to uppercase. It then stores the hash in two pieces, each of which is 7 bytes long. If your password is longer, it is truncated; if it is shorter, it is padded with null characters.

Each half of the hash uses DES to create two DES keys. The keys are then used to encrypt the password as two 8-byte values which are then concatenated into a single 16-byte LM hash value.

Do it!   **A-2:   Hashing data**

Questions and answers

1 How are Windows Vista password hashes stored?

2 When is a Windows Vista password stored as an LM hash?

Legacy connection

3 Why should NTLM be used instead of LM hashes whenever possible?

Identification and authentication

Explanation

In order for someone to use network resources, they need to identify themselves to the system. After identifying themselves with a user name, they are then authenticated before they are given access to resources.

The identity can be established by entering a user name. All usernames must be unique. The user then authenticates using one or more authentication methods such as passwords, tokens, and/or biometrics.

A secure authentication system doesn't allow someone to impersonate a valid identity. The important measures to take to prevent such exploitation include:

- Using strong authentication methods.
- Not allowing system access by bypassing authentication.
- Ensuring that stored authentication information is kept confidential and that its integrity hasn't been compromised.
- Encrypting all authentication sent over the network.

The identity and authentication process should balance the convenience for the user to gain access with the need for security. Assurance needs to be implemented so that the identity is properly authenticated and the identity is not compromised by an imposter while making sure that the identity is not rejected when it is legitimate.

Identity proofing

Before issuing a user a username and password, you need to verify that the person is who they say they are. Otherwise, all of the security measures you take won't amount to anything if you give someone access without verifying who they are in the first place.

Traditionally, this was done face-to-face with the person providing one or more proofs of identity such as a driver's license, photo ID, or Social Security card. Often when you want to establish a new user, it is done online, making the traditional method difficult or impossible.

Knowledge-based authentication (*KBA*) of a user involves asking the potential new user to provide information that only they would be likely to know. This includes such things as mother's maiden name, the city you were born in, or the school mascot for your high school. These aren't all that secure, but until recently, this was about the best to do if you weren't meeting face-to-face.

More often now, institutions are using *dynamic knowledge-based authentication*. In this method, a public database is queried, and the individual is asked to verify the information. This information isn't stored anywhere on the institution's servers, so the risk of the information being compromised later is not a problem for the institution doing the verification. An example of the types of information the potential user might be asked include the person's previous address, the amount of a bank loan, or other publicly available information. The user must answer several questions and get a high percentage of the answers correct.

Another identity proofing method is *out-of-band* (OOB). It makes use of a channel outside of the primary authentication channel. For example, the user initiates contact with the desired service or resource on the Web. A phone call is then made to the user at the number provided by the user. A code is then issued to complete the online transaction.

Single sign-on

A server that has already authenticated a user can pass that user's authentication on to another server so that the user doesn't need to sign on again in order to access resources. With this *single sign-on*, a user identifies themselves to a system and gets authenticated. The user is then authenticated to other resources on the strength of this initial process.

It can be done using an SSL certificate. A user's identity is mapped to the certificate which can also be used to identify the user. Another method is to use an LDAP-based directory model. In this case, all of the resources are secured within the directory.

Windows Live ID and Microsoft Passport are examples of single sign-on applications. The user signs on once and is given access to any resources that use Windows Live ID or the Microsoft Passport. This includes MSN Messenger, Hotmail e-mail account, MSN groups, and other sites and services that make use of Windows Live ID or Microsoft Passport.

Do it!

A-3:   Identifying the requirements of a secure authentication system

Questions and answers

1   Your company is creating a social networking site for pre-teens. You want to ensure that the site is secure for them and that no predators will be able to access the site. Adults including parents need to be able to access the site. How would you secure the site? What types of identity verification would you use?

2   Your company has an online sales site where visitors typically place $500 orders for products. Most customers make several purchases during the year. You need to make sure that the customer is actually who they say they are and that they will be able to pay for the products they are ordering. Some customers occasionally make purchases that are up to five times the cost of their usual purchases. You want to make it easy for the customer to shop your site.

Kerberos

Explanation

Kerberos is an authentication method that was developed at MIT as part of the Athena Project. This secure authentication method is named after the three-headed dog in Greek mythology that guards the gates of Hades. It provides authentication security on physically insecure networks.

Kerberos 5 is the current version in use. It is freely available within the United States and Canada. Kerberos can be downloaded from `itinfo.mit.edu/product.php?name=Kerberos`.

Kerberos provides a means to authenticate users and services over an open multi-platform network using a single login procedure. After the user is authenticated by the system, all subsequent commands and transactions can be carried out securely without any prompting for a password. The Kerberos system is composed of the following components.

Component	Description
Principal	A server or client that Kerberos can assign tickets to.
Authentication Server (AS)	Authentication service that gives ticket-granting tickets to an authorized service or user.
Ticket-Granting Server (TGS)	Service that provides authorized service or user with temporary session keys and tickets.
Key Distribution Center (KDC)	A server that runs AG and TGS services to provide initial ticket and ticket-granting ticket requests.
Realm	A boundary within an organization. Each realm contains an AS and a TGS.
Remote Ticket-Granting Server (RTGS)	The TGS in a remote realm.

The following table describes the types of data passed over the network during Kerberos processing:

Item	Description
Credentials	Ticket for the resource server along with the session key.
Session key	Temporary encryption key. It is used in communication between the client and the resource server. It lasts only the length of a single login session.
Authenticator	A record that usually lasts for five minutes that can't be reused. The record contains information to prove that the session key was recently created and is known only to the client and the server.
Ticket	Record used by a client to authenticate to a server. The record contains the identity of the client, session key, a timestamp, and a checksum. The record is secured with the resource server's secret key.
Ticket-Granting Ticket (TGT)	Ticket granted during the Kerberos authentication process. It is used to acquire additional tickets from the TGS.

The Kerberos process

Using encryption, Kerberos passes a user's credentials over unsecured channels and validates the user for network resources. The process is depicted in Exhibit 9-4.

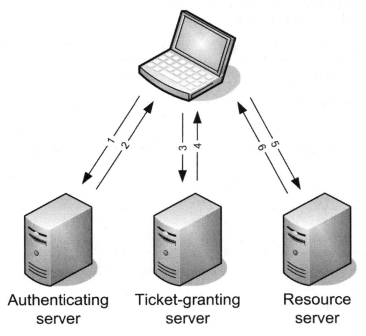

Authenticating   Ticket-granting   Resource
server   server   server

Exhibit 9-4: Kerberos authentication process

1. A user logs into their workstation with their username and password, and the workstation automatically requests a TGT from the AS. A database on the AS lists the valid users and servers within its realm along with their master keys.

2. When the AS receives the TGT request, it authenticates the user, uses their master key to encrypt a new TGT, and sends it back to the user's workstation. Since the user has a TGT, the user doesn't need to authenticate themselves again to gain access to additional services until the TGT expires. The TGT is valid during the current logon session, for a set time as configured by an account security policy, or until the user disconnects or logs off.

3. When the user requests additional services, a copy of the TGT is sent automatically by the workstation, along with the name of the server where the application being requested resides, an authenticator, and the time period that access is needed for each service, to the TGS requesting a ticket for each of the services needed.

4. After the TGS verifies the identity of the user, the session key is used to access the user's authenticator, and assuming the TGT matches the user to the authenticator, the TGS sends the tickets to enable the user to use the requested service.

5. Once the appropriate tickets are received from the TGS, the workstation verifies that each one is for a service that was originally requested, and sends a ticket to each relevant server requesting permission to use their services.

6. Each server receiving a service request verifies that the request came from the same entity to which the TGS granted the ticket. As each server determines that the user has the authority to use the requested service, it authorizes the user to begin using those services.

The TGT must be submitted each time the user needs additional services. When the validity period for using previously requested service expires, an entirely new TGT must be obtained.

Kerberos security weaknesses

Kerberos is, in general, a pretty strong authentication service. However, the Kerberos model is open to several weaknesses.

- Brute force attacks can be used against Kerberos authentication and are especially effective against weak passwords.
- Kerberos assumes that network devices are physically secure and that an attacker can't somehow get to a password between the user and the service to which the user is seeking access.
- If your password is somehow exposed through poor password protection, an attacker can easily access services to which the password granted you access.
- Kerberos is vulnerable to denial-of-service attacks.
- Because Kerberos makes use of timestamps, the clocks in network authenticating devices need to be "loosely synchronized" so that authentication can occur as it should.
- If an attacker gains access to the AS then the attacker can impersonate any authorized user on the network.

Do it!   **A-4:   Examining the components of Kerberos**

Questions and answers

1 List some of the Kerberos security vulnerabilities.

2 A subset of users in Kerberos is referred to as a:

   A   Peer

   B   Realm

   C   Server

   D   Client

4 Which of the following is not true in a Kerberized system?

   A   Once the user has been authenticated, the AS sends the user a ticket-granting ticket (TGT).

   B   Once the client has received a TGT, the client presents it to the TGS in order to receive a session key for each requested service.

   C   Once the client receives the appropriate ticket from the TGS, the client submits a request to the authentication server.

3 A user has been issued a logical token by the TGS. What privileges does this grant the user?

5 How long is a timestamp valid in a Kerberos authenticator?

   A   Eight hours

   B   One hour

   C   Twenty minutes

   D   Five minutes

   E   Two minutes

CHAP

Explanation

CHAP (*Challenge Handshake Authentication Protocol*) is an authentication method used by *Point-to-Point Protocol* (*PPP*) servers. CHAP validates the remote client's identity at the communication session start or at any time during the session.

CHAP uses a three-way handshake after establishing a link between the client and the server. The procedure is outlined in Exhibit 9-5.

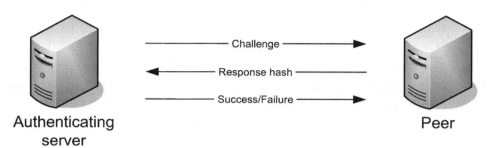

Exhibit 9-5: CHAP challenge-and-response process

1   A challenge message is sent from the authenticating server to the client.
2   The client replies with a value computed using a one-way hash function.
3   When the authenticating server receives the response it checks the value against its own calculation of the expected hash value. If the value matches, the server responds to the client with a success message. If the values don't match, the connection is terminated and a failure message is sent to the client.

At random times during the session a new challenge is sent by the authenticating server to the client. This is done to make sure the server is still connected to the same client. This helps protect against playback attacks. Each authentication request challenge contains different content. The exposure time during an attack is limited by the server's frequency and timing of challenges.

MS-CHAP is Microsoft's version of CHAP. There are two versions, MS-CHAPv1 and MS-CHAPv2, which is the only version supported in Windows Vista.

EAP

Extensible Authentication Protocol (*EAP*) is a PPP extension and is also used in wireless connections. It includes multiple authentication methods, such as token cards, one-time passwords, certificates, and biometrics. It runs over the data link layers without requiring use of IP.

EAP defines message formats rather than being an authentication mechanism. The EAP authentication framework provides common functions known as EAP methods. There are over 40 different EAP methods at this time. Some of them are:

- Lightweight Extensible Authentication Protocol (LEAP)
- EAP Transport Layer Security (EAP-TLS)
- EAP Flexible Authentication via Secure Tunneling (EAP-FAST)

PPPoE

The Point-to-Point over Ethernet protocol encapsulates PPP inside Ethernet frames. PPPoE allows users to establish a secure connection from one computer to another. PPPoE is used to connect multiple users to the Internet through DSL and cable modem connections.

Mutual authentication

Mutual authentication requires both the client and the server to authenticate to each other instead of just the client authenticating to the server like in other authentication systems. This is also known as two way authentication.

Both computers must trust the other's digital certificate in order to create the connection. This helps protect against phishing sites since the fraudulent site wouldn't be able to successfully authenticate the connection to the client. It also helps protect against other attacks such as man-in-the-middle attacks.

As an example of mutual authentication, a bank clearly has an interest in positively identifying an account holder prior to allowing a transfer of funds; however, you as a bank customer also have a financial interest in knowing your communication is with the bank's server prior to providing your personal information.

Kerberos allows a service to authenticate a recipient so that access to the service is protected. Conversely, it allows the recipient to authenticate the service provider so rogue services are blocked.

Do it!

A-5: Comparing authentication systems

Questions and answers

1 Put the following steps in the proper sequence.

The authenticator sends a new challenge to the peer at random intervals throughout the session to make sure that it is still communicating with the same peer.

The peer responds with a hash value.

The authenticating server sends a challenge message to the peer.

The authenticating server checks the response against its own calculation of the expected hash value.

The authenticating server responds with either a "success" or a "failure" message.

2 CHAP protects against _____ attacks by changing the content of the challenge message with each authentication request.

3 How does EAP improve on security for PPP connections?

4 Kerberos allows a service to authenticate a recipient so that access to the service is protected. Conversely, it allows the recipient to authenticate the service provider so rogue services are blocked. This is referred to as _____ authentication.

5 _____ is used to secure PPP connections over the Ethernet.

Topic B: Public key cryptography

This topic covers the following CompTIA Network+ 2009 exam objective.

Bridge objective

#	Objective
6.4	**Explain methods of user authentication**
	• PKI

Cryptography overview

Explanation

Cryptography is the science of encrypting and decrypting data. Encryption is a technique through which source information is converted into a form that cannot be read by anyone other than the intended recipient. Decryption is the opposite: converting an encrypted message back into its original form.

Encryption

Encryption is accomplished through an algorithm, which is a mathematical or physical means to transform the message. The algorithm to decrypt data might not be simply an inverse of the algorithm used to encrypt it. However, these two algorithms form a pair and are designed to work with each other to encrypt and decrypt data. The pair of algorithms that encrypt and decrypt data is called a *cipher*. RSA is an example of an encryption algorithm.

Plaintext is the original, unencrypted information. While the "text" part of that term might seem to imply alphanumeric content, binary information could be considered plaintext. For example, the contents of a Microsoft Word file are stored as binary characters, not ASCII text. Yet, an unencrypted Word file would be considered plaintext in contrast to an encrypted form of the file. Encrypted plaintext is known as *ciphertext*.

Ciphers

There are many ciphers, only a few of which will be covered here. The most basic varieties are substitution and transposition ciphers. In a substitution cipher, characters are replaced with other characters or with symbols. In transposition ciphers, the characters of the plaintext are rearranged.

A very simple substitution cipher is the ROT13 ("rotate 13") cipher in which characters are replaced with the character whose ASCII value is thirteen higher (an A becomes an N, B becomes O, and so forth). Decrypting involves simply "rotating to the left" to reverse the process.

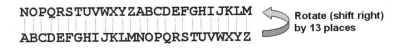

```
NOPQRSTUVWXYZABCDEFGHIJKLM          Rotate (shift right)
| | | | | | | | | | | | | | | | | | | | | | | | | |   by 13 places
ABCDEFGHIJKLMNOPQRSTUVWXYZ
```

Security+ is fun!   **Becomes**

Frphevgl+ vf sha!

Exhibit 9-6: The ROT13 cipher translocates characters

Character ciphers operate on each character in the plaintext. Block ciphers operate on groups of characters, sometimes though not always on whole words.

Keys

A key is a piece of information that determines the result of an encryption algorithm. For example, in the ROT13 substitution cipher, the key is knowing that the letters are shifted by 13 characters and not, for instance, 14.

Keys are also used with the decryption algorithm. In the case of the ROT13 cipher, the key is again simply knowing to rotate by 13 characters. In more complex ciphers, the key might be a starting value used in a mathematical operation and is likely to be some arbitrary and very large number.

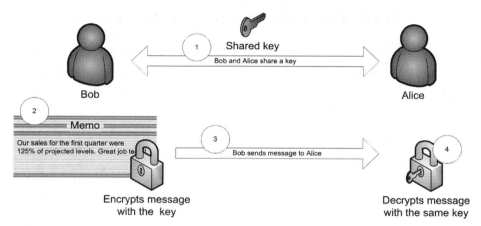

Exhibit 9-7: Symmetric encryption in action

When the same key is used to encrypt and decrypt a piece of data, the cipher is said to be symmetric. Asymmetric ciphers use different encryption and decryption keys; in fact, the encryption key can't be used to decrypt and vice versa.

Key management

A critical concern with any cipher is transmitting the key to the recipient so that he or she can decrypt the data. The issue is worse for symmetric ciphers, in which the sender and receiver of encrypted data must share the same key. These parties must create a secure means to share the key, which is no small task in the real world.

In addition, keys can vary. In some ciphers, a different key is used for each block or chunk of data within a larger message. In many cases, users would have separate keys for each person they need to communicate with. Sophisticated key management systems are often needed to share and securely store the enormous volume of keys involved in even routine business communications.

Users and organizations must also manage key storage and retention. For example, if Bob encrypts his work files, then leaves the company, there will need to be a means for authorized agents at the company to decrypt his files. That will require a means to recover his key.

In some operating systems, keys are stored as part of the user account. In such cases, key storage isn't the issue, but accessing it can be. Administrators will need a way to log on as the former employee to recover encrypted files. Some operating systems, such as Windows Server 2008, enable administrators to designate a data recovery agent, who has the necessary permissions to recover files encrypted by other users.

Public key cryptography overview

A symmetric cipher uses the same key for encrypting and decrypting a message. These ciphers suffer from the need to share keys. In fact, the cipher is only as secure as the means to share the key. If the key is lost or stolen, the ciphertext can easily be decrypted no matter how strong the cipher. An alternative, called asymmetric cryptography, attempts to eliminate the need to securely share a key by using two keys.

Asymmetric cryptography

Asymmetric cryptography uses two keys to eliminate the troubles associated with sharing the encryption key. What is encrypted by one key can be decrypted only by the other key. One key is kept private (secret), and the other is made public (distributed freely), hence the name public key cryptography.

Encrypting and decrypting the public key way

In symmetric encryption, the plaintext is transformed through some mathematical operation into the ciphertext. Then, the ciphertext and key are shared with the recipient who reverses the process to recover the plaintext. With multiple keys involved, public key cryptography works a bit differently.

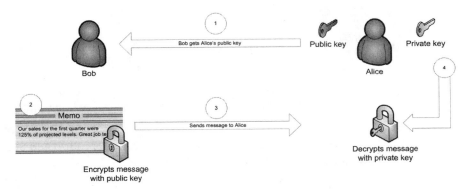

Exhibit 9-8: Asymmetric encryption in action

Let's say Bob wants to exchange a secret message with Alice. He begins by obtaining a copy of her public key. He uses that key in an encryption operation to generate the ciphertext. This operation is called a *padding scheme*, and is conceptually similar to the one-time pad cipher. Bob transmits the ciphertext to Alice. She uses her private key to reverse the padding scheme and decrypt the message.

Asymmetric keys

The private and public keys are mathematically related. For example, the RSA cipher begins with two very large randomly chosen prime numbers. These two numbers are essentially the user's private key. The numbers are multiplied together and the resulting product is published as the public key. While it is easy to compute the product of two numbers, it is computationally difficult to reverse the process—many combinations of numbers could be multiplied to reach the product and an attacker would have no way to know which pair were the correct numbers.

Public key cryptography characteristics

Public key cryptography has the following characteristics due to the nature of the computations involved in the algorithms:

- It is mathematically difficult and hopefully impossible to derive the private key from the public key. The more bits in the keys, the closer to impossible this operation becomes. A minimum of 1024-bits is often recommended.
- Data encrypted with the public key can be decrypted with only the private key. To reiterate, the public key cannot be used to decrypt a message encrypted with the public key.
- Data encrypted with the private key can be decrypted with only the public key. The private key cannot be used, but since the holder of the private key has or can regenerate the public key, this is not an impediment.

Asymmetric ciphers eliminate the worry over transmitting keys. One key is kept secret at all times. The other key in the pair is widely published. A wide range of operations, from encrypting data to digitally signing documents is possible in such a scheme, all without needing to share the secret private key.

Do it!

B-1: Exploring public key cryptography

Here's how	Here's why
1 In Windows Vista, use Internet Explorer to access **http://tinyurl.com/2t866c**	(Or, visit http://www.cs.pitt.edu/~kirk/cs1501/notes/rsademo/index.html.) This page offers a simplistic RSA public key encryption example. It uses extremely short keys and encrypts just a single letter. But the demo is still instructive for seeing how the full RSA system works.
2 At the bottom of the page, click **key generation page**	
3 From the list boxes, select two prime numbers	
Click **Proceed**	To generate a key pair. A new window opens showing you the results of various calculations.
Record the values for N, E, and D	N _____ E _____ D _____ Together, N and E are your public key; D and N are your private key.
Close the pop-up window	
4 At the bottom of the page, click **Encryption page**	

5 From the first list, select a letter to encrypt

This simple demonstration page enables you to encrypt just a single letter.

If you are working with a partner, record his or her values for N and E to the right

E _____

N _____

These are your partner's public key, with which you will encrypt the data.

Otherwise, use your values recorded previously

Enter your partner's values for N and E into the form

Click **Encrypt**

Record the encrypted data here: _____

Close the pop-up window

6 At the bottom of the page, click **Decryption page**

7 Exchange the encrypted message with your partner

You will decrypt your partner's message using your values for N and D. She will decrypt your message using her values for N and D.

In the form, enter the encrypted message your partner calculated

Enter your own values for N and D

These are your private key.

Click **Proceed**

A pop-up window is displayed with the decrypted message.

8 Compare the results with your partner

You both should have been successful in encrypting and decrypting the messages.

Close all open windows

Public key infrastructure

Explanation

PKI (public key infrastructure) offers two broad models for generating and administering public keys: centralized and decentralized management.

Centralized key-management systems place all authority for key administration with a top-level entity. This could be a *certificate authority* (*CA*) within an organization or a trusted third-party entity. This model gives the administrator system-wide control over each aspect of key management. This model typically appears in scenarios where a hierarchical or single-authority trust model is implemented, as in the case of X.509 certificates.

Decentralized key-management systems place responsibility for key management with the individual. The key and certificate are stored locally on the user's system or some other device, and the user controls all key-management functions. Decentralized systems do not provide all the functionality of centralized systems. For example, if a user loses or damages the private key, there is no way to recover the private key or the encrypted information. This model typically appears in scenarios where the Web of Trust model is implemented, as in the case of PGP certificates.

The decision to use centralized or decentralized systems depends on the size of the public-key infrastructure. If the number of keys that users retain on their key rings is limited, and the users are educated to properly protect their private keys, decentralized management works well. However, for a large organization, where thousands of keys might be generated, centralized management transfers the burden of private-key security from the end users to a trained individual or team.

Setup and initialization

The three main phases of the key life-cycle management process are: setup or initialization; administration of issued keys and certificates; and certificate cancellation and key history.

The setup or initialization process consists of:
1 Registration
2 Key pair generation
3 Certificate generation
4 Certificate dissemination

Registration

The registration process starts when a user approaches the CA with a specific request for a certificate. After verifying the identity and credentials of the user, the CA registers the user. Depending on the certificate practice statement, certificate policy, and privileges associated with a given certificate, the identity verification process might require a physical appearance at the CA or submission of documented proof of identity.

Key pair generation

Key pair generation involves creating matching private and public keys by using the same passphrase and different algorithms. Especially within the context of keys being used for non-repudiation services, the owner of the private key is entrusted with generating and storing such keys. In other scenarios, performance, usage, legalities, and algorithm specifications are the factors affecting the choice of location.

Multiple key pairs are often generated to perform different roles to support distinct services. A key pair can also be restricted by policy to certain roles based on usage factors such as type, quantity, category, service, and protocol. For instance, a certificate can be restricted to a particular function, such as signing or encryption. Multiple key pairs allow the CA to issue multiple certificates to the user for distinct functions.

Certificate generation

The responsibility of creating certificates lies with the CA, regardless of where the key pair is generated. A certificate binds an entity's unique *distinguished name* (*DN*) and other identifying attributes to its public key. The entity DN can be an individual, an organization or organizational unit, or a resource (for example, a Web server or site).

The certificate policy governs the creation and issuance of certificates. The public key needs to be transmitted securely to the CA if it was generated elsewhere by a party other than the CA.

Requests for keys and certificates require secure transmission modes. The IETF defines management and request message format protocols specifically for the purpose of transmitting public keys and certificates between the key owner and the CA. Alternatives such as the Public Key Cryptography Standard also exist.

Certificate dissemination

Dissemination involves securely making the certificate information available to a requester without too much difficulty. This is done through several techniques, including out-of-band and in-band distribution, publication, centralized repositories with controlled access, and so forth. Each method has its own benefits and drawbacks.

Depending on the client-side software, certificate usage, privacy, and operational considerations, the information requirements and dissemination methods vary. Several protocols are available that facilitate secure dissemination of certificates and revocation information. Enterprise domains widely use LDAP (Lightweight Directory Access Protocol) repositories with appropriate security controls, along with in-band distribution through S/MIME-based (Secure Multimedia Mail Extensions) e-mail. This hybrid approach maximizes the benefits. Even within the repository model, several configurations—such as direct access, interdomain replication, guard mechanism, border, and shared repositories—are possible and often used.

Administration of issued keys and certificates

The issued keys and certificates need to be administered properly after the initialization phase. The administrative phase involves the following:

- Key storage
- Certificate retrieval and validation
- Key backup or escrow
- Key recovery

Key storage

After the key pair has been generated, the private key must be safely stored to protect it from being compromised, lost, or damaged. There are several key-storage methods, generally categorized as hardware or software storage.

Hardware storage refers to storing the private key on a hardware storage medium, such as a smart card, memory stick, USB device, PCMCIA card, or other such device. These devices can be physically carried on the person, enforce encryption of the private key, and often provide the added benefit of on-board encryption and decryption processing. The disadvantage to this method is that the storage medium can be easily lost or stolen.

Software storage refers to storing the private key in a computer file on the hard drive. The owner encrypts the private key by using a password or passphrase, and stores the encrypted key in a restricted file. The user can enable auditing to track access to this file. Software storage is not considered reliable, because if the file is restored to a different medium (such as a floppy disk or FAT drive), the encryption is removed.

Certificate retrieval and validation

As the name implies, *certificate retrieval* involves access to certificates for general signature verification and for encryption purposes. Retrieval is necessary as part of the normal encryption process for key management between the sender and the receiver. For verification, retrieval is used as a reference where the certificate containing the public key of a signed private key is retrieved and sent along with the signature or is made available on demand. It's imperative to have an easy and simple mechanism to retrieve certificates; otherwise, the complexity makes the system unusable.

Validation is performed to ensure that a certificate is issued by a trusted CA in accordance with appropriate policy restrictions and to ascertain the certificate's integrity and validity (whether it's expired or has been revoked) before its actual usage. In most cases, all of this is achieved transparently by the client software before cryptographic operations using the certificate are carried out.

Note: Attempts to use revoked certificates are a likely sign of attempted break-in.

Key archive

Key archiving is the storage of keys and certificates for an extended period of time. It's an essential element of business continuity and disaster recovery planning, and it's the only solution that addresses lost keys and recovery of encrypted data. When used with additional services such as time stamping and notarization, a key-archive service meets audit requirements and handles the resolution of disputes.

Key archiving is typically undertaken by an organization's CA, a trusted third party, or, in some cases, the end entity (the user or computer that owns the key). Relying on the key's owner to manage archiving is generally unreliable due to the complexities involved. All private keys (current, expired, and revoked), with the exception of keys used for non-repudiation, are backed up to a key-archival server. The server requires strong physical security and at least the same security as the key-generating system.

Key escrow

Key escrow is a form of key archive that allows third-party access without the cooperation of the subject (such as for law enforcement or other government agencies). Copies of the private keys are stored in an off-site repository called a *key escrow agency*. In 1995, the U.S. government required that all parties keep copies of the key pairs with a key escrow agency. Almost immediately, the government was questioned about its intentions for requiring key escrows. Eventually, the government dropped the requirement.

Key escrow has severe implications on individual privacy because control of the private keys is passed to a third party.

Key recovery

Key recovery complements the key backup/escrow process. The recovery of lost, damaged, or archived keys allows access to encrypted messages and prevents permanent loss of business-critical information. This process is also automated to minimize user intervention and errors.

Many archive systems use the *M of N Control* to ensure that no single administrator can abuse the recovery process. This access-control mechanism creates a PIN number during the archive process and splits the number into two or more parts (N is the number of parts). Each part is given to a separate key-recovery agent (a person authorized to retrieve a user's private key). The recovery system can reconstruct the PIN number only if M number of agents provide their individual PIN numbers. For M of N Control to work, N must be greater than 1, and M must be less than or equal to N ($N > 1$ and $M \leq N$).

Certificate cancellation and key history

The final phase in the key and certificate life cycle management deals with cancellation procedures. This phase includes:

- Certificate expiration
- Certificate renewal
- Certificate revocation
- Certificate suspension
- Key destruction

Certificate expiration

Certificate expiration occurs when the validity period of a certificate expires. Every certificate has a fixed lifetime, and expiration is a normal occurrence. Upon expiration, a certificate can be renewed if the keys are still valid and remain uncompromised, or are destroyed. Most applications will reject a certificate if it's in an expired state.

Certificate renewal

Certificate renewal is the process of issuing a new certificate with a new validity period. All that's required is that the certificate owner use the old key to sign a request for a new certificate. To facilitate smooth transition and prevent service interruption, the renewal should be initiated when a certificate approaches three-quarters of its intended lifetime (or 30 days before expiration).

Many Certificate Authorities merely repackage the old public key with the new certificate. This is a bad practice because the longer you keep the same key pair, the more insecure it will become over time. Ideally, a new key should be generated with each renewal (also called a *certificate update*).

Certificate revocation

Certificate revocation implies the cancellation of a certificate before its natural expiration. Certificate owners and PKI administrators (with the approval of the certificate owner) can revoke a key for any number of reasons; for instance, a company changes ISP or moves to a new address, a contact leaves the company, or a private key is compromised or damaged.

The cancellation process is much easier than properly publishing and maintaining the revocation information after the fact. There are several ways in which the notification is accomplished. The primary method is through *certificate revocation lists* (*CRLs*). Essentially, CRLs are data structures containing revoked certificates. To maintain integrity and authenticity, CRLs are signed. Other methods include CRL distribution points, *certificate revocation trees* (*CRTs*), and Redirect/Referral CRLs.

Performance, timeliness, and scalability are some of the main factors that influence the revocation mechanisms. Instant-access methods through *Online Certificate Status Protocol* (*OCSP*) are also available. However, there is no guarantee that the real-time service is indeed providing an up-to-the-moment status. It's possible that the service might respond based on poorly updated databases. Additionally, many application implementations do not constantly check CRLs.

There are also exceptions for which such notification is deemed unnecessary. Two such exceptions involve short certificate lifetimes and single-entity approvals. In the former case, the accepted revocation delay might be more than the certificate lifetime, so the certificate might not require revocation at all. In the latter case, as requests are always approved by a single entity, it might not be necessary to publish the revocation separately.

The delay associated with the revocation requirement and subsequent notification is called *revocation delay*. Revocation delay must be clearly defined in the certificate policy because it determines how frequently or quickly the revocation information is broadcast and used for verification.

Certificate suspension

If a certificate is not used for a period of time, the CA will eventually revoke it. To prevent this from taking place, a certificate owner will *suspend* the certificate, temporarily revoking it. Often, this option is executed if an employee is on an extended leave of absence or a Web site is taken offline for renovations.

The suspension is published in the CRL or OCSP response with a status of "Certification Hold." At the appropriate time, the suspension can be undone.

Key destruction

CAs typically destroy certificates and any keys associated with them when certificates expire or get revoked. Another significant event warranting key destruction occurs before a certificate server or key archival server is sold or recycled. Key destruction is usually accomplished by overwriting the key data. One common method is *zeroization*, which overwrites the data with zeros.

Securing public-key management systems

Attacks on public-key systems typically target key-management systems rather than attempting to crack public-key encryptions. Therefore, these systems must be well protected. If a key-management system is compromised, the hacker can use the stolen keys to forge certificates and impersonate someone else. All trust associations are compromised as well.

Key life cycle describes the stages a key goes through during its life: generation, distribution, storage, backup, and destruction. *Encryption key management* describes the systems used to manage those keys throughout their life cycle. If any phase of a key's life is not managed properly, the entire security system can be compromised.

Do it!

B-2:   Understanding certificate life cycle and management

Exercises

1 What is the key life cycle?

2 What is a centralized key-management system?

3 Match each phase of key management below with its definition:

Certificate generation	Certificate renewal
Certificate revocation	Certificate validation
Key archival	Key escrow
Key pair generation	Key recovery
Key storage	Registration

A browser requests signature verification of a certificate.

A certificate is cancelled before its expiration date.

A certificate is reissued with a new validity period.

A key is retrieved from archive due to loss or damage of the original.

Matching private and public keys are created.

A private key is safely stored on a hardware or software medium.

The CA binds the requestor's identifying attributes to its public key.

The key is stored for an extended period of time.

The key is stored in an off-site repository for third-party access.

The user approaches the CA with a specific request for a certificate.

4 What is the difference between certificate revocation and suspension?

Topic C: Remote access

This topic covers the following CompTIA Network+ 2009 exam objectives.

#	Objective
6.3	**Explain the methods of network access security**
	• Tunneling and encryption
	• SSL VPN
	• VPN
	• L2TP
	• PPTP
	• IPSEC
	• Remote access
	• RAS
6.4	**Explain methods of user authentication**
	• AAA
	• RADIUS
	• TACACS+
	• Network access control
	• 802.1x
6.5	**Explain issues that affect device security**
	• Secure methods vs. unsecure methods
	• SSH

Bridge objective (6.3)

Bridge objective (6.4)

Bridge objective (6.5)

Remote network access

Explanation

Telecommuters and traveling employees often need access to your network beyond what a simple Internet connection can provide. For example, these users might need to access internal file storage locations, application servers, or printers. Your security needs might preclude the use of an Internet connection, or perhaps you want to use Active Directory integrated security, which is not available via the Internet. In these situations, remote access solutions such as RADIUS and TACACS+ might enable you to provide the needed connectivity solutions.

Remember, access security can be generalized into a three phase process:

1 Authentication
2 Authorization
3 Accounting

The remote access systems described in the upcoming sections typically provide solutions for all three AAA phases. Older systems often provided only authentication and authorization.

RADIUS

Remote Authentication Dial-in User Service (*RADIUS*) provides centralized AAA remote access services. RADIUS is a client/server system. While originally developed for dial-in user authentication, RADIUS is often applied to wireless and virtual private networking connections.

RADIUS client

The role of RADIUS client is provided by the network access server (NAS), sometimes called the remote access server (RAS). It accepts user connections and passes authentication requests to the RADIUS server. Once connections are authenticated, the RADIUS client acts as a middleman between the user's system and the RADIUS server for authorization and accounting functions. The RADIUS client could be located on the corporate LAN or at a remote site.

RADIUS server

The RADIUS server provides all AAA services, but communicates with the RADIUS client rather than directly with the end user's system. A RADIUS server can authenticate connections against a variety of information stores. These include a flat file, proprietary RADIUS database, UNIX password file, Network Information Service (NIS), or even Active Directory. The RADIUS server is located on the corporate LAN.

RADIUS authentication process

The authentication process involves actions by the user, the RADIUS client, and the RADIUS server. In general, the process works as follows:

1 The user connects to the NAS.
2 The RADIUS client (the NAS) requests authentication information via a user name/password or CHAP challenge.
3 The user supplies the log on credentials.
4 The RADIUS client encrypts the password, if necessary, and forwards the credentials to the RADIUS server.
5 The RADIUS server authenticates the user and replies with an Accept, Reject, or Challenge message.
6 The RADIUS client receives the message and acts accordingly:

- Accept: The user's connection is finalized.
- Reject: The user can be re-prompted for credentials, or if the maximum number of requests has been reached, the user can be disconnected.
- Challenge: The user can be prompted for further credentials, which are used to further tailor their connection and the services to which they have access.

Realms

In RADIUS, a realm defines a namespace. It also helps determine which server should be used to authenticate a connection request. Realm names are formatted like Internet domain names, though they have no actual relation to domains. A user's full RADIUS name might be janedoe@outlanderspices.com, where outlanderspices.com is the realm.

RADIUS defines three types of realms, which essentially define three configuration possibilities at your RADIUS client (the NAS):

- Named realm—You configure your client to use a specific RADIUS server for a given named realm. For example, authentications for outlanderspices.com go to RadServerA, while those for megaspices.com go to RadServerB.
- Default realm—You define the server to use for authentication for realms not listed explicitly in the client configuration. In other words, the user logon name contains a realm, but that realm is not listed in your client configuration.
- Empty realm—You define a realm to use when a customer's login attempts don't contain a named realm. This in effect defines which server to use for authenticating such requests.

Named realms can be cascaded, meaning joined together in a chain. For example, janedoe@outlanderspices.com@megaspices.com describes a cascade. Authentication requests are sent to the servers in order: first to the server configured to authenticate for the outlanderspices.com realm, followed by the server for the megaspices.com realm.

RADIUS communication security

The RADIUS client and server communicate over a channel that is secured via a shared secret key. That key is never sent over the network. Instead, the installer must configure each system with that key prior to deployment.

Furthermore, the user station's authentication messages, which are ultimately forwarded to the RADIUS server, are encrypted via the Extensible Authentication Protocol (EAP).

- If configuring multiple RADIUS client server pairs, use a unique secret key for each pair. This reduces the opportunity for spoofing-based attacks.
- Use a long secret key: RFC 2865 suggests at least 16 characters. Keys over 22 characters are required to provide sufficient complexity to thwart most dictionary-based attacks.
- The RADIUS server doesn't authenticate messages from the client, thus is open to IP spoofing based attacks. To prevent such attacks, configure your systems to use the MD5-hashed Message-Authenticator attribute in all Access-Request messages.
- Enable authentication attempt limits (the number of times a user can attempt to authenticate before being locked out) to prevent brute force and dictionary-based attacks.
- By default, RADIUS uses a relatively weak stream cipher with MD5-based hashing of user passwords. You can use IPsec with Encapsulating Security Payload (ESP) to provide more secure transport of RADIUS messages.

Benefits

The distributed client/server architecture of RADIUS provides the following benefits:

- Improved security—Authentication is centralized at the RADIUS server, and possibly integrated with your core network's authentication systems. This eliminates the need to configure each remote access connection point, eliminates potential duplicates, and reduces the opportunities for insecure configurations, such as short or empty passwords.
- Scalable architecture—A single RADIUS server can authenticate requests for many RADIUS clients. This means users can connect to various clients as they travel but still be authenticated by the same server.
- Interoperability—The RADIUS architecture is defined by widely accepted and long-established Internet standards. This enables you to mix and match products from various vendors. The standards also enable vendor-specific customizations without breaking core functionality. For example, you can get a product integrated with Active Directory that authenticates Windows, Macintosh, and Linux user stations.

Diameter

Diameter is a new protocol designed as a successor to RADIUS. It is backward compatible with that protocol. The name is a pun on RADIUS, as mathematically, the diameter is twice a circle's radius. Unlike the earlier protocol, Diameter is not typically written in all capital letters.

Diameter is defined by RFC 3588 and defines a minimum set of AAA services and functionality that must be provided. Vendors can extend Diameter to provide additional functionality. They do so by creating a Diameter Application. In these terms, an Application is not a program to be run on a computer but rather a protocol that works within the Diameter framework.

The following table describes the improvements Diameter provides over RADIUS.

Item	Improvement over RADIUS
Data flow	Uses windowing scheme to regulate the flow of UDP packets.
Error notification	Server can be configured to notify clients of problems by sending messages.
Message acknowledgement	Server can be configured to send message acknowledgements so that clients "know" that data has been received properly.
Processing requirements	Uses a more efficient 32-bit alignment scheme, which can be more efficiently handled by most devices.
Security	Supports end-to-end security through IPsec, TLS, or both. Message tampering can be detected and handled. Diameter supports challenge/response attributes which can be used to prevent authentication replay attacks. Diameter supports mutual authentication, through which the client ensures that it has connected with a legitimate server.

Do it!   **C-1:   Examining RADIUS and Diameter authentication**

Questions and answers

1   Name the benefits of using RADIUS authentication compared to configuring your network access servers to perform authentication.

2   True or false? A RADIUS client is the end-user's computer connecting to your network.

3   When configuring multiple RADIUS clients, you should use a unique _____ with each client-server pairing.

4   Because RADIUS uses a relatively weak stream cipher with MD5-based hashing of user passwords, you should use _____ to provide secure message transport.

5   A realm is a _____.

A   Domain

B   Name space

C   Scope of authority

D   MD5 hash key

6   Name at least one way Diameter provides better security than RADIUS.

7   True or false? Diameter is backward compatible with RADIUS.

LDAP and remote access

Explanation

LDAP (Lightweight Directory Access Protocol) is the industry-standard protocol for network directory services. LDAP systems store information about users, network resources, file systems, and applications. Applications and services can use an LDAP data store to locate and store such configuration information.

Many RADIUS and Diameter servers enable you to use LDAP as your remote access configuration repository. FreeRadius, for example, is one RADIUS server solution that features LDAP integration. Such a solution is possible because at their heart, RADIUS and Diameter are AAA protocols. Servers that implement these protocols typically provide a database component and tools to manage the configuration data. However, you can just as easily use your existing LDAP repository instead.

LDAP security

LDAP is a critical network service and is thus a prime target for internal and external attacks. Such attacks can be categorized in a number of ways. Perhaps most useful is to consider attacks against the LDAP systems themselves, typically for the purposes of shutting down or destroying the services, and attacks against the data cataloged within the LDAP database.

An attack against the LDAP data would enable a hacker to:

- Gain unauthorized access to data.
- Gain unauthorized access to network resources.
- Modify or delete the LDAP data.
- Impersonate LDAP functions to gain further and more privileged access to the network or its resources.

Sometimes such attacks are carried out by spoofing, hijacking valid sessions, or brute-force attacks against the authorization mechanisms.

An attack against the LDAP services would enable a hacker to:

- Prevent legitimate users from accessing resources (denial-of-service attack).
- Redirect access requests to imposter resources (trick a user into accessing the wrong shared folder).
- Hide his or her attempts to attack (or successful attacks) the data stored in the LDAP system.

Commonly, such attacks would be carried out by attacks against the LDAP server's operating system or by attacks against the LDAP control software. An attacker could also attack support servers, such as the database server that stores the data managed by the LDAP system.

LDAP authentication and authorization

To access the LDAP directory service, the client must first authenticate itself to the LDAP server by performing a Bind operation. LDAP supports three Bind methods:

- Simple Bind
- Simple Authentication and Security Layer (SASL)
- Anonymous Bind

In a Simple Bind, the client sends its distinguished name (DN) along with a plaintext password. Such connections should be protected through TLS (Transport Layer Security). During the Bind operation, the client specifies the LDAP protocol version to be used. This is typically LDAPv3, though other versions are possible.

Strong authentication methods are supported in a SASL Bind operation. For example, the client and LDAP server can use Kerberos authentication. Or, the client can send its security certificate over a TLS link.

In an Anonymous Bind, the client sends a message with empty DN and password. This resets the connection to a non-authenticated, or anonymous, state.

Do it!

C-2: Examining the role of LDAP in a remote access environment

Questions and answers

1 Why would you use LDAP in conjunction with a RADIUS or Diameter system?

2 Name at least two goals a hacker might have when attempting to access your LDAP data.

3 Describe the functional differences between an LDAP Simple Bind and Anonymous Bind operation.

4 To improve password security in LDAP Simple Bind messages, you should implement _____.

Terminal Access Controller Access Control System

Explanation

The *Terminal Access Controller Access Control System* (*TACACS*) is a proprietary authentication protocol developed by Cisco Systems. Like RADIUS, it is designed to provide centralized and scalable authentication. TACACS+ also provides authorization and accounting functions.

TACACS+ is the current version of the protocol, and while it shares the name with earlier versions, it is not compatible with them. TACACS and XTACACS are older and no longer supported protocols.

Comparing TACACS+ and RADIUS

TACACS+ uses TCP rather than UDP for messages. TCP is connection-oriented, providing for acknowledgement that requests have been received. Such acknowledgements provide, at minimum, an indication that a client or server might have failed if it doesn't respond within a predetermined time.

Unlike RADIUS, the message body is fully encrypted to provide greater security without resorting to IPsec or other means. TACACS+ uses TCP port 49.

Unlike RADIUS, however, it can provide these services independently. This means a TACACS+ server can use separate databases for each AAA function. It can interface with various services on a function-by-function basis. You can even use individual TACACS+ servers for each function.

TACACS+ supports username/password, ARA, SLIP, PAP, CHAP, and Telnet authentication messages by default. The protocol is also extensible so that vendors can add extra functionality, such as supporting Kerberos authentication messages.

Finally, TACACS+ offers multiprotocol support. In addition to TCP/IP, it supports AppleTalk Remote Access, NetBIOS Frame Protocol Control, Novell Asynchronous Services Interface, and X.25 PAD connections.

Do it!

C-3:   Examining TACACS+ authentication

Questions and answers

1 Name the benefits of using TACACS+ authentication compared to RADIUS.

2 Name the authentication message types supported by TACACS+.

3 TACACS+ uses TCP port _____.

802.1x

Explanation

802.1x is an extensible authentication protocol designed to let you control which devices have access to your network. By using 802.1x, you can prevent unauthorized workstations from connecting to your network. Furthermore, you can prevent users or attackers from attaching hubs and wired or wireless routers to your network (which they might do to extend your network or create unsecured access points).

802.1x adds strong authentication services to wired and wireless networks. It works in conjunction with a dedicated authentication server, such as a RADIUS or TACACS+ server. In wireless networks, it enables you to provide strong authentication even when using WEP encryption.

802.1x device roles

According to the 802.1x protocol, devices have one of three roles:

- Supplicant—the end user's PC or network device.
- Authenticator—a switch between the supplicant and remainder of the network.
- Authentication server—the RADIUS or TACACS+ authentication server that grants or denies access to the network.

When a supplicant attempts to connect to the network, it sends an authorization request which is passed from the authenticator to the server. The authentication server exchanges messages with the supplicant to establish an authenticated session. If granted, the server notifies the authenticator, which then allows network traffic to and from the supplicant.

If a supplicant attempts to transmit data without first authenticating, the authenticator (switch) blocks the traffic. It returns a message to the supplicant demanding that the device authenticate. Together this system prevents unauthenticated access to your network.

While the system works well in most cases, engineers at Microsoft discovered a flaw. Basically, once a session has been authenticated, further traffic is permitted without any checks. So, in theory, a hacker can insert his station into the network by hijacking an authenticated session. Adding IPsec encryption to the system would prevent such physical injection attacks. Of course, the rogue user would also need physical access to your network to accomplish this attack—but with a wireless network that could mean simply being close enough to make radio contact.

802.1x is an IEEE standard based on the EAP (Extensible Authentication Protocol). EAP is defined under RFC 3748. 802.1x is part of the larger 802 group of protocols.

Do it!   **C-4:   Examining how 802.1x adds security to your network**

Questions and answers

1   In 802.1x, the client's PC is known as the _____.

2   What happens when a new end-user station connects to an 802.1x-protected network?

3   To prevent physical injection attacks, you should use _____ in conjunction with 802.1x authentication.

4   True or false? 802.1x works only with wired network access points.

VPN security

Explanation

Remember, a *virtual private network* (*VPN*) is in essence a network transmitted across another network. VPNs enable the secure transmission of data over insecure networks. For example, employees can securely access corporate network resources via the Internet by using a VPN. This sort of VPN would be called a *remote access VPN*. You could also use a VPN to link the networks at two locations via the Internet. This would be described as a *site-to-site VPN*.

VPN technologies

VPNs use authentication, encryption, and tunneling technologies to create a secure communications channel across the public network. These technologies are used as described in the following table.

Technology	Role in a VPN
Authentication	Many VPNs use RADIUS, Diameter, TACACS+, or proprietary remote access authentication technologies to ensure that only authorized users can access the network.
Tunneling	Packets sent to and from the end user can be bundled within the packets of the public network. Consider a packet originating at a client's workstation. Equipment or software at her location inserts the packets into Internet packets and sends them via the Internet to the corporate VPN server. At the corporate LAN side of the connection, the interior packets are removed and forwarded onto the LAN. The process is reversed for data being transmitted to the client's station. In effect, the private network "tunnels" through the public network.
Encryption	VPNs can encrypt the entire client packet before putting it into the data field of the public network packet. This ensures that hackers and unintended recipients cannot decipher any valuable information. Various encryption technologies can be used, depending on the VPN solution you implement.

VPN security models

VPNs typically follow one of these three security models:

- Authentication before connection
- Trusted delivery network
- Secure VPNs

With authentication before connection, clients, network devices, and even servers must authenticate to the VPN system before being able to complete a connection. Tunneling is not typically used with this sort of system. This type of system is often used to provide access to additional resources to a subset of users over an existing LAN.

Trusted delivery networks are third-party private networks protected by various means. Clients and servers connect to this network, rather than connecting to the LAN via a public network. Security mechanisms on the provider's network provide assurance that data can be transmitted safely. Tunneling is not typically used on this sort of network.

Secure VPNs are the typical sort of network that enable secure connections over insecure public networks. Secure VPNs rely on tunneling, authentication, and encryption to protect private data. Secure VPNs are the focus of the remainder of this section of the course.

VPN protocols

Secure VPNs use various protocols for transmitting data securely. The most common protocols are listed in the following table.

Protocol	Information
PPTP	(Peer to Peer Tunneling Protocol) A VPN protocol developed by Microsoft. Once a link has been established, the client is added as a virtual node on the LAN and packets between the two are encrypted using Microsoft Point-to-Point Encryption (MPPE). In general practice, L2TP is preferred over PPTP.
L2TP	(Layer 2 Tunneling Protocol) A standardized tunneling protocol. It generally combines the best features of PPTP and L2F to provide tunneling over IP, X.25, Frame Relay, and ATM networks. L2TP relies on IPsec for encryption and RADIUS or TACACS+ for authentication. Currently at version 3, called L2TPv3.
IPsec	(IP Security) A standardized network protocol that encrypts data at the Network (OSI layer 3) layer of the protocol stack. Because it operates at the IP level, IPsec can provide security for both TCP and UDP traffic. Furthermore, applications do not need to be specially designed to work with this form of security.
SSL/TLS	(Secure Sockets Layer / Transport Layer Security) While SSL is commonly used in Web-based ecommerce, many vendors use this technology for secure VPN communications. SSL/TLS can either encrypt the entire protocol stack or be used to provide a proxy between client and network.

The following is a comparison of PPTP and L2TP:

Feature	PPTP	L2TP
Encryption	Native PPP encryption encrypts data, but negotiations are sent in plaintext.	Relies on IPsec or other encryption protocols.
Authentication	PPP authentication using PAP, CHAP, or MS-CHAP protocols.	Relies on RADIUS or TACACS+ for authentication.
Data protocols	IP	IP, IPX, SNA, NetBEUI
Port	1723 (TCP)	1701 (UDP)

IPsec

The IPsec protocol suite is made up of four separate protocols:

- *Authentication Header* (*AH*) ensures authenticity by signing packet data with MD5 or SHA-1 hashes and a shared secret key.
- *Encapsulating Security Payload* (*ESP*) ensures confidentiality by encrypting the packet using the DES or Triple-DES (3DES) cipher.
- *IP Payload Compression Protocol* (*IPComp*) compresses packet data before transmission.
- *Internet Key Exchange* (*IKE*) negotiates the shared secret keys.

While all four are typically used, systems could implement each sub-protocol independently.

IPsec encryption modes

IPsec enables two modes of encryption: transport and tunnel.

- *Transport mode* encrypts only the packet's data but not the header and is used in host-to-host (peer-to-peer) communications.
- *Tunnel mode* encrypts the entire packet (data and header). In this mode, source and destination addresses are hidden so that eavesdroppers cannot glean information about your internal network configuration. This mode should be used in a VPN.

Secure shell (SSH)

Programs such as Telnet and FTP send logon information in plaintext. For better security, you can use secure shell (SSH), which uses public key encryption to establish an encrypted and secure connection from the user's machine to the remote machine. By default, a server would listen on port 22 (TCP) for SSH connections.

SSH is a popular tool for remote command-line system access and management, and current implementations also support secure file transport (over Secure FTP or SFTP). To implement SSH, you will need both a server service and a client program. Most Linux distributions include an SSH daemon (service), but Windows does not. By visiting http://sshwindows.sourceforge.net/download/ you can download a free open-source Windows SSH server service.

For the client, there are a number of popular free tools for Linux and Windows systems. These include PuTTY (www.chiark.greenend.org.uk/~sgtatham/putty/) for Windows and Open SSH for Linux, BSD-variants, and Windows (by using the Cygwin POSIX-over-Windows framework).

The current protocol version, SSH-2, divides functionality into three primary layers:

- Transport layer, as defined in RFC 4253, manages the key exchange process.
- User authentication layer, as defined in RFC 4252, manages client authentication through various methods (public key, password, "keyboard interactive," Kerberos, and so forth).
- Connection layer, as defined in RFC 4254, manages communication channels. Each client-server connection can support multiple channels over which distinct operations can proceed—for example, you could have multiple command-line shells and a file transfer session over a single connection by using multiple channels.

VPN solutions

To create a VPN, you will need to select and set up two categories of components:

- Remote access communication options
- VPN hardware and software

Communication options

Remote access VPNs are most often implemented via the Internet nowadays. This means users will need a way to connect to the Internet, such as DSL, cable, or even dial-up. They will need an ISP account and of course the equipment required by the ISP for their connection—a cable modem or DSL router or analog telephone style modem.

Site-to-site VPNs are again most often implemented via the Internet. Few other shared public networks remain since access to the Internet became widespread. Thus, your remote offices will need a communications line to the Internet. Most often, this would be provided through an always-on connection. DSL, cable, ISDN, and T/E dedicated circuits are all common ways that companies provide Internet connectivity, though dial-up access is doable.

VPN hardware and software

VPN solutions are offered by many vendors. Some require dedicated access hardware, most commonly at the corporate LAN side of the connection. Many require special software to be installed on the client workstation.

Microsoft's VPN solution uses standard Windows components on the client side and Microsoft's version of a *remote access service* (*RAS*). Under Windows Server 2008, you can install the *Routing and Remote Access Service* (*RRAS*) components of the *Network Protection Services* (*NPS*) to create the server to which clients connect.

Cisco, Juniper Networks, and OpenVPN, provide commercial or open source VPN solutions to businesses and end users. Some are software only while others require specialized hardware components, such as a VPN concentrator.

Third-party service providers offer VPN solutions that work like this: The business creates a secure connection to the VPN provider's systems; the client connects to the provider's network via the Internet or dial-up. Such solutions eliminate the need to purchase, install, and maintain VPN systems. However, communications from the client to provider are not secure (though, communications over the provider's network are secure).

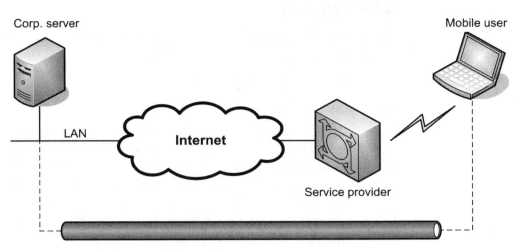

Exhibit 9-9: Service provider tunneling

Microsoft Routing and Remote Access Service (RRAS)

The Windows Server operating systems include VPN software in the form of the Routing and Remote Access Service (RRAS) component. With RRAS, you can enable VPN clients to connect to your network. The server on which you run RRAS should have two network adapters: one connected to the Internet and one to your LAN.

Do it!

C-5:   Comparing VPN protocols

Questions and answers

1 Give at least two reasons to choose L2TP over PPTP.

2 Name at least two obsolete or antiquated VPN protocols.

3 Which IPsec mode should be used for a VPN? Why?

4 Name an advantage and disadvantage of SSH over Telnet and FTP.

Topic D: Wireless security

This topic covers the following CompTIA Network+ 2009 exam objectives.

Bridge objective

#	Objective
6.3	**Explain the methods of network access security** • Filtering • ACL • MAC filtering • IP filtering
6.5	**Explain issues that affect device security** • Physical security • Restricting local and remote access

Bridge objective

Wireless networking

Explanation

Wireless networking provides a means to connect network nodes without installing network cabling. While many technologies exist for wireless networking, the 802.11 family of standards are the most widely implemented and least expensive.

802.11 standard

The *IEEE 802.11 standard* specifies a wireless computer networking technology that operates in the 2.4 through 2.5GHz radio frequency (RF) band. The IEEE 802.11 standards are defined at the Data Link layer of the Open Systems Interconnection (OSI) model.

The 802.11 standard defines an *access point* (*AP*) as a device that functions as a transparent bridge between the wireless clients and the existing wired network. The access point contains at least one interface to connect to the existing wired network (typically called the WAN port), and transmitting equipment to connect with the wireless clients.

APs often integrate other networking functions. Many include Gigabit Ethernet networking ports for connecting wired devices and thus function as switches. Many include routing capabilities, and such devices most often also include firewall functions. The popular Linksys WRT family of wireless routers are one such example of multi-function APs.

Many modern APs support multiple standards. For example, one AP might offer concurrent support for 802.11a, b, g, and n clients in addition to 100 Mbps wired network clients.

Wireless connections

To create a wireless LAN (WLAN), you must have both an AP and clients with wireless networking adapters. Most laptops have such adapters built in. You can easily add adapter cards and USB devices to desktop computers to enable wireless access. Printers with wireless networking support are becoming more commonplace, as well. Your AP and clients must support a common set of 802.11 standards.

When setting up your AP, you will assign a service set identifier (SSID), which is essentially a name for your wireless network. It is possible, and sometimes likely, that multiple wireless networks will be accessible from a given location. In such cases, clients can use the SSID to distinguish between WLANs and connect to a particular network.

An AP typically broadcasts the SSID. In this way, clients can discover the presence of a nearby AP. Such broadcasts typically identify the security mechanisms in place to enable clients to auto-configure connections.

Wireless networking security

There are four components to security on a wireless network:

- Access control
- Encryption
- Authentication
- Isolation

Access control

You can control which clients can access your AP through various techniques. The simplest, and least effective, is to simply turn off SSID broadcasts. This "hides" the presence your AP. However, the SSID is also included in routine client-to-AP traffic. Thus, it's easy for appropriately configured devices to detect SSIDs that aren't explicitly broadcast.

A stronger means of access control is to enable a MAC filter on your AP. The MAC address is the hardware-level address of a client's network adapter. On most APs, you can enter a list of permitted MACs, or blocked MACs, to limit connections.

As with the SSID, valid MAC addresses are transmitted across the wireless network. Thus, a malicious user could detect a valid MAC address and then configure his computer to impersonate that MAC address and thus gain access to your AP.

Encryption

You can encrypt communications between your AP and clients. Various techniques exist, with some more secure than others. To make a connection, clients must use the same encryption scheme and possess the appropriate encryption key. Once connected, a static or dynamically-changing key provides on-going encryption.

In theory, encryption blocks unapproved connections to your AP. Additionally, as long as the encryption scheme is sufficiently strong, your data streams are kept private from eavesdroppers. As you will see, not all wireless encryption systems are sufficiently robust to actually provide these protections.

Authentication

Through RADIUS or other systems, you can enable client authentication over your wireless network. Using a system essentially like the user name and password you use when you log on, your AP could authenticate the identity of wireless networking clients.

Authentication provides much stronger access control protection than SSID hiding or MAC and IP address filtering. You should still use encryption with authentication. Without it, eavesdroppers could access the data that legitimate clients transmit once those clients have connected to the AP.

Authentication typically requires the use of additional software or hardware devices, such as a RADIUS server.

Isolation

Isolation is a means of segregating network traffic. There are two types: wireless client isolation and network isolation.

With wireless client isolation, also called AP isolation, wireless clients are put onto individual VLANs so that they cannot access each other. This is commonly used in public wireless networks to prevent one user from accessing another user's computer. Imagine the risk you face in a library or coffee shop where another user might attempt to access your shared folders or even mount brute force attacks on your PC over the Wi-Fi hotspot network.

You might also want to provide network isolation. For example, you might want to permit wireless clients to access the Internet and your corporate mail server, which is on your wired network. However, you might also want to prevent wireless clients from accessing other wired nodes, such as your file servers.

Some APs offer network isolation through custom routing configurations. You can also enable such isolation through your general network design and firewall configuration.

Wireless network vulnerabilities

Through careful technology selection and configuration, you can prevent unwanted access to your AP as well as block client-to-client access over your wireless network. You should also consider vulnerabilities in your APs. As with other networking devices, APs include these common vulnerabilities:

- Physical access
- Firmware vulnerabilities
- Default administrator accounts

Just as you should prevent physical access to your switches, routers, and servers, you should prevent physical access to your AP. You should use lockable enclosures for your APs or mount them in physically secure locations, such as a locked room. Unlike wired devices, you must take care to consider how these physical safeguards will affect the wireless signal propagation.

You should check often for firmware upgrades. After careful testing, implement upgrades as they become available. You might also consider third-party router firmware, such as the open source DD-WRT firmware.

As with wired devices, make sure to change the passwords on all administration interfaces on your APs. Typically, APs provide Web-based administration interfaces. Make sure to change the password on such interfaces because the default passwords for most APs are widely published on the Internet.

Additionally, make sure to change the passwords for Telnet, SSH (secure shell), and SNMP interfaces. In many cases, APs support such interfaces, yet their documentation and built-in administration tools provide little information on their availability. Third-party AP firmware typically offers easier access to managing these interfaces.

Additional risks associated with wireless networks include:

- The authentication mechanism is one-way, so it is easy for an intruder to wait until authentication is completed and then generate a signal to the client that tricks the client into thinking it has been disconnected from the access point. Meanwhile, the intruder begins to send data traffic to the server pretending to be the original client.

- The client connection request is a one-way open broadcast. This gives an intruder the opportunity to act as an access point to the client, and act as a client to the real network access point. This allows an intruder to watch all data transactions between the client and access point, then modify, insert, or delete packets at will.

Data emanation

Nearly all computing devices emit electromagnetic radiation. Processors and chips, as well as electronic signals flowing through wires, create electronic signals. Unintentionally, such emanations can transmit data. With the right equipment, someone could capture and decode these emanations and reconstruct the data they represent.

Decoding data emanations is not likely. The signals are weak and don't travel far, requiring the eavesdropper to be very close to the "leaky" equipment. Additionally, it is computationally difficult to reconstruct data from the electromagnetic noise. Eavesdropping in this way is perhaps the stuff of spy movies rather than a real-world security concern. However, if you must run an extremely secure network, you should consider the risks associated with data emanation.

Do it!

D-1: Identifying wireless networking vulnerabilities

Questions and answers
1 Why should you enable encryption on your wireless network?
2 Why might you *not* want to use AP isolation?
3 Speculate on the equipment that would be needed to eavesdrop on network communications via data emanation.

Wi-Fi scanners

Explanation

Wireless access points, when set up right out of the box, have no security configured. By default, they broadcast their presence—in essence saying "Hey, my name is xxx, here I am!" Unsecured access points in an otherwise secure network are sometimes called "rogue access points" and represent a large vulnerability.

You can purchase Wi-Fi scanners, which detect the presence of wireless signals within range. These devices often provide lights or other indicators that describe what security is in place on the network. You can also use software such as Airsnort or NetStumbler on a laptop to scan for WLANs.

The stated purpose of such tools is to help "road warriors" find wireless networks for legitimate networking purposes. In many cities, free wireless networks are available for public use. However, these tools are often used by people looking to use wireless networks without permission.

Wardriving is the practice of scanning for open wireless access points in a region. Several Web sites provide detailed information locating unsecured networks. These sites provide locations, sometimes on city maps for the convenience of others looking for open access links to the Internet.

Warchalking is the process of marking buildings, curbs, and other landmarks indicating the presence of an available access point and its connection details by utilizing a set of symbols and shorthand. Some common warchalking symbols are shown in Exhibit 9-10.

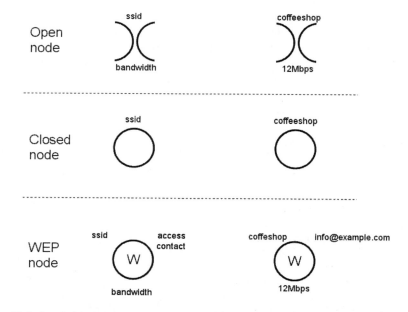

Exhibit 9-10: Warchalking symbols

Do it!   **D-2:   Scanning for insecure access points**

Here's how	Here's why
1 You arrive at work to see the following symbol painted onto the sidewalk. What does it mean? 	
2 Using a Wi-Fi scanner, scan the area for wireless networks	
3 What security measures are in place?	

Unit summary: Network access control

Topic A   In this topic, you learned about the basics of **authentication**. You learned about one-, two-, and three-factor authentication, and you learned about the **Kerberos** and **NTLM** authentication protocols. You also learned how **EAP**, **CHAP**, and **PPPoE** are used in authentication.

Topic B   In this topic, you learned about the basics of **PKI**. You learned basic **cryptography** and key management concepts, and you learned the basics of **certificate** management and certificate lifecycles.

Topic C   In this topic, you learned how to secure remote network access. You learned how **RADIUS** and **TACACS** provide **authorization** and **accounting** functions for network access, and you learned how **802.1x** helps you control wireless network access.

Topic D   Finally, in this topic, you learned how about **wireless** network standards, and you learned about different wireless network **vulnerabilities**.

Review questions

1 What are the three steps of the AAA model?

2 Compare one-, two-, and three-factor authentication.

3 Which is more secure, an LM hash or an NTLM hash? Why?

4 Why would an administrator use password cracking tools?

5 True or false? Kerberos authenticates users and servers over an open multi-platform network using a single login procedure.

6 Which of the following is a reason to revoke a certificate?

   A A newer certificate has been issued to the user or computer.

   B The private key has become known to someone other than the holder.

   C The user or computer is no longer employed by the company.

   D All of the above.

7 According to the 802.11 standard, an access point is _____.

8 What are the four components of wireless security?

9 True or false? To enable remote access to your network, you must provide services for authentication, authorization, and accounting.

10 In RADIUS terminology, what is the name given to the system that provides authentication services for remote computers?

11 In RADIUS terminology, what is the name given to the system that provides connectivity services for remote computers?

12 What is a RADIUS realm?

13 Diameter provides better security than RADIUS by providing end-to-end security using _____ or _____.

14 What are the three LDAP Bind methods?

15 True or false? TACACS+ is backward compatible with TACACS and XTACACS.

16 TACACS+ uses _____ rather than UDP for messages.

17 TACACS+ provides better message security than RADIUS because it encrypts _____.

18 For Windows Server 2008, Microsoft's RADIUS server is called _____.

19 VPNs generally use _____, _____, and _____ to enable secure remote connections across insecure networks.

20 What are the three VPN security models?

21 Name two VPN protocols.

22 What are the two IPsec encryption modes?

23 True or false? You can safely distribute your public key to others.

24 CHAP is an authentication scheme used by _____ servers to validate the identity of the remote user.

Independent practice activity

In this activity you capture passwords using Network Monitor while logged in to the domain.

1 Start the Windows Server 2008 virtual machine.

2 Switch to Network Monitor on the Vista host, start Network Monitor.

3 Begin capturing packets.

4 On Windows Server 2008, log off and log in to the domain netadmin## with a password of P@$$word.

5 Switch to Network Monitor on the Vista host. Stop capturing packets and locate the login process. Network Monitor records this traffic under the KerberosV5 protocol.

6 Determine if you can tell anything about the user's name or password.

7 Close Network Monitor. Don't save the capture.

8 In the Windows Server 2008 virtual machine, close Server Manager. Close and save the state.

9 After cracking the passwords on your network you find that one of your users has used Password, another has used his last name, and another has used paSSw0rd. Make suggestions on better passwords they might haven chosen.

10 List some of the Kerberos security weaknesses.

Unit 10
Monitoring

Unit time: 120 minutes

Complete this unit, and you'll know how to:

A Monitor the network.

B Read event logs to monitor network activity.

Topic A: Monitoring resources

This topic covers the following CompTIA Network+ 2009 exam objectives for Network+.

Bridge objective

Bridge objective

#	Objective
4.4	**Conduct network monitoring to identify performance and connectivity issues using the following** • Network monitoring utilities
6.3	**Explain the methods of network access security** • Remote access • RDP • VNC • ICA

There are different methods for monitoring and assessing the status of network devices, depending on the type of device and the device manufacturer. This includes from checking for blinking lights on the most basic of hubs, to sitting down at a computer or server to check its status, to using Telnet or other command-line tool to communicate with a router.

Windows computers

Explanation

In Windows Server 2008, Reliability and Performance Monitor contains an important tool called Resource Overview that you can use to assess and maintain the health of your system.

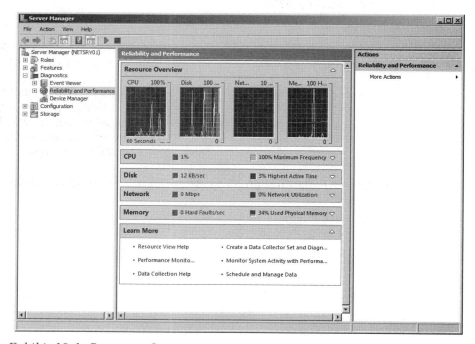

Exhibit 10-1: Resource Overview

As shown in Exhibit 10-1, Resource Overview is the first tool you see when you select Reliability and Performance. It provides real-time graphs and detailed information about four key components:

- CPU—Displays CPU utilization.
- Disk—Displays the disk input/output statistics.
- Network—Details network traffic.
- Memory—Displays memory statistics, including the percent of memory used and the number of hard page faults.

Under the graphs are corresponding sections that you can expand to see more detailed information. Just click the associated graph to see more detailed information about that component's current performance.

To display Resource Overview, in Server Manager, expand Diagnostics and select Reliability and Performance.

Do it!

A-1: Viewing real-time performance data in Resource Overview

Here's how	Here's why
1 Start the Windows Server 2008 virtual machine and log on as **netadmin##**	
2 Open Server Manager	
Click **Continue**	
3 Expand Diagnostics and select **Reliability and Performance**	To display the Resource Overview.
4 Observe the four graphs	Each graph is scrolling to the left, showing you the level of activity for each component.
5 Click the Network graph	To display the details below. You can see the current network activity, including bytes sent and received, and the other network devices and computers with which your sever has established connections.
6 Click the Network graph again	To close its details section.

Performance Monitor

Explanation

You use Performance Monitor, shown in Exhibit 10-2, to monitor computer performance in real time, one-second intervals, or in the form of saved reports of real-time data. Hundreds of computer performance variables called *counters* are available for you to measure and assess a computer's performance, including:

- Create a baseline to compare system performance over time.
- Monitor system resource use.
- Locate performance problems.
- Identify performance bottlenecks.

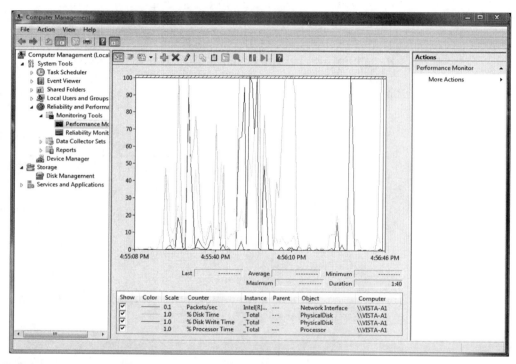

Exhibit 10-2: Performance Monitor real-time graph

The counters are categorized by *performance object*, which is any resource that you can measure. Some of the more commonly used performance objects:

- Network Interface
- Memory
- Paging File
- PhysicalDisk
- Process
- Processor
- TCPv4 and TCPv6
- UDPv4 and UDPv4

Bottlenecks

A bottleneck occurs when a shortage of a specific system or network resource causes a performance degradation. Sometimes slow network response time can be traced to problems with the network adapter or networking settings on a specific server. Other times you can trace the bottleneck to a network device, such as a router. You can use Performance Monitor on a Windows Server 2008 server to identify potential network problems to help you determine if the server is creating a bottleneck.

You can identify some common network performance problems by using the following counters:

Counter	Use to
IPv4 and IPv6	Measure rates at which IP datagrams are sent and received.
Network Interface	Measure how many packets are sent and received over a TCP/IP connection, and monitor for connection errors.
Redirector	Monitor network connections that originate on the server.
Server	Monitor communication between the server and the network.
TCPv4 and TCPv6	Measure rates TCP segments are sent and received using the TCP protocol
UDPv4 and UDPv6	Measure the rates UDP datagrams are sent and received using the UDP protocol.

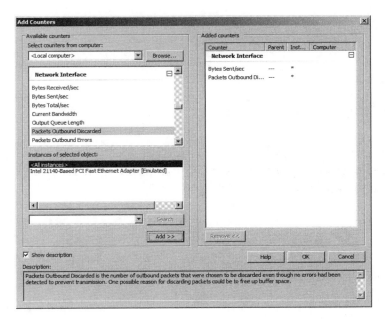

Exhibit 10-3: Adding counters

Real-time monitoring

To monitor resources in real time, you add counters to the Performance Monitor graph. To add counters, right-click the graph and choose Add Counters to open the dialog box you see in Exhibit 10-3. In the Add Counters dialog box:

1 Select whether you want to monitor resources on the local computer or a remote computer.

2 In the list of performance objects, expand the performance object that contains the counter you want to add.

3 Select the counter.

4 If necessary, select an instance of the counter. Instances are unique copies of a performance object (for example, a specific network card or hard disk).

5 Click Add.

6 When you've added all the counters you want to the Added Counters list, click OK.

Do it!

A-2: Monitoring network performance

Here's how	Here's why
1 In the console tree, expand **Reliability and Performance** Under Monitoring Tools, select **Performance Monitor**	
2 Observe the empty graph	After you add counters, this is where the real-time data will be displayed. Under the graph is a currently empty list of the counters displayed in the graph.
3 Right-click the empty graph and choose **Add Counters...**	
4 Expand **Network Interface**	To expand that performance object and display its associated counters.
5 Select **Bytes Total/sec**, and observe the "Instances of selected object" box	Depending on the number of network adapters in the server, you might see more than one instance.
Check **Show description**, and observe the counter's description at the bottom of the window	You can get a quick idea of what the counter measures using this information.
Verify that **<All Instances>** is selected, and click **Add**	To add Bytes Total/sec to the list of added counters.
6 Select **Packets Outbound Errors** and click **Add**	To add it to the list of counters.
Select **Packets Received Errors**, and click **Add**	You use both these counters to monitor for errors with packets being sent and received.

7   Scroll up, collapse **Network Interface**, and expand **IPv4**

It's easier to scroll when you don't have performance objects expanded.

Select **Datagrams/sec**, and click **Add**

8   Collapse IPv4, and under IPv6, add **Datagrams/sec**

9   Add **TCPv4: Segments/sec and TCPv4: Connection failures** to the Added counters list

(Repeat the procedure of expanding the performance object, selecting the counter, and then clicking Add.)

Add the **TCPv6: Segments/sec** and **TCPv6: Connection Failures** counters to the list

10   After you've added all the counters, click **OK**

11   Observe the graph

The real-time monitoring has begun. In a moment you'll generate some activity to see how the graph spikes when you access the network from the server.

Observe the list of counters

You can see all the counters you added, and each has been assigned a different color. You can uncheck one of the checkboxes to remove the counter's display on the graph. It won't delete the counter, but it will temporarily hide it.

12   Open Internet Explorer and access several Web pages

To generate network activity.

Switch back to Server Manager and observe the Performance Monitor graph

The network activity is displayed in graphical form. You can use these counters, and the others related to network performance, to help determine the server's network capabilities, and to help troubleshoot any problems you might be having accessing the server. Issues not directly related to the server might indicate problems with the network itself.

Performance Monitor configuration

Explanation
Like any Windows utility, you can customize the Performance Monitor graph in dozens of ways to help you better see and understand the data it's displaying. The following table describes some of the more useful buttons in the toolbar above the graph.

Button	Use to...
	Open saved log files and display them in Performance Monitor.
	Change the Performance Monitor display from a line graph to a histogram to a text-based report.
	Add and delete counters.
	Highlight counters so you can see their lines on the graph more easily.
	Display the Performance Monitor Properties dialog box.
	Freeze and restart the real-time display.
	Update data, one click (or increment) at a time.

You can also use the Performance Monitor Properties dialog box to configure Performance Monitor and the display of data. The following table describes the tabs and the settings you can configure on each.

Tab	Use to configure
General	The display of components, such as the legend and the toolbar; how much data is displayed in the histogram and report views; whether Performance Monitor should collect samples automatically; how often samples should be collected; and the duration of samples that should be displayed.
Source	Whether the data source to be displayed is real-time data or from a saved log file.
Data	How data is displayed, including which counters should be displayed, and the color, scale, width, and style of the line displayed for each counter.
Graph	Graph elements such as the view, scroll style, title and vertical axis labels, and scale.
Appearance	General appearance values, including colors and font.

Do it!   **A-3:   Configuring Performance Monitor**

Here's how	Here's why
1 In the Performance Monitor toolbar, click 🔲	To open the Properties dialog box.
2 Activate the **General** tab and observe the settings	You can configure some display options and the performance sample interval.
3 Change Sample every to **2**, and the Duration to **30**	**Graph elements** Sample every 2 seconds Duration: 30 seconds The data will now update every two seconds and the graph will display 30 seconds of data.
Click **OK**, and observe the changes in the line graph	(If necessary, refresh the Web page in Internet Explorer.) It updates more slowly than it did at the one-second interval.
4 Open the Properties box, and change the Sample every and Duration settings back to **1** and **100**, respectively	
5 In the Properties box, activate the **Data** tab	
Select the **Bytes Total/sec** counter and change line width to the thickest choice	
Select the **TCPv4 Segments/sec** counter, and change color to a dark color (if necessary) and the line style to the style shown	Style: [———] ▼
6 Activate the **Graph** tab	
Change the scroll style to **Scroll**, and change the vertical scale maximum to **50**	
7 Click **OK**, and observe the changes	(Refresh a Web page.)

8 In the Performance Monitor toolbar, click 🖼️ ▾	To change the line graph to a histogram. A histogram is another way to display the data graphically.
Click 🖼️ ▾ again	To change the histogram to a text-based report. The data is still presented in real time, but it's text-based rather than graphical representation.
Return the display to a line graph	
9 In the list of counters, select the **Bytes Total/sec** counter, and then click 🖊️	To highlight the counter.
Click the button again	To turn off highlighting.
10 Click ⏸️	To freeze the display.
Click ⏭️ a few times	To update the data manually.
Click ▶️	To unfreeze the display.
11 In the list of counters, select the **IPv6 Datagrams/sec** counter and click ❌	To delete the counter.

Data Collector Sets

Explanation

A *Data Collector Set* (*DCS*) is a mechanism that logs a computer's performance for review at a later time. This later time could be immediately after you run the DCS or several hours, days, or weeks later. You can use a Data Collector Set to obtain a performance baseline or troubleshoot performance issues.

The set takes a snapshot of a computer's performance by collecting three types of data:

- Performance counters
- Event trace data (used for debugging and performance tuning)
- System configuration information from the Registry

Windows Server 2008 contains three built-in DCSs that you can use to log a computer's performance:

- LAN Diagnostics
- System Diagnostics
- System Performance

After the DCS has run, you can then review the performance counters in Performance Monitor and the rest of the data in the form of a text-based report.

To start a Data Collector Set:

1   In Server Manager, under Reliability and Performance, expand Data Collector Sets, and expand System.

2   Right-click the Data Collector Set you want to run and choose Start. (To see the system objects the Data Collector Set examines, select it and view the objects in the details pane.) You can see the Data Collector Set is running by the small green arrow that appears on it in the tree pane.

3   If it's necessary to stop the Data Collector Set, right-click it and choose Stop. Otherwise, you know the Data Collector Set is done when the small green arrow disappears.

Do it!

A-4:   Running a Data Collector Set

Here's how
1   In the console pane, under Reliability and Performance, expand Data Collector Sets, and then expand System. Select LAN Diagnostics and click Start.
2   Switch back to Internet Explorer and browse to several different Web sites.
3   Switch back to Server Manager and stop the LAN Diagnostics Data Collector Set.

Viewing Data Collector Set reports

Explanation

Data Collector Set reports are stored in the Reports node under Reliability and Performance in the tree pane, as shown in Exhibit 7-1. You can drill down in the tree pane and select a report to view its contents in the details pane.

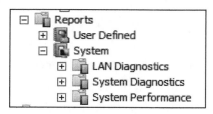

Exhibit 10-4: Data Collector Set reports

To quickly view a report for a Data Collector Set you've just run, right-click the Data Collector Set and chose Latest Report. It will select the latest report in the tree pane, and display the data in the details pane.

To view data in Performance Monitor:

1   On the Performance Monitor toolbar, click the View Log Data button to open the Performance Monitor Properties dialog box with the Source tab activated, as shown in Exhibit 7-2.

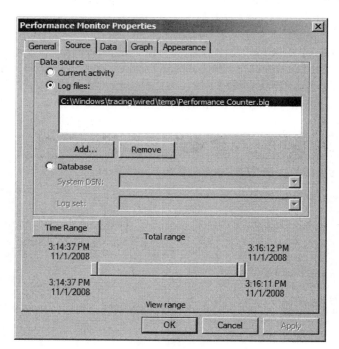

Exhibit 10-5: Opening a log file in Performance Monitor

2   Under Data source, select Log files, and then click Add.

3   Browse to find the log you want to view, select it, and click Open. If the log covers a large period of time and you want to view just a select interval, click Time Range and select the interval you want to view.

4   Click OK. You can view the recorded data in Performance Monitor just as if it were running live.

Do it!

A-5:   Viewing a Data Collector Set report

Here's how	Here's why
1 Right-click the **LAN Diagnostics** and choose **Latest Report**	To display the report you just created.
2 Observe the console tree	The report has been selected, and you can see where it's stored in the Reports node in the tree pane.
3 Scroll to observe all the captured data, expanding sections as necessary	You can see the large amount of data that was captured to create this report.
4 In the tree pane, select **Performance Monitor**	
In the toolbar, click ▨	To open the Performance Monitor Properties dialog box with the Source tab activated.
5 Select **Log files**, and click **Add...**	You're going to view the data captured by the Data Collector Set.
Browse to C:\Windows\tracing\wired\temp	
6 Select **Performance Counter** and click **Open**	
7 Click **Time Range**	You can use this setting to select the range of time you want to view in the graph.
8 Click **OK**	To display the data in Performance Monitor.
Observe the line graph	You can see the performance data for the entire time the Data Collector Set ran.

Reliability Monitor

Explanation

In addition to knowing how well your system components are operating, it's also helpful to know the overall reliability of your system, including not just the hardware components, but any applications and the Windows Server 2008 operating system itself. Reliability Monitor is one tool you can use to assess the stability of your system over a period of time and pinpoint any components that might be causing system problems.

Reliability Monitor tracks the following events that affect system stability:

- Software installs and uninstalls
- Application failures
- Hardware failures
- Windows failures
- Miscellaneous failures

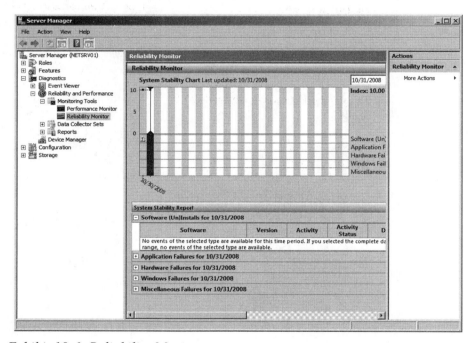

Exhibit 10-6: Reliability Monitor

Reliability Monitor, shown in Exhibit 10-6, provides two features that you can use to track and troubleshoot system health:

- System Stability Chart—A calendar-based chart that tracks reliability and the events above that affect reliability over a 28-day period. Each day Reliability Monitor assigns a number to system stability, called the *Stability Index*, from 1.0 (least stable) to 10.0 (most stable), and you can track the rise and fall of the index and match that number to the logged events to help determine what exactly is affecting system stability. You can also choose to view specific date ranges, and see a current average index.

- System Stability Report—This report provides details for the day you select in the System Stability Chart. You can use the report to see details about the events that affected the Stability Index that day.

To open Reliability Monitor, in Server Manager, under Reliability and Performance, expand Monitoring Tools, and select Reliability Monitor.

Do it!

A-6: Determining a system's Stability Index

Here's how	Here's why
1 Under Reliability and Performance, Monitoring Tools, select **Reliability Monitor**	
2 Observe the System Stability Chart	You can see the Stability Index represented by a black line, with a dot on each day to indicate that day's number. If there have been any events, they're logged as an icon to show either an informational event, a warning, or an error.
3 If possible, select a day with an icon and observe the System Stability Report	To see the event details for that day. Only event categories that logged events will open in the report. You can use this information to track problems and maintain system stability.
4 Select any other days with icons	To view the events on those days.
5 What's your current Stability Index? Is it trending up or down? Why?	
6 How might you increase the Stability Index?	
7 Close Internet Explorer	

Remote Desktop

Explanation

As you've already seen in this topic, you can often just sit down at a networked computer to determine its status, but sometimes you'll need to use a remote connection to determine a computer's status. Remote Desktop in Windows is a tool you can use to connect to a computer from a remote location and then work as if you were physically sitting at that computer. *Virtual Network Computer* (*VNC*) is another remote desktop software. You can also use the *Independent Computer Architecture* (*ICA*) protocol to connect to and remotely manage desktops on servers and clients.

Before you can connect using Remote Desktop in Windows, however, you must first permit Remote Desktop connections on the remote computer. Then you can use the Remote Desktop client to connect to the remote computer. You can enable support for Remote Desktop connections in Windows Server 2008, Windows Vista (Ultimate, Business, and Enterprise), Windows Server 2003, and Windows XP Professional. Remote Desktop connections are implemented through the Remote Desktop Protocol (RDP).

If you want to connect to computers from outside the corporate network, you'll need to first configure a way for these users to connect to the network. Most organizations do so by setting up a Virtual Private Network (VPN) to the corporate network. You can then use the VPN to connect to the corporate network first, and then run Remote Desktop Connection to connect to the networked computer.

Remote Desktop support

Enabling Remote Desktop requires that you first enable Remote Desktop itself and then define the users you want to permit to connect to the computer via a Remote Desktop connection. To accomplish both tasks on Windows Vista computers, complete the following steps:

1 In Control Panel, click the System and Maintenance link.

2 Under System, click the Allow remote access link.

3 In the User Account Control dialog box, click Continue. Windows Vista opens the System Properties dialog box and displays the Remote tab.

4 To enable support for Remote Desktop, select either of the following options, as shown in Exhibit 7-3:

   • Allow connections from computers running any version of Remote Desktop (less secure). Select this option if you will be connecting to the Windows Vista computer from an older version of Windows such as Windows XP Professional.

   • Allow connections only from computers running Remote Desktop with Network Level Authentication (more secure). Select this option if you will be connecting to the Windows Vista computer from another Windows Vista computer. Network Level Authentication (NLA) is a new authentication method introduced in Windows Vista that is more secure. Specifically, it requires complete user authentication before permitting a user to start a full Remote Desktop connection and attempt to log on.

5 Click Select Users, and add the users to whom you want to grant remote access right.

Note: By default, when you enable Remote Desktop on a Windows Vista computer, it automatically updates Windows Firewall to permit Remote Desktop connections to the computer.

Exhibit 10-7: Enable Remote Desktop support in the System Properties dialog box

To enable Remote Desktop on a Windows Server 2008 computer:

1 In Server Manager, select the Server Manager console root.

2 Under Server Summary, click Configure Remote Desktop.

3 Select either of the following options:

- Allow connections from computers running any version of Remote Desktop (less secure).

- Allow connections only from computers running Remote Desktop with Network Level Authentication (more secure).

4 Click Select Users, and add the users to whom you want to grant remote access right.

Remote Desktop Connection

After you enable support for Remote Desktop on a computer, you can connect to it by using the Remote Desktop Connection utility. To establish a connection from a Windows Vista computer, use the following steps:

1 Click Start, All Programs, Accessories, and then Remote Desktop Connection.

2 In the Computer text box, type the name or IP address of the computer to which you want to connect.

3 Click Connect.

4 By default, Remote Desktop Connection prompts you to enter a user name and password to log on to the remote computer. Enter the requested information and then click OK. You are now connected to the desktop of the remote computer.

You can configure a number of options in the Remote Desktop Connection dialog box. To configure these options, start Remote Desktop Connection and then click Options. You use the options in this dialog box to customize and also secure the remote connection.

The following table describes the options you can configure on each tab.

Tab	Use to
General	Save the settings you've configured to an RDP file for use when re-establishing a connection to the same remote computer.
Display	Configure the size of the window and color settings Remote Desktop Connection uses when displaying the desktop of the remote computer.
Local Resources	Specify whether you want Remote Desktop Connection to play the remote computer's sound over the local computer's sound card. You can also define whether you want to print to the printers defined on the remote computer or the printers configured on your local computer.
Programs	Configure Remote Desktop Connection to automatically start a program when it establishes a connection to the remote computer.
Experience	Specify the speed of your connection to the remote computer. Remote Desktop Connection determines which Windows features it displays during your remote session based on the speed of this connection. For example, you can specify whether you want Remote Desktop Connection to display the background (wallpaper) defined on the remote computer. These settings are used to optimize the performance of Remote Desktop Connection.
Advanced	Configure the behavior of Remote Desktop Connection when authentication fails. You can also configure Remote Desktop Connection to enable you to connect to a Terminal Services Gateway so that you can then connect to a remote computer behind a firewall.

Ending a Remote Desktop session

After you establish a connection with a remote computer by using Remote Desktop Connection, you can work in the window displayed just as you would if you were sitting at that computer. When you're done, it's important that you log off from your session instead of disconnecting if you no longer want your programs to run on the remote computer.

When you disconnect from the remote computer, you leave all programs running on the remote computer, which can be a security risk. You disconnect by clicking Start and then on the "X" button (or by closing the Remote Desktop Connection window). When you log off from the remote computer, you close your session (and all running programs) and then disconnect from the remote computer. Log off from the remote computer by clicking Start, the right-pointing arrow, and then Log Off.

Do it!   **A-7:   Implementing Remote Desktop connections**

Here's how	Here's why
1 On Windows Server 2008, in Server Manager, select the Server Manager console root	
In the details pane, under Server Summary, click **Configure Remote Desktop**	
2 In the System Properties box, below Remote Desktop, select **Allow connections only from computers running Remote Desktop with Network Level Authentication (more secure)**	
Click **OK**	To acknowledge that the Remote Desktop Firewall exception will be enabled. This exception will allow the Remote Desktop Protocol (RDP) to pass through Windows Firewall on the server computer.
3 Click **Select Users**	
Click **Add**	
4 In the Enter the object names to select text box, type **netadmin##**	Where netadmin## is the name of the student the instructor assigned to work with you in this activity.
Click **OK**	
Click **OK**	To close the Remote Desktop Users dialog box
Click **OK**	To close the System Properties dialog box.
5 Minimize the Windows Server 2008 virtual machine window	
6 In Windows Vista, click **Start** and choose **All Programs**, **Accessories, Remote Desktop Connection**	

7	In the Computer text box, type **netsrv##** and then click **Connect**	Where netsrv## is the computer name of your partner's Windows server.
	When prompted, enter **networkplus.class\ netadmin##** and a password of **!pass1234**	To connect to the desktop of your partner's netsrv## computer using your domain account.
	Click **OK**	
8	Observe the netsrv## computer	Notice that you can work as if you were seated in front of the computer itself. Remote Desktop is a great way to connect to servers and other computers throughout the network from your own Windows Vista desktop.
9	Click through Server Manager	To see what capabilities you have when connected remotely.
	When you're done, log off	(Click Start, point to the right-pointing arrow, and choose Log Off.) To return to your Windows Vista desktop.

Topic B: Event Viewer

This topic covers the following CompTIA Network+ 2009 exam objective.

Bridge objective

#	Objective
4.4	**Conduct network monitoring to identify performance and connectivity issues using the following** • System logs, history logs, event logs

Event Viewer

Explanation

Event Viewer, shown in Exhibit 10-8, is a Windows utility that enables you to monitor events that occur on your system. The events that are recorded can help you determine the cause of problems you're having with a particular application, a component of the operating system, or networking.

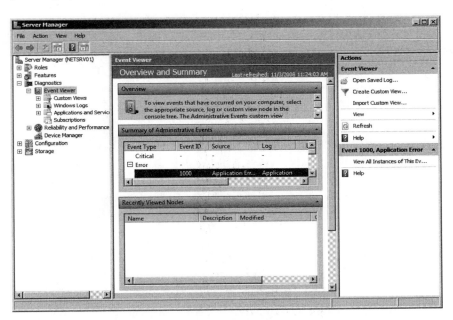

Exhibit 10-8: Event Viewer in Server Manager

In Windows Server 2008 and Windows Vista, events are kept in two sets of logs, Windows Logs and Applications and Services Logs. The Windows Logs contain administrative events, which provide information that network technicians and administrators can use when troubleshooting issues with a computer. These events and suggested solutions are usually documented on Microsoft's TechNet, MSDN, or Knowledge Base Web sites, or in other support Web sites, newsgroups, and publications.

The Windows Logs are described in the following table.

Windows Log	Contains
Application	Events logged by individual applications. The types of events an application logs in Event Viewer are determined by the application's developers and might vary considerably among applications and vendors.
Security	Events relating to the security of your computer.
Setup	Events related to application setups.
System	Events reported by Windows system components. The operating system determines which components report errors to the Event Viewer log.
Forwarded Events	Events forwarded from remote computers, which are forwarded as a result of an event subscription.

The Applications and Services Logs contain application- and component-specific logs, including logs for Internet Explorer and hardware components. These applications and components may also write to the Windows Logs but have their separate logs for events that don't necessarily have a system-wide impact. There are four types of Applications and Services events: administrative, operational, analytical, and debug.

- *Administrative events* are the same as the administrative events you'll find in the Windows Logs.

- *Operational events* and *analytical events* are used by applications or utilities to diagnose and solve a problem or trigger a task. These events can't be handled by administrative intervention. Analytical events are hidden by default.

- *Debug events* are typically used by developers when testing and diagnosing problems during the development process. These events are also hidden by default.

Within the Application and Services Log is a Microsoft folder, and within that folder is a Windows folder. Inside the Windows folder are dozens of additional logs for other Windows components and services.

To view the analytical and debug logs, in Event Viewer, choose View, Show Analytic and Debug Logs. This is a toggle menu choice; select it again to hide the logs.

Event information

Each of the Windows Logs displays the following event information for each recorded event.

Item	Description
Source	The program, system component, or individual component of a large program that recorded the event.
Event ID	An ID that identifies the type of event. Event IDs are coded into the operating system and individual applications and can be used by product support personnel to troubleshoot problems.
Level	The type of event that is recorded: Error, Warning, Information, Success Audit (Security Log only), or Failure Audit (Security Log only).
User	The name of the user who was logged on when the event was recorded. Many components run under a system account, so you might see SYSTEM in this column, even if a user is physically logged on when the event occurs.
OpCode	Shows the point in an activity that a program was performing that the event was recorded.
Logged	The date and time the event was logged.
Task Category	Additional information about the component that logged the event.
Keywords	Words that you can use to search for more information about the event.
Computer	Name of the computer where the event occurred.

Event types

There are several types of events, which are listed in the following table.

Type	Records
Critical	Events that record the complete failure of an application or component.
Error	A significant problem; for example, a service fails to start.
Warning	An event that is not a significant or immediate problem but could become a significant problem in the future; for example, disk space is running low.
Information	The successful operation of a task; for example, a network driver loads successfully.
Success Audit (Security Log only)	A successful security event; for example, a user logs on successfully.
Failure Audit (Security Log only)	An unsuccessful security event; for example, a user attempts to log on but fails to submit proper credentials.

Double-clicking an individual event opens an Event Properties dialog box with a description of the event. You can use the arrow buttons to view information about the previous (up arrow) or next (down arrow) event.

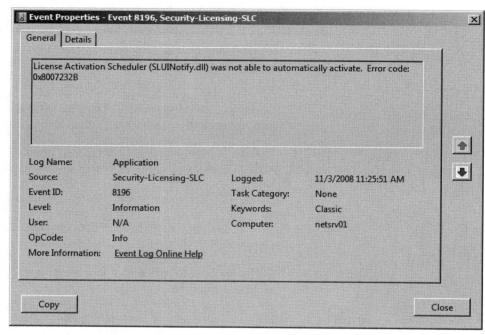

Exhibit 10-9: An Event Properties dialog

To open Event Viewer in Windows Vista, in Control Panel, click System and Maintenance. Then, click Administrative Tools, and double-click Event Viewer. Or right-click Computer on the Start menu, and choose Manage. In Computer Management, in the tree pane, select Event Viewer.

To display Event Viewer in Windows Server 2008, in Server Manager, under Diagnostics, expand Event Viewer—then Windows Logs, and select the log you want to view.

Do it!

B-1: Viewing the event logs

Here's how	Here's why
1 Switch to the Windows Server 2008 virtual machine window. Log on as netadmin##	
2 In the console tree of Server Manager, expand **Diagnostics**	
3 Select **Event Viewer** Observe the details pane	You can view a summary of administrative events, and double-click a listed event for more details. You can also go back to logs you've recently viewed under Recently Viewed Nodes, and you can see a summary of all the available logs.
4 Expand **Event Viewer**	
5 In the console tree, expand **Custom Views**	You can create and save custom views to help organize events. By default there's already an Administrative Events custom view.
6 Expand **Windows Logs**	
7 Select **Application** Observe the column headers	(You can maximize the window to view the details pane information.) The most important identifying information is displayed.
8 Observe the events Double-click the first event	The events are listed from the newest to the oldest, by default. To open the Event Properties dialog box, which displays a more detailed description of the event. You can use detailed event information to determine why an application, service, hardware device, or Windows Vista component failed and may be disrupting or preventing communication on the network.
9 Click 🔽 Click **Close**	To move to the next event in the Application log. To close the Event Properties dialog box and return to Event Viewer and the Application log.

10 In the console tree, select **Security** and scroll through the list of events	To view security-related events on the computer. You can see the events related to logons and logoffs.
Select **System** and scroll through the list of events	To view the events recorded by the operating system and its components.
11 Expand **Applications and Services Logs**	To view the default Applications and Services Logs. Some applications, such as Microsoft Office, may install additional logs under the category.
12 Expand **Microsoft**, and then expand **Windows**	
Expand the subcategories and scroll to view the logs	You can see dozens of logs covering all types of services and components. Chances are you won't be using these logs very often unless you're troubleshooting events related to a specific component that's interfering with network communication.
13 Choose **View**, **Show Analytic and Debug Logs**	To display the analytical and debug logs under Applications and Services Logs. You can see logs are now displayed for the Encrypting File System and other Windows Vista services.
Hide the analytical and debug logs	
14 Close Server Manager	

Remote logs

Explanation

Although you can sit in front of a Windows Server 2008 computer to scan its event logs, you can also connect to it remotely across the network and right from your desk. This might be more convenient if the other computer is several floors, buildings, or miles away.

To read the logs, you must have the necessary permissions on the remote computer. An account with administrative rights to the local computer (local Administrators group or other administrative account, such as a domain-level administrative account) is one way. Another way is to use the built-in local group Event Log Readers. You can use the group to grant permissions to read the logs without granting any unnecessary administrative rights. You can log on to the local computer and make the connection using the same account, or you can specify another user account to use in order to make the connection.

You must also provide a Windows Firewall exception for Remote Event Log Management. Without this exception, you won't be able to connect to the remote computer using Event Viewer; instead you'll receive an error message. (This requirement is generally true for any firewall you might be using.)

To make the connection from a Windows Vista computer, in Event Viewer, select the Event Viewer node in the tree pane. Then click "Connect to Another Computer" in the action pane.

Do it!

B-2: Viewing event logs on a remote computer

Here's how	Here's why
1 On Windows Server 2008, open Control Panel	
Double-click **Windows Firewall**	You're going to create an exception for remote event log management.
2 In the left pane, click **Allow a program through Windows Firewall**, and click **Continue**	
3 On the Exceptions tab, check **Remote Event Log Management**	Without this exception, you won't be able to make the connection using Event Viewer.
Click **OK**, and close Windows Firewall and Control Panel	
4 On Windows Server 2008, open Event Viewer	(In Control Panel, click System and Maintenance, Administrative Tools, and double-click Event Viewer.)
In the console tree, select the **Event Viewer (Local)** node	
5 Right-click and choose **Connect to Another Computer...**	
In the Select Computer dialog box, type **netsrv##**	(Where ## is your partner's unique number.)
Click **OK**	To make the connection.
6 Observe the Event Viewer node and the heading above the details pane	Both show that you're connected to your partner's NETSRV##.NETWORKPLUS.CLASS computer. Because your user account is a domain administrator, you didn't have to configure any special permissions to access the event logs on the remote server.
7 Browse through the event logs on the remote computer	

8 When you're done, click
   **Connect to Another
   Computer...**

   Select **Local computer**, and   To re-connect to your nethost## computer.
   click **OK**

9 Close all open windows

Event forwarding

Explanation

While it's easy enough to connect to a single computer to check its event logs while you're troubleshooting a problem, when you have multiple computers you need to monitor, it's not so easy to connect to each one over and over again. To help make things easier, you can use event forwarding to subscribe to events on other computers and have them collected in Event Viewer on your computer. That way you have quick and easy access to only the events you need to see on specific computers you're trying to troubleshoot.

Event forwarding requires one or more source (or forwarding) computers and a collecting computer—the computer where you collect the events, which will likely be your own computer or that of another help desk technician or administrator. On the collecting computer, you create a subscription that specifies exactly which type of events you want to collect. Those events are collected and displayed in Event Viewer under the Subscriptions node.

At a high level, in a domain environment, configure event forwarding using the following steps:

1 Configure the source computers.
2 Configure the collecting computer.
3 Create an event subscription on the collecting computer.

We'll cover these steps in more detail in the following sections.

Source computers

On each source computer, you must enable and configure the Windows Remote Management (WinRM) service and create a Windows Firewall exception to allow the WinRM service to accept incoming connections using TCP port 80. Fortunately, there's a simple method that let's you accomplish these tasks: open an elevated command prompt, and enter `winrm quickconfig`. You'll see the changes that the command will make to the WinRM service. Just confirm the changes, and you're done configuring the WinRM service.

Next, you must add the computer account of the collecting computer to the local Administrators group on each source computer. To accomplish this:

1 On each source computer, open Computer Management.
2 Expand Local Users and Groups, and select Groups.
3 In the details pane, right-click Administrators and choose Properties.
4 Click Add, and in the Select Users, Computers, or Groups dialog box, click Object Types. Check Computers, and click OK.
5 Type the name of the collector computer and click Check Names. Select the correct computer account, and click OK.

After you've made these two changes on each source computer, you can configure the collecting computer.

Collecting computers

On the collecting computer, you need to enable the Windows Event Collector (Wecsvc). Again, there's an easy command you can use: open an elevated command prompt and enter `wecutil qc`.

Do it!   **B-3:   Configuring source and collecting computers**

Here's how	Here's why
1 On Windows Server 2008, open the Start menu and in the Search box type **cmd**	You're going to configure netsrv## as the source computer and nethost## as the collecting computer.
Press `CTRL` + `SHIFT` + `⏎ ENTER`	
Click **Continue**	To open an elevated command prompt.
2 Enter **winrm quickconfig**	
Type **y** and press `⏎ ENTER`	To confirm that you want to make the changes to configure the WinRM service.
Close the command prompt window	
3 Open Server Manager, expand Configuration, Local Users and Groups, and select **Groups**	You need to add the computer account for nethost## to the local Administrators group.
4 Right-click **Administrators** and choose **Properties**	
Click **Add**	
5 Click **Object Types**	You can't search for computer objects by default, so you need to enable this feature before you can add the computer account for netsrv##.
Check **Computers** and click **OK**	
6 In the text box, type **nethost##**, and click **OK**	(Where ## is your assigned student number.) To add the computer account to the Windows Vista local Administrators group.
7 Click **OK**	To close the Administrators Properties dialog box.
8 On Windows Vista, open an elevated command prompt	
At the command prompt, enter **wecutil qc**	
Enter **y**	To confirm that you want to change the startup mode for the Wecsvc.
9 Close the Command Prompt window	

Subscriptions

Explanation

Now that the source and collecting computer are configured, you can create a new event subscription on the collecting computer. To create a new subscription:

1 On the collecting computer, open Event Viewer.

2 In the tree pane, select Subscriptions, and in the action pane, click Create Subscription to open the Subscription Properties dialog box you see in Exhibit 10-10.

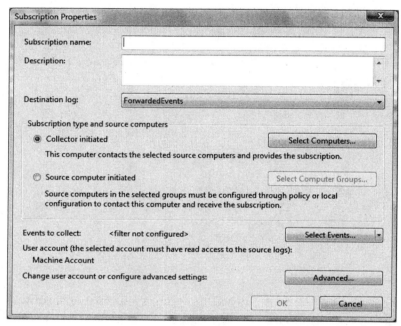

Exhibit 10-10: Event subscription properties for a Windows Vista computer

3 Type a name and description for the new subscription.

4 In the Destination Log list, select the log where you'd like the new subscription to be displayed. By default, Forwarded Events is selected, but you can choose just about any location.

5 Next to the Collector Initiated, click Select Computers. Click Add, type the name of the computer you want to add, and click OK.

6 Next to Events to collect, click the Select Events drop-down arrow. You can choose Edit to open the Query Filter dialog box, shown in Exhibit 10-11, where you can specify the exact types of events you want to collect. Or you can choose "Copy from existing Custom View" to use the criteria in a custom filter you've already created.

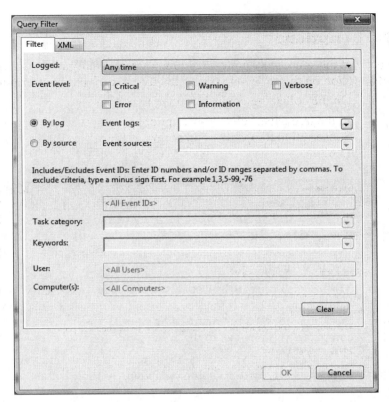

Exhibit 10-11: Filtering events

7   Next to "Change user account or configure advanced settings," click Advanced to open the Advanced Subscription Settings dialog box shown in Exhibit 10-12. You can choose to use the computer account or specify a user account. Select any event delivery optimization settings, or which protocol you'd like to use, and then click OK.

8   Click OK.

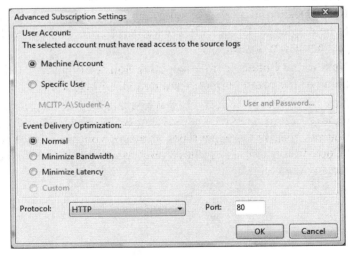

Exhibit 10-12: Advanced settings

Advanced subscription settings

You can choose to use the computer account for the collection computer, or you can use a specific user account. When using computer accounts, you never have to worry about expired passwords or user accounts being deleted or disabled if someone leaves the organization. On the other hand, if you use a user account that's a member of the Domain Admins group, you don't have to add it to the Event Log Readers local group on the source computers because Domain Admins already have rights to read event logs on domain computers.

You can also use the Advanced Subscription Settings dialog box to optimize event delivery for your network setup, choosing a setting based on how you want to configure the manner, speed, and frequency at which events are collected.

- **Normal:** Use this setting in a normal network configuration, when you don't need to worry about network bandwidth and event collection time isn't critical. Using this setting, the collecting computer pulls events from source computers five events at a time. If 15 minutes pass between collections, then any available events are collected.

- **Minimize Bandwidth:** Use this setting when you're trying to conserve network bandwidth, such as if you're operating over a wide area network or if you have a local area network with particularly heavy traffic. Using this setting, source computers push events to the collecting computer every six hours.

- **Minimize Latency:** Use this setting if you need to receive new events quickly. Using this setting, the source computers will push events every 30 seconds.

And finally, you can choose the protocol and port to use for event forwarding and WinRM communications. The default is HTTP, but you can choose to use HTTPS in networks that require an increased level of security. Be sure to configure an appropriate Windows Firewall exception if you choose to use HTTPS on port 443, because the `winrm quickconfig` command will create an exception automatically for only HTTP on port 80.

Do it!

B-4: Creating an event subscription

Here's how	Here's why
1 On Windows Vista, open Event Viewer	(In Control Panel, System and Maintenance, Administrative Tools.)
2 In the console tree, select **Subscriptions**	
In the Actions pane, click **Create Subscription...**	To open the Subscription Properties dialog box.
3 In the Subscription Name text box, type **Events from netsrv##**	
4 Observe the Destination Log drop-down list	**Forwarded Events**
	The events will be collected in the Forwarded Events log, which is under Windows Logs in the console tree.
5 Next to Collector Initiated, click **Select Computers**	
Click **Add Domain Computers**	
Type **netsrv##** and click **OK** twice	To add your netsrv## computer to the list.
6 Click the **Select Events** drop-down arrow, and choose **Edit...**	To open the Query Filter dialog box. You're going to collect all the events from the System log from the past 12 hours.
7 In the Logged drop-down list, select **Last 12 hours**	
8 Next to Event level, check **Critical**, **Error**, **Warning**, and **Information**	You might not normally collect information events, but we will for classroom purposes.
9 Next to By log, display the Event logs drop-down list	
Expand Windows Logs, and check **System**	System ▾ ☑ Windows Logs ☐ Application ☐ Security ☐ Setup ☑ System ☐ Forwarded Events ☐ Applications and Services Logs

10	Click in a blank area of the dialog box	To close the drop-down list.
11	Observe the criteria at the bottom of the Query Filter dialog box	You can enter specific event numbers, keywords, and user and computer names to make your filter even more narrow.
12	Click **OK**	To create the filter.
13	Click **Advanced**, and observe the options	In the Advanced Subscription Settings dialog box, you can choose to use a specific user account if you don't want to use a computer account (the default) to perform the collection operations. You can also configure the delivery optimization options, and assign another protocol (HTTPS) and port number.
14	Click **Cancel**	To close the dialog box without making any changes.
15	In the Subscription Properties dialog box, click **OK**	To create the subscription using the settings you've defined.
16	Observe the subscription in Event Viewer	You can see the subscription you just created. To change any of the settings, re-open the Subscription Properties dialog box.

Do it!

B-5:   Examining forwarded events

Here's how

1   In Event Viewer, under Windows Logs, select Forwarded Events.

2   Scroll through the list of events, and examine some of the different events from the Windows Server 2008 computer (netsrv##).

3   When you're done, close all open windows on Windows Vista.

On Windows Server 2008, close Server Manager.

Close and save the state of the Windows Server 2008 virtual machine.

Device and application logging

Explanation

In addition to the logging enabled by Windows and the Reliability and Performance console, you should consider enabling logging on your non-Windows servers and network devices. For example, your router or wireless access point probably provides logging capabilities. You should examine its logging capabilities and enable those that will help you capture needed information without adversely affecting performance.

Component	Information to log
Antivirus software	Signature version and update date, last scan date and time, positive detections, date and time the software is disabled or shut down.
Router	Dropped packets, errors, logons/logoffs, and configuration changes.
Firewall	Blocked access requests, blocked application requests, malformed packets, invalid requests, management actions (such as opening ports).
Wireless access point and RADIUS	Failed log on attempts, RADIUS access rejections, malformed packets, invalid requests.
DNS server	DNS record update, update request failures, zone transfer requests, zone transfer failures.
Domain controller	Failed log on attempts, failed and successful administrator logons, requests for privilege escalations.

Do it!

B-6: Discussing device and application logging

Questions and answers

1 Identify a challenge associated with enabling logging on devices and remote servers. Then, speculate on solutions to that challenge.

2 Speculate on information you should log that isn't included in the preceding table.

3 Let's say you enable logging of data on users' personal firewall software. Why would you want to monitor management actions, such as opening ports?

Unit summary: Monitoring

Topic A   In this topic, you monitored performance and reliability using **Performance Monitor**. You also used a **Data Collector Set** to collect system performance data, and you used **Reliability Monitor** to determine a computer's **Stability Index**.

Topic B   In this topic, you monitored computer performance using **Event Viewer**. You viewed **event logs** on the local computer and then connected to a remote computer to view the event logs. You then configured **event forwarding** between two computers, and created a **subscription** to collect events from a remote computer.

Review questions

1 True or false? Events are collected in event reports.

2 Which of the following are default Windows Logs? (Choose all that apply.)

   A Application

   B Hardware

   C Media Player

   D Security

3 Which of the following are types of events reported in Event Viewer? (Choose all that apply.)

   A Critical

   B Error

   C Logon

   D Logoff

4 True or false? Event Viewer is a Computer Management component.

5 Analytical and _____ logs are hidden by default and generally used only by developers.

6 Which of the following is the local group you can use to grant permissions to view event logs on a remote computer?

   A Event Log Managers

   B Event Log Admins

   C Event Log Readers

   D Event Log Browsers

7 You use the `winrm` _____ command to enable and configure the Windows Remote Management service on a source computer.

8 True or false? You must enable the Windows Event Collector service on the source computer when configuring event forwarding.

9 For which port must you create a Windows Firewall exception when using HTTP in event forwarding?

A 45

B 80

C 180

D 443

10 For which port must you create a Windows Firewall exception when using HTTPS in event forwarding?

A 45

B 80

C 180

D 443

11 You use the `wecutil` _____ command to enable and configure the Windows Event Collector service on a collecting computer.

12 To collect events on the collecting computer, you must create a _____.

13 In event forwarding, under normal settings, the collecting computer uses a _____ method to obtain events from a source computer.

14 Which of the following event delivery optimization settings might you use when collecting events from a branch office that's connected over a slow WAN link?

A Minimize Latency

B Minimize Bandwidth

C Maximize Bandwidth

D Maximize Latency

15 When monitoring a computer using Performance Monitor, you must add _____ to display real-time data on the line graph.

16 You'd use the LAN _____ Data Collector Set to troubleshoot network performance.

17 Which of the following display types can you use to display data in Performance Monitor?

A Line graph

B Pie chart

C Histogram

D Pictogram

18 True or false? The System Diagnostics Data Collector Set runs for exactly 5 minutes.

Independent practice activity

In this activity, you will monitor events in Event Viewer, configure event forwarding, and run a Data Collector Set.

1 Configure netsrv## as a collector computer and nethost## as a source computer.

2 Create a subscription on netsrv## that collects information events from the system log on nethost##. Observe the events.

3 Use a Data Collector Set to capture network diagnostic information from the nethost## computer.

4 When finished, close all open windows. Close and save the state of the Windows Server 2008 virtual machine.

Unit 11
Troubleshooting

Unit time: 240 minutes

Complete this unit, and you'll know how to:

A Explain the basic troubleshooting steps and prepare toolkits for troubleshooting.

B Troubleshoot the physical and logical network.

C Implement a network troubleshooting methodology based on a given scenario.

Topic A: Troubleshooting basics

This topic covers the following CompTIA Network+ 2009 exam objectives.

#	Objective
4.3	**Given a scenario, evaluate the network based on configuration management documentation** • Compare wiring schematics, physical and logical network diagrams, baselines, policies and procedures and configurations to network devices and infrastructure • Update wiring schematics, physical and logical network diagrams, configurations and job logs as needed
4.4	**Conduct network monitoring to identify performance and connectivity issues using the following:** • Network monitoring utilities
4.6	**Given a scenario, implement the following network troubleshooting methodology** • Information gathering – identify symptoms and problems • Identify the affected areas of the network • Determine if anything has changed • Establish the most probable cause • Determine if escalation is necessary • Create an action plan and solution identifying potential effects • Implement and test the solution • Identify the results and effects of the solution • Document the solution and the entire process
4.7	**Given a scenario, troubleshoot common connectivity issues and select and appropriate action** • Logical issues • Issues that should be identified but escalated • Switching loop • Routing loop • Route problems • Proxy arp • Broadcast storms • Incorrect VLAN

Bridge objective (for 4.4)

Bridge objective (for 4.7)

Bridge objective

#	Objective
5.3	**Given a scenario, utilize the appropriate hardware tool**

- Cable testers
- Protocol analyzer
- Certifiers
- TDR
- OTDR
- Multimeter
- Toner probe
- Butt set
- Punch down tool
- Cable stripper
- Snips
- Voltage event recorder
- Temperature monitor

Troubleshooting is the process of determining the cause of, and ultimately the solution to, a problem. By applying a logical, consistent method to the troubleshooting process, you make your job easier and shorten the time it takes to discover the root of a problem.

Troubleshooting problems can be a daunting experience. To troubleshoot a problem, learn as much as you can about the equipment you support. In addition, approach the situation in a straightforward and logical manner.

Information gathering

When a user reports a problem on the network or on his or her system, listen carefully to what's being said. This points you in the right direction. Sometimes, however, the key to identifying the problem is to determine what isn't being said.

Learn to ask open-ended questions to help identify symptoms and problems. Open-ended questions can't be answered by a simple yes or no. Instead of asking "Are you able to log in to the network?" try "What happens when you try to log in to the network?" Open-ended questions typically encourage the user to provide greater detail about what occurred prior to, during, and after the problem occurred.

Keep in mind that users might flavor their observations with their own interpretations when reporting a problem. These interpretations might not be completely accurate. Error messages, if you don't understand what they're telling you, can be misleading. Learn to recognize the relevant information.

Another problem is that all errors might not be reported. This is especially true if users have reported minor problems in the past and never received any type of response or follow-up. These small difficulties might, however, be leading up to a major failure.

While defining a potential problem, you might realize that there could be a quick solution to the malfunction. Try these quick fixes before proceeding. They might save you time by immediately resolving the problem.

Make sure that you speak to users in a professional manner. Don't become impatient or condescending. Many support professionals work from a script or checklist when speaking with users to remind themselves of pertinent and appropriate areas of inquiry. Make sure that you set expectations with the users, providing them with a timeline for correction.

Identify the affected area

As mentioned before, it's very important to identify who and how many users are affected by a problem. Once you've identified the area that's affected, you can use this information to help you in the troubleshooting process.

Understanding the area that's affected by the problem helps you determine the priority of the issue and whether you may need assistance from other support personnel. It also might give you clues as to the cause of the problem and help you make your questions more specific.

To help with identifying the area that's affected, you can also try to recreate the problem. For example, try the function yourself on the user's workstation to verify that it isn't an operator error. Have the user try to perform the function on another, similar workstation to determine if it's a machine-specific problem. Repeat the factors involved in the original occurrence as closely as possible. Keep variables to a minimum while you're working.

You won't be able to reproduce the problem in all situations. If the problem is physical or data damaging, you don't want to. If it's irregular, you might not be able to. In situations like this, you must depend heavily on intuitive logical processes.

Determine if anything has changed

One of the most helpful troubleshooting tools is identifying the changes that have occurred between the time that all was well and the time the problem started. Often, users make changes to their systems and cause unintended problems along the way. Or, the IT department may have made a network environment change that's now causing problems.

Often, when you ask a user about changes they may have made, their first reaction is to deny having made any changes, either because they truly can't remember or because they aren't comfortable admitting that they made changes. Try to get the user to think about it, help him feel ok about any changes he may have made, and ask leading questions that might prompt the user to provide relevant information. The troubleshooting process isn't a good time for admonitions about not making changes.

You can also try to identify changes at the user's workstation yourself if certain standards apply to all workstations or groups of workstations in your organization. Further, think about changes you or other systems administrators have made to the network recently to determine if they could have a part in the problem at hand.

Meticulous attention to change management documentation can help you determine what, if anything, has changed in the larger network:

- **Wiring schematics:** You can use these to help determine where the physical network might be causing the issues you're investigating.
- **Physical and logical network diagrams:** These documents can give you a high-level view of the physical network and its devices, and the IP addressing information associated with each network host.
- **Baselines:** A set of baselines can help you narrow down a problem to a specific device when you begin to investigate devices and their current performance.
- **Policies and procedures:** These documents can help you determine the best way to proceed according to company policy and how configurations to network devices and infrastructure can be modified and how the changes should be documented.

Establish the most probable cause

Next, you need to attempt to isolate and select the most likely source of the problem. A systematic approach to problem solving is generally the best approach. That is, based on the type of problem, determine what parameters should be eliminated first. Upon elimination, check whether the problem still exists. If so, eliminate the next obvious parameter. Repeat the procedure until the problem disappears.

To isolate the cause of failures, you must be familiar with the following components:

- Workstation hardware
- Workstation operating systems
- Workstation applications
- Network operating systems
- Cabling

Complicating the process is the fact that components might work properly when tested separately or fail only in certain specific combinations. In addition, it's seldom possible to isolate all components that you want to test. It's necessary to isolate as much as possible, keeping variables to a minimum.

When isolating the cause, it's helpful to determine its scope on the network. To determine the scope, it's generally best to answer the following questions in order:

- Does the problem exist across the enterprise?
- Is the problem related to the logical arrangement of resources?
- Does the problem exist across a WAN link?
- Does the problem exist in the local area network?
- Does the problem exist at the workstation?

Determine if escalation is necessary

You won't be able to solve every problem, either because you don't have he necessary access rights, or because it's a problem with a system that is administered by a different department. At this point, you must determine if the problem needs to be escalated to a higher level of support, or to a different administrator, such as a server administrator or a security administrator.

There are several issues that you might need to escalate to the network administrator:

- Switching loop, which occurs when misconfiguration or broken link causes packets to loop endlessly between switches.

- Routing loop, which is a similar problem with communication between routers.

- Route problems: Outdated routing tables or misconfigured routers and routing protocols.

- Proxy ARP: Proxy ARP occurs when one host answers ARP requests for another. In this way, the answering host masks its identity and forwards the ARP request itself. Misconfiguration can cause lost network and Internet communications.

- Broadcast storm: Caused by an extremely high level of broadcast radiation, which is a combination of broadcast and multicast network traffic. A broadcast storm can inundate network resources and choke off regular network traffic.

- Incorrect VLAN: Incorrect settings on a VLAN switch can cause network clients to lose connectivity, either because they're receiving the wrong network configuration settings or because the VLAN itself has failed due to misconfiguration. Typically VLAN configuration will be escalated to the network administrator for a solution.

Create an action plan

After the problem has been isolated and you've determined that the problem doesn't need to be escalated, determine the appropriate course of action to eliminate the cause and identify possible effects. Experienced technicians draw on their past experiences to help them formulate a correction. At times, the problem might be large enough to merit a formal plan of correction. If this is the case, you should carefully set forth a plan containing all steps necessary to correct the problem.

Implement a solution and test the result

Once you've formulated an action plan, it's time to fix the problem. First and foremost, ensure that the operational needs of your business are met. This might mean having the user work at another system while repairs are being made. The first priority is to keep the users productive while you fix the problem.

To make the process of fixing the problem the most efficient, use troubleshooting tools that are at your disposal. These include system logs and monitoring utilities, online or printed documentation, support CDs, telephone support, online knowledge bases, data analyzers, and so forth.

It might also be necessary to bring in a third-party service provider to assist with correcting the problem. You'll find that any background work you've done up to that point helps streamline the process. It also helps reduce costs incurred by implementing the solution.

After you've implemented the correction, you must verify that it resolved the issue. This needs ample testing. For example, if the problem is at a user's workstation, test the workstation locally and after it's attached to the network. After you feel certain that the problem is resolved, have the user test it in your presence. The problem's been corrected only when the user feels confident it's been corrected.

Solving the problem doesn't always determine the cause. You need to look at underlying factors, such as system environment, and correct these as well.

Identify the results of the solution and its effects

Once you've tested the results of the solution you implemented, you need to identify its results as well as its effects. This helps with the final step of documenting the problem and solution and with future troubleshooting.

At this point, you should be clear as to what the actual results of your solution are and how it effects the user, the network, and so on. In many cases, this simply means that everything is back to how it was before. In some cases, however, implementing the solution may have created a changed environment for the user or resulted in changes in the network.

Document the problem and the solution

Finally, document the symptoms, cause, and solution, as well as the process you used to arrive at the solution. This becomes a valuable tool when troubleshooting problems in the future. Documentation provides a company with trend information and a knowledge base that can be used to address future issues. Documentation includes wiring schematics, network diagrams, baselines, polices and procedures (if the network issues relate to company-wide policies), and configuration changes to network devices and infrastructure.

In addition, after you've resolved the problem, make sure that the resolution doesn't create additional problems. Verify the stability of the computing environment through follow-up with the users. Talk to the users. Check whether they're happy with your resolution of the problem.

Continual failure to give feedback to users reporting problems typically results in employee distrust and dissatisfaction with the IT department. This is damaging to the IT department's ability to troubleshoot future issues, not to mention the efficiency of the network.

Do it!

A-1:   Discussing troubleshooting procedures

Questions and answers

1 Why is it important to document problems and their resolutions?

2 When identifying a problem, why is it important for the network administrator to ask open-ended questions?

3 What should you do to check if a problem reported to you is machine specific?

Problem and resolution tracking

Explanation

It's important to maintain information about the problems you need to resolve and the resolution to those problems. You must keep track of all open issues so that you and your support technician teammates don't let customers slip through the cracks. Having a record of past resolutions can assist you when you encounter similar problems in the future.

Tracking options

The options for tracking problems and resolutions are nearly endless. You can do something as simple as a pen-and-paper-based system in a 3-ring binder to an off-the-shelf problem-tracking and resolution database system to a custom-built application. It all depends on the size of the user base you're supporting and the needs of the organization.

Whichever system you use, it's recommended you maintain a backup copy in a secure location so that if something happens to the original, you have access to the copy from another location. A system on a server could be unavailable due to server problems, network problems, or computer workstation problems. Any system could be unavailable due to fire or natural disaster problems.

Important information you should consider tracking in your system includes:

- User name
- User location
- Operating system
- Hardware platform
- Date call was received
- Date user was visited
- Time spent on problem
- Date problem was resolved
- Detailed description of the problem
- Detailed description of steps to resolve the problem
- Summary of problem (using keywords or a one-line summary)
- Summary of resolution (using keywords or a one-line summary)

Help desk software

Many vendors offer software to help manage problem-tracking and help desk functions. Companies like IBM, Computer Associates, and others offer large-scale commercial problem tracking applications.

Many smaller companies offer similar packages aimed at smaller company needs or for targeted vertical markets. For example, you can find applications designed specifically to support the tracking needs of Web site hosting companies or software developers.

Visit `www.helpdesk.com/software-helpdesk.htm` for a long list of help desk software publishers and their Web sites. Further information, particularly on the smaller vendor products, is also available at `http://linas.org/linux/pm.html`.

Do it!   **A-2:   Tracking problems and resolutions**

Here's how
1 Use Internet Explorer to search the Web for a problem-tracking system
2 List the features in the solution you found:
3 Are there any features you'd like that aren't included in this solution?
4 Would your company be more likely to develop its own database to track problems or to purchase some type of problem-tracking system? Would it be very basic or an integrated solution with modules for tracking assets as well as problem-tracking? Explain your reasons.

Hardware toolkit

Explanation

Network support technicians need tools that perform a wide variety of functions. Pre-assembled repair toolkits are available for amateurs and for professionals. These specialty hardware tool kits contain versions of the tools appropriate for working with networking components. You can also assemble a toolkit yourself containing the following items.

- A variety of screwdrivers—You should have large and small versions of flat-blade, Phillips, and Torx screwdrivers.
- Small and large needle-nosed pliers—These are useful for grasping objects.
- Tweezers—Also used for grasping objects.
- Three-pronged "grabber"—For picking up screws or other objects in areas too small to get your fingers into.
- A small flashlight—A small penlight or a light that can be clamped to the computer case can prove quite useful.
- Antistatic bags to protect components that are sensitive to static electricity.

    ⚠ Never lay a component on the outside of an antistatic bag. The bag is designed to collect static charges on the outside of the bag, so if you lay the component on the bag, it's likely that they'll discharge onto the component.

- Small containers—For holding screws and small components that are easily lost.
- Grounding wrist straps and ESD static mats—To protect the equipment from any static you might be carrying on your body.

    ⚠ A grounding wrist strap should never be worn when working on the interior of a monitor, but in all other cases this is a highly recommended ESD protection tool.

- Anti-static sprays—Useful if your clothes are staticky.

The following additional items are important for every toolkit.

Item	Used to
Multimeter	Test equipment with readings of ohms, amps, and volts. Comparing the readings with the appropriate values for a component helps determine if there's a problem with the component.
Nut driver	Remove hex-head nuts.
Cable stripper	Remove the outer insulation from network cables and expose the wires inside them. Usually, this item also includes wire cutters to cut the cable or wire.
Snips	Cut or trim cables.
Punch down tool	Connect wires to a punch down block.
Crimper	Crimp a connector onto a network cable. It comes in varieties for RJ-11, RJ-45, and coaxial cable.
Butt set	Test and verify telephone lines.
Time-domain reflectometer (TDR)	Locate problems in metallic wires, such as coaxial cable and twisted-pair network cables.

Item	Used to
Optical time-domain reflectometer (OTDR)	Locate faults in optical fiber.
Certifier	Test and verify network cable speeds by sending data packets across the network. You can use certifiers to verify network segments are operating at optimal levels.
Temperature monitor	Monitor temperature in various environments, especially in rooms that contain networking devices. High temperatures can cause damage to some network devices, including servers. Monitors can be configured to warn you when the temperature has exceeded a specific limit to allow you to take corrective action.
Voltage event recorder	Measure electrical-related properties to determine whether there's an adequate power supply and the quality of that power supply.

Software toolkit

Most people think of hardware toolbox tools when you speak of assembling a toolkit for a network technician. However, there are several software tools without which no troubleshooting toolkit would be complete, especially when you're troubleshooting clients and servers and their network connections.

Item	Description
Common drivers disk	If your company has standardized a specific set of equipment with common drivers, having a disk that you can carry with you can make it easy to install the drivers quickly if you have to remove them to fix a problem, or if they become corrupted. While many companies place this information on a central server location, if you can't access the server due to the problem you're trying to fix, having it on the server won't do you any good.
Virus protection software	You should include a boot disk from which you can boot a system that has been infected with a boot virus. Norton and McAfee are examples of companies that make virus protection software from which you can create such a disk. Follow their directions for how to clean the virus from the system. The virus protection software CD in some cases is what to boot from when you need to clean a system, so configure CMOS to be able to boot from CD.
Boot disk	A bootable floppy disk or boot CD-ROM is useful if you can no longer boot from the hard drive. On this CD or floppy disk, you should have basic commands that enable you to perform simple tasks.
Operating system CD or DVD	Having a copy of the operating system CD enables you to get to the CAB files that you might need when installing or repairing some piece of hardware. It's also useful if you need to boot from the CD or if files or drivers have been corrupted and need to be replaced.
Common problems	If you have a set of common problems that you encounter and need documentation on how to fix them, a CD or flash drive with that information can prove valuable. If this is in a searchable format, then you can easily locate the information you need to fix a problem you've encountered in the past.

Web sites for the manufacturers of the equipment you support should be included somewhere in your toolkit. A bookmark list, a paper list, or a document containing the URLs is useful. Being able to access the support sites directly is beneficial when you need to obtain updated drivers or look for solutions to problems you encounter. Another useful site is drivers.com. You can download drivers for many components including ones from companies no longer in operation.

A CD binder is useful for carrying these tools with you. They come in a variety of sizes. You could also copy the files to a USB flash drive instead of to a CD if you preferred.

Do it!

A-3: Identifying common toolkit components

Here's how	Here's why
1 Open a Web browser and go to a search site	You'll examine the components of a hardware technician's toolkit.
2 Search for **computer maintenance tool kit**	
3 Compare your results with those of other students	Tool kits range from a modest price for a few tools to comprehensive kits for a facility specializing just in hardware repairs.
4 Which tools would you include in your tool kit for your job?	
5 When would you use a crimper? A punch down tool?	
6 What software tools would you include in your troubleshooting kit?	
7 When would you use a certifier? A temperature monitor?	
8 Search for diagnostic software. What are some examples you find?	
9 In addition to the software mentioned in the text, are there any other tools you would include?	

Topic B: Troubleshooting the network

This topic covers the following CompTIA Network+ 2009 exam objectives.

#	Objective
4.5	**Explain different methods and rationales for network performance optimization**

Bridge objective

- Methods
  - QoS
  - Traffic shaping
  - High availability
  - Caching engines
  - Fault tolerance
- Reasons
  - Latency sensitivity
  - High bandwidth applications
    - VoIP
    - Video applications
  - Uptime

4.6   Given a scenario, implement the following network troubleshooting methodology

- Information gathering – identify symptoms and problems
- Identify the affected areas of the network
- Determine if anything has changed
- Establish the most probable cause
- Determine if escalation is necessary
- Create an action plan and solution identifying potential effects
- Implement and test the solution
- Identify the results and effects of the solution
- Document the solution and the entire process

#	Objective

Bridge objective

4.7   Given a scenario, troubleshoot common connectivity issues and select an appropriate solution

Physical issues:

- Cross talk
- Nearing crosstalk
- Near End crosstalk
- Attenuation
- Collisions
- Shorts
- Open impedance mismatch (echo)
- Interference

Logical issues:

- Port speed
- Port duplex mismatch
- Incorrect IP address
- Wrong gateway
- Wrong DNS
- Wrong subnet mask
- Issues that should be identified but escalated:
  - Switching loop
  - Routing loop
  - Route problems
  - Proxy arp
  - Broadcast storms

Wireless issues

Bridge objective

5.1   Given a scenario, select the appropriate command line interface tool and interpret the output to verify functionality

- Traceroute
- Ipconfig
- Ifconfig
- Ping
- Arp ping
- Arp
- Nslookup
- Host
- Dig
- Mtr
- Route
- Nbtstat
- Netstat

#	Objective

Bridge objective

5.3 **Given a scenario, utilize the appropriate hardware tools**

- Cable testers
- Protocol analyzer
- Certifiers
- TDR
- OTDR
- Multimeter
- Toner probe

- Butt set
- Punch down tool
- Cable stripper
- Snips
- Voltage event recorder
- Temperature monitor

Troubleshooting wired connections

Explanation

There can be many sources of problems with wired connections—some are physically based, such as a bad network cable; and some are software based, such as an invalid TCP/IP address.

Electrical interference

One common problem that occurs on networks that degrades data signals is electrical interference. *Network noise* is any electrical signal on the network cable that isn't part of the sender's original signal. Noise is generated both internally and externally.

Internally, twisted pair cables produce relatively little electrical interference—the twists cancel each other out. Any variation in the thickness of the wire, in the cable insulation, or the capacitance of wires or insulation causes a mismatch and creates noise between the pairs. When you use good quality cables, you minimize the internally-produced noise, but don't remove it altogether.

Electrical interference can come from many external sources. You should always install cables in separate conduits away from items such as electric motors (like those found in lifts/elevators), fluorescent lights, and air conditioners. In areas where there's an abundance of electrical noise, you can use shielded cables or other technologies such as fiber optic cables to avoid interference.

When a data signal travels down a conductor, it creates an electric field, which interferes with any wires close by. This is called *crosstalk*. Crosstalk gets larger at higher frequencies and with parallel wires. The twists in twisted pair cables cancel this effect; however, it's important that the twists are symmetrical and that adjacent pairs have different twists. Remember, there are different types of crosstalk, as described in the following table.

Crosstalk	Description
Near End Crosstalk (NEXT)	Crosstalk that originates up to 30 meters from the source of the signal. This is a typical problem on cable connectors or patch panels, where you untwist the wires to make the connection. Always keep the section of untwisted cable to a minimum; even a very short piece of untwisted cable can introduce a large amount of crosstalk.
Far End Crosstalk (FEXT)	Crosstalk that occurs at the far end of the cable. FEXT is greater on short cables than on long cables because signals attenuate by the time they reach the far end of the cable and are weaker.
Equal Level Far End Crosstalk (ELFEXT)	A calculated value of the crosstalk between pairs measured at the far end of the cable. ELFEXT takes into account the amount of signal loss and is calculated for each pair of cables. ELFEXT is slightly different for each pair. If you have a very high ELFEXT, it indicates excessive attenuation or high far-end crosstalk.
Pair to Pair Crosstalk	The value a signal on one pair of cables has on the others. To calculate pair to pair crosstalk, you place a signal on one pair and then measure the disturbance on the others. You calculate 12 sets of measurements—each pair at the near and far ends.
	Measure NEXT for pairs 1 to 2, 1 to 3, and 1 to 4; measure NEXT for pairs 2 to 3, 2 to 4, and 3 to 4. Repeat at the other end of the cable. The worst value you calculate out of the 12 sets is the crosstalk for the cable.

Other physical issues

In addition to crosstalk and interference, you should be aware of the additional issues described in the following table.

Physical issue	Description
Attenuation	The decrease in signal strength along the length of a network wire. The longer the wire, the greater the degree of signal attenuation. You can solve this problem by shortening the length of cable or by inserting a device such as a repeater. Attenuation is expressed in negative decibels (dB).
Collisions	On Ethernet networks, collisions are the result of multiple network hosts transmitting data simultaneously. A certain amount of collisions are expected in any network, but too many collisions can cause a bottleneck and prevent the transmission of data.
Open impedance mismatch (echo)	Line echo is typically the result of impedance mismatch, which is caused by the termination or wiring conversion from four-wire telephone circuits to two wires.

Cable testing devices

You can use a cable testing device, as shown in Exhibit 11-1, to test the physical cables and network functions, such as how a network handles varying loads of data, and whether the network throughput matches the cable and device ratings. You can purchase cable testing devices for your particular LAN or purchase one that's compatible with multiple network types. For example, testing devices are available for 10 and 100 Base-T networks.

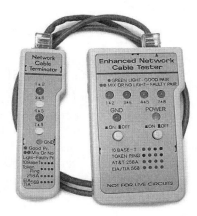

Exhibit 11-1: A cable testing device

Examples of physical cable tests that your cable testing device might be able to perform include:

- Locating miswired cables, open cables, and shorts
- Locating missing cables
- Locating cables that don't support your network type (for example, 100 Base-T)
- Testing hub connections
- Testing PC connections
- Testing installed cables
- Testing patch cables
- Locating and tracing inactive cables

Examples of network function tests that your cable testing device might be able to perform include:

- Verifying if PC is ON, if it appears as a PC, and maximum speed
- Verifying if hub is ON, if it appears as a hub, and maximum speed
- Verifying PC to hub speed and data transmission and port speed or duplex mismatch
- Verifying hub to hub data transmission
- Determining if straight-thru or crossover patch cable is required
- Finding speed bottlenecks on LANs
- Monitoring LAN link between two devices

You can also install software on computers in your network to test for load and throughput bottlenecks on the network. Some are freely downloadable, while others are available for purchase.

Network analyzers

A *network analyzer*, sometimes called a protocol analyzer, shown in Exhibit 11-2, is a portable device that can be hand-carried to a network location and set up to monitor and diagnose problems with a network. A network analyzer can help you troubleshoot difficulties that can occur because of problems with the hardware or software. A network analyzer can identify problems with:

- Cabling
- Jacks
- Network cards
- Hubs
- Other hardware that works at the lower levels of the OSI model

A network analyzer also can diagnose problems with TCP/IP, including TCP/IP packet errors. It can analyze where a packet is coming from or going to, and if the protocols within the packet are used correctly. The packets can be captured and analyzed at any point on the network, such as when the cabling is connected to a wall jack. The analyzer can be attached between the cable and the jack, and can read and analyze packets as they pass.

Exhibit 11-2: A portable network analyzer

One problem that you might encounter when using a network analyzer is that the analyzer can capture too much data, making it difficult to wade through all the data to search for what applies to the problem at hand. For that reason, a network analyzer allows you to specify filters that weed out data that isn't involved in the problem. A network analyzer can be a laptop computer with a proprietary operating system and other software specifically designed to capture and analyze packets on a network.

Network optimization

Fixing network problems can be as easy as replacing a worn cable, but sometimes network problems require bigger fixes. For example, some network communication problems require a reconfiguration of the entire network either for all network communication or for specific types.

- Many networks have servers that contain highly sensitive data that must be available around the clock. To increase the amount of uptime for these servers and provide a high level of availability, a network administrator must build in a level of fault tolerance, which simply means that there is a way to quickly recover from a server or network problem. For example, a server farm provides a high level of fault tolerance by spreading sensitive data and applications across a number of different servers. If one server were to fail, the remaining servers would still provide services to network users.

- To increase response times for Internet users, and to reduce the load on gateway servers, you can deploy a proxy servers that use a caching engine to store frequently requested Web addresses. These severs can store Web content that users access frequently, and return that content to the users faster than they could retrieve the content directly from the Web.

- Many applications, such as *Voice over IP (VoIP)* and video applications, are particularly prone to *latency sensitivity*, which is caused when the network breaks the packets in to variable sizes that may be transmitted out of sequence. This can cause *jitters* in the video or voice transmissions that can severely reduce the quality of both, potentially rendering them useless. *Quality of Service (QoS)* mechanisms and policies on the network can be used prioritize video and VoIP transmission to ensure that the packets receive priority over other types of network traffic, which can help reduce and eliminate jitters and other types of interference.

When troubleshooting network problems, you should be aware of these issues and escalate them if necessary.

Do it!

B-1: Testing the physical network

Here's how	Here's why
1 Follow your instructor's directions to attach your cable tester to your computer's network cable	You're going to test the section of cable between your computer and the classroom hub.
2 Follow your instructor's directions to attach your cable tester to the network cable ending at the classroom hub	
3 Follow your instructor's directions to test the section of cable and read the tester's display	
4 Follow your instructor's directions to remove the cable tester and reattach the cables	
5 Follow your instructor's directions to connect the network analyzer to the network	You're going to conduct load and throughput testing.
6 Follow your instructor's directions to conduct load testing and throughput testing	
7 Follow your instructor's directions to remove the network analyzer	

Troubleshooting wireless network connections

Explanation

As with other types of troubleshooting, troubleshooting wireless network connections begins with identifying the components that make up the wireless communication process. These components include:

- The Windows operating system and the network adapter driver
- The wireless network adapter
- The wireless radio frequency signal
- The wireless access point

Problem isolation

Your task is to isolate the problem by using isolating questions. Questions you should ask include:

- Can you see the wireless network adapter in Device Manager? Does Device Manager report that the adapter is working properly? If it doesn't, you should suspect a problem with the network adapter driver or even the card itself. You should also verify whether the wireless network adapter's radio has been turned off. If Device Manager reports that the network adapter is working properly, you should suspect a problem with its configuration or the wireless access point.
- Is the computer's wireless network connection configured to use the appropriate encryption method for the wireless access point? If it isn't, modify the configuration of the wireless network connection to use the correct security settings.
- Is the computer detecting the wireless access point? If so, what is the strength of the wireless signal? (You can determine the strength of the wireless signal by using the Connect to a wireless network wizard.) If the wireless signal is weak, this is an indication that the computer might be too far from the wireless access point. The wireless access point might also be experiencing interference from the environment (such as metal file cabinets). You might also try installing equipment designed to boost the signal strength of the wireless access point.
- Is the wireless access point configured correctly? Specifically, is it configured to use the appropriate encryption algorithm for the network cards in use in your environment? For wireless access points configured to use WPA or WPA2 with a pre-shared key, has anyone changed this key on the wireless access point? If so, you must enter the new key in your profile for connecting to the network.

The following table lists common problems with your wireless connection that you might encounter.

Symptom	Probable cause	Suggested solution
Unable to connect to infrared wireless device	Out of range, obstructions blocking ports, infrared serial port disabled in BIOS or operating system.	Move closer. Remove obstructions and gently clean the infrared port windows. Use the BIOS setup utility and Device Manager to confirm that the infrared port is enabled.
Unable to connect to radio wireless device	Out of range, interference from electrical motors or equipment, drivers not installed, wireless router turned off, security settings prevent connections.	Move closer and move away from sources of interference. Use Device Manager to confirm that the wireless device is installed and that there are no conflicts. Confirm that your router is turned on. Confirm that you have sufficient permissions to connect to the wireless device.
Unable to connect to Bluetooth wireless device	Out of range, interference from electrical motors or equipment, drivers not installed, security settings prevent connections.	Move closer and move away from sources of interference. Use Device Manager to confirm that the wireless device is installed and that there are no conflicts. Confirm that you have sufficient permissions to connect to the wireless device.

Do it!

B-2: Troubleshooting wireless networking

Questions and answers

1 A user reports that she doesn't see any wireless networks when she runs the Connect to a wireless network wizard. What are some things you should check on her computer?

2 Several users report this morning that they are unable to connect to the network. These users connect wirelessly via a wireless access point. What are two things you should check to troubleshoot this problem?

3 Users report that they are intermittently losing their connections to the wireless network. What should you check?

Troubleshooting TCP/IP

Explanation

One of the most common complaints you'll hear from users is that they can't get to something on the network, or "the Internet is down." When you hear a complaint about network connectivity, your first step should be to check the user's network connection and TCP/IP settings.

If you find there's a problem on the client computer, it's your job to fix it, usually by correcting TCP/IP properties. If you suspect a problem with the network as a whole or with a particular server on the network, you'll need to contact the appropriate individual, typically the network administrator, to escalate the problem.

TCP/IP utilities

TCP/IP includes a group of utility tools that can be used to troubleshoot problems with TCP/IP. The following table lists the utilities and the purpose of each.

Utility	Purpose
ARP (Address Resolution Protocol)	In IPv4, manages the IP-to-Ethernet address translation tables that are used to find the MAC address of a host on the network when the IP address is known. In IPv6, the Neighbor Discovery Protocol (NDP) is used to provide ARP functionality.
ARP ping	Uses ARP packets to ping a host on the local network segment. Network hosts must respond to ARP pings, even if they're protected by a firewall. You can use ARP ping in place of the ICMP ping described below.
Dig (Domain Information Groper)	A Unix/Linux tool used to query DNS servers.
Getmac	Displays the NIC's MAC address (new in Windows XP).
Host	A Unix/Linux DNS lookup utility used to determine a host's name or IP address. When the host name is entered, the host command will return the host's IP address. When an IP address is entered, host will return the host's name.
Ifconfig	A Unix/Linux utility used to display a host's IP addressing information.
IPConfig	Displays the IP address of the host and other configuration information. Some parameters are:

`ipconfig /all`—Displays all information about the connection.

`ipconfig /release`—Releases the current IP address.

`ipconfig /renew`—Requests a new IP address.

`ipconfig /?`—Displays information about ipconfig. |

Utility	Purpose
FTP (File Transfer Protocol)	Transfers files over a network.
Mtr	Unix/Linux utility that combines the functionality of ping and traceroute.
Nbtstat	Displays NetBIOS over TCP/IP statistics, NetBIOS name tables, and the NetBIOS name cache. You can use this utility with switches to remove or correct NetBIOS name cache entries.
Netstat	Displays a list of a computer's active incoming and outgoing connections.
Nslookup	Reports the IP address of an entered host name, or the host name of an entered IP address.
Ping (Packet Internet Groper)	Verifies a connection to a network between two hosts using Internet Control Message Protocol echo requests.
Route	Allows you to manually control network routing tables.
Telnet	Allows you to communicate with another computer on the network remotely, entering commands on the local computer that control the remote computer.
Trace Route	Traces and displays the route taken from the host to a remote destination; tracert is one example of a trace-routing utility.

Most of these commands are entered from a command prompt. To open a Command Prompt window in any Windows version, run the cmd command. From the Command Prompt, you can enter a Windows or DOS command, including any of those in the previous table. You can view the results of the non-Unix commands in the window.

Do it!

B-3: Identifying TCP/IP utilities used for troubleshooting

Questions and answers

1 A user opens a browser window and attempts to contact your intranet server at www.networkplus.class. The user receives a message that it can't be found. What's the first TCP/IP utility you should try?

2 You have received complaints from users in one location that load time for the company's intranet Web site is slow. No one in any other location is reporting a problem. What TCP/IP utility can you use to diagnose the problem?

Ipconfig

When a user complains of network problems, you should first check the TCP/IP settings on the user's computer. When using any version of Windows, use ipconfig, as shown in Exhibit 11-3, to display and modify the current configuration of the TCP/IP stack. Several switches can be added to the ipconfig command line that can display information (ipconfig /all), release the IP address (ipconfig /release), and renew the IP address (ipconfig /renew) for all connections. The following table contains some common switches.

IPConfig parameter	Use to
/release [*adapter name*] /release6 [*adapter name*]	Release a leased IPv4 or IPv6 address (respectively) so that it returns to the pool of available addresses on the DHCP server. You can optionally specify the name of the network connection for which you want to release the leased address. If you don't specify a connection name, Windows Vista releases the leased IP addresses for all network connections.
	You might use this option when a computer is unable to obtain an address from a DHCP server (typically when the server is unavailable) or if you want to force the computer to obtain a new lease (because the DHCP server's IP addressing parameters have changed).
/renew [*adapter name*] /renew6 [*adapter name*]	Renew a leased IPv4 or IPv6 address. As with the /release parameter, you can optionally specify the name of the network connection for which you want to renew the IP address lease. If you don't specify a network connection name, Windows Vista attempts to renew all leased IP addresses for all network connections configured to use DHCP.
	Use this option to attempt to renew a computer's IP address lease. If the computer can't communicate with the DHCP server from which it obtained its IP address, or you have disabled the scope (pool) of IP addresses from which the computer obtained its IP address, the DHCP server denies the computer's lease renewal request. At this point, the computer then starts all over with the IP address leasing process by broadcasting a DHCP request packet.
/flushdns	Delete all name resolution information (consisting of host names and their IP addresses) from the client's DNS Resolver cache. For example, you might use this parameter to troubleshoot name resolution problems that occur after you change a server's IP address. If computers still have the server's name and old IP address in the DNS Resolver cache, they won't be able to communicate with the server until this cache is deleted.
/displaydns	Display the contents of the DNS Resolver cache.
/registerdns	Renew all IP address leases from DHCP servers and re-register the computer's host name and IP address on your network's DNS servers.

Check to see if the IP address and subnet mask are correct, and verify the default gateway and DNS server addresses. When you verify this information, you might find that the computer has no IP address configured or has configured itself with an APIPA address. If so, this gives you a couple of options:

- If IP addressing information is assigned by a DHCP server, suspect a problem with a DHCP server itself or with the network between the user's computer and the DHCP server. First, verify that the network card is working correctly and is attached to the network cable, which is in turn plugged into the appropriate network port on the wall or floor. Try to release and then renew the IP address from the DHCP server. If you can verify these things, and you can't get an IP address from the DHCP server, then escalate the call to the appropriate network administrator.

- If IP addressing is assigned manually, assign the correct information, such as IP address, default gateway, subnet mask, or DNS server address and test to see if connectivity is restored.

```
Command Prompt                                                    _ □ X

Microsoft Windows [Version 6.0.6001]
Copyright (c) 2006 Microsoft Corporation.  All rights reserved.

C:\Users\Host Administrator>ipconfig /all

Windows IP Configuration

    Host Name . . . . . . . . . . . . : nethost01
    Primary Dns Suffix  . . . . . . . : networkplus.class
    Node Type . . . . . . . . . . . . : Hybrid
    IP Routing Enabled. . . . . . . . : No
    WINS Proxy Enabled. . . . . . . . : No
    DNS Suffix Search List. . . . . . : networkplus.class

Ethernet adapter Local Area Connection:

    Connection-specific DNS Suffix  . :
    Description . . . . . . . . . . . : Intel(R) 82566DC-2 Gigabit Network Connec
tion
    Physical Address. . . . . . . . . : 00-1D-09-24-F5-97
    DHCP Enabled. . . . . . . . . . . : No
    Autoconfiguration Enabled . . . . : Yes
    Link-local IPv6 Address . . . . . : fe80::690e:5c3a:7771:89b6%8(Preferred)
    IPv4 Address. . . . . . . . . . . : 192.168.100.214(Preferred)
    Subnet Mask . . . . . . . . . . . : 255.255.255.0
```

Exhibit 11-3: Ipconfig on a Windows computer

UNIX Ifconfig

A command similar to ipconfig used by UNIX is called ifconfig. Like its Windows counterparts, this UNIX command displays the IP address of the host and other configuration information. You can also use ifconfig to disable and enable network cards and release and renew the IP addresses assigned to these cards. For example, at a UNIX command prompt:

- Type `ifconfig -a` to show all configuration information.

- Type `ifconfig en0 -168.92.1.1` to release the given IP address from the TCP/IP connection named en0. In this example, en0 indicates the first Ethernet connection of the system.

- To assign a static IP address to this Ethernet connection, type `ifconfig en0 168.92.1.1.5`.

Do it!

B-4: Using Ipconfig to display TCP/IP settings

Here's how	Here's why
1 On Windows Vista, click **Start**, choose **Run**, and enter **cmd**	To open a Command Prompt window. You're going to use Ipconfig to view your IP address settings.
2 At the command prompt, enter **ipconfig**	To view your current IP address, subnet mask, and default gateway, as shown here.

```
C:\Users\hostadmin01>ipconfig

Windows IP Configuration

Ethernet adapter Local Area Connection:

        Connection-specific DNS Suffix  . : networkplus.class
        Link-local IPv6 Address . . . . . : fe80::3585:ffb7:fa18:8e72%11
        IPv4 Address. . . . . . . . . . . : 192.168.157.17
        Subnet Mask . . . . . . . . . . . : 255.255.255.0
        Default Gateway . . . . . . . . . : 192.168.157.1
```

This is a quick way to find a computer's basic IP address information.

3 At the command prompt, enter **ipconfig /all**	To view extended IP addressing information, as shown here.

```
C:\Users\hostadmin01>ipconfig /all

Windows IP Configuration

        Host Name . . . . . . . . . . . . : nethost01
        Primary Dns Suffix  . . . . . . . : networkplus.class
        Node Type . . . . . . . . . . . . : Hybrid
        IP Routing Enabled. . . . . . . . : No
        WINS Proxy Enabled. . . . . . . . : No
        DNS Suffix Search List. . . . . . : networkplus.class

Ethernet adapter Local Area Connection:

        Connection-specific DNS Suffix  . : networkplus.class
        Description . . . . . . . . . . . : Broadcom NetXtreme Gigabit Ethernet
        Physical Address. . . . . . . . . : 00-1E-C9-47-59-31
        DHCP Enabled. . . . . . . . . . . : Yes
        Autoconfiguration Enabled . . . . : Yes
        Link-local IPv6 Address . . . . . : fe80::3585:ffb7:fa18:8e72%11(Preferred)
        IPv4 Address. . . . . . . . . . . : 192.168.157.17(Preferred)
        Subnet Mask . . . . . . . . . . . : 255.255.255.0
        Lease Obtained. . . . . . . . . . : Monday, December 08, 2008 1:43:26 PM
        Lease Expires . . . . . . . . . . : Sunday, December 14, 2008 1:43:25 PM
        Default Gateway . . . . . . . . . : 192.168.157.1
        DHCP Server . . . . . . . . . . . : 192.168.157.5
        DNS Servers . . . . . . . . . . . : 192.168.157.5
        NetBIOS over Tcpip. . . . . . . . : Enabled
```

It can be easier to view this information at the Command Prompt than to click through a few dialog boxes to find the same information in the Windows GUI.

Ping and basic TCP/IP connectivity

Explanation

While you're in the MS-DOS prompt or Command Prompt window, you can use another tool to verify basic TCP/IP connectivity. *Ping* (*Packet Internet Groper*) is a simple program that allows one computer to send a test packet to another computer and then receive a reply. You use ping to discover if another computer is available for communication on a TCP/IP network.

After you have verified the computer has a valid IP address, you can use the ping command to see if you can communicate with another computer on the network. You'll need to know the NetBIOS name, DNS name, or IP address of the other computer—perhaps a router or server that you know is operational. At the MS-DOS or command prompt, enter

        ping *computer*

where `computer` is the other computer's name or IP address. A successful result looks similar to Exhibit 11-4.

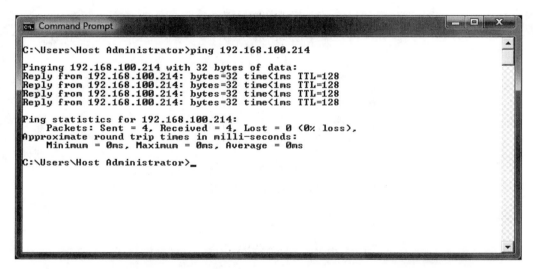

Exhibit 11-4: Successful Ping results

When you issue ping from the command prompt, followed by an IP address or a domain name, ping communicates over a TCP/IP network to another node on the network. It sends an Internet Control Message Packet (ICMP) Echo Request and expects to receive an ICMP Echo Reply in return. Packets are exchanged and then reported on the screen to verify connectivity on the network. ICMP is a software component of the Network layer of the OSI model. If the ping is successful, you know that the two nodes are communicating at the Network layer. If communication is happening at this layer, you also know that all layers underneath the Network layer are working.

If you can't use ping successfully, try these options:

- If you tried to ping using a domain name, use the IP address of the remote host instead. If that works, the problem is with name resolution.
- Try to ping a different computer. Can you communicate with any other computer on the network?
- If not, use ipconfig to verify that the computer has been assigned an IP address.
- Verify all network configuration settings.
- Reboot the computer to verify that TCP/IP has been loaded.
- Try removing TCP/IP and reinstalling it. Perhaps the initial installation was corrupted.
- Check the physical connections. Is the network cable plugged in or is there a telephone connection? Do you get a dial tone?

If all these fail to produce results, you might need to escalate the issue.

Do it!

B-5: Testing TCP/IP connectivity

Here's how	Here's why
1 On Windows Vista in the Command Prompt window, type **ping 127.0.0.1** and press (↵ ENTER)	(It should still be open from the previous activity.) This is the loopback address and verifies that TCP/IP is working on this computer. Pinging the loopback address tests a computer's own basic network setup. You should receive four successful responses.
2 Type **ipconfig /all** and press (↵ ENTER)	Record your IP address and your default gateway address. IP address: Default gateway address:
3 Ping your IP address	This verifies TCP/IP communication can be sent out on to the network cable from your NIC card and back in again. You should receive four successful responses.
4 Ping the instructor's computer	It verifies you have connectivity to other computers on your local subnet. You should receive four successful responses.
5 Ping the IP address of your classroom's gateway	This verifies that you can reach the gateway that connects you to other subnets. You should receive four successful responses.

6 How does being able to successfully ping the IP address of your default gateway help you when troubleshooting?

7 Users are complaining that they are unable to access one of your organization's file and print servers (even though they had just been using this server). You discover that another person in desktop support moved the server to a new subnet. What might be the cause of users not being able to access this server? How can you resolve the problem?

NSLookup

Explanation

When two computers communicate with each other using TCP/IP across the network, Domain Name System (DNS) server is responsible for resolving the names you specify to their associated IP addresses. Active Directory domains also use DNS to provide users and computers with access to the network's resources.

To verify that your computer can communicate with its DNS server(s), enter `nslookup [host or FQDN]`. Your computer succeeds in communicating with the DNS server if the server responds with the IP address of one or more computers. You'll sometimes see multiple IP addresses for a given fully qualified domain name (FQDN) such as www.cnn.com. In this example, the Web site administrators have configured multiple Web servers to host its content. DNS servers then use a technique referred to as "round robin" to balance the workload across those servers.

Tracert

If a user is telling you he or she can't access resources on the network, you should verify that the user's computer has the correct network client installed: either "Client for Microsoft Networks" or "Client for NetWare Networks." Verify that the client software is configured properly. You should also verify "File and Printer Sharing" is installed and enabled on the computer the user is trying to access.

You can also perform an additional test on the network using the tracert command to check the network path between two computers. At an MS-DOS or command prompt, enter `tracert computer` where `computer` is the name or IP address of a destination.

Do it!

B-6: Using NSLookup and tracert

Here's how	
1 At the command prompt, enter **nslookup**	To test your DNS configuration. In class, you get the classroom DNS server's IP address returned.
	In other environments, depending on the configuration, you might see a DNS server name and IP address returned, or you might see just an IP address and an error message telling you that nslookup can't find the server name. This is a DNS server configuration issue.
2 Enter **nslookup** followed by a Web address	Try www.yahoo.com. You should see DNS addressing information for that domain.
3 Enter **nslookup netdc.networkplus.class**. What does this command tell you if it succeeds?	
4 Enter **exit**	To exit nslookup.
5 Enter **tracert [IP_address of the classroom server]**	To trace the path to the DNS server in your network. This is a short path, so the results are returned promptly.
6 Enter **tracert www.yahoo.com**	To trace the route to Yahoo's Web server. This takes a while longer.
7 Close the Command Prompt window	

Windows Network Diagnostics

Explanation

One of the tools built into Windows Vista and Windows Server 2008 for troubleshooting network problems is Windows Network Diagnostics. This utility automates many of the steps for troubleshooting TCP/IP and network connectivity. You can access Windows Network Diagnostics by using a number of methods. For example, as shown in Exhibit 11-5, you see the Network and Sharing Center of a computer that isn't able to connect to the Internet. You could launch Windows Network Diagnostics on this computer by either clicking the "Diagnose and repair" link in the Tasks pane or clicking the red "X" displayed on the connection to the Internet. Other methods for launching Windows Network Diagnostics include:

- Right-click on the Network icon in your system tray and choose "Diagnose and repair."

- In the Network Connections window, right-click on the appropriate network connection and choose Diagnose.

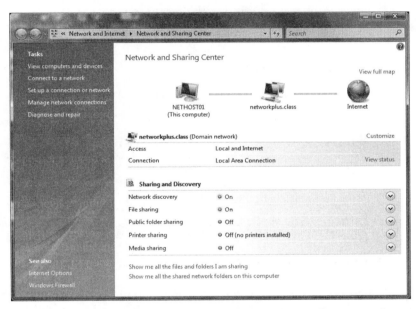

Exhibit 11-5: The Network and Sharing Center provides you with access to Windows Network Diagnostics

Windows Network Diagnostics tasks

When you run Windows Network Diagnostics, it attempts to diagnose many of the common problems encountered on TCP/IP networks. For example, Windows Network Diagnostics can typically identify problems such as an incorrect subnet mask or default gateway address, a DNS server that is down, a disabled network adapter, or a network adapter that you need to reset, as shown in Exhibit 11-6. Click one of the options displayed to see if it solves the problem.

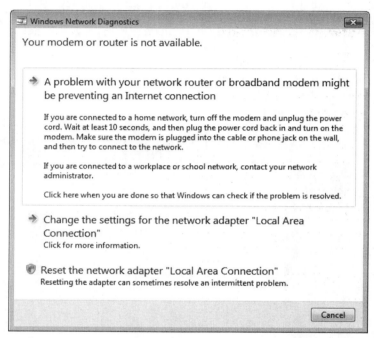

Exhibit 11-6: Network Diagnostics helps you to resolve many common TCP/IP problems

Wireless networks

Windows Network Diagnostics can help you resolve problems with your wireless networks too. Windows Network Diagnostics will attempt to identify the cause of the problem you're experiencing, and then walk you through the steps to correct this problem. In addition, Windows Network Diagnostics records information about the problems it detects in the System log with the Event ID of 6100. You can review these events to help identify the cause of the problem with the wireless network.

Do it!

B-7: Troubleshooting with Network Diagnostics

Here's how	Here's why
1 On nethost##, click **Start** and then right-click **Network**	To open the Network and Sharing Center.
Choose **Properties**	
2 In the Tasks pane, click **Manage network connections**	
3 In the Network Connections window, right-click **Local Area Connection** and choose **Properties**	
Click **Continue**	
4 On the Networking tab, select **Internet Protocol Version 4 (TCP/IPv4)**	
Click **Properties**	To open the Properties dialog box for the TCP/IP protocol.
5 Enter a non-working IP address and invalid gateway and DNS server addresses	To deliberately misconfigure your computer so that it cannot connect to the Internet. You will troubleshoot the "problem" in upcoming steps.
Click **OK**	To save your changes.
Click **Yes**	You'll see that Windows Vista already recognizes a problem.
Click **Close**	
Close the Network Connections window	
6 In the Network and Sharing Center, click **Diagnose and repair**	To open Windows Network Diagnostics so that you can diagnose why your computer can't access the Internet.
7 Read the message box	Windows cannot communicate with the Primary DNS Server. It can't repair the problem automatically.
Click **Cancel**	
8 Click **Manage network connections**	

9 Right-click **Local Area Connection** and choose **Properties**

Click **Continue**

On the Networking tab, select **Internet Protocol Version 4 (TCP/IPv4)**

Click **Properties** — To open the Properties dialog box for the TCP/IP protocol.

10 Configure your computer to use DHCP to obtain both an IP address and DNS server address — So that your computer can connect to the Internet.

Click **OK** and **Close** — To save your changes.

11 Close Network Connections

12 Verify that you can connect to the Internet — (Use Internet Explorer or observe the connection information reported in Network and Sharing Center.)

13 Close all open windows

14 You have just run Windows Network Diagnostics to help you identify the problem with a computer's wireless connection. You want to view the information reported by the utility in the computer's event logs. Which event log should you check?

Topic C: Troubleshooting scenarios

This topic covers the following CompTIA Network+ 2009 exam objectives.

#	Objective
4.6	**Given a scenario, implement the following network troubleshooting methodology**
	• Information gathering – identify symptoms and problems
	• Identify the affected areas of the network
	• Determine if anything has changed
	• Establish the most probable cause
	• Determine if escalation is necessary
	• Create an action plan and solution identifying potential effects
	• Implement and test the solution
	• Identify the results and effects of the solution
	• Document the solution and the entire process
4.7	**Given a scenario, troubleshoot common connectivity issues and select an appropriate solution**
	• Physical issues
	• Logical issues
	• Wireless issues

Bridge objective

Network technicians are responsible for handling almost all the problems relating to the network. There are several types of problems relating to the network, and each of them has to be dealt with in a different way.

Remote Desktop troubleshooting

Explanation

As with troubleshooting other types of network problems, it's important that you approach troubleshooting Remote Desktop by identifying the components that make up such connections. These components include:

- The Windows computer on which you've enabled Remote Desktop so that a user can connect to it from a remote location.
- The configuration of Remote Desktop itself, including the types of connections it supports and the users to which you've given the necessary permissions.
- The computer with which you're connecting to the remote Windows computer.
- The DNS server that is responsible for resolving the remote computer's name to its IP address.
- The physical network.

The next step is to ask the isolating questions that help you to narrow down the source of the problem. These questions include:

- Can you connect to other shared network resources? If you can, you can be sure that the user's network card, cable, and wall jack, along with the hubs, routers, and other cabling components are working properly.

- Can you connect to a shared folder on the remote computer to which you attempted to connect with Remote Desktop Connection? If you can, you know that the network card, cable, and wall jack for the remote computer are working properly as well.

- Can you connect using Remote Desktop Connection by specifying the remote computer's IP address instead of its computer name? If you can, suspect a problem with the DNS server.

- Is Remote Desktop configured properly? Verify that you've configured Remote Desktop to require the appropriate authentication method based on the type of computer from which the user establishes the Remote Desktop connection; make sure the user has the necessary permissions to connect via Remote Desktop; and verify that the Remote Desktop exception is enabled in Windows Firewall. Be aware that if you're configuring Remote Desktop on a computer that isn't a member of a domain, any user who attempts to use Remote Desktop Connection to connect to that computer must have a password defined.

- Is the remote computer configured to sleep or hibernate after a certain period of inactivity? If so, you can't connect via Remote Desktop while the computer is asleep or hibernating. You can resolve this problem by reconfiguring the Power Management settings in Control Panel.

- Is Remote Desktop Connection configured properly? Or is there a problem with the computer the user is using to connect to the remote computer? For example, the computer on which the user is running Remote Desktop Connection must have enough available RAM to run the program. Try closing some of the user's programs if necessary.

Do it!

C-1: Troubleshooting Remote Desktop connectivity

Questions and answers

1 A user reports that she is unable to connect to her desktop computer using Remote Desktop Connection when she is away from her desk. You have determined that the network is functioning correctly. When the user attempts to connect to her desktop computer, she receives an error stating that authentication failed. What might be the problem?

2 A user who is in a meeting wants to connect to his computer using Remote Desktop Connection. When he attempts to do so, he is unable to contact his computer. You have verified that the user can connect to other network resources; however, the user is not able to connect to a shared folder on his computer. What might be the problem?

Inability of a user to access a shared resource

Explanation

A network technician can give various types of access rights to users as per the requirements. One common problem is that the user can't access a shared resource.

Do it!

C-2: Troubleshooting the inability of a user to access a shared resource

Questions and answers

Scenario: As a network administrator at Outlander Spices, your sales personnel need access to a file share on the network that contains the data used by the contact management system. You've created the directory and given access to a special group of users called Sales. The Sales group contains user accounts for the members of the Sales team. After providing access to these files, an employee from the Sales department reports that she can't access the resource.

1 What should you do as a part of identifying the exact issue?

2 The other employee reports a failure. What step should be taken to recreate the problem?

3 Both indicate that they saved proposals to the corporate file server within the last several minutes. Now, what should you do to isolate the cause?

4 As part of formulating the correction, you notice that only the Administrators group has been given rights to log in to the contact management system. As the problem has been identified, how can you implement the correction?

5 How can you confirm the correction?

6 You get a positive response. As the network technician, what should you do after solving the problem?

7 What feedback do you give to the employees?

Preventing illegal attempts to access an account

Explanation   A network administrator can set policies to lock accounts in case of repeated bad logon attempts. This procedure is generally followed to prevent illegal attempts to access an account.

Do it!   ## C-3: Troubleshooting access to an account

Questions and answers

Scenario: You're the network administrator at Outlander Spices. The network consists of a single Windows domain. Sally, a secretary to the president, reports that she receives a message on her Windows Vista computer indicating that she can't log on to the network. You've also set password restrictions so that users must alter their passwords every 90 days. Passwords must be at least 9 characters in length, and the account is locked out after 5 bad login attempts.

1 To identify the exact issue, what action do you take?

2 In response to your attempt to recreate the problem, she reports that she can't log on at other workstations either. What do you do to isolate the cause?

3 As a part of formulating the correction, you notice that her account is locked out. What do you do to implement the correction and confirm it?

4 This time she's successful. What should you do after solving the problem?

Connectivity issues

Explanation   In a networked environment, connectivity failures might occur due to many factors. Some of the common causes can be:

- Faulty cables
- Hardware failure
- Problems with RAS
- Compatibility issues with other operating systems

Do it!

C-4: Troubleshooting hardware problems

Questions and answers

Scenario: Tim reports that this morning when attempting to access network resources he was unable to do so. The network is configured in a Star topology.

1 How can you identify the exact issue?

2 He's able to do so. What does that indicate?

3 How can you recreate the problem?

4 The attempt fails. How do you isolate the cause in this situation?

5 It appears to be connected. What do you check next?

6 You note that it isn't. What do you do next?

7 As part of formulating the correction, when you touched the cable, you noted that the link light on the hub corresponding to Tim's computer flickers. You disconnected and reconnected the cable at the patch panel and at the hub, but the link light doesn't remain on. Wiggling the patch cable causes the link light to flicker. How do you implement the correction?

8 The link light on Tim's network adapter came on and stayed on. How can you test that the problem is solved?

9 He's able to access the network resources. After documenting the problem and the solution, what feedback do you give Tim?

Network problems relating to adding or removing services

Explanation

Problems might occur in a network when services, such as DNS and DHCP, are added to or removed from the network. Making a change of this sort typically involves updating both the server and client environment and can be a complex task.

Do it!

C-5: Troubleshooting a network problem relating to adding or removing services

Questions and answers

Scenario: Outlander Spices has seen large growth in the past year. As a result, many new employees have been hired, and the number of workstations connected to the network has increased accordingly. Prior to this growth, IP addresses had been assigned manually at the Windows XP and Windows Vista workstations in the network. Recently, DHCP was added and configured in the network to ease the administrative burden of managing workstation IP addresses. Shortly thereafter, another new employee was hired and a workstation added to the network for him by one of the 1st tier network support personnel. On his first day, the new employee calls to state that, upon booting his machine, he received a message that an IP address conflict exists and that the local interface has been disabled. Although he's able to access the local workstation, he can't access the network or any network resources.

1 What's the first step in troubleshooting this scenario?

2 You find that an IP address was assigned manually. What do you do next?

3 After changing the setting, what do you do?

4 He's able to do so. What is the next step you take?

5 After correcting the issue, what do you do?

Unit summary: Troubleshooting

Topic A

In this topic, you learned the basics of **troubleshooting**: how to gather information, form a resolution, and implement it. You also learned how to track problems and build hardware and software **toolkits** to help in your troubleshooting practice.

Topic B

In this topic, you learned to troubleshoot the network. You learned to troubleshoot the **physical network** by troubleshooting **cables** and **wireless devices**. Then you learned to troubleshoot the **logical network** by troubleshooting **TCP/IP** and network communications.

Topic C

In this topic, you worked through several troubleshooting scenarios. You practiced **troubleshooting Remote Desktop** issues and network connectivity from local and remote locations.

Review questions

1 At a minimum, which IPv4 address components must you configure in order to communicate on your local subnet?

   A IP address

   B Subnet mask

   C Default gateway

   D DNS server address

2 Which utility enables you to reset a computer's network adapter?

   A Network Map

   B Windows Network Diagnostics

   C IPConfig

   D Local Area Connection

3 True or false? Network Map is enabled by default in Windows Vista computers within an Active Directory domain.

4 What steps can you take to minimize electrical interference on your wired LAN?

use-fiber

5 What might be the cause if you are unable to connect to radio wireless device?

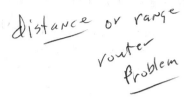

distance or range
router
problem

6 Which command displays the IP address of the host and other configuration information?

A Getmac

B Ipconfig

C Nslookup

D Ping

7 Which type of crosstalk is a calculated value of the crosstalk between pairs measured at the far end of the cable?

A Near End Crosstalk (NEXT)

B Far End Crosstalk (FEXT)

C Equal Level Far End Crosstalk (ELFEXT)

D Pair to Pair Crosstalk

8 List four physical cable tests you can perform using a cable testing device.

wrong cable

patch cable

9 List four network function tests you can perform with a cable testing device.

hub
switch
✓ if on

10 A network analyzer can detect problems with what four pieces of hardware?

Jacks
cabling
switch
NIC

11 What information does the command ipconfig report?

IP address

12 What command should you enter to view the Host Name and DNS Server address?

/ALL

13 Which command would you use to verify name resolution (DNS) settings?

A ipconfig

B ping

C nslookup

D tracert

Independent practice activity

In this activity, you will discuss and apply various troubleshooting techniques.

1 List the steps in a generic troubleshooting procedure.

Note: Form teams and discuss the following questions. There are no definite answers for these questions.

2 A user is unable to access the network from his or her workstation. Role-play troubleshooting this user's problem.

3 On an IP network that's connected to the Internet through a router providing network address translation, Jim reports that he can't browse the Internet. List the steps to resolve the problem.

Appendix A
Certification exam objectives map

This appendix covers these additional topics:

A CompTIA Network+ 2009 Edition certification exam objectives with references to corresponding coverage in this course manual.

Topic A: Comprehensive exam objectives

Explanation
This section lists all CompTIA Network+ 2009 exam objectives and indicates where each objective is covered in conceptual explanations, activities, or both.

1.0 Network Technologies

Objective		Conceptual information	Supporting activities
Bridge objective 1.1	**Explain the function of common networking protocols**	Unit 1, Topic A	A-6
	TCP	Unit 5, Topic A	A-6, A-8
	FTP	Unit 5, Topic A	A-5, A-9
	UDP	Unit 5, Topic A	A-7, A-8
	TCP/IP suite	Unit 5, Topic A	A-1
	DHCP	Unit 5, Topic B	B-3, B-4
	TFTP	Unit 5, Topic A	
	DNS	Unit 2, Topic B Unit 5, Topic B	B-3
	HTTP(S)	Unit 5, Topic A	
	ARP	Unit 5, Topic A	A-3
	SIP (VoIP)	Unit 5, Topic A	
	RTP (VoIP)	Unit 5, Topic A	
	SSH	Unit 5, Topic A	
	POP3	Unit 5, Topic A	
	NTP	Unit 5, Topic A	
	IMAP4	Unit 5, Topic A	
	Telnet	Unit 5, Topic A	A-10
	SMTP	Unit 5, Topic A	A-10
	SNMP2/3	Unit 4, Topic A	
	ICMP	Unit 5, Topic A	A-4
	IGMP	Unit 5, Topic A	
	TLS	Unit 9, Topic C	C-1, C-2

Objective		Conceptual information	Supporting activities
Bridge objective	1.2 **Identify commonly used TCP and UDP default ports**		
	TCP ports		
	FTP — 20, 21	Unit 5, Topic A	A-5
	SSH — 22	Unit 5, Topic A	
	TELNET — 23	Unit 5, Topic A	
	SMTP — 25	Unit 5, Topic A	
	DNS — 53	Unit 5, Topic A	
	HTTP — 80	Unit 5, Topic A	A-5
	POP3 —110	Unit 5, Topic A	
	NTP — 123	Unit 5, Topic A	
	IMAP4 — 143	Unit 5, Topic A	
	HTTPS — 443	Unit 5, Topic A	
	UDP ports		
	TFTP — 69	Unit 5, Topic A	
	DNS — 53	Unit 5, Topic A	
	BOOTPS/DHCP — 67	Unit 5, Topic A	
	SNMP — 161	Unit 5, Topic A	

	Objective	Conceptual information	Supporting activities
	1.3 **Identify the following address formats**		
	IPv6	Unit 2, Topic B Unit 5, Topic B	B-2 B-1, B-2, B-3, B-4
	IPv4	Unit 2, Topic B Unit 5, Topic B	B-2 B-1, B-2, B-3, B-4
	MAC addressing	Unit 2, Topic B Unit 5, Topic A	B-2
Bridge objective	**1.4** **Given a scenario, evaluate the proper use of the following addressing technologies and addressing schemes**		
	Addressing Technologies		
	Subnetting	Unit 5, Topic B	B-2
	Classful vs. classless (e.g. CIDR, Supernetting)	Unit 5, Topic B	B-2
	NAT	Unit 5, Topic B	
	PAT	Unit 5, Topic B	
	SNAT	Unit 5, Topic B	
	Public vs. private	Unit 5, Topic B	
	DHCP (static, dynamic, APIPA)	Unit 5, Topic B Unit 5, Topic C	B-1, B-3, B-4 C-1, C-2
	Addressing schemes		
	Unicast	Unit 5, Topic B	
	Multicast	Unit 5, Topic B	
	Broadcast	Unit 4, Topic A Unit 5, Topic B	
Bridge objective	**1.5** **Identify common IPv4 and IPv6 routing protocols**		
	Link state		
	OSPF	Unit 4, Topic A Unit 5, Topic A	
	IS-IS	Unit 4, Topic A	

Objective			Conceptual information	Supporting activities
		Distance vector		
		RIP	Unit 4, Topic A Unit 5, Topic A	
		RIPv2	Unit 4, Topic A Unit 5, Topic A	
		BGP	Unit 4, Topic A	
		Hybrid		
		EIGRP	Unit 4, Topic A	
Bridge objective	**1.6**	**Explain the purpose and properties of routing**		
		IGP vs. EGP	Unit 4, Topic A	
		Static vs. dynamic	Unit 4, Topic A	A-3
		Next hop	Unit 4, Topic A	
		Understanding routing tables and how they pertain to path selection	Unit 4, Topic A	A-3
		Explain convergence (steady state)	Unit 4, Topic A	
Bridge objective	**1.7**	**Compare the characteristics of wireless communication standards**		
		802.11 a/b/g/n		
		Speeds	Unit 1, Topic B Unit 6, Topic B	B-1
		Distance	Unit 6, Topic B	B-1
		Channels	Unit 6, Topic B	B-1
		Frequency	Unit 6, Topic B	B-1
		Authentication and encryption		
		WPA	Unit 6, Topic C	C-1
		WEP	Unit 6, Topic C	C-1
		RADIUS	Unit 6, Topic C	C-1
		TKIP	Unit 6, Topic C	C-1

2.0 Network Media and Topologies

Objective		Conceptual information	Supporting activities
Bridge objective	**2.1 Categorize standard cable types and their properties**		
	Type		
	CAT3, CAT5, CAT5e, CAT6	Unit 1, Topics A and B	A-4 B-2
		Unit 2, Topic A	A-2, A-3
	STP, UTP	Unit 1, Topic A	A-4
	Multimode fiber, single-mode fiber	Unit 1, Topics A and B	A-4 B-2
		Unit 2, Topic A	A-1
	Coaxial	Unit 1, Topics A and B	A-4 B-2
		Unit 2, Topic A	A-4, A-5
	RG-59	Unit 1, Topics A and B	
		Unit 2, Topic A	
	RG-6	Unit 1, Topics A and B	
		Unit 2, Topic A	
	Serial	Unit 2, Topic A	
	Plenum vs. Non-plenum	Unit 2, Topic A	A-6
	Properties		
	Transmission speeds	Unit 1, Topic B	
		Unit 2, Topic A	
	Distance	Unit 1, Topic B	
		Unit 2, Topic A	
	Duplex	Unit 1, Topics A and B	
		Unit 2, Topic A	
	Noise immunity (security, EMI)	Unit 1, Topic A	
		Unit 2, Topic A	
	Frequency	Unit 2, Topic A	

		Objective	Conceptual information	Supporting activities
Bridge objective	**2.2**	**Identify common connector types**		
		RJ-11	Unit 2, Topic A	A-2
		RJ-45	Unit 2, Topic A	A-2, A-3
		BNC	Unit 2, Topic A	A-4, A-5
		SC	Unit 2, Topic A	A-1
		ST	Unit 2, Topic A	A-1
		LC	Unit 2, Topic A	A-1
		RS-232	Unit 2, Topic A	
		RG-59	Unit 2, Topic A	
		RG-6	Unit 2, Topic A	
Bridge objective	**2.3**	**Identify common physical network topologies**		
		Star	Unit 1, Topic B	B-1, B-3
		Mesh	Unit 1, Topic B	B-1, B-3, B-4
		Bus	Unit 1, Topic B	B-1, B-3
		Ring	Unit 1, Topic B	B-1, B-3
		Point to point	Unit 1, Topic B	B-1
		Point to multipoint	Unit 1, Topic B	B-1
		Hybrid	Unit 1, Topic B	B-1, B-3
Bridge objective	**2.4**	**Given a scenario, differentiate and implement appropriate wiring standards**		
		568A	Unit 2, Topic A	
		568B	Unit 2, Topic A	
		Straight vs. cross-over	Unit 2, Topic A	
		Rollover	Unit 2, Topic A	
		Loopback	Unit 3, Topic C	

Objective		Conceptual information	Supporting activities
Bridge objective	**2.5 Categorize WAN technology types and properties**		
	Type		
	Frame relay	Unit 1, Topic B	B-4
	E1/T1	Unit 1, Topic B	B-4
	ADSL	Unit 1, Topic B	B-4
	SDSL	Unit 1, Topic B	B-4
	VDSL	Unit 1, Topic B	B-4
	Cable modem	Unit 1, Topic B	B-4
	Satellite	Unit 1, Topic B	B-4
	E3/T3	Unit 1, Topic B	B-4
	OC-x	Unit 2, Topic A	
	Wireless	Unit 1, Topic B	B-3, B-4
		Unit 6, Topic A	A-1
	ATM	Unit 1, Topic B	B-4
	SONET	Unit 2, Topic A	
	MPLS	Unit 4, Topic B	
	ISDN BRI	Unit 1, Topic B	B-4
	ISDN PRI	Unit 1, Topic B	B-4
	POTS	Unit 1, Topic B	B-4
	PSTN	Unit 1, Topic B	B-4
	Properties		
	Circuit switch	Unit 1, Topic B	B-4
	Packet switch	Unit 1, Topic B	B-4
	Speed	Unit 1, Topic B	B-4
	Transmission media	Unit 1, Topic B	B-4
	Distance	Unit 1, Topic B	B-4

	Objective	Conceptual information	Supporting activities
Bridge objective	**2.6 Categorize LAN technology types and properties**		
	Type		
	Ethernet	Unit 1, Topic B	B-2, B-3
	10BaseT	Unit 1, Topic B	B-2, B-3
	100BaseTX	Unit 1, Topic B	B-2, B-3
	100BaseFx	Unit 1, Topic B	B-2, B-3
	1000BaseT	Unit 1, Topic B	B-2, B-3
	1000BaseX	Unit 1, Topic B	B-2, B-3
	10GBaseSR	Unit 1, Topic B	B-2, B-3
	10GBaseLR	Unit 1, Topic B	B-2, B-3
	10GBaseER	Unit 1, Topic B	B-2, B-3
	10GBaseSW	Unit 1, Topic B	B-2, B-3
	10GBaseLW	Unit 1, Topic B	B-2, B-3
	10GBaseEW	Unit 1, Topic B	B-2, B-3
	10GBaseT	Unit 1, Topic B	B-2, B-3
	Properties		
	CSMA/CD	Unit 1, Topic B	B-3
	Broadcast	Unit 1, Topic B	B-3
	Collision	Unit 1, Topic B	B-3
	Bonding	Unit 1, Topic B	B-2
	Speed	Unit 1, Topic B	B-2, B-3
	Distance	Unit 1, Topic B	B-2, B-3
		Unit 3, Topic B	B-1
	2.7 Explain common logical network topologies and their characteristics		
	Peer to peer	Unit 1, Topic A	A-1
	Client/server	Unit 1, Topic A	A-1, A-2
	VPN	Unit 1, Topic B	
	VLAN	Unit 4, Topic A	

Objective		Conceptual information	Supporting activities
Bridge objective	**2.8** **Install components of wiring distribution**		
	Vertical and horizontal cross connects	Unit 3, Topics A and B	B-1
	Patch panels	Unit 3, Topics A and B	A-2
	66 block	Unit 3, Topics A and B	A-2 B-2
	MDFs	Unit 3, Topic A	A-2
	IDFs	Unit 3, Topic A	A-2
	25 pair	Unit 3, Topics A and B	A-2 B-2
	100 pair	Unit 3, Topics A and B	A-2 B-2
	Demarc	Unit 3, Topic A	A-2
	Demarc extension	Unit 3, Topic A	A-2
	Smart jack	Unit 3, Topic A	
	Verify wiring installation	Unit 3, Topic C	
	Verify wiring termination	Unit 3, Topic C	

3.0 Network Devices

Objective		Conceptual information	Supporting activities
Bridge objective	**3.1 Install, configure and differentiate between common network devices**		
	Hub	Unit 4, Topic A	A-4
	Repeater	Unit 4, Topic A	A-1
	Modem	Unit 2, Topic B	B-4, B-5, B-6
	NIC	Unit 2, Topic B Unit 5, Topic B Unit 6, Topics A and C	B-1, B-3 B-3
	Media converters	Unit 4, Topic A	A-5
	Basic switch	Unit 4, Topic A	A-2
	Bridge	Unit 4, Topic A	A-2
	Wireless access point	Unit 1, Topics A and B Unit 6, Topics A and C	A-5 C-1, C-2
	Basic router	Unit 3, Topic A Unit 4, Topic A	A-1 A-3
	Basic firewall	Unit 4, Topic A	A-6
	Basic DHCP server	Unit 5, Topic B Unit 5, Topic C	B-3 C-1, C-2
Bridge objective	**3.2 Identify the functions of specialized network devices**		
	Multilayer switch	Unit 4, Topic B	B-1
	Content switch	Unit 4, Topic B	B-1
	IDS/IPS	Unit 4, Topic B	B-2
	Load balancer	Unit 4, Topic B	B-1
	Multifunction network devices	Unit 4, Topic B	
	DNS server	Unit 5, Topic B	B-2
	Bandwidth shaper	Unit 4, Topic B	B-3
	Proxy server	Unit 4, Topic A	
	CSU/DSU	Unit 3, Topics A and B	A-1

	Objective		Conceptual information	Supporting activities
Bridge objective	**3.3**	**Explain the advanced features of a switch**		
		PoE	Unit 4, Topic A	
		Spanning tree	Unit 4, Topic A	
		VLAN	Unit 4, Topic A	
		Trunking	Unit 4, Topic A	
		Port mirroring	Unit 4, Topic B	B-2
		Port authentication	Unit 6, Topic B	
Bridge objective	**3.4**	**Implement a basic wireless network**		
		Install client	Unit 6, Topic C	C-3
		Access point placement	Unit 6, Topic A	
		Install access point	Unit 6, Topic C	C-2
		Configure appropriate encryption	Unit 6, Topic C	C-2
		Configure channel and frequencies	Unit 6, Topic C	C-2
		Set ESSID and beacon	Unit 6, Topic C	C-2
		Verify installation	Unit 6, Topic C	C-3

4.0 Network Management

Objective		Conceptual information	Supporting activities
4.1	**Explain the function of each layer of the OSI model**		
	Layer 1 – physical	Unit 1, Topic C	C-1
	Layer 2 – data link	Unit 1, Topic C	C-1
	Layer 3 – network	Unit 1, Topic C	C-1
	Layer 4 – transport	Unit 1, Topic C	C-1
	Layer 5 – session	Unit 1, Topic C	C-1
	Layer 6 – presentation	Unit 1, Topic C	C-1
	Layer 7 – application	Unit 1, Topic C	C-1
Bridge objective **4.2**	**Identify types of configuration management documentation**		
	Wiring schematics	Unit 7, Topic B Unit 11, Topic A	B-4
	Physical and logical network diagrams	Unit 7, Topic B Unit 11, Topic A	B-4
	Baselines	Unit 7, Topic B Unit 11, Topic A	B-4
	Policies, procedures and configurations	Unit 7, Topic B Unit 11, Topic A	B-4
	Regulations	Unit 7, Topic B Unit 11, Topic A	B-4
4.3	**Given a scenario, evaluate the network based on configuration management documentation**		
	Compare wiring schematics, physical and logical network diagrams, baselines, policies and procedures and configurations to network devices and infrastructure	Unit 11, Topic A	
	Update wiring schematics, physical and logical network diagrams, configurations and job logs as needed	Unit 11, Topic A	

	Objective	Conceptual information	Supporting activities
Bridge objective	**4.4 Conduct network monitoring to identify performance and connectivity issues using the following:**		
	Network monitoring utilities (e.g. packet sniffers, connectivity software, load testing, throughput testers)	Unit 10, Topic A Unit 11, Topic B	A-1 through A-7 B-1
	System logs, history logs, event logs	Unit 10, Topic B	B-1 through B-6
Bridge objective	**4.5 Explain different methods and rationales for network performance optimization**		
	Methods:		
	QoS	Unit 11, Topic B	
	Traffic shaping	Unit 4, Topic B	B-3
	Load balancing	Unit 4, Topic B	
	High availability	Unit 11, Topic B	
	Caching engines	Unit 11, Topic B	
	Fault tolerance	Unit 11, Topic B	
	Reasons:		
	Latency sensitivity	Unit 11, Topic B	
	High bandwidth applications	Unit 11, Topic B	
	VoIP	Unit 11, Topic B	
	Video applications	Unit 11, Topic B	
	Uptime	Unit 11, Topic B	
	4.6 Given a scenario, implement the following network troubleshooting methodology		
	Information gathering – identify symptoms and problems	Unit 11, Topic A Unit 11, Topic C	A-1 C-1 through C-5
	Identify the affected areas of the network	Unit 11, Topic A Unit 11, Topic C	A-1 C-1 through C-5
	Determine if anything has changed	Unit 11, Topic A Unit 11, Topic C	A-1 C-1 through C-5
	Establish the most probable cause	Unit 11, Topic A Unit 11, Topic C	A-1 C-1 through C-5

Objective	Conceptual information	Supporting activities
4.6	**(continued) Given a scenario, implement the following network troubleshooting methodology**		
	Determine if escalation is necessary	Unit 11, Topic A Unit 11, Topic C	A-1 C-1 through C-5
	Create an action plan and solution identifying potential effects	Unit 11, Topic A Unit 11, Topic C	A-1 C-1 through C-5
	Implement and test the solution	Unit 11, Topic A Unit 11, Topic C	A-1 C-1 through C-5
	Identify the results and effects of the solution	Unit 11, Topic A Unit 11, Topic C	A-1 C-1 through C-5
	Document the solution and the entire process	Unit 11, Topic A Unit 11, Topic C	A-1 C-1 through C-5
Bridge objective **4.7**	**Given a scenario, troubleshoot common connectivity issues and select an appropriate solution**		
	Physical issues:	Unit 1, Topic B	
	Cross talk	Unit 2, Topic B Unit 11, Topic B	B-1
	Near End crosstalk	Unit 2, Topic B Unit 3, Topic C Unit 11, Topic B	B-1
	Attenuation	Unit 2, Topic B Unit 11, Topic B	B-1
	Collisions	Unit 1, Topic B Unit 11, Topic B	B-1
	Shorts	Unit 3, Topic C Unit 11, Topic B	B-1
	Open impedance mismatch (echo)	Unit 11, Topic B	B-1
	Interference	Unit 2, Topic B Unit 11, Topic B	B-1

Objective	Conceptual information	Supporting activities
4.7 **(continued) Given a scenario, troubleshoot common connectivity issues and select an appropriate solution**		
Logical issues:		
Port speed	Unit 11, Topic B	
Port duplex mismatch	Unit 11, Topic B	
Incorrect VLAN	Unit 4, Topic A Unit 11, Topic A	
Incorrect IP address	Unit 11, Topic B	B-4, B-5
Wrong gateway	Unit 11, Topic B	B-4, B-5
Wrong DNS	Unit 11, Topic B	B-4, B-5
Wrong subnet mask	Unit 11, Topic B	B-4, B-5
Issues that should be identified but escalated:		
Switching loop	Unit 11, Topic A	
Routing loop	Unit 11, Topic A	
Route problems	Unit 11, Topic A	
Proxy arp	Unit 11, Topic A	
Broadcast storms	Unit 11, Topic A	
Wireless Issues:		
Interference (bleed, environmental factors)	Unit 6, Topic A	A-1
Incorrect encryption	Unit 6, Topic C	C-2, C-3
Incorrect channel	Unit 6, Topic C	C-2, C-3
Incorrect frequency	Unit 6, Topic C	C-2, C-3
ESSID mismatch	Unit 6, Topic C	C-2, C-3
Standard mismatch (802.11 a/b/g/n)	Unit 6, Topic B	
Distance	Unit 6, Topic A	A-1
Bounce	Unit 6, Topic A	A-1
Incorrect antenna placement	Unit 6, Topic A	A-1

5.0 Network Tools

Objective		Conceptual information	Supporting activities
Bridge objective	**5.1** **Given a scenario, select the appropriate command line interface tool and interpret the output to verify functionality**		
	Traceroute	Unit 11, Topic B	B-6
	Ipconfig	Unit 5, Topic A Unit 11, Topic B	A-2, A-3 B-4
	Ifconfig	Unit 5, Topic A Unit 11, Topic B	
	Ping	Unit 5, Topic A Unit 11, Topic B	A-4 B-5
	Arp ping	Unit 11, Topic B	
	Arp	Unit 5, Topic A Unit 11, Topic B	A-3
	Nslookup	Unit 11, Topic B	B-6
	Host	Unit 11, Topic B	
	Dig	Unit 11, Topic B	
	Mtr	Unit 11, Topic B	
	Route	Unit 11, Topic B	
	Nbtstat	Unit 11, Topic B	
	Netstat	Unit 2, Topic B Unit 11, Topic B	B-2
Bridge objective	**5.2** **Explain the purpose of network scanners**		
	Packet sniffers	Unit 5, Topic A Unit 7, Topic A Unit 8, Topic B	A-6, A-7
	Intrusion detection software	Unit 4, Topic B Unit 8, Topic B	B-2 B-7, B-8
	Intrusion prevention software	Unit 4, Topic B Unit 8, Topic B	B-2 B-7, B-8
	Port scanners	Unit 7, Topic A	A-4

	Objective	Conceptual information	Supporting activities
Bridge objective	**5.3** **Given a scenario, utilize the appropriate hardware tools**		
	Cable testers	Unit 2, Topic A Unit 3, Topic C Unit 11, Topic B	A-3, A-4 C-1 B-1
	Protocol analyzer	Unit 5, Topic A Unit 5, Topic B Unit 11, Topic A Unit 11, Topic B	A-6, A-7 B-1
	Certifiers	Unit 11, Topic A	
	TDR	Unit 3, Topic C Unit 11, Topic A	C-1
	OTDR	Unit 3, Topic C Unit 11, Topic A	C1
	Multimeter	Unit 11, Topic A	
	Toner probe	Unit 11, Topic A	
	Butt set	Unit 11, Topic A	
	Punch down tool	Unit 3, Topic B Unit 11, Topic A	B-2
	Cable stripper	Unit 2, Topic A Unit 3, Topic B Unit 11, Topic A	A-3, A-4 B-2
	Snips	Unit 11, Topic A	
	Voltage event recorder	Unit 11, Topic A	
	Temperature monitor	Unit 11, Topic A	

6.0 Network Security

Objective			Conceptual information	Supporting activities
Bridge objective	**6.1**	**Explain the function of hardware and software security devices**		
		Network based firewall	Unit 4, Topic A	A-6
		Host based firewall	Unit 4, Topic A	A-6
		IDS	Unit 4, Topic B	B-2
		IPS	Unit 4, Topic B	B-2
		VPN concentrator	Unit 8, Topic B Unit 9, Topic C	
Bridge objective	**6.2**	**Explain common features of a firewall**		
		Application layer vs. network layer	Unit 8, Topic B	B-1
		Stateful vs. stateless	Unit 8, Topic B	
		Scanning services	Unit 8, Topic B	
		Content filtering	Unit 8, Topic B	B-1
		Signature identification	Unit 8, Topic B	
		Zones	Unit 8, Topic B	B-2
Bridge objective	**6.3**	**Explain the methods of network access security**		
		Filtering:		
		ACL		
		MAC filtering	Unit 8, Topic B Unit 9, Topic D	
		IP filtering	Unit 8, Topic B Unit 9, Topic D	
		Tunneling and encryption		
		SSL VPN	Unit 9, Topic C	
		VPN	Unit 9, Topic C	C-5
		L2TP	Unit 9, Topic C	C-5
		PPTP	Unit 9, Topic C	C-5

Objective		Conceptual information	Supporting activities
6.3	(continued) Explain the methods of network access security		
	IPSEC	Unit 8, Topic B Unit 9, Topic C	B-4 C-5
	Remote access		
	RAS	Unit 9, Topic C	
	RDP	Unit 10, Topic A Unit 11, Topic C	A-7 C-1
	PPPoE	Unit 9, Topic A	A-5
	PPP	Unit 9, Topic A	
	VNC	Unit 10, Topic A	
	ICA	Unit 10, Topic A	
Bridge objective 6.4	**Explain methods of user authentication**		
	PKI	Unit 9, Topic B	B-1, B-2
	Kerberos	Unit 9, Topic A	A-4
	AAA	Unit 9, Topic A	
	RADIUS	Unit 6, Topic C Unit 9, Topic C	C-1 C-1
	TACACS+	Unit 9, Topic C	C-3
	Network access control		
	802.1x	Unit 6, Topic C Unit 9, Topic C	C-1 C-3
	CHAP	Unit 9, Topic A	A-5
	MS-CHAP	Unit 9, Topic A	A-5
	EAP	Unit 9, Topic A	A-5

	Objective		Conceptual information	Supporting activities
Bridge objective	**6.5**	**Explain issues that affect device security**		
		Physical security	Unit 8, Topic B	B-9, B-10
		Restricting local and remote access	Unit 8, Topic B Unit 9, Topic C	B-9, B-10 C-1 through C-5
		Secure methods vs. unsecure methods		
		SSH, HTTPS, SNMPv3, SFTP, SCP	Unit 8, Topic B Unit 9, Topic C	 C-5
		TELNET, HTTP, FTP, RSH, RCP, SNMPv1/2	Unit 8, Topic B Unit 9, Topic C	 C-5
	6.6	**Identify common security threats and mitigation techniques**		
		Security threats		
		DoS	Unit 7, Topic A	A-3, A-4
		Viruses	Unit 7, Topic A	A-1
		Worms	Unit 7, Topic A	A-1
		Attackers	Unit 7, Topic A Unit 7, Topic B	
		Man in the middle	Unit 7, Topic A	A-5
		Smurf	Unit 7, Topic A	A-3
		Rogue access points	Unit 6, Topic C	
		Social engineering (phishing)	Unit 7, Topic A Unit 7, Topic B	A-2
		Mitigation techniques		
		Policies and procedures	Unit 7, Topic B	B-1 through B-4
		User training	Unit 7, Topic B	B-5, B-6
		Patches and updates	Unit 8, Topic A	A-3, A-4, A-5

Appendix B
CompTIA Network+ Acronyms

This appendix covers these additional topics:

A Acronyms that appear on the CompTIA Network+ exam.

Topic A: Acronym list

Explanation

The following is a list of acronyms that appear on the CompTIA Network+ exam. Candidates are encouraged to review the complete list and attain a working knowledge of all listed acronyms as a part of a comprehensive exam preparation program.

Acronym	Spelled out
AAA	Authentication Authorization and Accounting
ACL	Access Control List
ADF	Automatic Document Feeder
ADSL	Asymmetric Digital Subscriber Line
AH	Authentication Header
AM	Amplitude Modulation
AMI	Alternate Mark Inversion
APIPA	Automatic Private Internet Protocol Addressing
ARP	Address Resolution Protocol
ATM	Asynchronous Transfer Mode
BDF	Building Distribution Frame
BERT	Bit-Error Rate Test
BGP	Border Gateway Protocol
BNC	British Naval Connector/Bayonet Niell-Concelman
BootP	Boot Protocol/Bootstrap Protocol
BRI	Basic Rate Interface
CHAP	Challenge Handshake Authentication Protocol
CIDR	Classless Inter-Domain Routing
CNAME	Canonical Name
CRAM-MD5	Challenge-Response Authentication Mechanism – Message Digest 5
CSMA/CA	Carrier Sense Multiple Access/Collision Avoidance
CSMA/CD	Carrier Sense Multiple Access/Collision Detection
CSU	Channel Service Unit

Acronym	Spelled out
dB	Decibel
DHCP	Dynamic Host Configuration Protocol
DLC	Data Link Control
DNS	Domain Name Service/Domain Name Server/Domain Name System
DoS	Denial of Service
DDoS	Distributed Denial of Service
DSL	Digital Subscriber Line
DSU	Data Service Unit
E1	E-Carrier Level 1
EAP	Extensible Authentication Protocol
EGP	Exterior Gateway Protocol
EIGRP	Enhanced Interior Gateway Routing Protocol
EMI	Electromagnetic Interference
ESSID	Enhanced Service Set Identifier
ESP	Encapsulated Security Packets
FDM	Frequency Division Multiplexing
FHSS	Frequency Hopping Spread Spectrum
FM	Frequency Modulation
FQDN	Fully Qualified Domain Name/Fully Qualified Distinguished Name
FTP	File Transfer Protocol
GBIC	Gigabit Interface Converter
Gbps	Gigabits per second
HDLC	High-level Data Link Control
HTTP	Hypertext Transfer Protocol
HTTPS	Hypertext Transfer Protocol Secure
Hz	Hertz
IANA	Internet Assigned Numbers Authority

Acronym	Spelled out
ICA	Independent Computer Architecture
ICMP	Internet Control Message Protocol
IDF	Intermediate Distribution Frame
IDS	Intrusion Detection System
IEEE	Institute of Electrical and Electronics Engineers
IGMP	Internet Group Multicast Protocol
IGP	Interior Gateway Protocol
IKE	Internet Key Exchange
IMAP4	Internet Message Access Protocol version 4
IP	Internet Protocol
IPS	Intrusion Prevention System
IPsec	Internet Protocol Security
IPv4	Internet Protocol version 4
IPv6	Internet Protocol version 6
ISDN	Integrated Services Digital Network
IS-IS	Intermediate System-Intermediate System
ISP	Internet Service Provider
IT	Information Technology
Kbps	Kilobits per second
L2F	Layer 2 Forwarding
L2TP	Layer 2 Tunneling Protocol
LACP	Link Aggregation Control Protocol
LAN	Local Area Network
LC	Logical Connector
LDAP	Lightweight Directory Access Protocol
LEC	Local Exchange Carrier
LED	Light Emitting Diode
LLC	Logical Link Control

Acronym	Spelled out
MAC	Media Access Control/Medium Access Control
Mbps	Megabits per second
MBps	Megabytes per second
MDF	Main Distribution Frame
MDI	Media Dependent Interface
MDIX	Media Dependent Interface Crossover
MIB	Management Information Base
MMF	Multimode Fiber
MPLS	Multi-Protocol Label Switching
MS-CHAP	Microsoft Challenge Handshake Authentication Protocol
MT-RJ	Mechanical Transfer-Registered Jack
MX	Mail Exchanger
NAT	Network Address Translation
NetBEUI	Network Basic Input/Output Extended User Interface
NetBIOS	Network Basic Input/Output System
NIC	Network Interface Card
nm	Nanometer
NNTP	Network News Transfer Protocol
NTP	Network Time Protocol
OCx	Optical Carrier
OS	Operating System
OSI	Open Systems Interconnect
OSPF	Open Shortest Path First
OTDR	Optical Time Domain Reflectometer
PAP	Password Authentication Protocol
PAT	Port Address Translation
PC	Personal Computer

Acronym	Spelled out
PKI	Public Key Infrastructure
PoE	Power over Ethernet
POP3	Post Office Protocol version 3
POTS	Plain Old Telephone System
PPP	Point-to-Point Protocol
PPPoE	Point-to-Point Protocol over Ethernet
PPTP	Point-to-Point Tunneling Protocol
PRI	Primary Rate Interface
PSTN	Public Switched Telephone Network
PVC	Permanent Virtual Circuit
QoS	Quality of Service
RADIUS	Remote Authentication Dial-In User Service
RARP	Reverse Address Resolution Protocol
RAS	Remote Access Service
RDP	Remote Desktop Protocol
RFI	Radio Frequency Interface
RG	Radio Grade
RIP	Routing Internet Protocol
RJ	Registered Jack
RSA	Rivest, Shamir, Adelman
RSH	Remote Shell
RTP	Real Time Protocol
SC	Standard Connector/Subscriber Connector
SCP	Secure Copy Protocol
SDSL	Symmetrical Digital Subscriber Line
SFTP	Secure File Transfer Protocol
SIP	Session Initiation Protocol

Acronym	Spelled out
SLIP	Serial Line Internet Protocol
SMF	Single Mode Fiber
SMTP	Simple Mail Transfer Protocol
SNAT	Static Network Address Translation
SNMP	Simple Network Management Protocol
SOA	Start of Authority
SOHO	Small Office/Home Office
SONET	Synchronous Optical Network
SPS	Standby Power Supply
SSH	Secure Shell
SSID	Service Set Identifier
SSL	Secure Sockets Layer
ST	Straight Tip
STP	Shielded Twisted Pair
T1	T-Carrier Level 1
TA	Terminal Adaptor
TACACS+	Terminal Access Control Access Control System+
TCP	Transmission Control Protocol
TCP/IP	Transmission Control Protocol/Internet Protocol
tcsh	turbo C shell
TDM	Time Division Multiplexing
TDR	Time Domain Reflectometer
Telco	Telephone Company
TFTP	Trivial File Transfer Protocol
TKIP	Temporal Key Integrity Protocol
TLS	Transport Layer Security
TTL	Time to Live

Acronym	Spelled out
UDP	User Datagram Protocol
UNC	Universal Naming Convention
UPS	Uninterruptible Power Supply
URL	Uniform Resource Locator
USB	Universal Serial Bus
UTP	Unshielded Twisted Pain
VDSL	Variable Digital Subscriber Line
VLAN	Virtual Local Area Network
VNC	Virtual Network Connector
VoIP	Voice over IP
VPN	Virtual Private Network
VTP	Virtual Trunk Protocol
WAN	Wide Area Network
WAP	Wireless Application Protocol/Wireless Access Point
WEP	Wired Equivalent Privacy
WINS	Windows Internet Naming Service
WPA	Wi-Fi Protected Access
www	World Wide Web
Zeroconf	Zero Configuration

Course summary

This summary contains information to help you bring the course to a successful conclusion. Using this information, you will be able to:

A Use the summary text to reinforce what you've learned in class.

B Determine the next courses in this series (if any), as well as any other resources that might help you continue to learn about network installation, configuration, and management.

Topic A: Course summary

Use the following summary text to reinforce what you've learned in class.

Unit summaries

Unit 1

In this unit, you learned the basic components that make up a **local area network**. You learned about the different types of networks—**peer-to-peer** and **client/server** and how you can connect computers on a LAN together using different types of cabling or wireless signals. You also examined the characteristics of the different network architectures (**Ethernet** and **Token Ring**) and how those architectures can be arranged physically (**Bus, Ring, Star, Hybrid**). You learned how LANs can be connected together in **Wide Area Networks (WANs)**. Finally, you examined the layers of the **OSI model**, which is used to standardize network technologies.

Unit 2

In this unit, you learned about the various wired computer-to-computer connections in a LAN. You examined and connected different types of wired cables and connectors— **fiber optic**, **twisted pair**, and **coaxial**. You learned about the more stringent requirements for cabling you'll run in a **plenum**. You then installed and created network connections through both a **network interface card** and a **PCI internal modem**.

Unit 3

In this unit, you learned how to connect networks and network segments together. You learned the functions of **Network Access Points (NAPs)** and **Internet Service Providers (ISPs)**. You also learned how to physically wire a building for network access from the **demarc**, through the **telecommunications room**, to the **workstation drops**. You learned about the tools that you can use to verify your LAN wiring and to diagnose wiring problems.

Unit 4

In this unit, you identified the functions of basic internetworking devices such as **repeaters**, **hubs**, **bridges**, **switches**, **routers**, and **brouters**. You also learned about internetworking devices specific to Ethernet and Token Ring networks. You examined specialized internetworking devices such as **multilayer switches**, **IDS** and **IPS** devices, as well as **hardware firewalls**. You also looked at how to use **traffic shapers** to control network traffic in order to optimize performance or increase usable bandwidth.

Unit 5

In this unit, you examined the components that make up the **TCP/IP protocol suite** and how it relates to the **OSI model**. You identified the functions of various major protocols in the suite and at which layer in both the TCP/IP architecture model and the OSI model that each protocol operates. You configured the **Internet Protocol (IPv4 and IPv6)** and its properties on your network connection. You installed and configured a **DHCP server** on a Windows Server 2008 computer to lease **IP addresses** and **TCP/IP configuration parameters** to clients.

Unit 6

In this unit, you learned how to install and configure a **wireless network**. You distinguished between the wireless technologies of **radio**, **Bluetooth**, and **infrared**. You also compared the various wireless standards available under the main **802.11** standard. You configured both a **wireless access point** and a **wireless client**, and then verified connectivity.

Unit 7

In this unit, you learned about common **security threats**, and you learned what these attacks are and how devastating they can be to a network. You also learned how to **mitigate** security threats. You learned about **security policies** and **incident response policies**. Finally, you then learned about **educating users** and providing them with important security information.

Unit 8

In this unit, you used **Windows Update** to apply **patches** and **hot fixes** and **service packs**. You then determined whether your **BIOS** needed to be updated, and you examined **Windows Firewall** configuration. Next, you learned how to secure network devices. You learned about **network-based firewalls** and how they're used to protect the internal network. You learned about the different types of firewalls and which firewall configurations are the most secure, and you learned about **Intrusion Detection Systems (IDS)** and **Intrusion Prevention Systems (IPS)**. Finally, you learned about physically securing your systems using **locks** and **surveillance**.

Unit 9

In this unit, you learned about the basics of **authentication**; you learned about one-, two-, and three-factor authentication; and you learned about the **Kerberos** and **NTLM** authentication protocols. You also learned how **EAP**, **CHAP**, and **PPPoE** are used in authentication. Next, you learned about the basics of **PKI**, and you learned how to secure remote network access. You learned how **RADIUS** and **TACACS** provide authorization and accounting functions for network access, and you learned how **802.1x** helps you control wireless network access. Finally, you learned about wireless network standards, and you learned about different wireless network vulnerabilities.

Unit 10

In this unit, you monitored **performance** and **reliability** using **Performance Monitor**. You also used a **Data Collector Set** to collect system performance data for viewing at a later time, and you used **Reliability Monitor** to determine a computer's **Stability Index**. Next, you monitored computer performance using **Event Viewer**. You viewed event logs on the local computer and then connected to a remote computer to view the event logs. You then configured event forwarding between two computers and created a subscription to collect events from a remote computer.

Unit 11

In this unit, you learned the basics of **troubleshooting**: how to gather information, form a resolution, and implement it. You also learned how to **track problems**, and about building hardware and software **toolkits** to help in your troubleshooting practice. Next, you learned to troubleshoot the network, including the **physical network** (cables and wires) and the logical network (TCP/IP settings). Finally, you worked through several troubleshooting scenarios. You practiced troubleshooting **Remote Desktop** issues and network connectivity from **local** and **remote** locations.

Topic B: Continued learning after class

It is impossible to learn how to install, configure, and maintain a network in a few days. To get the most out of this class, students should begin network installation, configuration, and management tasks as soon as possible. We also offer resources for continued learning.

Next courses in this series

This is the only course in this series.

Other resources

For more information, visit www.axzopress.com.

Glossary

10-Mbps Ethernet (Twisted Pair Ethernet)
Ethernet standard operating at a speed of 10 megabits per second (Mbps) of data.

100-Mbps Ethernet (Fast Ethernet)
Ethernet standard operating at a speed of 100 Mbps.

1000-Mbps Ethernet (Gigabit Ethernet)
Used for large, high-speed LANs and heavy-traffic server connections; it operates at a speed of 1000 Mbps (1 gigabit per second).

10GbE (10 Gigabit Ethernet)
The fastest of the Ethernet standards, with a data rate of 10 gigabits per second.

802.1x
A port-based, authentication framework for wired and wireless access to Ethernet networks.

802.11a
An improved version of the original Wi-Fi technology and is also based on the same IEEE 802 standard.

ACL (access control list)
Controls the permissions to allow or deny user access to a folder or printer.

amplifier repeater
A repeater that simply amplifies all incoming signals and passes them on.

anycast
An IPv6 address that identifies a group of interfaces, typically on separate nodes, and then delivers anycast packets to the nearest interface as identified by the routing protocol distance measurement.

APIPA (Automatic Private IP Addressing)
The non-routable network 169.254.0.0 used by Windows clients to automatically generate an address in this range if they are configured to obtain an IPv4 address from a DHCP server and are unable to contact one.

AppleTalk
A routable network protocol supported by Apple Macintosh computers.

ARP (Address Resolution Protocol)
Converts logical IP addresses to physical MAC addresses as part of the packet delivery process.

ATM (Asynchronous Transfer Mode)
A very fast network technology that can be used with LANs as well as WANs; it uses fixed-length packets, called cells, to transmit data, voice, video, and frame relay traffic across virtual circuits.

authentication
Positive identification of the entity, either a person or a system, that wants to access information or services that have been secured.

authorization
A set level of access granted to an entity so that it can access the resource.

back-to-back firewall
The DMZ network is located between two firewalls, the two firewalls between the Internet and the DMZ, and the DMZ and the intranet each have two network cards, as does the server within the DMZ.

backbone
A high-speed network link connecting network segments.

BASE-CX
Ethernet standards run over shielded copper twisted-pair cable.

BASE-R
Ethernet standards run over fiber optic cable.

BASE-T
Ethernet standards run over shielded or unshielded twisted-pair cable.

BASE-W
Ethernet standards run over fiber optic cables; uses the same types of fiber and support the same distances as 10GBASE-R standards; however, Ethernet frames are encapsulated in SONET frames. Referred to as Wide Area Network Physical Layer (WAN PHY).

BASE-X
Ethernet standards run over fiber optic cable.

bastion host
Computers that stand outside the protected network and are exposed to an attack by using two network cards, one for the DMZ and one for the intranet. Network communication isn't allowed between the two network cards in the bastion host server.

biometrics

Uses something about a user, such as a fingerprint, retinal scan, or voice print, to secure an account or resource.

Bluetooth

A short-range wireless technology limited to transmission distances of about 100 meters or less.

bridge

An internetworking device that connects two different LANs and makes them appear to be one; or segments a larger LAN into two smaller pieces.

buffer overflow

An attack which manipulates the maximum field input size variable and then enters data much larger than the database is prepared to accept causing memory reserved for other data to be overwritten.

bus topology

Each node is connected to the next by a direct line so that a continuous line is formed.

CA (certificate authority)

The person or entity responsible for issuing certificates.

cable

WAN connection technology that connects over the same lines that carry cable television signals.

cable scanner

A device used to find cable faults. Comes in analog and digital versions.

cable tracer

A device used to detect cables hidden behind walls or underground.

cable wire map tester

A device used to verify that each TP wire is connected to the correct pin.

cellular

WAN connection technology that connects through a cell phone or laptop's cellular network PC card on a cellular phone network.

channel access method

Determines the physical methodology by which data is sent across the transmitting media.

CHAP (Challenge Handshake Authentication Protocol)

An authentication method used by Point-to-Point Protocol (PPP) servers. CHAP validates the remote client's identity at the communication session start or at any time during the session.

CIDR (Classless Inter-Domain Routing)

Allows you to use variable-length subnet masking (VLSM) to create additional addresses beyond those allowed by the IPv4 classes.

circuit switching

A dedicated line is allocated for the transmission of data between two network nodes.

client/server network

A network with computers called servers, which hold data and provide a wealth of services that users can share.

coaxial cable

Contains a layer of braided wire or foil between the core and the outside insulating layer.

composite cable

Combines Cat5 or Cat6 and other transmission cables within a single PVC jacket.

consolidation point

The point in a horizontal run where two cables are interconnected using a reusable connector such as a punch-down block.

continuity tester

A device used to verify an electrical connection between two points.

CRL (certificate revocation list)

A data structure containing revoked certificates.

cross-connect

A location where signals are distributed to various destinations.

crossover cable

A TP cable where one end is wired using 568A and the other using 568B, allowing you to directly connect two computers.

crosstalk

Alternating electrical current flowing through a wire creates an electromagnetic field around the wire which affects the current flow in any adjacent cables.

CS (certificate server)

Maintains a database, or repository, of certificates.

CSMA/CA (Carrier Sense Multiple Access with Collision Avoidance)

Channel access method which doesn't detect collisions as much as it attempts to avoid collisions.

CSMA/CD (Carrier Sense Multiple Access with Collision Detection)

The most common implementation of channel access; includes carrier sensing, multiple access, and collision detection. Examples include: Ethernet and 802.3.

CSU/DSU (Channel Service Unit/Digital Service Unit)

A two-in-one device that cleans and formats data before sending it on a T1 line. The Channel Service Unit (CSU) acts as a safe electrical buffer between the LAN and a public network accessed by the T1 line. The Digital Service Unit or Data Service Unit (DSU) ensures that the data is formatted correctly before it's allowed on the T1 line.

custom subnetting

Creating several smaller networks from a large network by taking bits from the host ID and adding them to the network ID.

DCS (Data Collector Set)

A Performance Monitor feature that gathers information for a period you specify so that you can review a computer's performance over time.

DDoS (Distributed Denial of Service)

A network attack in which the attacker manipulates several hosts to perform a DoS attack.

dead zone

A network between two routers that uses another network protocol other than TCP/IP.

demarc

The point at which the communications network owned by one company connects to the communications network owned by another company. Also called demarcation point.

demarc terminating device

Device responsible for the code and protocol conversions, as well as the buffering required for communications to and from an ISP and your internal network. Also referred to as the network terminating interface (NTI), network terminating unit (NTU), network terminating device (NTD), smart jack, or an MPOE (minimum point of entry).

demodulation

The process a modem uses to convert analog data received from a phone line to digital.

DHCP (Dynamic Host Configuration Protocol)

An automated mechanism to assign IP addresses to clients. There are two version—the original DHCP, which is used for IPv4 addressing, and Dynamic Host Configuration Protocol for IPv6 (DHCPv6), which is used for IPv6 addressing.

Diameter

A successor to RADIUS; a new protocol which defines a minimum set of AAA services and functionality.

DMZ

An area between the private network (intranet) and a public network (extranet) such as the Internet.

DNS (domain name system)

Used to resolve host names to IP addresses, find domain controllers, as well as resources on the Internet such as Web servers and e-mail servers.

DOS (Denial of Service)

An attack which consumes or disables resources so that services to users are interrupted.

DSL (Digital Subscriber Line)

WAN connection technology that uses high-speed connections made over regular analog phone lines.

dual-homed firewall

(See bastion host.)

dual-homed host

(See bastion host.)

dumpster diving

Digging useful information out of an organization's trash bin.

DUN (Dial-up networking)

WAN connection technology that uses a modem to connect through regular, analog phone lines.

E lines

The European equivalent of the American T-lines.

EAP (Extensible Authentication Protocol)

Includes multiple authentication methods, such as token cards, one-time passwords, certificates, and biometrics, and runs over the data link layers without requiring use of IP.

encryption

A technique through which source information is converted into a form that cannot be read by anyone other than the intended recipient.

Ethernet bonding

Combines the bandwidth of two network interface cards as a cost-effective way to increase bandwidth available for data transfers for critical servers, such as firewalls and production servers.

Ethernet hub

An internetworking device that takes the signal transmitted from one computer and propagates it to all the other computers on the network configured as an Ethernet star.

Event Viewer

The Windows logging utility.

eye scanner

A biometric hardware security device that scans the surface of a user's retina to obtain the blood vessel patterns found there, then compares it to a database of user names and passwords.

fiber optic cable
Carries light-based data through strands of glass or plastic.

fingerprint scanner
A biometric hardware security device that scans a user's finger and compares the print to a database of user names and passwords.

firewall
Software or hardware used to control information that's sent and received from outside the network.

frame relay
Packet-switching communication protocol designed for long-distance digital data transmission rather than the circuit-switching technology used by the telephone system.

FTP (File Transfer Protocol)
An OSI Application layer protocol used to upload and download files, as well as request directory listings from remote servers.

full-duplex
Data can be transmitted across the medium in both directions at the same time.

global unicast address
A routable and reachable address on the IPv6 Internet; beginning with the binary values 001 (2000::/3) through 111 (E000::/3). (The IPv6 version of an IPv4 public address.)

half-duplex
Data is transmitted across the medium in both directions, but only in one direction at a time.

hardening
The process of modifying an operating system's default configuration to make it more secure from outside threats.

hash
A unique fixed-length mathematical derivation of a plaintext message.

HIDS (host intrusion detection systems)
Typically software based systems for monitoring the health and security of a particular host. HIDS monitor operating system files for unauthorized changes, watch for unusual usage patterns, or failed logon requests.

horizontal cross-connect
The junction point for the workstation cables.

host
A computer.

host ID
The portion of an IP address which represents a unique host on a network.

hotfix
Fixes errors in the operating system code.

HTTP (Hypertext Transfer Protocol)
An OSI Application layer protocol which defines the commands that Web browsers can send and how Web servers are capable of responding.

hybrid topology
Two or more different types of network topologies are combined together into one network.

ICMP/ICMP6 (Internet Control Messaging Protocol)
An OSI Network layer protocol used to send IP error and control messages between routers and hosts.

IDF (intermediate distribution frame)
A network rack containing the devices connecting a floor's internal wiring to the MDF.

IDS (intrusion detection system)
Installed inside your network to monitor both internal traffic and traffic that has passed through your firewall; it uses a monitoring port to look at data packets sent on the network.

IFCONFIG
A UNIX-based version of IPCONFIG—a command-line utility used to display and modify the current TCP/IP stack.

IGMP (Internet Group Management Protocol)
An OSI Network layer protocol used for the management of multicast groups.

IMAP4 (Internet Message Access Protocol version 4)
An OSI Application layer e-mail protocol used to retrieve e-mail messages; provides more features than POP3.

infrared
A wireless technology that uses pulses of invisible infrared light to transmit signals between devices, offering relatively low-speed, line-of-sight connections between devices.

inoculation
The process of calculating and recording checksums to protect against viruses and worms.

IP (Internet Protocol)
An unreliable connectionless protocol, functioning at the Network layer of the OSI model.

IPCONFIG

A command-line utility used to display and modify the current TCP/IP stack.

IPS (intrusion prevention system)

Installed on the perimeter of your network to monitor for and stop threats before they are passed on your network; shuts down suspicious traffic on the wire.

IPv4 address

A 32-bit address consisting of a series of four 8-bit numbers separated by periods, which identifies a computer, printer, or other device on a TCP/IP network, such as the Internet or an intranet.

IPv6 address

A 128-bit address, written in the hexadecimal equivalent values for each of its 16 bytes, which identifies a computer, printer, or other device on a TCP/IP network, such as the Internet or an intranet.

IPX/SPX (Internetwork Packet Exchange/Sequenced Packet Exchange)

A routable, proprietary protocol that was the native protocol in early versions of Novell NetWare.

ISDN (Integrated Services Digital Network)

Uses a telephone line to transmit data, but unlike POTS, the data isn't converted to analog form. An ISDN line is digital and consists of two phone circuits, both carried on one pair of wires along with a slower, third circuit used for control signals.

ISP (Internet Service Provider)

A business that provides connectivity to the Internet.

Kerberos v5

The primary authentication protocol used in Active Directory Domain Services environments.

key

A piece of information that determines the result of an encryption algorithm.

key life cycle

The stages a key goes through during its life: generation, distribution, storage, backup, and destruction.

LAN (local area network)

A specifically designed configuration of computers and other devices located within a confined area, such as a home or office building, and connected by wires or radio waves that permit the devices to communicate with one another to share data and services.

LDAP (Lightweight Directory Access Protocol)

The industry-standard protocol for network directory services.

link-local address

An IPv6 self-assigned address using the Neighbor Discovery process. (The IPv6 version of IPv4's APIPA.)

loopback connector

A device used to check cables for broken or shorted wires, and wall jack to network switch connections.

MAC (Media Access Control) address

A unique address permanently embedded in a NIC by the manufacturer, used to identify the device on the LAN.

man-in-the-middle

An attack that tricks e-mail servers into sending data through a third node.

man-trap

A set of doors that are interlocked—when one door is opened, the other door can't be opened.

MDF (main distribution frame)

A network rack that contains the devices used to manage the connections between external communication cables and the cables of your internal network.

media converter

An internetworking device that provides a connection between one network media type and another without changing the channel access method.

mesh topology

All nodes in the mesh have independent connections to all other nodes in the mesh.

MLS (multi-layer switch)

An internetworking device that combines Layer 2 data switching with Layer 3 routing using an application-specific integrated circuit (ASIC).

modem

A device that enables you to connect your computer to another computer through a phone line.

modem bonding

Combining multiple dial-up links over POTS for redundancy or increased throughput.

modulation

The process a modem uses to convert data into an analog signal to be sent over a phone line.

monitoring

The ongoing process of gathering information.

multicast

An IPv4 or IPv6 address that sends information or services to all interfaces that are defined as members of the multicast group.

multimode
Optic fibers which support many transmission (propagation) paths.

MUTOA (Multiuser telecommunications outlet assembly)
Centrally mounted workstation outlets (in a wall, not the ceiling).

mutual authentication
Requires both the client and the server to authenticate to each other instead of just the client authenticating to the server like in other authentication systems.

NAC (Network Access Control)
A process or architecture through which computers are verified to be in compliance, and brought into compliance if they fall short, before they are permitted access to the network.

NAP (Network Access Point)
A major Internet connection point that's used to connect and route traffic between smaller commercial backbones.

NAT (network address translation)
Modifies network address information in the packets it transmits from an internal network onto the Internet, allowing a single address from a router to rewrite originating IP addresses from the internal network so that they all appear to come from the router's IP address.

NetBEUI
A non-routable, proprietary Microsoft protocol that's supported in Windows 9x/Me, Windows NT, and Windows 2000.

network ID
The portion of an IP address which represents the network on which a device resides.

Network Monitor
A simple protocol analyzer for Microsoft Windows operating systems.

NEXT (near end crosstalk)
Occurs when the signal from one pair of wires interferes with the signal on another pair of wires.

NIC (network interface card)
Provides the communication channel between your computer's motherboard and the network.

NIDS (Network intrusion detection systems)
Devices or systems designed to monitor network traffic on a segment or at a network entry point, such as a firewall. NIDS monitor network traffic volumes, watch for malicious traffic, and suspicious patterns.

node
A device on a network with an address that can be accessed to send or receive information.

NTLM
A challenge-response protocol that's used with operating systems running Windows NT 4.0 or earlier.

NTP (Network Time Protocol)
An OSI Application layer protocol that provides the mechanisms to synchronize time and coordinate time distribution in a large, diverse internet operating at rates from mundane to light wave.

one-factor authentication
Use of a single type of authentication; typically something you know.

OSI (Open Systems Interconnection) model
A standard means of describing a network operating system by defining it as a series of layers, each with specific input and output.

OTDR (optical time-domain reflectometer)
Version of TDR for optical cable.

packet switching
Data is broken up into packets before it's sent over the network; each packet is transmitted individually and is able to follow different routes to its destination.

PAP (Password Authentication Protocol)
An insecure authentication method used by the Point to Point Protocol (PPP) for remote dial-up access.

password
A secret code associated with a username, used to authenticate a user.

password crackers
Applications you use (or attackers use) to attempt to determine or decipher the passwords associated with user accounts.

PAT (Port Address Translation)
Translates TCP or UDP communications made between hosts on a private network and hosts on a public network, allowing a single public IP address to be used by many hosts on a private network.

patch
Temporary or quick fix designed to fix a security vulnerability, compatibility or operating issue.

peer-to-peer network
Consists of several client computers that are connected to a network for simple file and printer sharing in a small office or home office.

phishing

An attack where an e-mail that appears to be from a trusted sender directs the recipient to a Web site that looks like the company's site they are impersonating and then records the user's logon information.

physical token

A material object, such as a smart card, that stores a cryptographic key, which might be a digital signature or biometric data.

PKI (public key infrastructure)

A formalized and feature rich system for sharing public keys, distributing certificates, and verifying the integrity and authenticity of these components and their issuers.

plaintext

Original, unencrypted information.

plenum

An enclosure in a building that's used to move air for heating, cooling, or humidity control.

PoE (Power over Ethernet)

A method for transferring both electrical power and data to remote devices over twisted-pair cable in an Ethernet network.

point-to-multipoint connection

There are multiple connections that connect a single node to multiple nodes.

point-to-point connection

There's a dedicated connection between two nodes—only those two nodes communicate over the connection.

POP3 (Post Office Protocol version 3)

An OSI Application layer e-mail protocol used to download and delete messages from the mail server.

port address

A number between 0 and 65,535 that identifies a program running on a computer.

port scanner

A tool that examines a host or network to determine which ports are being monitored by applications on the scanned hosts.

POTS (plain old telephone service)

The network of the world's public circuit-switched telephone networks (public switched telephone network—PSTN).

preset lock

A lock that's opened or closed with a metal key, or by turning or pressing a button in the center.

protocol

A language that computers, servers, and network devices use to communicate with each other.

proxy server

A server that acts as an intermediary between computers on a network and the Internet.

punchdown block

Used to terminate station cables and cross-connect to other punchdown locations. There are two types—the 110 block and the older 66M block.

radio

A wireless technology that use signals sent over electromagnetic radio waves to transmit data between devices, allowing transmissions to pass through most nonmetallic obstructions and around corners.

RADIUS (Remote Access Dial-in User Service)

Uses a specialized server for authentication and WEP for data encryption.

RARP (Reverse Address Resolution Protocol)

Converts physical MAC addresses to logical IP addresses.

realm

A defined namespace in RADIUS, which helps determine which server should be used to authenticate a connection request.

repeater

A basic internetworking device which boosts the electronic signal from one network cable segment or wireless LAN and passes it to another; helping you to physically extend network segments or wireless coverage.

RG-6

Coaxial cable used to deliver cable television signals to and within homes.

RG-8

50-ohm stranded core coaxial cables used for backbones.

RG-11

75-ohm solid core cables with dual shielding (foil and braided wires) used for backbones.

RG-58

Coaxial cabling used for Ethernet networks.

RG-59

Coaxial cabling used for low-power video and RF signal connections.

ring topology

Each node is connected to a central device by two wires.

RIP/RIP2 (Routing Information Protocol)

An OSI Network layer protocol responsible for defining how paths are chosen through the internetworking of one computer to another and how routers can share information about the networks of which they are aware.

rollover cable

A TP cable where the wires in each end are the reverse of one another; used to connect a computer's serial port to the console port of a router or managed switch.

ROT13 ("rotate 13")

A symmetric cipher in which characters are replaced with the character whose ASCII value is thirteen higher.

router

An internetworking device that opens the MAC (Media Access Control) layer envelope and looks at the contents of the packet delivered at the MAC layer to make decisions on how to send data through the network.

RS-232

Serial cable connector.

RSA

The best known asymmetric public key cipher where two users each generate a pair of keys: a private and public key pair. To send a secure message to the second user, the first user obtains the second user's public key and encrypts the message with it. Only second user's private key can be used to decrypt the message.

satellite

WAN connection technology that uses connections made by sending and receiving signals from satellites in orbit around the earth.

screened host

A router used to filter all traffic to the private intranet but also to allow full access to the computer in the DMZ.

security policy

Defines rules and practices that the organization puts in place to manage and protect information within the organization.

segment

The portion of the network on either side of two network transmission devices.

service pack

A collection of updates as a single installation.

S-HTTP (Secure HTTP)

An OSI Application layer protocol used to secure Internet transmissions by securing the individual data packets themselves.

signal-regenerating repeater

A repeater that reads the signal and then creates an exact duplicate of the original signal before sending it on. Also called an intelligent repeater.

Simplex

Data is transmitted across the medium in a single direction.

single-mode

Optic fibers which support only a single transmission path.

single sign-on

A user logs on once to gain access to multiple systems without being required to log on each time another system is accessed.

site-local address

An IPv6 private address; begin with FE with C to F for the third hex digit.

site-to-site VPN

Links the networks at two locations via the Internet.

SLA (service-level agreement)

A contract documenting the service level between a service provider and the end user.

SMTP (Simple Mail Transfer Protocol)

An OSI Application layer e-mail protocol used to send and receive e-mail messages between e-mail servers; and send e-mail from an e-mail client to an e-mail server.

smurf

An attack where a host is flooded with ICMP packets.

SNAT (source network address translation)

The process that a router or firewall uses to rewrite source and destination addresses of IP packets as they pass through.

social engineering

An attack which exploits trust in the real world between people to gain information that attackers can then use to gain access to computer systems.

SONET (Synchronous Optical NETwork)

An ANSI standard protocol for signal transmission on optical networks, which is divided into categories based on a base signal (Synchronous Transport Signal or STS) and an optical carrier (OC) level.

spoofing

An attack where a user appears to be a different user that is sending messages. Also, presenting credentials that don't belong to you in order to gain access to a system.

spyware

Software that gets installed on a system without the user's knowledge and gathers personal or other sensitive information; potentially changing the computer's configuration.

SSH (Secure Shell)

A popular tool for remote command-line system access and management, with current implementations supporting secure file transport (over Secure FTP, or SFTP).

SSH (Secure Shell)

An OSI Network layer protocol used to exchange data between two network nodes over a secure channel.

SSL (Secure Sockets Layer)

An OSI Application layer public-key/private-key encryption protocol used to transmit data securely over the Internet over TCP/IP.

star topology

Each node is connected to a central network transmission device such as a hub or a switch, which serves as a distribution device.

straight-through cable

A TP cable where both ends follow either 568A or 568B wiring standard.

subnet mask

Used to identify the network ID and host ID portions of an IP address.

supernetting

Creating one large network from several smaller ones by taking bits from the network ID and giving them to the host ID.

symmetric cipher

Uses the same key to encrypt and decrypt a piece of data.

SYN flood

An attack where a server is inundated with half open TCP connections which prevent valid users from being able to access the server.

T lines

A leased digital communications line provided through a common carrier; the leased lines are permanent connections that use multiplexing, a process of dividing a single channel into multiple channels that can be used to carry voice, data, video, or other signals. Several variations of T-carrier lines are available; the most popular are T1 and T3 lines.

TACACS+ (Terminal Access Controller Access Control System)

A proprietary authentication protocol developed by Cisco Systems that provides centralized and scalable authentication, along with authorization and accounting functions.

TCP (Transmission Control Protocol)

An OSI Transport layer protocol used to transmit information across the Internet, providing acknowledged, connection-oriented communications, as well as guaranteed delivery, proper sequencing, and data integrity checks.

TCP/IP (Transmission Control Protocol/Internet Protocol)

A routable, non-proprietary protocol that's the protocol of the Internet, and the predominant Windows network protocol.

TCP/IP architecture

A four-layer reference model is used to describe the TCP/IP protocol suite.

TCP/IP hijacking

An attacker takes over an established session between two nodes that are already communicating.

TDR (time domain reflector)

A device used to verify impedance and termination in a cable.

Telnet

An OSI Application layer terminal emulation protocol that is primarily used to remotely connect to UNIX and Linux Systems.

TFTP (Trivial File Transfer Protocol or Trivial FTP)

An OSI Application layer protocol used to send and receive files to a single computer or multiple computers simultaneously.

three-factor authentication

Authentication based on three items; typically something you know, something you have, and something you are.

three-homed firewall

The entry point to the DMZ requires three network cards—one network card is connected to the Internet, one to the DMZ network (or perimeter network), and the final network card to the intranet. Traffic is never allowed to flow directly from the Internet to the private intranet without filtering through the DMZ.

thicknet cable

RG-8 or RG-11 cable.

thinnet cable

RG58/U coaxial cable.

traffic shaper

Software that controls network traffic in order to optimize performance or increase usable bandwidth. Also called a bandwidth shaper.

Trojan horse

An application designed to appear harmless, but delivers malicious code to a computer.

twisted-pair cable

Composed of four pairs of copper wires, with the wires in each pair are twisted around each other, then twisted together and bundled within a covering.

two-factor authentication

Authentication based on two items; typically something you know plus either "something you have" or "something you consist of."

UDP (User Datagram Protocol)

An OSI Transport layer protocol used to provide connectionless, unacknowledged communications.

update

Enhancement to the operating system and some of its features.

VLAN trunking

The ability of a single network adapter in a switch to virtualize "n" number of network adapters.

VoIP (Voice over IP)

Used to make telephone calls over a data network such as the Internet.

VPN (Virtual private network)

WAN connection technology that uses encryption and security protocols to create a private network over a public network.

war chalking

The process of marking buildings, curbs, and other landmarks indicating the presence of an available access point and its connection details by utilizing a set of symbols and shorthand.

wardriving

Driving around with a laptop system configured to listen for open wireless access points.

Web spoofing

Users are tricked into visiting a Web site that looks and acts like an official, legitimate Web site. The imposter Web site is set up to dupe the victim into providing information such as user names, passwords, credit card numbers, and other personal information.

WEP (Wired Equivalent Privacy)

A wireless encryption technology which uses a 64-bit or 128-bit symmetric encryption cipher where a key is configured on both the WAP and the client.

Wi-Fi (Wireless Fidelity)

The most widely used wireless technology at present; began as 802.11b IEEE standard, although most implementations have been upgraded to use the newer 802.11g.

Wi-Fi hijacking

A hacker configures his or her computer to present itself as a wireless router to intercept a user's communication.

WiMAX (IEEE 802.16 Air Interface Standard)

A point-to-multipoint broadband wireless access standard that's emerging as the wireless connection standard for long distances.

Wireless Auto Configuration

Windows clients dynamically select the wireless network to which a connection attempt is made, based on configured preferences or default settings.

WLAN (Wireless LAN)

Uses radio waves or infrared light instead of cables to connect network nodes.

workstation drop

A horizontal cable run without splice points, cable junctures, or taps to an individual workstation.

worm

A program that replicates itself over the network without a user's intervention.

WPA (Wi-Fi Protected Access)

A wireless encryption technology that uses the RC4 symmetric cipher with a 128-bit key. WPA Personal uses a "pre-shared key" (PSK), which simply means you must enter a passphrase onto both the AP and clients.

X.25

Packet-switching communication protocol designed for long-distance analog data transmission rather than the circuit-switching technology used by the telephone system.

Index

I-4 CompTIA Network+, 2009 Edition